An Irish Heart

INTERIOR of St PATRICK'S CHURCH

An Irish Heart

How a Small Immigrant Community Shaped Canada

Sharon Doyle Driedger

A PHYLLIS BRUCE BOOK
HARPERCOLLINS PUBLISHERS LTD

A Phyllis Bruce Book, published by HarperCollins Publishers Ltd.

Originally published in hardcover by HarperCollins Publishers Ltd: 2010
This trade paperback edition: 2011

HarperCollins Publishers Ltd
2 Bloor Street East, 20th Floor
Toronto, Ontario
M4W 1A8

www.harpercollins.ca

Library and Archives Canada Cataloguing in Publication

Doyle Driedger, Sharon, 1947-
An Irish heart : how a small immigrant community
shaped Canada / Sharon Doyle Driedger.

ISBN 978-0-00-639488-4

1. Griffintown (Montréal, Québec)–History.
2. Irish–Québec (Province)–Montréal–History.
3. Irish Canadians–Québec (Province)–Montréal–History.
I. Title.
FC2947.52.D74 2011   971.4'280049162   C2010-907028-3

Printed in the United States
RRD 9 8 7 6 5 4 3 2 1

Map on page 211 by Dawn Huck
Text design by Sharon Kish

For my family
and
in memory of my father and those who have gone before us

They are flying, flying, like northern birds, over the sea for fear;
They cannot abide in their own green land, they seek a resting here.
—Thomas D'Arcy McGee

CONTENTS

PART ONE

Across the Ocean Wild and Wide

ONE

Leaving Ireland

Sail on, sail on, thou fearless bark,
Wherever blows the welcome wind;
It cannot lead to scenes more dark,
More sad, than those we leave behind.
—Thomas Moore

THE IRISH CALL IT THE HARBOUR OF TEARS. From time beyond memory, countless thousands have sailed away from their beloved Ireland from the Cove of Cork, a rare natural harbour tucked into the wild, jagged cliffs of the southwest coast. And as if the land itself were reluctant to let them go, two arms of the River Lee reach inward from the cove, embracing the island city of Cork and caressing the long quays where so many have cried through anguished farewells.

Never did Cork's harbour see more weeping and wailing than in Black '47. In that single, sad year, more than ten thousand men, women and children left famine-struck Ireland from that port alone, in an unprecedented exodus of more than a quarter of a million Irish to North America. Nearly half embarked for Canada, carried away on

*Emigrants bound for Quebec, Boston and other ports
wait on a quay at Cork Harbour.*

a haphazard fleet of decrepit cargo vessels. Thousands would perish on the grim voyage, their typhus-ridden bodies dumped into the sea. Thousands more would die within days and weeks of landing in the New World.[1]

On Thursday, May 20, 1847, in a gentle Irish rain, Michael Daley and Mary Walsh of Kilbany Parish, Limerick, with their twelve-year-old son, Michael, boarded the barque *Avon*, bound for Quebec. Thomas Reilley and Mary Barry, of Cork Parish in County Roscommon, went too, with their daughters, Mary, 5, Bridget, 7, and Helena, 12. So did Margaret and John Brien of Mondaniel Parish, County Cork, with their children Ellen, 15, Patrick, 14, and William, 12. By the time Captain Michael Johnston signalled the mate to pull anchor, 552 passengers, all but two of them in steerage, were crammed into the dangerously overcrowded vessel.

The *Avon*, built in Boston in 1831, would prove to be one of the deadliest of the coffin ships. But as the boat slipped down the River Lee, hope flickered in the exiles' sunken eyes. The *Avon* would take them away—far from the stink of potatoes rotting in black fields; from the feel of freshly-dug tubers collapsing into slimy mush in their hands; and from the sight of emaciated bodies lying dead by the road, half eaten by rats.

Gaunt and threadbare, the passengers pressed together on the open deck, trying to keep their footing in the swaying vessel, taking in the noise and bustle of the busy port, the shouts and banter of the busy crew. The barque's imposing canvas spread to the wind and the *Avon* heaved forward, past the tightly packed buildings along the quays, past the marshes, out into the cove. On shore, people and cattle in coastal villages went silent, then faded into the misty distance. Past Mizen Head, out into the Atlantic. One last look at Ireland: a thin flat line on the horizon. Then down into the hold, clutching boxes and chests containing a few humble possessions, holy water and a clump of turf or shamrock tucked in for God and good luck.

The misery trailing in their wake had yet to surface.

Passengers press onto the upper deck as an emigrant ship leaves Liverpool, port of departure for thousands of Irish.

ADVENTURE AND AMBITION HAD ALREADY PROPELLED hundreds of thousands of Irishmen across the sea to Canada. The first Hibernian émigrés arrived long before the Great Famine, landing in the colony of Newfoundland, the Maritimes and settlements along the St. Lawrence, centuries earlier, with the French and the British, rivals competing for control of North America's lucrative fur trade and fisheries.

The Irish started spending summers at Newfoundland fishing stations in the early 1600s. Each spring, British fishing boats en route to the Grand Banks would stop at Waterford, Cork and other ports in the south of Ireland, to take on provisions and to hire young Irishmen to work for the season in "Talamh an Eisc"—Gaelic for "land of the fish"—the Irish name for Newfoundland.

The wanderlust that had led the Irish to Newfoundland prompted many to move on again; and they gradually fanned out into Nova Scotia, New Brunswick, Prince Edward Island, Anticosti and the Magdalen Islands. A few Irish sailed directly to Halifax in 1749, with some 2500 settlers sponsored by British authorities who were eager to establish a fortified town on the Nova Scotia coast. And they were soon joined by indentured workers from the Newfoundland fishery, trying to escape their harsh contracts. Within a decade, their numbers had increased to nearly three thousand, enough to lead one British resident to complain that "the common dialect spoke at Halifax is wild Irish."

Irishmen had begun to trickle into Quebec in the seventeenth century. O'Sullivan, Casey, O'Brennan and other Irish names appear in land documents and census records as early as 1625. Nearly one hundred of the twenty-five hundred families registered in the parishes of New France in the late 1600s originated in Ireland. By then, members of the legendary Irish brigade known as the Wild Geese had made their way to the French colony.

The Irish Catholics soldiers had found a ready ally in France, after their exile from Ireland in 1691. They had lost the infamous Battle of the Boyne on July 1, 1690, a turning point in an epic struggle for the

English crown. The war, fought on Irish soil, had pitted supporters of the deposed Catholic King James against those of "King Billy," the Protestant William of Orange. The Irish army, largely Catholics, had resisted their oppressors for more than a year after their bitter defeat at the Boyne. But the soldiers were forced out of Ireland en masse after the Battle of Limerick in 1691—a Protestant victory that would usher in centuries of oppression of Ireland's Catholics under increasingly severe Penal Laws.

Irish emigration to Canada began in earnest after the French lost their hold on North America. Louisbourg fell to the British in 1758, followed by Quebec in 1759 and Montreal in 1760. Almost as soon as the hostilities ended, British entrepreneurs looked to the colonies for business opportunities. And the Irish came streaming in behind them, encouraged by the British who were eager to populate their newly acquired territories with loyal subjects.

So many sons of Erin had settled in the Maritimes, that when the British decided to carve a new colony out of Nova Scotia in 1784, William Knox, the province's Irish-born undersecretary of state, proposed naming it New Ireland after his native land. King George III demurred, choosing instead to call it New Brunswick in honour of a German prince.

Most of the Irish who arrived in the final decades of the eighteenth century were ambitious Protestants from the northern counties, so-called Ulster Scots. In the seventeenth century, the British government had invited trusty Protestants to settle lands confiscated from Irish Catholics. But the Ulster Scots, fervent Presbyterians, had resisted pressures to join the Anglican Church of Ireland, and over time they found themselves increasingly marginalized. Though never as oppressed as Ireland's Catholics, tens of thousands seized the opportunity to emigrate to Canada. Most would achieve at least modest success, and some, like John McCord, one of the earliest arrivals, would win, and occasionally lose, great wealth in the young colonies.

McCord, a well-connected merchant from Newry, one of Ireland's busiest ports, sailed to Quebec City as early as the summer of 1760 to arrange provisions for the British troops. By the fall of that year, he had moved his wife and two sons, John and Thomas, then 10 and 12 years old, to the colony. And in no time at all, the canny McCord had parlayed his way into the home, and business, of an expelled French merchant. By 1763, he had acquired the title to the Frenchman's property, moved into his residence and was using his warehouse and dock to serve his former customers.

The enterprising Irishman who had kept an ale-house in a small town in Northern Ireland also set up sheds near the barracks to sell spirits to the soldiers. Profits from his trade in rum, sugar, tea, spices and other goods, allowed McCord to acquire servants, a few slaves and other accoutrements of the traditional British colonial lifestyle. But a political misstep would lead to the decline of his business—and near bankruptcy. The McCord dynasty would have a second chance, several decades later, when John's younger son, Thomas, stumbled onto a potential fortune in Montreal, in a wild Irish working-class suburb called Griffintown.

Few emigrants ventured into the treacherous seas during the Napoleonic wars at the beginning of the nineteenth century. And Catholic sailors, grateful for a safe Atlantic crossing, kept to the long tradition of placing a carved wooden replica of their boats in Notre-Dame-de-Bon-Secours, Montreal's oldest chapel, which overlooked the waterfront. But Our Lady of Good Help saw a sudden surge in the number of ships from the British Isles after the conflict ended in 1815. It was the beginning of the largest wave of immigration in Canadian history. Over the next four decades, one million immigrants would land in British North America—the great majority of them Irish.

"Canada became the great landmark for the rich in hope and poor in purse. . . . Men who had been hopeless of supporting their families in comfort and independence at home thought that they had only to come out to Canada to make their fortunes," Susanna Moodie wrote in *Roughing It in the Bush,* her classic account of her emigrant experience. "The infection became general. A Canada mania pervaded the middle ranks of British society."

The Irish caught the craze and soon outnumbered the English and Scots in the dash across the Atlantic. Once again, Ulster Protestants, disenchanted by Northern Ireland's continuing political strife and an economic depression, led the way. But the bright future of the New World now attracted a cross-section of Irish society: tradesmen and teachers, lawyers and labourers, doctors and merchants, from the north and the south. A large contingent settled in Quebec City and in Montreal, within range of Notre-Dame-de-Bon-Secours.

Thousands of small farmers of modest means struck out for Upper Canada, where they found "nothing but unbroken forest," Nicholas Flood Davin notes in his 1877 history, *The Irishman in Canada,* which touts their achievements: "Men have come here who were unable to spell, who never tasted meat, who never knew what it was to have a shoe on their foot in Ireland, and they tell me they are masters of 1000, or 2000, or 3000 acres, as the case may be, of the finest land in Canada."

The Irish influx into Canada tripled from an average of about ten thousand a year in the 1820s to roughly thirty thousand in the 1830s. And each year, spurred on by sporadic crop failures and increasing competition for land, a larger proportion of poor Catholics from the south and west of Ireland stepped ashore in Quebec and New Brunswick. Perhaps as many as half travelled on prepaid tickets, as early emigrants helped bring family members to Canada.

Each spring, as soon as the ice broke, timber ships would begin a procession up the St. Lawrence. Thousands of emigrants, mostly Irish, would emerge from putrid steerage quarters, hungry, filthy and exhausted after their long voyage. French Canadians called them *bas de soie,* mocking the hearty emigrants with their homespun knee britches and bare calves.

In the early years, Quebec City, the last stop before the river narrowed and ran into shallow, treacherous rapids, felt the brunt of the passing hordes. But with the opening of the new Lachine Canal in 1825, Montreal became a more convenient transfer point for the journey to Upper Canada. The crush of emigrants shifted to that city, briefly jamming its inns and taverns and boarding houses, and blanketing the wharves and the riverbank each summer.

Many sought lodgings in Griffintown, an Irish working-class suburb on the southwest fringe of the city. John McCord's son Thomas had wrangled with another Irishman over control of the district, and his residence, and a few other fine homes, stood as a fading testament to his ambitions. Yet few moneyed travellers wandered into the rough-and-tumble neighbourhood, a growing jumble of wooden houses set amid soap factories, brickyards, foundries, tanneries and other noxious industries clustered near the mouth of the Lachine Canal. Irish navvies had built the canal in the 1820s, and settled near its banks, along with a smattering of French, English and Scots. Here they eked out a living as labourers, carters, servants, coachmen, carpenters and factory hands.

Griffintown naturally became a jumping-off point for new emigrants en route to Upper Canada. Every summer, the population of the small settlement swelled from several hundred to several thousand, as Irish expatriates welcomed kith and kin into their small wooden houses and shanties. It was not unusual for as many as ten families to crowd into a single flat or cottage. The hospitable Irish often ignored the Board of Health, and their own safety, to welcome their countrymen—or to reap a small income from the boarders. The situation became even more extreme in 1831, when the influx surged to more than fifty thousand—roughly equivalent to the population of Montreal and Quebec City combined. That year, inspectors found fifty people in a two-room house in Griffintown, twenty-seven of them suffering from contagious typhus.

In 1832, the year Susanna Moodie emigrated from England, a partial famine had pushed the number of emigrants up to a record 66,339. Moodie, like many of her class, scoffed at the "extravagant expectations" of some of the steerage passengers she encountered. She considered them coarse fellows, like the one in a "long, tattered great-coat" who "leaped upon the rocks, and flourishing aloft his shillelagh, bounded and capered like a wild goat from his native mountains. 'Whurrah! My boys!' he cried. 'Shure we'll all be jintlemen.'"

In fact, many of the later arrivals, in the 1830s and '40s, had little hope of owning their own piece of land. Often the sons of poor tenant farmers, they had no capital and much of the best land had already been settled. "A great proportion speak only Erse," wrote Dr. George Douglas in 1846, describing the Irish emigrants he had encountered in his position as medical superintendent of the Grosse Isle quarantine station. "They come out ignorant of everything beyond the use of the spade." Most settled for work as farmhands or canal diggers, lumberjacks or longshoremen.

In an odd twist of fate, Napoleon had indirectly helped launch the largest and longest wave of Irish emigration to Canada. In 1807, the French general signed a treaty with Russia, blocking Britain's lumber imports from northern Europe. Forced to find an alternate supply, England turned to the vast, forested colonies of British North America. Soon a steady and expanding stream of ships was transporting timber from New Brunswick and Quebec to British ports. Most vessels returned in ballast to the thinly populated provinces—until ship owners realized they could profit by filling the holds with human cargo.

Low fares—only two or three pounds for a passage to the ports of Quebec, Saint John and St. Andrews—put the New World within reach of Ireland's lowly tenant farmers. But travellers on the timber ships had to settle for primitive, makeshift accommodation. On arrival at a British or Irish port, the crew would unload timber from New

Brunswick or Quebec. Then the ship's carpenter would quickly convert the hold into steerage quarters: nailing crude planks over the bilges for a temporary floor; hammering rough boards into place along the sides, for two or more rows of narrow sleeping berths. The better ships provided straw for bedding. Some installed privies in the steerage quarters, others on the open deck—or none at all. Passengers would bring their own food to supplement the ship's meagre rations (on some vessels, none were provided), and the crew distributed water and cooking fuel during the journey.

Despite the perils and hardships of transatlantic journeys in rough, poorly regulated timber ships, most travellers in the Age of Sail lived to tell their tale. Like the jaunty Irishman Susanna Moodie noticed, brandishing his shillelagh on the rocks at Grosse Isle, the sturdy, spirited emigrants of the 1830s managed to survive the foul water and cramped conditions of a typical month-long journey. When cholera spread across Europe in the early 1830s, inevitably it surfaced on emigrant ships and claimed lives. Still, the death rate averaged less than 1 per cent a year in the decade leading up to the Famine. But in Black '47, as Famine refugees, half-starved and weakened by malnutrition and disease, rushed down to the sea, the typhus fever then raging in Ireland spread to the ships, and the rate climbed to 16 per cent, according to one official estimate—though still an understatement, some doctors claimed. The toll soared to more than 25 per cent for emigrants sailing out of Cork and Liverpool.

The blight struck first in 1845, destroying more than a third of Ireland's potato crop in a crazy-quilt pattern across the country, black fields next to green. But initial reports, in August, that the mysterious fungus had appeared in a few spots in Ireland did not, at first, create widespread alarm. Not every region depended on the potato. In the northeast, farmers tended to rely on oatmeal, a traditional staple. And peasants in many parts of the country supplemented the potato diet with fish, oatmeal, cabbage and eggs. Hardest hit would be Ireland's poorest population, those in the western counties who subsisted on the potato alone. And only in the autumn did the extent of the damage become known, as the harvest progressed and even apparently healthy plants produced decaying tubers.

Irish cottiers, of course, had always known hunger. The familiar gnawing pangs came every year in the months between the end of the old crop and the harvest of the new potatoes, and grew worse in occasional partial crop failures. A tenant farmer blessed with a thriving garden could feed a family of six for an entire year from the harvest of a single acre of potatoes; he could sell his pig to pay the rent on his tiny patch of land and the obligatory tithes to the local Protestant minister; the pittance left over might buy milk or a few scraps of clothing. But that tenuous existence—a way of life for more than three million people, about a third of Ireland's population—fell apart for the unlucky farmer facing a patch of rotting black plants. Without the potato, he was forced to buy food. If he bought food, he would not be able to pay the rent.

Many chose to feed their families and the number of evictions soared to tens of thousands. The chaotic, heart-wrenching scenes played over and over, like a recurring nightmare, in the poorest areas of Ireland. "House tumbling," as it was commonly called, followed a familiar pattern. The landlord's agent would supervise the ouster on horseback, under the protection of the sheriff and constabulary. A few pathetic victims, led to believe they would be paid for their efforts, helped tear down their own houses. But most tenants had to be dragged out: sobbing, pleading women clinging to doorposts; children crying and screaming; men swearing and belligerent, held back by constables while crowbar-wielding wreckers ripped off the roof and tore down the walls.

Before driving the evicted tenants off the estate, the agent might offer admission to the workhouse. Most refused to go to the despised institutions that separated wives from husbands, parents from children, and demanded hard labour for scant food. Nor could they turn to neighbours, who were forbidden to take them in. The homeless would

*A landlord's agent, on horseback, ignores tenants' pleas, while a wrecking crew,
protected by the sheriff and constabulary, demolish their cottage.*

build a scalp, a crude shelter in a ditch, topped with sticks and clumps
of turf, or a scalpeen, fashioning a roof over a hole dug within the foundations of their razed house.

The exodus to North America began calmly in the spring of 1846.
The better-off farmers went first. Ignoring the widespread hope that was
sprouting up along with the vigorous green plants in the potato fields,
they travelled down the roads to Cork City, Dublin and other port
towns, often whole families together, their baggage and sea-stores piled
high on carts. The first ships from Ireland arrived in Quebec at the end
of April 1846. Alexander Carlisle Buchanan, the chief emigrant agent,
observed that the passengers appeared "well-to-do, healthy." Most, he
noted with relief, had "ten to thirty pounds in their possession."

The blight struck again that year, in August, just before the harvest.
Almost overnight, the bright green leaves of the potato plants with-
ered and died. This time the fungus rolled across virtually every potato
field in the country. Father Theobald Mathew, the popular Catholic

temperance leader, wrote to a British official, describing what he had seen on his travels through County Cork: "On the 27th of last month [July] I passed from Cork to Dublin and this doomed plant bloomed in all the luxuriance of an abundant harvest. Returning on the third instant [August] I beheld with sorrow one wide waste of putrefying vegetation. In many places the wretched people were seated on the fences of their decaying gardens, wringing their hands and wailing bitterly at the destruction that had left them foodless."

Ireland's poor fell into despair. Food prices skyrocketed with the return of the blight in 1846; riots broke out in some districts as the starving attacked the "gombeen men," the local merchants accused of hiking their prices. Many tenant farmers had sold or pawned all of their belongings, even their bedding and clothes, after the failure of the previous year's crop. Now they were scavenging for cabbage leaves, turnip cuttings, nettles and weeds; they were devouring putrid potatoes, diseased animal scraps and even grass—anything to stay alive. Already weak and ragged, their pitiful resources depleted, anxious cottiers saw emigration as their only hope of survival.

Reckless with fear, thousands embarked for North America, many with barely enough money to pay for the passage. The fare on a Canadian emigrant ship averaged three pounds—an impossible dream for the destitute. Tenant farmers used the funds from the sale of their small holdings to emigrate, often with little left over to buy food for the voyage. Large numbers sailed with prepaid passage certificates sent by family and friends in North America, or with the assistance of charities, parishes or landlords. Thousands travelled first to England, then sailed from Liverpool to North America, after working to earn the money for the passage.

In Quebec, officials became alarmed at the swarms of destitute Irish stepping ashore at the onset of a Canadian winter, some so needy that the government agent had to pay their sixpence fare on the steamer to Montreal, from where they would proceed to Upper Canada. The exodus escalated through the fall of 1846 and—for the first time—the winter months. The frozen St. Lawrence blocked travel to Quebec, but as many as thirty thousand sailed to ports in the United States during the stormy season. Appalled by the influx of destitute emigrants, the Americans tightened ship regulations under a new Passenger Act; as a result, the fare to New York increased to seven pounds. In the spring of 1847, cheaper fares would redirect the exploding emigrant traffic to Quebec and New Brunswick.

While emigrant ships set out across the wild Atlantic, horrific reports of extreme starvation emerged from Mayo, Galway, Cork and other hard-hit counties. In Skibbereen, in December 1846, a local magistrate encountered a swarm of two hundred famished residents, "phantoms, such frightful spectres as no words can describe," he reported. "Their demoniac yells are still ringing in my ears, and their horrible images are fixed upon my brain." That same day, police entered a nearby house, believed to be abandoned, to find two frozen corpses lying on the floor, gnawed by rats.

Bitter northeast winds blew over normally temperate Ireland that winter, adding to the misery. By January 1847, more than seven hundred thousand paupers toiled on public works—a government scheme introduced in March 1846, designed to relieve the distress of the Famine without encouraging dependency. Ravenous farmers, clad in rags, laboured in heavy rains and blowing snow, building piers and roads to nowhere, for about ten pence a day, barely enough to pay for a single meal for a family of six. Destitute widows and children received only four pence a day for breaking stones. By the spring of 1847, the government would have spent five million pounds on the make-work projects, most of it in the potato-dependent counties in the West.

But onsite engineers reported that "however willing," the workers were "too feeble to perform tasks"; they "were fainting and falling down dead from exhaustion." Still, hordes of hungry applicants kept vigils outside the lodgings of Board of Works officials; the pittance from the public works provided their only hope of eating. Lineups for work-houses, the last resort of the hopeless, grew longer. In January, the over-crowded workhouse in Leitrim turned away two cartloads of orphans whose parents had starved to death.

That same month, the government decided it would stop hiring the destitute on public works. Instead, they would help fund soup kitchens, to be set up by relief committees in workhouses. But the able-bodied destitute would not be eligible for the free soup if they owned more than a quarter-acre of land—a requirement that forced even more Irish tenants off their tiny plots.

Local relief committees struggled to feed thousands of ravenous pau-pers as the public works wound down. In Killarney, one soup kitchen served ten thousand people. By the end of January, in West Cork, a relief committee was ladling out seventeen thousand pints of soup each day; a charitable group dispensed another fourteen thousand pints. In the first months, the effort fed barely one-tenth of the needy. In remote

Starving children scrounge for potato remnants in a barren field at Cahera in a distressed region of County Cork in 1847.

Emigrants seek the ritual blessing of the parish priest before leaving their village.

rural districts, the poor had to walk miles to the nearest centre; then stand in line for hours, sometimes overnight, for a serving of watery broth and a hunk of bread. Thousands, utterly destitute, far from the nearest soup kitchen, with no hope of employment, gave up, took to their beds and slowly starved to death. By July 1847, some three million were lining up for daily rations. That summer, the government revised the Irish Poor Law and shifted the entire financial burden to Irish landlords, already suffering heavy losses from unpaid rents.

Hordes of starving bog-dwellers moved into the towns. As many as five thousand beggars wandered the streets of Cork. In December, Father Mathew, who ran a soup kitchen in Cork, estimated that, in that city alone, one hundred a week were dying from starvation.

More than 1 million Irish perished in 1847, the worst year of the Great Famine, though most died not from literal starvation, but from typhus, dysentery, scurvy and other "Famine diseases" caused by severe malnutrition.

THE EVACUATION OF IRELAND began in earnest in February of 1847, a few months before the *Avon* set sail for Quebec. Emigrants, like Michael Daley and his family, thronged the roads, hundreds at a time, travelling to the port towns together, carting their pitiful belongings, their departure made more urgent by the horrific deaths and degradation of their neighbours and countrymen. At Castlebar, people lay in the streets, green froth dribbling from their mouths after eating grass. In the parish of Kilglass, seven bodies were found in a hedge, half-eaten by dogs.

The parish priest of Kenmare found several corpses in a cabin; one man, barely alive, was in bed, next to his wife and two children—both dead—while a starving cat ate a dead infant. A British naval commander, on a mission for the Society of Friends, delivered a cargo of meal to Schull in southwest Ireland; he later reported that all of the parish's eighteen thousand residents had been reduced to living skeletons, suffering swollen limbs, diarrhea and other signs of extreme starvation. Rats chewed on bodies buried in a mass grave without coffins, covered with just a few inches of soil. The police shot two dogs that were tearing a body to pieces. One had a heart and part of a liver in its mouth.

Frantic to escape, uneducated and gullible farmers became easy victims for ruthless brokers and their agents who travelled from village to village selling tickets to North America. Others went at the expense of landlords eager to shed their estates of worn-out paupers, whom they shipped as cheaply as possible. Passenger Acts set health and safety standards, but, in the scramble to transport the mass exodus of 1847, ship owners and agents blatantly ignored the law. All of them downplayed the distance and inconvenience of the voyage.

Now in this port, and will be despatched for Quebec, direct from Anderson's Quay, Cork, on the 7th May, the Fine fast-sailing copper-fastened first class brig *Emily*. Parties wishing to emigrate should avail of this very favourable opportunity, as this vessel will be comfortably fitted up, is six feet between decks, and passengers found in the usual allowance of breadstuffs and water.

So read the ad for the *Emily* in the May 1, 1847, edition of *The Constitution, or, Cork Advertiser*. In fact, the "fast-sailing" *Emily* took fifty-one days to reach Grosse Isle; and nine of the 157 passengers who signed up for the "very favourable opportunity," died on the passage; six more succumbed in quarantine.

Unscrupulous speculators chartered small, unseaworthy ships, sold more tickets than permitted by law, then sent off unsuspecting passengers from out-of-the-way western ports to avoid official inspection. In County Mayo, where 90 per cent of the population subsisted on the potato, ship-brokers found ready buyers for passage to Montreal on the *Elizabeth & Sarah,* a decrepit barque. Local businessmen had chartered the seventy-three-year-old vessel and sent misleading circulars through the district in 1846, at the beginning of the Famine panic. The ship, scheduled to depart on May 1, finally left on May 26, with 276 passengers—dozens over the legal limit. The delay forced emigrants to spend scarce funds on lodgings. And that was only the beginning of their troubles. The rickety berths on the *Elizabeth & Sarah* collapsed after a few days at sea. Only thirty-six sleeping compartments remained intact, and four of them were reserved for the crew. Passengers had to sleep on the damp, filthy floor, on a vessel described by one survivor as "horrible and disgusting beyond the power of language to describe."

Shipwrecks took the lives of more than three hundred Irish emigrants en route to British North America in Black '47. But typhus, a deadly infection that kills 70 per cent of its victims, caused most of the fatalities on the coffin ships. Spread through the excretions of infected body lice, typhus can enter the bloodstream through the slightest scratch or break in the skin after a louse bite; dried to a fine dust, it can be inhaled or enter through the eyes. A single infected louse carried unknowingly onto the ship could kill dozens of passengers.

Steerage passengers spent several weeks confined in the dark, airless holds of emigrant ships. The hatch, their only source of light, was shut tight in stormy weather.

The highly contagious disease ran rampant among passengers huddled together in damp, squalid holds. Many owned only the clothes on their backs, often the lice-infested castoffs of relatives who had died of typhus. Some captains failed to enforce hygiene regulations, which called for a general cleanup and the airing of bedding on deck in fine weather. Straw mattresses often remained in place for the entire voyage, as did the accumulated excretions of passengers suffering from seasickness, dysentery and other disorders. The overflow collected on the floor, in the tight space between the berths, piled high with boxes, chests and the food stores of those who could afford to supplement the ship's rations. Lack of privies added to the passengers' degradation, and to the mire in the steerage quarters. The scanty water supply doled out by the crew each day—two quarts, by law—was barely enough for cooking and drinking. Cleanliness was a luxury paid for by thirst.

Typhus turned ships into floating charnel houses. "The moaning and raving of the patients kept me awake nearly all the night. It made my heart bleed to listen to the cries for 'Water, for God's sake water,'" wrote Robert Whyte, who paints a grim picture of the hellish conditions in steerage on an infected emigrant ship en route to Quebec in *The Ocean Plague: Or, A Voyage to Quebec in an Irish Emigrant Vessel*. As a cabin passenger, the author heard about the horrors below from the crew: "The mate, who spent much of his time among the patients, described to me some of the revolting scenes he witnessed in the hold; but they were too disgusting to be repeated."

One quick, accidental glance below left a searing impression: "Passing the main hatch, I got a glimpse of one of the most awful sights I ever beheld," Whyte wrote. "A poor female patient was lying in one of the upper berths—dying. Her head and face were swollen to a most unnatural size; the latter being hideously deformed."

No record survives of the agony on the *Avon*, as 136 passengers sickened and died from typhus on the voyage. Did Michael Daley tell his wife, Mary Walsh, when he felt the reeling in his head—the first sign of typhus? Or had Mary already fallen victim to the disease? No one recorded the terror and helplessness of twelve-year-old Michael Daley as he watched his parents succumb to the malady the Irish call "black fever" or "ship fever," then stood on deck as their bodies were slipped into the deep.

Typhus blocks circulation and causes a stench that makes even doctors retch. Swelling begins in the feet and progresses up the body. Gangrene sets in. Putrid sores erupt on the skin. Faces darken and bloat beyond recognition. Mothers and fathers, husbands, wives and children were forced to share narrow sleeping berths with the stricken and dying. How long did they lie beside a corpse before a grieving, brave soul dared to move it?

The *Avon* dropped anchor at the Grosse Isle quarantine station some thirty miles below Quebec City, on Monday, July 12. Fifty-four days after sailing out of Cork, the sea-weary exiles had reached the New World, the "land of heart's desire," where no one went hungry and meat and potatoes filled every pot. The small, hilly island, one of many scattered along the channel at a point where the St. Lawrence loosens its girth, sat tantalizingly close. But most of the survivors—passengers and crew—were too sick, too feeble, to climb up out of the dark, reeking confines of steerage. Their moans and feverish ravings were barely audible through the open hatch. The dead lay silent in the hold. The *Avon*'s sails flapped lonely in the breeze.

So, in the summer of 1847, did young Michael Daley and thousands of other Irish emigrants uprooted by the Great Famine land in Canada: penniless and hungry, diseased and demeaned, thrown among strangers.

TWO

ᐧᐧᐧᐧ

Sorrow, Sorrow, Oh My Sorrow

In the beginning of July, with the thermometer at 98 in the shade,
I have seen hundreds landed from the ships and thrown rudely by the
unfeeling crews on the burning rocks, and there I have known them
to remain whole nights and days without shelter or care of any kind.
—Father Bernard O'Reilly

ON TUESDAY, JULY 13, 1847, UNDER A BLISTERING HOT SUN, Father Bernard O'Reilly and Father Jean Harper climbed into a small boat and rowed out to the *Avon*. Gulls screeched and wheeled overhead as the two Catholic priests paddled through the debris floating around Grosse Isle: filthy straw mattresses, barrels, featherbeds, cloaks and shoes thrown overboard in cleanups ordered by ships' captains as they waited for inspection by government officials. As they drew near the emigrant ships, the stench intensified, a smell so strong that a Grosse Isle physician had once claimed it was visible—"a stream of foul air issuing from the hatches as dense and palpable as seen on a foggy day from a dung heap."

After a few words with the captain on the deck of the *Avon,* the black-cassocked clergymen donned their vestments and, carrying their black bags containing holy water, blessed oil and candles, descended into the darkness and oppressive heat of the steerage quarters to comfort the sick and anoint the dying. Next, they boarded the *Triton,* a vessel out of Liverpool that had lost about ninety of its 462 passengers at sea. In two hours, the priests administered the last rites to some two hundred passengers on the two ships.

"The *Avon* and the *Triton* have scarcely a truly healthy person on board; those who were very sick could not and were not landed when I left," Father O'Reilly testified at an inquiry into the management of the quarantine station, in Montreal a few days later. "Ships have been for several days at anchor before the inspecting Physician had it in his power to visit them: I know too that after the first inspection, the sick on board have been for days without medical attendance—this I heard from the Captains of the *Avon* and the *Triton.*"

Nearly a week would pass before a doctor boarded the vessel. The medical superintendent, Dr. George Douglas, and his small band of weary assistants could not possibly keep up with the flood of Famine emigrants. Two hundred and twenty-seven ships, carrying more than fifty thousand passengers, had stopped at the quarantine station since it opened for the year in mid-May. Now more than a dozen vessels stood offshore with the *Avon,* their captains waiting, impatient to unload the sick and proceed upriver to Quebec City and Montreal. At least three thousand passengers—most of them suffering from ship fever and dysentery—needed immediate medical attention, food and fresh water.

By the time the *Avon* arrived, nearly eight hundred emigrants had died onboard vessels waiting for inspection. The corpses posed a problem, Dr. Douglas knew. There were instances, he wrote in one report, "where both passengers and seamen refused to remove the dead and the Captain himself had to go down and carry up corpses on his back."

Artist's sketch of emigrant ships standing in the quarantine grounds at Grosse Isle. In 1847, officials inspected 398 vessels and detained 284, several of them for more than twenty days.

Sometimes, he noted, "the dead had to be dragged out with boat hooks, their nearest relatives refusing to touch them." The captain of the *Erin's Queen,* anchored near the *Avon,* had to pay sailors a sovereign per corpse for their removal. A grim procession of boats ferried the dead to the island for burial, their bodies wrapped in canvas and piled like cargo, or placed in crude coffins, sailors' handiwork, nailed together from the planks of their berths.

As early as May 24, Father Bernard McGauran, the outspoken young hospital chaplain, had complained about the "heart-rending" situation at Grosse Isle in a letter to Archbishop Joseph Signay, in Quebec City: "Doctor Douglas does not want to receive any more on the island. Since we truly have no place for them, he forces the captains to keep them on board, and we have at present thirty-two of these vessels which are like floating hospitals, where death makes the most frightful inroads, and the sick are crowded in among the more healthy, with the result that all are victims to this terrible sickness." The angry young priest from

County Sligo directed his frustration at the hard-pressed Dr. Douglas and urged Signay to press the authorities "to force this inhuman person to pitch tents on the farms where at least the healthy could be landed."

Stands of poplar, fir and beech lined Grosse Isle's rocky shore, obscuring the tragedy unfolding on the picturesque island. The mass grave, a six-acre field where more than fifteen hundred Irish emigrants had been buried over the past two months, was mercifully out of sight, on the western end of the island. The tall, white spires of the island's two chapels, one Catholic, one Protestant, turned into makeshift hospitals, gave no hint of the hell below. Priests said mass in the sacristy, their prayers broken by the cries of the sick.

Many of the fifty-nine clergymen who ministered to the sick at Grosse Isle that summer gave searing accounts of the emigrants' misery. On July 13, Father William Moylan, a twenty-five-year-old Irish curate, told the inquiry that during his twelve days on the island, he had seen,

One of several sheds built to house the 8,691 emigrants hospitalized at Grosse Isle in 1847. More than three thousand patients died on the island in the hospitals alone.

in the old hospital sheds, two and sometimes three patients in the same bed, in long rows of bunks. "The planks of the upper tier not being close together, the consequence is, that the filth of the upper patients fell on the lower ones," the priest testified. "Corpses were allowed to remain all night in the places where death had occurred, even when they had a companion in the same bed."

Glimpsed through the trees, from a distance, the dozens of military tents pitched at the northwest end of the island took on an almost jaunty air. In early July, Father O'Reilly paid a visit to the site and found a dirty holding place where three thousand passengers from infected vessels were to be decontaminated before boarding steamers for Montreal. There, among those presumed well, he administered the last rites to upwards of fifty people in a few hours, and saw many more "spectre-like wretches" in need of the sacrament. "Being considered healthy, they had to look out for themselves and were lying in beds they had brought from home or on planks, or on the damp ground," he told the inquiry.

THE EMIGRANTS' FAITH INSPIRED THE CLERGYMEN as they made their rounds from the sheds to the ships to the tents. "The blessings they give us and their marks of affection are so lively and so cordial that they fill us with courage and conviction," Father Elzéar-Alexandre Taschereau wrote to Archbishop Signay. "Most of them have for a bed the boards or a few filthy wisps of straw that do more harm than good: still, how many more, after a month and a half of the crossing, are wearing the same clothes and the same shoes that they had when they came on board ship, and which they have not taken off, day or night? I have seen people whose feet were so stuck to their socks that I could not anoint them!" Father Taschereau reported. "I saw a child playing with the hand of his mother who had just died."

Fewer than 10 per cent of the Famine emigrants were Protestant. Still, seventeen Anglican clergymen ministered to them at Grosse Isle over the summer. "We witness most deplorable scenes—but the poor people are so glad to receive our ministrations and in not a few instances, in the midst of dirt, sickness, want and affliction, are so resigned and full of faith, that it is soothing to visit them," Anglican Bishop George Jehoshaphat Mountain wrote in a letter to his son in June 1847. The bishop had counted no more than three hundred emigrants of his faith at the quarantine station during a one-week stay on the island, "dispersed, ashore and afloat, and so intermingled with Romanists, sometimes two of different faith in one bed." At the end of his tour of duty at Grosse Isle, he had to destroy his vermin-infested clothing.

A quick check of the pulse. A glance at the tongue—a whitish coating suggested fever. Weary doctors, forced to examine thousands of passengers, had little time to make proper diagnoses. "The medical inspection on board was slight and hasty," declared Stephen E. De Vere, a wealthy Limerick landowner who travelled steerage to Upper Canada in June, to witness firsthand the conditions on the sailing ships. In his scathing letter of November 30, 1847, later brought to the attention of a British parliamentary committee, he stated: "The doctor walked down the file on deck, he selected those for hospital who did not look well, and after a very slight examination ordered them on shore. Some were detained in danger who were not ill; and many were allowed to proceed who were actually in fever."

The *Avon* spent thirteen days in quarantine at Grosse Isle. By the time medical authorities boarded the vessel, twenty-six emigrants had died. The doctors admitted 390 of the passengers to the hospital sheds and sent the remaining few to the decontamination tents. Most of them also fell ill and had to be transferred to the hospital.

Margaret and John Brien of County Cork were among the 110 *Avon* passengers who died at Grosse Isle, either on the ship or in the sheds and tents on the island. Their three young children, like more than a thousand others orphaned at the station that summer, were given over to the

Irish orphans Bridget, Mary and Helena Reilley. Their parents died before reaching their destination, but the three sisters from County Cork survived the crossing on the Avon *and were taken in by the Augustinian nuns of the Hôpital Général de Québec.*

care of strangers. A French-Canadian family from Lotbinière adopted fifteen-year-old Ellen. An Irish family in Valcartier took in her twelve-year-old brother, William. Patrick, fourteen, was placed with a French-Canadian family in St. Nicolas but after a short time he was returned to the authorities. By December, he too had found a permanent home with an Irish family in Valcartier, about fifty-five miles from their sister's village. The Ladies of the Hôpital Général in Quebec City adopted the orphaned Reilley girls, Helena, Bridget and Mary, aged 12, 7 and 5.

Of the 552 Irish who boarded the *Avon* in Cork Harbour, only 306 left Grosse Isle alive. In his report, Dr. Douglas gave them, and passengers on other vessels from Cork and Liverpool, a slim chance of survival: "Of this comparatively small number, I am convinced a great proportion would fall ill at various places on their route." A.C. Buchanan, the chief emigration agent, had also forewarned authorities in Montreal and Quebec in early June that thousands of Irish would fall sick within three weeks of leaving Grosse Isle: "All the passengers from Cork and Liverpool are half dead from starvation and want before embarking; and the least bowel complaint, which is sure to come with change of food, finishes them off without a struggle. . . . Good God! What evils will befall the cities wherever they alight."

To ease the overcrowding in the hospital sheds, toward the end of July authorities decided to land only the sick on Grosse Isle and to transfer healthy emigrants from infected vessels directly onto steamers bound for Montreal. The plan tore families apart. "The screams pierced my brain; and the excessive agony so rent my heart that I was obliged to retire to the cabin," wrote Whyte, witness to a wrenching separation scene when sailors, following orders, removed the sick from the ship to the quarantine hospital. "The husband—the only support of an emaciated wife and helpless family—torn away forcibly from them, in a strange land; the mother dragged from her orphan children, that clung to her as she was lifted over the bulwarks, rending the air with their shrieks; children snatched from their bereaved parents, who were perhaps ever to remain ignorant of their recovery, or death."

By August, many patients were diagnosed—and separated from their families—without the benefit of even a cursory medical exam. John Wilson, a steamboat operator, hired to transport some eighty thousand emigrants from Grosse Isle to Montreal, Ottawa and Kingston that summer, later testified that Dr. Douglas relied on him to sort the sick from the healthy: "He was worn out trying to do impossibilities. He was compelled to instruct me and the captains of the steamers what people to pass by the color of their tongues." In the hurried confusion, in early August, one determined emigrant managed to keep his dead wife at his side. He carried her body, wrapped in a featherbed, unnoticed, onto a steamer bound for Quebec.

Father O'Reilly watched in anger as his hapless countrymen were loaded carelessly into riverboats, as many as a thousand on a single vessel: "When they left the station they were *literally crammed* onboard the steamers, exposed to the cold night air, or the burning summer's sun, and in this state the most robust constitution must soon give way to an unbroken series of hardships," he testified.

Hired fiddlers and dancers stood at the prow on most of the steamboats that carried the weary emigrants upriver to Quebec, Montreal and beyond, their lively jigs and reels underscoring the melancholy journey.

THE GOVERNMENT HAD ESTABLISHED the Grosse Isle quarantine station in 1832 with the Irish in mind. News of a cholera epidemic sweeping across Europe had alarmed officials already straining to cope with the annual tide of emigrants. Quarantine stations popped up at ports along the coast of British North America, the only defence against the deadly, incurable new malady.

Grosse Isle descended into chaos almost as soon as it opened. Nearly thirty thousand emigrants, in more than four hundred ships, had arrived at the quarantine station by the end of the first week of June 1832. Long lines of vessels stood at anchor while soldiers tried to enforce the cumbersome rules. An officer and inspecting physician rowed out to the incoming ships to check for signs of disease. A military guard transferred sick passengers and their baggage to the not-quite-finished cholera hospital. And while crewmen scoured tainted ships, healthy steerage passengers were required to go ashore to wash themselves, their bedding and belongings, a rule that led to bedlam as boatloads of emigrants competed for space along the shore.

"A crowd of many hundred Irish emigrants had been landed during the present and former day and all this motley crew—men, women, and children, who were not confined by sickness to the sheds (which greatly resembled cattle-pens)—were employed in washing clothes or spreading them out on the rocks and bushes to dry," writes Susanna Moodie in *Roughing It in the Bush*, describing a scene she witnessed during a brief stop at Grosse Isle on August 30, 1832. "The men and boys were in the water, while the women, with their scanty garments tucked above their knees, were tramping their bedding in tubs or in holes in the rocks, which the retiring tide had left half full of water. . . . Those who did not possess washing tubs, pails or iron pots, or could not obtain access to a hole in the rocks, were running to and fro, screaming and scolding in no measured terms."

Moodie recognized the folly of the rule that obliged apparently healthy emigrants from tainted vessels to mingle on the crowded shore. Still, the author, steeped in upper-class Victorian sensitivities, expressed no little contempt for the emigrants forced to perform the required ablutions in public: "The people who covered the island appeared perfectly destitute of shame, or even a common sense of decency. Many were almost naked, still more but partially clothed. We turned in disgust from the revolting scene."

Cholera soon slipped through the elaborate military and medical net. Rumours of an outbreak spread after the arrival of the *Carricks* from Dublin on May 9, 1832, with several cases of a suspicious fever. But the first confirmed cases surfaced not at Grosse Isle, but in Quebec City's Lower Town, on June 8, in a boarding house run by an Irishman named Roach. The victims, recent emigrants from Ireland, had landed in the city by mischance. They had left Grosse Isle on the evening of June 7, on the *Voyageur,* bound for Montreal. But the steamer, weighed down with more than seven hundred emigrants, hit stormy weather, and passengers panicked when the vessel appeared to be sinking. Unable to control the hysterical travellers, the captain turned back and, in the middle of the night, dropped nearly two hundred soaking wet Irish emigrants on the wharf at Quebec City. The next morning, several showed clear signs of malignant cholera. The disease spread rapidly through Quebec City.

John Kerr, an emigrant from Derryaghy, near Belfast, remained on board the *Voyageur* for the wild, stormy ride to Montreal. But by the time the steamer unloaded its 550 passengers on June 9, Kerr had died of cholera. A passenger named McKee had also contracted the disease. Carried from the *Voyageur* to a waterfront tavern, he died less than twenty-four hours later, surrounded by a crowd with a morbid interest in the horrific symptoms of the mysterious malady.

CHOLERA EXPLODED IN MONTREAL. The day McKee died, the disease broke out, seemingly at random, across the city and in the surrounding suburbs. On June 15, 1832, the Board of Health reported 1,204 cases and 230 deaths from cholera. The next day, the *Canadian Courant* painted a sad picture of Montreal:

> Calashes [*sic*] bearing the Ministers of religion to different parts of the suburbs, were met at full speed at almost ever corner, women with terror in their countenances, and many of them weeping, were to be seen in every street, some walking at a rapid pace, some running; persons bearing medicines were hastening towards their respective abodes, carts containing coffins with dead bodies, each accompanied by four or five persons, were passing frequently. . . . Business seemed paralysed. Merchants who had come to our market fled in every direction, and many of our citizens left town and in fine a panic of almost indescribable nature seemed to have taken hold of the whole body of citizens.

Into this city of twenty-five thousand souls caught in the grip of cholera came an unprecedented flood of strangers. Nearly thirty thousand Irish emigrants made their way upriver in the first three weeks of June. Almost every boat delivered new cases of cholera. And, as the *Courant* reported on June 16, "Almost every door was shut against them."

Political turmoil had already poisoned the atmosphere in Montreal. On May 21, in the middle of a bitter election campaign, barely three weeks before cholera hit the city, British troops had shot and killed three French Canadians, supporters of the Patriote Party that was attempting to oust the English Tories. When it became clear, a few weeks into the epidemic, that the city's English residents had remained largely unscathed and that cholera was killing more French Canadians than emigrants, nationalists suspected a British plot.

Even boatmen shunned the travellers. Throngs of emigrants bound for Upper Canada were stranded in Montreal after crews deserted their vessels to avoid contact with them. Traffic picked up again in early July, after the initial panic subsided, but magistrates in Upper Canada tried to enforce their own quarantine rules. Armed guards patrolled roads leading into Belleville, Kingston, and Cornwall; other towns along the rivers and lakes refused to allow boats to land goods or passengers.

During an eight-day journey from Montreal to Prescott by batteau in late June, one party had to sleep in the open after they were turned away from inns along the way. One of the travellers later complained in the *Cobourg Star*, July 4, 1832: "When we came to Prescott we were all wet with rain, and went to a tavern, hoping to dry ourselves; but we were so many, standing in their way. They did not want us there, so we were forced to remain as we was."

Spurned on all sides, the pitiful army of emigrants stranded in Montreal in June sought lodgings in Griffintown, by now a well-known stopover for new emigrants en route to Upper Canada. Emigrant sheds had become fixtures in towns and cities across North America in the early decades of the century, as large waves of Irish crossed the Atlantic. Members of benevolent organizations—or, as the cynical claimed, those eager to help the indigent move along—built the shelters as temporary accommodation and sometimes helped pay for their transportation inland. So, in 1831, did the Montreal Emigrant Society erect two sheds for destitute emigrants in Griffintown, on the St. Ann Common, a narrow strip of land between the Lachine Canal and the St. Lawrence River.

In the first days of the cholera epidemic of 1832, thousands crowded into the large, barnlike structures, with dirt floors and holes cut here and there for windows. "No farmer would consider them as comfortable accommodation for his cattle," Benjamin Workman, editor of the *Canadian Courant*, wrote on June 20, after a visit to the sheds. And, yet, a week earlier, despite the offer of a vacant seminary in the town, the city's powerful Board of Health forced out the emigrants and turned the sheds into a cholera hospital.

At first, patients lay on the bare ground, without beds or bedding; men, women and children, scattered along the sides of the building— the sick and dying next to the dead. A team of doctors visiting from Philadelphia described the makeshift hospitals as "mere charnel houses, where the destitute and houseless might die beneath a roof instead of the canopy of heaven. In the St. Ann's shed, the day of our arrival, 117 patients had been admitted, of whom 101 had died, and during our stay nine to 10 more deaths ensued."

The evicted slept out in the open, in the streets, on the wharves and fields along the edge of the river; huddled under blankets, boards and sticks, their numbers increasing daily, as ships continued to stream up the St. Lawrence. To accommodate them, in late June the Montreal Emigrant Society—led by Peter McGill, a prominent businessman who would become the city's second mayor in 1840—decided to build two more large sheds in Griffintown. By then the epidemic was taking more than a hundred victims a day, and terrified local residents, already living in the shadow of the dreaded cholera hospitals, objected. But the committee—made up, as critics pointed out in public meetings, of "gentlemen who did not live in the neighbourhood"—ignored their protests. The new emigrant sheds were foisted on Griffintown.

Blame for the epidemic also fell on the residents of the impoverished Irish neighbourhood and the emigrants who sought shelter there. In the absence of a medical explanation, the elite presumed cholera was a disease of the lower classes, of the unclean, the immoral, the intemperate. The unsavoury Irish caused their own misfortune, or so Catharine Parr Traill—an author, like her sister Susanna Moodie—heard after landing in Montreal on August 21. "To no class, I am told, has the disease proved so fatal as to the poorer sort of emigrants. Many of these, debilitated by the privations and fatigue of a long voyage, on reaching Quebec or Montreal indulged in every sort of excess, especially the dangerous one of intoxication; and as if purposely paving the way to certain destruction, they fell immediate victims to the complaint. In one house, eleven persons died, in another seventeen; a little child of seven years old was the only creature left to tell the woful tale," Traill wrote in *The Backwoods of Canada.*

In September, at the end of the epidemic, the Board of Health reported 1,904 deaths from cholera in Montreal. But the city's health commissioner, Dr. Robert Nelson, later placed the death toll closer to four thousand, explaining in his 1866 book, *Asiatic Cholera,* that at the height of the scare, illiterate carters trundled the dead off to the trenches, uncounted. The official tally in Quebec City was 2,208. Hundreds more died in Upper Canada, where the figures remain incomplete. But, even with those dismal statistics, the cholera epidemic of 1832 would prove to be only a grim dress rehearsal for the unprecedented catastrophe of Black '47.

IN THE SORROWFUL SUMMER OF 1847, more than sixty thousand Irish refugees streamed into Montreal, a city of fifty-four thousand. Frail, emaciated, their clothing soiled and ragged, the emigrants filed down the gangways of the steamers and sailing ships, brigs and barques that had cleared Grosse Isle, as many as two thousand in a single day. Fitzgeralds. O'Neills. Kellys. Connollys. Boyles. Men, women and children bearing Irish names, scant baggage and frayed hopes. They wound their way past a tangle of ropes and boxes, through the shouts and chatter of French-Canadian dock workers, onto the busy stone wharves at the port of Montreal.

Carriages collected the few cabin passengers and transported them to one of the better hotels in the old town. But more than half of the others arrived destitute, their last few pounds gambled on a passage out of famine-struck Ireland. Others came buoyed by landlords' false assurances, only to find no trace of an agent with the promised money, food, clothing, or land for their fresh start in the New World. Hordes of bewildered emigrants huddled together in the passenger shed at the docks, not knowing where to turn. Too sick, too weak from hunger, to carry on, some simply crept under the shed and collapsed.

The office of the government emigrant agent, a vital source of information about employment, provisions and, if needed, medical advice, was a mile away, at the emigrant sheds in Griffintown. Most eventually found their way there: past Bonsecours Market, past the Hôtel-Dieu and other fine stone buildings along the cobblestoned riverfront; along Wellington or Gabriel or William streets, or any of the other dirt roads that led into the gritty Irish district.

If the weary emigrants of 1847 had glanced up at Mount Royal as they walked toward Griffintown, they might have caught a glimpse of the spire of St. Patrick's, the stately new church on the hill. On March 17, just a few months before their arrival, ten thousand Montrealers had marched in a grand procession to celebrate its opening—a strong display of respect for the city's numerous Irish Catholics. Irish gentlemen, lawyers, doctors, merchants and other professionals who shared their national heritage, and their faith, lived in fine homes on the slopes of Mount Royal, a mile and a world away from the emigrant sheds.

BUT THE CITY'S LARGEST CONTINGENT OF IRISH lived in working-class Griffintown. There, as in past years, many of the newcomers found kin and countrymen willing to welcome them into their small flats and cottages. One Irishman, head of a family of six, jammed nine boarders into his rented two-room flat on Ann Street. However, some residents began to worry as the typhus began to spread. In June, the man's landlord, Robert Everett, complained to the Board of Health that one of the roomers was "sick of what we believe is ship fever, which creates alarm among my other tenants." The board instructed the chief of police to send an officer to the house, and "if any sick person be found, to send them to hospital or to Doctor Munro."

By June 10, six thousand Famine emigrants had disembarked at Montreal. Two thousand of them quickly moved on to destinations in Upper Canada and the United States, joining family and friends long settled in North America. But thirty-five hundred made it only as far as the old emigrant sheds in Griffintown. They crammed into the rambling structures, with the overflow camping out in the muddy yard, exposed, along with their pathetic baggage, to the thunderstorms that punctuated that unusually hot summer. "Pitiable in the extreme is their situation during the present rains," wrote a *Gazette* reporter after a visit that week. "Numbers were lying about on their wet bedding and boxes, the subjects of excessive weakness, generally brought on from violent dysentery. They manifested a state of apathy and indifference to personal cleanliness, the result of great and protracted suffering."

Squeezed into a small strip of swampy ground between the Lachine Canal and the St. Lawrence River, little more than one thousand feet long and twenty feet wide, the ramshackle buildings quickly descended into squalor. "The food is altogether unfit for the poor famishing wretches. Hard black biscuit, surely, is not proper food. There is no soup kettle," the *Pilot* reported. The emigrants had to fetch drinking water from the canal or the river.

Scores fell ill with typhus and other ailments. Partitions went up in the sheds, an attempt at hasty, makeshift hospitals for the seriously ill. "We met with one poor heartbroken man whose children were in the hospital at Grosse Isle and whose wife was uttering her last sigh in our sheds," a *Gazette* reporter wrote. "Rows of roughly constructed beds, each containing two patients, line the long narrow sides of the sheds. . . . There ought to be four times the number of sheds and also an increased number of careful attendants; persons in attendance are some of them unfeeling and do not obey the doctors."

Government regulations required the healthy to move out of the sheds after a few days. And by mid-June, hordes of impoverished refugees were roaming the streets of Montreal. Some tried to sell their paltry possessions to buy food, inadvertently spreading disease in their lice-infected featherbeds, blankets and clothing. On June 18, one newspaper noted "an enormous increase in begging in the city during the last few days," and advised readers "to send to the sheds all those they find about the streets soliciting alms." The next day, a policeman rescued two brothers who tried to commit suicide by jumping off a wharf into the river. At the stationhouse, the men told police they were destitute, without hope, and wanted to end their misery.

Authorities assisted, even pressed, the new arrivals to proceed to Upper Canada, loading them onto barges and riverboats and shipping them up the Rideau Canal or the St. Lawrence as far as the Great Lakes, into the rural areas, into the next jurisdiction. "Sometimes the crowds were stowed in open barges and towed after the steamer, standing like pigs upon the deck of a Cork and Bristol packet," Stephen De Vere noted in his celebrated letter.

Passengers travelling by barge through the canals faced long delays, waiting for a steamer to tow them. Biddy Macavaray left Montreal on July 14 with about sixty other emigrants, heading up the Rideau Canal en route to Kingston. Four passengers died before the barge reached the dock at Bytown. Macavaray lay sick on the deck for sixteen days, ignored by the captain through numerous delays, including a twenty-four-hour stop to wait for a shipment of wheat. The unfortunate woman died ten minutes after landing in Kingston on July 30.

Twenty-eight towns and villages in Upper Canada set up shelters

In Toronto, fever victims were housed in the emigrant sheds shown at left.
The Third Parliament Buildings of Upper Canada appear on the right
in this view from the southeast corner of Front and Simcoe streets.

to provide food and lodging, at public expense, for up to six days. But most of the shelters were soon transformed into hospitals, as thousands fell ill along the way. The death toll from typhus fortunately decreased as the emigrants moved inland. Still, more than 3,048 died in fever sheds in Upper Canada, with most of the fatalities concentrated in Kingston, Bytown, Hamilton and other large centres.

Toronto managed to contain the contagion with strict public health measures. But, thousands of the more than thirty-eight thousand emigrants who reached the city fell ill, and 1,110 died in the fever sheds thrown up along the lakefront. The *Memoir of Captain M.M. Hammond, Rifle Brigade* (1858) includes a letter that the British army officer wrote on August 26, 1847, to his mother in England, describing the scene:

My dear Mother,

   . . . Here the fever sheds are in the centre of the town; about six hundred are sick, and you may see them, as you pass, lying in their beds within a few feet of the roadside. The disease is confined almost entirely to the poor emigrants themselves, and, through mercy, has not extended itself to the town's people. The great thing to keep off the infection seems to be cleanliness and ventilation; and that they have thoroughly established.

A shortage of boats, for a time, trapped thousands of emigrants in Montreal, in the midst of the pestilence. Some tried to strike out on their own and fell uncounted on the roads and rivers, leaving a trail of nameless corpses.

Emigrants continued to stream into Montreal from Grosse Isle, hundreds so sick they collapsed on the wharf. The urgent need for additional sheds prompted Montreal's mayor, John Easton Mills, a handsome, personable American, to pitch in and help the carpenters in the sweltering heat. By early July, a hodgepodge of buildings—a dozen sheds (ten of them used as hospitals), a surgery, a ropewalk and seven outhouses—covered the long narrow site near the Wellington Street bridge.

Carpentry shops turned out scores of caskets. "One of the common daily sights in Wellington Street, in those sad days, were the coffins on their way to the Emigrant Hospital," the chief of police recalled in a memoir. Hundreds of plain deal coffins "piled up in the hospital yard, awaiting the daily toll of the dead, who were always buried at night." Each day, at least two dozen emigrants were laid in a mass grave near the sheds. "Trenched," the Irish called the now routine burials.

Gawkers and idlers hovered in the cramped space between the canal and the fever sheds, trying to catch a glimpse of the wretched emigrants. But the sight of the skeletal patients, their extremities swollen, their skin blistered and blue-black with gangrene, proved too repulsive for many of the well-intentioned souls who came to care for them. In early June, Rev. Mark Willoughby, pastor of Trinity Anglican Church, invited members of his congregation—including several officers from the nearby British garrison—to assist in the hospital sheds. On June 28,

Maximilian Montagu Hammond described his experience as a volunteer in a letter home to England (later included in his memoir):

> I went once to see one of these places (we have since been forbidden to go near them) and never shall I forget the sight. The room I saw was crowded with these poor creatures, some of them lying two in a bed. They were in every stage of disease, from those who just came in, to those who were on the point of expiring. Outside the door was a pile of coffins of different sizes, all ready to receive the dead. Two were nailed up waiting for the dead cart to carry them off; and all this in sight of the patients. The doctor begged me to walk through the other wards where the worst cases were, but I declined. . . . Don't fear my catching the fever. I am not going near the sheds again—being forbidden—even if I wished it.

Jacob Ellegood had just been appointed junior assistant at the Anglican Christ Church in June, when the fever-laden vessels began to dock at Montreal. At least 90 per cent of the emigrants were Roman Catholic, but the genial young cleric toiled in the sheds along with Catholic priests and several other Anglican clergymen. The emigrants' faces, deformed by the plague, remained forever etched in his memory. Decades later, he would recall his stupefied reaction: "When I first entered the sheds and saw a row of black faces, I said to the doctors: 'For heaven's sake, what are these? Are they wild animals?' 'They are human beings' was the reply."

"Well, we all did our best, but what did it amount to?" Ellegood wrote in an article reflecting on his long career. "I saw them dying by the dozen, by the score. While I bent over to take a last message, they died. While I held their hands, they died."

The nuns provided most of the nursing care. Moved by the sight of the sick emigrants lying on the wharf, only two blocks from the convent, Mother Elizabeth McMullen, superior general of the Grey Nuns,

Nuns nurse Irish fever victims in the Montreal hospital sheds in this 1848 painting, Le Typhus, *by Théophile Hamel. Bishop Ignace Bourget commissioned the work for the Chapel of Notre-Dame-de-Bon-Secours.*

had already resolved to volunteer the services of her nursing order when Father Joseph Connolly, pastor of St. Patrick's Church, asked her to assume the work. On June 7, Mother McMullen consulted the emigration agent. Relieved at her offer, he authorized the nuns to care for the patients, and to hire additional medical assistants, as needed. The emigration agent then led them out, in a heavy rain, through mud up to their knees, to the hospital shed on the riverbank, or, as the nuns would describe it in their annals, *l'Ancien Journal,* "the decrepit wooden shack, 'decorated' with the name of hospital." There they encountered "hundreds, scattered all over the ground, or on bare boards, men, women, children, lying helter-skelter, the dying and the dead under the same cover, while others lay in agony on the shore, or on pieces of wood, thrown here and there along the river."

That evening at the convent, some forty nuns in heavy grey habits, their solemn faces framed in starched white linen, gathered around after dinner and listened as Mother McMullen described their new mission in the sheds: "Sisters, the stench emanating from them is too great for even the strongest constitution. The air is filled with the groans of the sufferers. Death is there in its most appalling aspect. Those who thus cry aloud in their agony are strangers, but their hands are outstretched for relief. Sisters, the plague is contagious." Visibly shaken, Mother McMullen told her charges: "In sending you there I am signing your death warrant, but you are free to accept or refuse."

The next morning, eight Grey Nuns accompanied Mother McMullen to the sheds; the others would go in turn. The nuns recorded their impressions of that first day at the hospital. "I nearly fainted when I approached the entrance to this sepulchre," wrote one. "The smell suffocated me. I saw a number of beings with distorted features and discoloured bodies lying heaped together on the ground like so many corpses." Another recalled: "We could hear the groaning of the sick, the death rattles of the dying, even before we entered. . . . We spread out through this strange labyrinth. . . . We ran to this one, to that one. . . . We held one poor woman in the throes of death, her suckling infant still latched to her breast. . . . We lifted cadavers away from those who were still breathing."

The nuns set to work. They cut away the rank clothing stuck to the spectre-like figures; washed filth and blood and pus from their gaping sores. They rushed from one emergency to another, a few dozen nursing sisters, attendants, and selfless volunteers, including many local Irish, trying to care for hundreds of patients, men, women and children, literally piled on one another, three and four to a bed. It took the nuns weeks to establish a semblance of order by placing men, women and children in separate sheds, on beds of straw. They fed the patients government-supplied rations of bread, tea and meat, and, with water taken from the river, made soup in a twelve-gallon cauldron kept on a flame in the middle of the courtyard.

By June 23, a special children's shed held more than five hundred Irish orphans. At least eighty were newborns, suckling infants lifted from the stone-cold breast of a dead mother. Unable to feed them, the nuns laid the hungry, wailing babies four to six in a berth. Few wet nurses would risk their lives, and those of their own children, to breast-feed an infant in the infected sheds. By the end of June, many had died of starvation. Older siblings tried to calm hysterical toddlers, calling out for sick—or dead—parents. One nun discovered several little brothers and sisters who had run off and found their father in a nearby hospital shed; the children played and talked and caressed his corpse, unaware that he had died.

On Saturday, July 11, Bishop Ignace Bourget helped transfer 250 of the orphans from the sheds into temporary shelters, under the care of the Sisters of the Good Shepherd and the Sisters of Providence. "It was one of the most touching moments of my life," he would declare months later in a pastoral letter, recalling the warm summer evening when he sat in the first of a long line of carts, surrounded by the poor helpless children, hoping, by example, to inspire Catholic families to adopt them. Two nuns sat in each vehicle, holding the babies, some just a few days old, in their arms. "At the head of this numerous family of orphans, we travelled through the streets of the city to take them to hospices that had been prepared for them. The spectacle of these hundreds of children, emaciated by hunger, covered in rags and succumbing to attacks of this terrible malady that had deprived them of their parents was too poignant to ever forget."

Sadly, nine of the children died that night, on beds of straw in a hastily set-up shelter in an empty house on St. Catherine Street, named after Saint Jérôme-Emilien, patron saint of orphans. The chance of the other children finding homes was quickly diminishing.

By July, many had become leery of adopting Irish orphans for fear of bringing typhus into their homes. The sad story of a French-Canadian woman—one of many cases reported in the newspapers—served as a cautionary tale for the kind-hearted. The mother of nine took an Irish orphan into her modest home in a Quebec suburb, caring for the child, even after it developed symptoms of ship fever, as if it were her own. "The child recovered," the paper noted. "But its benevolent guardian was infected with the disease, under which she sank, leaving behind her nine orphans."

Typhus was also depleting the ranks of the religious working in the fever sheds. When the matins bell rang at the Grey Nuns' convent one morning in late June, two of the nuns failed to appear for prayers. One by one, the Sisters fell ill, until, a few weeks later, the moans of thirty delirious nuns filled the infirmary. On June 26, the Sisters of Providence replaced the Grey Nuns in the fever sheds. And, with permission from the bishop, on July 2, the cloistered Sisters of the Hôtel-Dieu, les Hospitalières de Saint-Joseph—forbidden by the board of health from accepting typhus cases in their hospital—left their sanctuary to help nurse the emigrants until the Sisters too caught the fever.

On July 10, the *Pilot* provided a grim tally of the casualties: forty-eight nuns, five doctors and eight medical students had contracted typhus. "To which gloomy and sickening record we must add the number of 1,586 persons, of all ages and sexes, lingering on beds of wretchedness and corruption, in many cases without an attendant to afford a drop of water, or even attend those decent formalities which the sad solemnities of death require."

Bishop Bourget and his vicar, Father Armand de Charbonnel—later appointed Bishop of Toronto—took turns on the night shift in the sheds; both contracted typhus and eventually recovered. But at least eight of the priests, five of them from St. Patrick's parish, who served in the fever sheds in Montreal that summer, lost their lives. The last, Father John Richard Jackson, known affectionately as the "Father of the Irish," died of typhus on July 23, after days and nights serving in the sheds. Only the pastor, Father Joseph Connolly, survived.

"No one can predict when this plague will end. It seems to be outstripping all our medical resources," wrote Father Felix Martin, superior of the Jesuits in Canada, in a letter to Rev. Augustus Thébaud, pleading with his counterpart at Fordham to send English-speaking priests to Montreal. Father Thébaud approached several of his priests. "I asked them whether they were willing to start immediately on this errand. It was my duty to place before their eyes the dangers they were going to encounter, the probability of never coming back." A few hours later, four Jesuits set out for Montreal. Only three would return.

By mid-July, typhus was running rampant in Montreal. The epidemic was no longer confined to emigrants and the nuns and priests, doctors and nurses attending them. In the week ending July 17, more people died of typhus in the city (239, including seventy-six emigrants) than in the fever sheds (164). "There was scarcely a street in the city in which there were not five cases of fever," a member of the Medical Immigrant Commission remarked.

In Griffintown, the contagion appeared in almost every house. One Jesuit priest called it a "hotbed of the plague, even worse than the sheds." Father Ferard, one of three priests who stayed in a house in the neighbourhood to minister to the sick and dying, later recalled, "Large numbers of emigrants, regarding the sheds as tombs, would seek out the hospitality of their compatriots established in Griffintown. Moved out of compassion, they would welcome them, and with them, the seeds of death; whole families would fall victim to the hospitality they had extended. Without cease, they would call us from one house or another, as many as seventeen times in a single night or a single morning."

Rev. Henry Wilkes, pastor of the Zion Church, stood up at a public meeting to complain about Griffintown's lodging houses, citing one "whereon the low flat, and in a small room without the least opening for ventilation, three or four persons were found together in the worst stage of the typhus fever. On the flat above the state of things was even worse; crowds of children, all diseased, were huddled together."

The Board of Health repeatedly called for the construction of a wall around the fever sheds and parts of Griffintown, to keep Irish emigrants out of the city, but lacked the power to enforce that or any other of its recommendations. Its members resigned en masse in mid-August, out of "a sense of self-respect."

As THE DEATH TOLL CLIMBED, public fear and rage exploded in frequent, noisy protests. Furious Montrealers gathered at the Champ-de-Mars parade grounds, demanding to know why officials allowed sick emigrants to land in the city. Rumours began to circulate that outraged citizens were planning to descend on the fever sheds and burn them down or throw them into the river. The threat was not without precedent: during the cholera epidemic of 1832, Quebec City officials constructed emigrant sheds near the new Marine Hospital—then rebuilt them after angry citizens tore them down.

A partisan press fed the panic. *The Witness,* a pro-British, Protestant Montreal weekly, asserted that the emigrants "were plague-stricken because they were Catholic." Another editorial suggested that the inmates of the sheds had deliberately spread the disease. Several accused the Irish of abusing public charity: "Cases of ten, twenty, thirty sovereigns being found on the bodies of deceased persons who, when almost in the Agonies of death, beseeched for charity are quite common," claimed one newspaper.

Another alleged that inmates of the sheds sold their daily allotment of bread and meat—three-quarters of a pound of each, for adults; a half-pound per child: "It is the custom of some of the immigrants to leave the sheds at a very early hour in the morning, taking with them portions of their over plus allowance of oatmeal and loaves of bread and selling them at the petty stores in Griffintown for the sum of a few coppers which most likely is expended afterwards in liquor."

The mayor created an uproar with his proposal to build more sheds at Windmill Point, on an empty tract of land in Point St. Charles, across the canal from Griffintown, a half-mile west of their current location. The bilingual Mayor Mills faced formidable opposition. The

View of the Montreal emigrant sheds at Windmill Point,
from the top of the Victoria Bridge.

Board of Health and a committee of influential citizens launched a counter-campaign to remove the sheds to Boucherville Island, twelve miles downstream. On July 10, three thousand citizens turned out to a public meeting at Bonsecours Market to oppose the mayor's plan. "Danger to the city is hourly increasing," declared Benjamin Holmes, one of many prominent citizens critical of the Windmill Point site. Others accused the mayor of converting part of one of the city's suburbs into "a second Grosse Isle."

On July 13, thousands assembled at Bonsecours Market a second time, to sign a petition demanding, among other things, the removal of the emigrant sheds; leading citizens presented the document to city council and the governor general on July 19.

But Mills, who was chairman of the Joint Immigrant Commission, the government-appointed body that included five physicians, stood firm. More than one hundred men were set to work, building the new sheds on the riverbank at Windmill Point. The mayor discounted critics' concerns that the emigrants' "foul effluvia and excrements of disease" would contaminate their drinking water, pointing out that it was already polluted—with the waste of the city's more than fifty thousand residents, regularly thrown into the notorious Little River St. Pierre, which drained into the St. Lawrence above the water pipes. More important, he declared: "To speak of removing from 1800 to 2000 men on the verge of death a distance of about ten or eleven miles is as monstrous as it is unnatural."

At the beginning of August, nearly one thousand patients were transferred to the first three new hospitals at Windmill Point. Editorials praised the spacious, airy buildings, which were well ventilated, with numerous windows and doors along two sides. Plans called for ninety beds, arranged in three rows, eighteen inches apart. There would be room enough, in each one-hundred-by-thirty-foot shed, for each patient to have a bed. There would be separate wards for men and women, and for Catholics and Protestants.

But the scent of freshly cut wood soon dissipated. In mid-August, a surge of arrivals from Grosse Isle swamped the new site and the stink of death and disease infiltrated the new sheds. "After a few weeks' service these wooden structures contained colonies of bugs in every cranny; the wool, the cotton, the wood were black with them," one witness observed.

Carpenters worked overtime to build more sheds, as the number of patients climbed to a high of nearly two thousand. By the end of the summer, twenty-one buildings stood on the six-acre site: nineteen hospitals, as well as a massive two-hundred-by-twenty-foot storage shed and a surgery, with kitchens and living quarters for medical staff.

In August, officials began to divert steamboats arriving from Grosse Isle away from the central city wharves. Emigrants, both sick and healthy, were received at a temporary wharf at the mouth of the Lachine Canal in Griffintown, then taken by barge the short distance to Windmill Point. Patients went directly to the new hospital sheds half a mile away on the riverbank.

A paling went up around the landing site and policemen stood guard at the gate to prevent infected emigrants from roaming into the city. The canal itself formed another barrier; guards were posted on all the bridges to further isolate the new arrivals. Plans included a chapel, which would give emigrants, almost all of them Roman Catholics, no excuse to enter the city. Passengers with sick relatives were permitted to wait in the old Griffintown sheds, which were also fenced in and linked to Windmill Point by a new road that wound for about a mile along the edge of the river.

Officials herded healthy emigrants onto boats for Lachine, a transfer point for the westward journey, as quickly as possible. Additional open shelters, with separate sheds for bathing and washing clothes, were constructed for passengers waiting to board river barges for Upper Canada. Meanwhile, thousands of emigrants, waiting for transportation upriver, spent days waiting in the open sheds, isolated on the banks of the St. Lawrence.

In a further effort to control the disease, toward the end of July medical authorities had ordered members of the public to remove anyone suffering from typhus, including friends and family members, from their premises. Emigrants and residents of Griffintown were to be admitted to the sheds at Windmill Point, others to city hospitals.

The crackdown hit hardest in Griffintown, where hundreds had found shelter among kin and countrymen in the area's numerous boarding houses. "There is scarcely a low shanty—and there is an abundance of them in that locality—which do not contain persons afflicted with the disease," one newspaper reported on August 5. Police, often accompanied by the mayor, went knocking on doors and searched stables and outhouses.

Tales of encounters with ship fever victims became part of Griffintown lore. The terror inspired by the appearance of a young emigrant at the

busy intersection of Notre Dame and McGill streets left an indelible impression on Margaret Dowling, herself a child during the Famine years. Dowling's account of the scene, of the poor waif standing on the corner and holding a tin cup in her hand, while a policeman cleared pedestrians out of the area, survived through several generations, often told by Dowling's grandson, John Loye—although, in the retelling, fear had shifted to sympathy for the emigrant girl.

One early November morning, as the mayor prepared to leave his mansion on Beaver Hall Hill to go to the fever sheds, a sense of foreboding overcame his wife and she burst into tears. Mills took her in his arms to console her. He had, after all, been going to the fever sheds almost daily to oversee construction and to help tend the patients. But today's visit would be his last. Mills, who was fifty-one, contracted typhus and died on November 12, just as ice closed the St. Lawrence, and only days after the last of the steamers had arrived from Grosse Isle, dangerously late, delivering hundreds of starving, near-naked tenants from the Irish estate of British Foreign Secretary Lord Palmerston.

The funeral for Montreal's "martyr mayor" drew the largest turnout in the history of the city. Council members wore mourning bands for thirty days in memory of the steadfast leader who had faced down angry citizens and stood firm when so many, overtaken by fear, were demanding that he turn the wretched emigrants away from the city.

Over the course of that summer, close to one thousand Montreal residents had died of typhus. The victims included at least eight Catholic priests, thirteen nuns and seven Anglican clergymen who had sacrificed their lives to care for the Irish. Typhus, of course, killed thousands of emigrants at Montreal. According to one official report, by the end of the year, 3,579 had perished in the fever sheds. But doctors and other observers believed the actual number was much higher, noting that many emigrants had died outside the sheds. Sister Mary Martine Reid, one of the Grey Nuns who nursed the fever patients and witnessed hundreds of burials that summer, placed the death toll at more than six thousand—the number that appears on the Black Stone, a monument erected on the mass grave at Windmill Point.[2]

In time, a collection of humble brick rowhouses, known as Goose Village, rose on the site of the fever sheds. The flocks of geese that nested on the riverbank may have inspired the name. But, surely, others say, this sorrowful spot so close to the half-forgotten bones of the Irish emigrants harks back to the Flight of the Wild Geese, the tragic expulsion of Ireland's brave soldiers to France in 1691—and the beginning of the centuries-long exodus that culminated here in 1847.

TYPHUS TOOK ITS GREATEST TOLL in the fever sheds at Montreal and Grosse Isle. But Black '47 cast a shadow over the entire country. Tragedy trailed the unfortunate emigrants out of famine-struck Ireland, cornered them on the coffin ships and struck them down in ill-prepared quarantine stations along the entire coast of Canada, from Miramichi to Montreal.

One hundred and six Famine ships would set sail for New Brunswick in 1847, bringing sixteen thousand Irish to Saint John, the second largest point of entry after Quebec. More than twelve thousand emigrants were quarantined at Partridge Island. And 601 of them were buried on the barren rocky isle in that sorrowful summer. Hundreds more breathed their last in the city's hospitals and poorhouses.

It may not be mere coincidence that Middle Island, the site of a quarantine station on the Miramichi River, just a mile downstream from Chatham, New Brunswick, is the same size and shape as a nearby lake. Local legend holds that leprechauns created the cursed island, scene of so much suffering by their countrymen, when, to make a lake, they scooped out a chunk of land and threw it in the river. More than one hundred Irish emigrants died on the small, eighteen-acre island, a former quarantine station hurriedly put back into use in 1847 after several ships arrived at the dock.

The disastrous typhus epidemic that decimated so many Famine emigrants in Canada barely touched the United States. No cases appeared in Boston and only fourteen hundred were reported in New York, a tiny percentage of the many thousands who entered the port. Nor did the like occur again in Canada. After the catastrophe of 1847, the great tide of Irish emigration shifted below the border.

In fact, an estimated thirty thousand—or more, by some counts—of the Irish who landed in Canada in 1847 immediately crossed the border, joining the hundreds of thousands of their countrymen who had been migrating to the United States since it won its independence from Britain in 1776. Most headed to Boston, New York and other northeastern cities, attracted by the ready employment on the docks, in the factories, on the railways or in domestic service. Half-a-million Irish immigrants poured into New York City between 1845 and 1850, and many of them clustered together in the cramped, dilapidated tenements of Five Points and Mulberry Bend, Manhattan's poorest, roughest districts.

In Canada, Irish emigrants typically dispersed into the rural areas. Between 1815 and 1846, three-quarters of a million Irish had sailed to the colony with plans, and, often, savings enough to set up as farmers with a grant of free or cheap Crown-owned land. But the Famine emigrants interrupted that long-established pattern. By the middle of the nineteenth century, the choice agricultural districts had already been settled, and the possibility of buying property remained a distant dream for the impoverished refugees of 1847. The poorest and sickest—among them a large number of widows and orphans, as well as blind, lame and frail elderly people—never got beyond their port of arrival. Nevertheless, large numbers of healthy emigrants, encouraged and assisted by government agents, followed earlier generations of Irish into the countryside to join established relatives or to seek employment as field labourers or as servants in farmhouses.

At the beginning of the season, farmers readily hired the new arrivals. On July 4, 1847, a few weeks after landing in Saint John, New

Brunswick, on the plague-stricken *Aeolus,* John Mullowney wrote to his parents in North Sligo, Ireland, with the good news that he and his sisters had survived the crossing and found employment:

> My dear parents,
> We sailed on Sunday morning from Roughly Head, and on that evening it began to blow a heavy storm, and continued for the space of three days very strong. We had it very stormy for a week and all the passengers gave up hopes of being safe, but I had confidence in the Lord and the Blessed Virgin Mary and my holy father, St. Dominic, that they would not see us perish. One night I put on my habit and surplice and went around all my friends and neighbours to leave them the last farewell. I went to my bed and gave myself up to the Lord, but thanks be to God, we arrived safe on land. . . .
>
> As soon as we landed the captain sent them all into an old Poor House and provided them with plenty of provisions. William Clancy died there and Robert Henry of Raghelly. Thanks be to God, all our friends arrived safe. Dear father and mother, we are all at service. Mary is hired at a place called Misspeek, ten miles out from the city and Margaret is within two miles of her. I would get £23 per year, but I would not go until I saw them all at service. I am at service twenty-three miles out from the city at a place called Quaco on the parish of St. Martin with a very religious man. His name is Timothy Cusack from the Co. Tipperary, Ireland. I get six dollars per month. . . .
>
> No more at present from your loving son and daughters
> —John Mullowney, Mary and Margaret

But opportunities for employment in the rural areas disappeared as the summer progressed, despite the need for labourers during harvest season. "The panic which prevails in Montreal and Quebec is beginning to manifest itself in the Upper Province, and farmers are unwilling to hire even the healthiest emigrants because it appears that since the warm weather has set in typhus has broken out among those who were taken into service at the commencement of the season as being perfectly free from disease," Governor General Lord Elgin explained in a letter to Lord Grey on July 13. One month later, Elgin reported: "The sick have been cast back in crowds into the towns, and the doors of the farmhouses have been closed against even those who are reported to be free from taint."

Throngs of emigrants began to retreat from the countryside. "This city . . . seems to have been made a sort of rallying point for those who cannot get employment in this section of the country," a Hamilton newspaper declared. "We state, on the authority of the health officer, that there are *one thousand persons sick and destitute* within the limits of the city! Many of these wretched beings are huddled together in damp cellars *without food or clothing!* . . . Everyday the poor emigrants are seen coming into the city to seek the shelter they cannot find in the country."

By November, the chief emigration agent had shut down most of the sheds in Upper Canada. Nearly penniless and often ill, the most unfortunate refugees congregated in towns and cities, crowding into the poorest neighbourhoods or into clusters of crude shacks on the fringes. In Ireland, evicted peasants took shelter in rubble and ditches, topped by sticks and mud and branches. In Canada, lost Irish souls built shanties out of slabs of lumber and other discards on unoccupied land. Slabtowns, Corktowns, Shantytowns, Paddytowns and Cabbagetowns sprang up from Kingston to Saint John. "I often wished to be at home again Bad and all as we were," Bryan Clancy wrote in a letter to his family in Ireland from Saint John on November 17, 1847. "This place is Different to our opinions at home any new passengers except they have friends before them are in Distress."

By late fall, snow filled the deep ruts etched into Griffintown's dirt roads by the tens of thousands of Famine emigrants who passed through the city in 1847. Most had travelled on to Upper Canada before ice jammed the St. Lawrence and closed the Lachine Canal. But heartbreak, illness and destitution kept several thousand Irish exiles in Montreal. Bereft of wives, husbands, children, their health depleted, thousands lacked the will or the means to move on.

Many, like William Taylor, placed want ads for missing relatives and waited for a response that might never come:

Information wanted of Abraham Taylor, aged 12 years, Samuel Taylor 10 years, and George Taylor, 8 years old, from County Leitrim, Ireland, who landed in Quebec about five weeks ago— their mother having been detained at Grosse Isle. Any information respecting them will be thankfully received by their brother, William Taylor, at this office. (*Montreal Transcript,* Sept. 11, 1847).

One Irishwoman, a Mrs. McKay, who had been separated from her children at Grosse Isle, went to the sheds at Windmill Point in the fall, at the end of her convalescence, to inquire about them. The nun in charge realized, after questioning Mrs. McKay, that the children had been given up for adoption. "Ah, Sister, I have the consolation of knowing my children are still alive. The Lord is good," the destitute woman said. She walked away with the names of her children's new guardians, but without the means to recover them.

More than three-quarters of the Famine emigrants who lingered in Montreal gravitated to Griffintown, where Father Pierre Pinsonneault, almoner of the poor assigned by his Sulpician order to serve the Irish, rented a building on Colborne Street to accommodate the most destitute. Vincent Franklin and his wife, a kindly Griffintown couple who were already sheltering a dozen orphans rescued from the sheds, moved into the establishment, known simply as "The House" to assist the fifty families that had taken up residence in its fifteen apartments. Editorials condemned it as a "breeding ground for disease." But, The House survived as shelter for several years, despite press opposition and other, more dire threats.

The Grey Nuns, charged by the bishop to care for the poor in Griffintown, saw the number of needy increase tenfold to nearly sixteen hundred that year, as impoverished Irish emigrants crowded into the neighbourhood's shabby boarding houses, damp cellars and unheated attics. The nuns who had set up a home for orphans on Murray Street in December 1846, organized another shelter for destitute women discharged from the sheds. And when the government finally closed down the sheds in April 1848, the nuns convinced the agents to keep one of them open as a night shelter for those emigrants too frail to earn even a subsistence living. Besides providing food, fuel and clothing in regular home visits, they distributed more than seventy-two kettles of soup every day in the winter of 1848, one of the coldest on record.

In January 1848, the long-suffering Famine emigrants faced yet another trial when the St. Lawrence spilled over its banks. For three days, from January 14 to 17, as much as ten feet of water flowed through the streets of Griffintown, Point St. Charles and the lower parts of the old town. Enormous blocks of ice smashed into houses, loosening door frames and foundations and knocking a number of rickety wooden structures into the swirling deluge. Typhus victims, still languishing in the fever sheds, had to be evacuated after ice and water swept through the ramshackle buildings on the river's edge. The flood forced out some six hundred and fifty Irish orphans living in two of the sheds, under the care of the Sisters of Providence; the nearby mass grave, where thousands of typhus victims lay buried, disappeared under a few feet of water.

Three hundred and thirty-two more emigrants had died by the end of March. Spring would bring more hardship, more illness, and the stirrings of new hope. The able-bodied Irish—in Griffintown and elsewhere—sought work as day labourers, dock workers, factory hands, carters and domestic servants. And, within a generation or so after the Famine, most had recovered the health and the means to move on. The Slabtowns, Corktowns and other loose Irish Catholic ghettos that had popped up across the country in Black '47 gradually disappeared.

But Montreal's Griffintown—one of Canada's oldest Irish communities, settled long before the Famine—would endure for more than a century after Black '47. In the heart of a French-speaking city dominated by a powerful Anglo-Scots elite, the working-class urban neighbourhood clung stubbornly to its Hibernian character. Irish canallers, after all, had shaped the physical geography of the original old shantytown. And between 1815 and 1847, at least a quarter of a million Irish emigrants had trod its streets, shaking off the sorrows of Ireland as they made their way west, while thousands of unfortunates, struck down by cholera and typhus, had breathed their last in its fever sheds.

The flood-prone wedge of land, covering little more than a square mile at the mouth of the Lachine Canal, seemed an unpropitious setting for a spirited, rural people. Yet Griffintown would become the mythical heart of the Irish of Montreal and, some would say, of Canada. It was in Griffintown, after all, where the silver-tongued young journalist Thomas D'Arcy McGee, a future Father of Confederation, would find his first and most enthusiastic supporters and, later, his deadliest enemies. The Griffintown Irish would retain an ardour for Ireland that became renowned across North America—and would beckon some of Ireland's great orators and heroes, the likes of Charles Stewart Parnell, to an audience of intensely patriotic expatriates. They also helped foment one of the country's most violent strikes and some of its wildest elections, shaping, through their solidarity, the future of Canada.

THREE

The Rise of Griffintown

*The extreme south-western portion of Montreal is occupied
almost exclusively by the Irish population. It is called Griffintown,
from a man of that name who first settled there and leased a
large tract of ground from the Grey Nuns for ninety-nine years.
Griffintown comprises a little world within itself.*
—from *Picturesque Canada: The Country As It Was and Is* (1882)

NEARLY TWO CENTURIES BEFORE BLACK '47, a Frenchman, Paul de Chomedey, Sieur de Maisonneuve, had surveyed the flat, damp meadowland the Irish would call Griffintown. The founder of Montreal stepped onto the riverbank only a few hundred yards away, on a point of land where the St. Lawrence meets a stream, later named the Little River St. Pierre. Mount Royal rose in the background, its gentle slopes swathed in a spring-green forest. Struck by the peace and beauty of the setting on that glorious morning of May 17, 1642, de Maisonneuve, a devout Catholic, fell to his knees in prayer. He had found the site for God's new settlement, Ville-Marie de Montréal.

The tall, imposing French soldier and his hardy band of pioneers immediately set to work, pitching tents and felling trees to build the palisade that would shelter them over the winter. The nameless place that would in time become Griffintown fell just outside the pale, unclaimed, in hostile Iroquois territory.

In time, stone fortifications would replace the primitive wooden fort at Ville-Marie and Montreal's sturdy limestone buildings would rise within its walls. Griffintown would grow willy-nilly on the marshy terrain to the southwest. Even after the city's walls started to come down in the early 1800s, Griffintown seemed, at least to some Montreal authorities, an afterthought, a catch-all home for the poor and the troublesome, a place apart—and distinctly Irish.

But for the first century and a half—until an Irish Protestant scooped it up—French Catholic nuns held much of Griffintown-to-be. Sponsored by the pious, Paris-based Société Notre-Dame de Montréal, de Maisonneuve had come to New France on a mission: to convert the native peoples and to provide them, and the settlers, with schools and hospitals. As seigneur of the Island of Montreal, he granted large tracts of land to numerous religious orders—the Jesuits, the Recollets, the Congrégation de Notre-Dame and several other communities of Catholic priests, nuns and lay brothers who had come to help establish a mission colony in New France.

On August 8, 1654, just a few years after Oliver Cromwell invaded Ireland and confiscated most of its fertile fields for British soldiers and adventurers, Jeanne Mance, then 48, took possession of the Nazareth Fief, a one-hundred-and-twelve arpent (ninety-four-acre) tract that would eventually form the heart of Griffintown. Mance, a pious lay nurse who had assumed the care of the sick of the colony, built a small hospital, known as the Hôtel-Dieu, on the property, just ten minutes from the fort, on a traditional hunting and trapping ground criss-crossed with ancient Indian trails. There, assisted at first by colonists, and, after 1759, by an order of nursing nuns, she treated settlers maimed and wounded

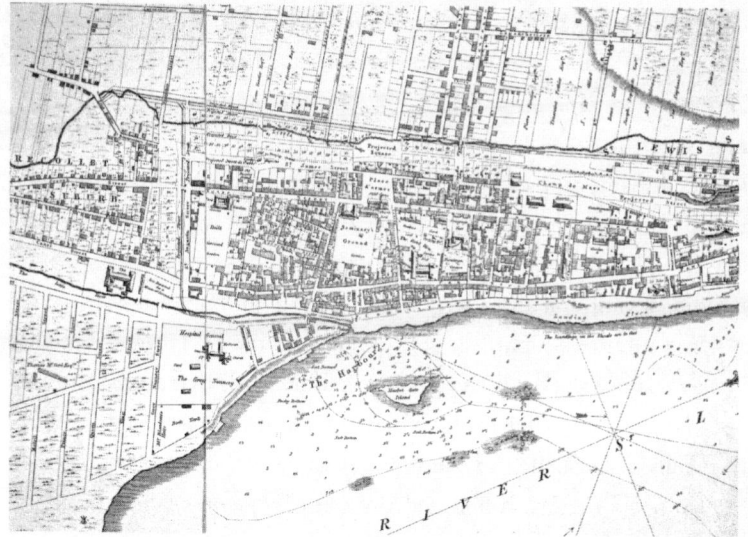

Thomas McCord's estate on the Nazareth Fief appears on the lower left of this 1815 map by cartographer Joseph Bouchette. The outlines of the ancient fortifications that once surrounded Old Montreal (top right) remain visible.

in Iroquois attacks, only a short distance from the fever sheds where, two centuries later, future generations of nuns would care for thousands of Irish refugees wracked by cholera and typhus.

In time, peace came to the colony, and, once the fur trade was established, prosperity. Still, the Sisters of the Hôtel-Dieu (Religieuses Hospitalières de Saint-Joseph) struggled to support themselves and their charitable works by farming part of the fief, raising tobacco and other crops. A 1781 survey of Montreal described the nuns' property, which bordered the Sulpicians' St. Gabriel Farm, as mostly prairie, only partly arable; it also mentioned a stone house and barn surrounded by meadows, and notes that part of the fief had been subdivided. The nuns had leased lots to such prominent Montrealers as Charlotte Guillemin, a widow who married James McGill, a Scottish fur trader and founder of the university that bears his name. The wealthy built country residences on the fief, but remarks in early notaries' documents suggest some disappointment in the district, situated on a flood plain, and prone to dank air and thin soil. But the practical nuns and their new seigneurs—the Gentlemen of Saint-Sulpice (la Compagnie des Prêtres de Saint-Sulpice), who became owners of the Island of Montreal in 1663 after the Société Notre-Dame de Montréal withdrew—put the low-lying land to good use, setting up an icehouse and a bakery, and building a windmill and a ferry dock on the adjoining commons.

On a summer's night, the soft gurgling of the St. Lawrence might be heard across the fields and pastures and orchards that dotted the fief, as the river slowed after a roiling downstream rush over the rapids. But the ebullient social life and commerce of the French fur traders, centred in Montreal's narrow, cobblestoned streets, frequently spilled through the city gates into the nuns' peaceful rural domain. In the spring, during the annual fur fairs, the large commons at the foot of the fief came alive as hundreds of native people set up camp along the riverbank to trade with local merchants.

The fur trade eventually moved inland and voyageurs had to paddle into the heart of the continent to barter for the valuable pelts. Not even the most experienced canoeist could navigate upstream through the turbulent Lachine Rapids that ran from the just above the fief to the west end of the island. So the long expeditions into the heart of the continent began on foot from Montreal. In the spring months, boisterous brigades of voyageurs would burst out of the west gate and strike out on a road that crossed the fields of the Nazareth Fief—the first stretch in a nine-mile portage trail that skirted the rapids—carrying their canoes and chanting the first of the songs that put the rhythm in their paddles:

> *Je prends mon canot, je te lance*
> *À travers les rapides, les bouillons.*
> *Là, à grands pas il s'avance.*
> *Il ne laisse jamais le courant.*

The Sulpicians made the first attempt to build a canal to bypass the Lachine Rapids—the main obstacle to Montreal's commercial ambitions—in 1689. Dollier de Casson, the superior of the seminary, commandeered indebted tenants to dig a mile-long channel from the St. Lawrence, at Lachine, to the Little River St. Pierre. But the work ended abruptly when some fifteen hundred Iroquois warriors attacked Lachine on August 4, killing twenty-four colonists and taking more than seventy prisoners. A second attempt a decade later failed after funding ran out. The construction of a canal would wait more than a century, until the arrival of thousands of Irish emigrants willing to undertake the back-breaking task, Canada's first major public work.

The fief would gain a reputation for rowdiness when the hard-working, hard-drinking Irish navvies came to build the canal in the early nineteenth century. But notoriety came much earlier, ironically, with the construction of a chapel. On May 11, 1697, Pierre Le Ber, the pious brother of Blessed Jeanne Le Ber, destined to become one of Canada's first saints, purchased one arpent of land on the edge of the Nazareth Fief to build a chapel in honour of Saint Ann. Le Ber helped design the structure, modelled after Montreal's Notre-Dame-de-Bon-Secours church. The first mass was celebrated in the stone chapel, a short distance from the town, on the road to Lachine, on November 17, 1698.

French Canadians shared a great devotion to Saint Ann and her feast day, on July 26, became a major celebration. Canteens opened to provide food and drinks for the hundreds of pilgrims who travelled to the little chapel, and some vendors began to sell liquor. By 1736, after several incidents of fighting and disorderly conduct, authorities banned the sale of alcohol in the area, known locally as the Quartier Ste.-Anne. Pilgrimages petered out by the end of the century and the abandoned chapel eventually burned down. But its legacy survived: St. Ann would replace the Nazareth Fief as the official name of the district. And the area's reputation for drunken revelry would linger on.

ON SEPTEMBER 8, 1760, the French Regime would come to an end when British soldiers marched past the little St. Ann chapel. War had broken out between France and England in 1756. During the conflict, Britain sent two armies to New France. Quebec fell on September 18, 1759, after the Battle of the Plains of Abraham. But the French continued to resist the enemy for another year. Finally, on September 7, 1760, with Montreal surrounded on all sides, the French governor, the Marquis de Vaudreuil, surrendered to the British. The bulk of the troops had assembled to the southwest of the city, and the next day some two thousand redcoats marched across the Nazareth Fief, drums blaring, and entered Montreal through the Recollet Gate, at the corner of Notre Dame and (what would later be called) McGill Street.

The conquest did not bring immediate change to the Nazareth Fief. The British made significant concessions to the French-Canadian population of New France, then numbering about sixty-five thousand, by guaranteeing their property rights and freedom of religion. The new authorities allowed the colony's six orders of nuns to maintain their hospitals, schools and homes for the aged. So the Sisters of the Hôtel-Dieu retained ownership of the Nazareth Fief.

The British did curtail the activities of the influential Jesuits, who they suspected might sway the population against them, as well as the Recollet priests, who served as chaplains in the French army. Denied the right to accept new recruits, both orders faced slow extinction under the new regime. Within a few decades, after the last of the monks died, the Recollets abandoned their stone monastery, built in 1713. The Recollets' property, immediately north of the Nazareth Fief, would later be swept up into Griffintown.

But the British commander, General James Murray, did tolerate the priests of the Seminary of St. Sulpice. Convinced that French Canadians would rebel if they were deprived of all their priests, he allowed the Sulpicians to continue in their dual role as curés and seigneurs of Montreal. The priests retained their feudal rights and continued to collect land dues, but only, they were made to understand, "at the King's pleasure."

While British officials engaged in a careful game of diplomacy with the Sulpicians, go-getting British and American entrepreneurs flocked to Montreal, eager to take over the French Canadians' lucrative fur trade. The newcomers, mostly Highland Scots, fierce rivals all, formed the North West Company in 1776, to compete with the French-Canadian traders, as well as with the long-established Hudson's Bay Company. Many of the Nor'Westers, based in Montreal, emerged from the cutthroat struggle with great wealth, capital that would transform the city.

Grand plans for canals and other money-making ventures began to percolate in business and government circles. Eager to boost Montreal's potential as the colony's centre of commerce, speculators began to invest in real estate in strategic locations around the city. But the Nazareth Fief sat untouched for nearly thirty years, until an Irish Protestant cast a capitalist eye on the nuns' farmland.

Thomas McCord had moved to Montreal from Quebec City in 1774, at the age of twenty-four, intent on making his fortune as a merchant. Born in County Antrim, Ireland, he came to Canada as a boy, with his father, John McCord Sr., in 1760. While McCord Sr. had quickly achieved financial success in Quebec City, he eventually lost his business.[3] He narrowly avoided bankruptcy by transferring his assets to his elder son, John Jr., and moved to Montreal, where he lived with Thomas until his death on October 10, 1793.

Thomas, an ambitious merchant and land speculator, risked a number of import-export schemes. He invested in a distillery with George King in a partnership that lasted, on and off, until 1793. But the distillery burned down, and profits eluded him. McCord lacked his father's mercantile expertise, although the son outshone the father socially and politically—more useful skills, perhaps, in the jostling power struggles of the emerging colony. Moving in the circles of the city's wealthy

English, Scottish and Irish Protestant elite, he acquired impressive credentials. McCord joined the Freemasons and, in 1788, reached the rank of provincial grand secretary. That same year, he became a justice of the peace. He was also a lieutenant with the local British militia. In the 1790s, he became a city magistrate, one of a powerful group of twenty men that managed the city.

In the 1780s, the well-connected McCord began to speculate in land, buying small lots outside the city. But he made potentially the most lucrative real estate deal of his life when he acquired the Nazareth Fief, held by the Sisters of the Hôtel-Dieu. The nuns' farmland, located close to the port of Montreal on the heavily travelled road to Lachine, would surge in value if the much-talked-about plans for a canal became a reality. On July 23, 1792, the ambitious Irish Protestant met with Sister Gabrielle d'Ailleboust, superior of the Sisters of the Hôtel-Dieu, and three other nuns, to sign a ninety-nine-year lease on the property. The nuns would use the rent—twenty-five pounds a year—to replace the income they had earned from farming the property, known as the Grange des Pauvres, since the revenue was used to feed the poor and maintain their nearby hospital.

McCord moved into an existing large, three-storey stone manor on the fief. He leased the property's windmill and wooden house to a local miller and sublet a small woodlot to a business partner. But McCord, then occupied by business and political pursuits, made no other attempts to develop the land. Instead, he relaxed into the life of a gentleman farmer on the property, which came with stone stables, a barn and fenced pastures overlooking the St. Lawrence. He ordered seeds and roots from England and planted raspberry and gooseberry bushes, nursing them and other non-native vegetables, fruits and flowers through the extremes of Montreal's climate.

McCord gradually expanded his real estate holdings in the area. In April 1793, he leased an eight-acre tract on the adjoining St. Ann Fief, in perpetuity, from the Sisters of the Congrégation de Notre-Dame. Three

years later, he acquired a one-hundred-foot strip of land that separated the property from the St. Lawrence.

But by 1796, McCord had accumulated a massive £3,000 debt, more than £2,000 due to business losses. He owed a significant sum to his former partner, George King, following the collapse of their import-export business in 1793. And, in 1795, with the failure of a joint venture in a local distillery with several prominent fur traders, among them James McGill and Levy Solomon, McCord sank further into debt.

In December 1796, on the brink of bankruptcy, McCord set sail for Ireland, supposedly to sell some real estate. Before he left, he sublet most of his properties, including his residence, for fourteen years, for six times more than he paid the nuns. He entrusted his affairs to his attorney, Patrick Langan, a personal friend and his niece's husband.

McCord's stay in Ireland stretched to nearly a decade. He spent the first two years in Newry, his childhood home, then relocated to Dublin. Political turmoil, he would explain, had flattened real estate sales. In fact, the Rebellion of '98, one of Ireland's bloodiest insurrections, erupted while McCord was in the Irish capital, and he joined the Dublin yeomanry and served on the side of the British.

Leaders of the United Irishmen, a popular movement committed to independence for Ireland, had planned a nationwide insurrection on the night of May 23. But the yeomanry, tipped off by informers, blocked the attack on Dublin Castle, and the British army quickly quashed the uprisings outside the city. It appeared doomed from the start, but the rebellion, supported by the United Irishmen's unprecedented coalition of Catholic and Protestants, more than half a million strong and of every class, continued until the end of September.

Small, scattered bands of rebels rose up to fight rampaging British troops, who were burning and destroying villages in an effort to crush the revolution. The fabled "boys of Wexford," armed with pitchforks, mounted a fierce but ultimately futile battle against a cavalry equipped with artillery. And in September, Wolfe Tone, leader of the United

Irishmen, arrived on the coast with a fleet of nine ships and three thousand French soldiers, only to face a final defeat.

Some six hundred soldiers died in the Rebellion of '98. On the rebel side, the toll mounted to more than twenty-five thousand, many of them women and children. Wolfe Tone, sentenced to death as a traitor, joined the ranks of Irish martyrs when he died in prison on November 19, 1798. The failed uprising led to a further crackdown by the British. In 1801, the government tightened its control over Ireland with the Act of Union, which abolished the Irish Parliament. And now, the United Irishmen would have to face yet another foe: in 1795, a few years before the rebellion, Irish Protestants had revived the Orange Order, a fraternal society that would mount a formidable opposition to their Catholic countrymen at home and abroad for at least another century.

AT THE END OF THE HOSTILITIES, Thomas McCord travelled to London for his marriage, on November 27, 1798, to Sarah Solomon, daughter of his former Montreal business associate. The couple would have five children; their two surviving sons were born in Ireland, John Samuel in 1801 and William King in 1803. There, McCord made yet another attempt to establish a business, this time exporting Irish linens to Canada and, with the assistance of Langan and a brother-in-law, importing potash, wheat and skins to Ireland. It, too, failed. "Misfortunes are said never to come singly and indeed I may have fully verified the observation," McCord wrote from Dublin to Montreal lawyer James Reid on July 31, 1801. "You have no doubt heard from Mr. Langan or some other of my friends the fatal termination of a mercantile connection from which I one time had such flattering expectations," he continued in his fine, elegant script. As for his bankruptcy, McCord told the Montreal lawyer that he had at least found "some satisfaction" in that, "it was out of my power to prevent it and I have the pleasure of saying to my friends that my conduct throughout the whole of this unfortunate [event] has been such to ensure me the friendship of all the creditors."

Meanwhile, in Montreal, Langan took advantage of McCord's absence to acquire his assets through some financial sleight-of-hand. The clever trustee recognized an opportunity in 1799 when King and other former partners threatened to sue McCord for debts arising out of the failed Montreal Distillery Company. But Langan's first move was to consolidate McCord's real estate holdings by leasing two small parcels of land adjacent to the fief from the Sulpicians and the Congrégation de Notre-Dame in 1801. He then proceeded to buy up his uncle's debts and, in 1803, sued him for default. In the subsequent sheriff's sale, Langan purchased McCord's property leases. Before the end of the year, he had sold them to Mary Griffin, then living in McCord's manor with her husband, Robert, owner of a soap factory on the fief.

By the early 1800s, the Nazareth Fief had lost much of its appeal to the gentry. Wealthy Montrealers had begun to look toward the slopes of Mount Royal for country estates, away from the swampy, flood-prone flats along the St. Lawrence. The Little River St. Pierre, which wound its way across the Island of Montreal and slid along the fortifications at the edge of the fief before draining into the St. Lawrence, had become a cesspool. Residents would throw their garbage into the stream, expecting spring floods to flush it away. But the refuse tended to pile up in Griffintown, at the bridge that connected the fief to the city. Still, the land's proximity to the city had increased its commercial appeal and its value.

Mary Griffin shrewdly anticipated the need for cheap housing for the workers in her husband's factory. Soon after acquiring Thomas McCord's unexpired lease, she paid a visit to the convent of the Hôtel-Dieu and presented the nuns with her plans for the property. On April 10, 1804, the sisters gave Griffin their blessing and signed the documents allowing her to subdivide one-third of the Nazareth Fief into

Silhouette of Robert Griffin. The Irish businessman, who owned a soap factory near Wellington and Nazareth streets in the early 1800s, lent his name to the Montreal working-class district.

small lots. Under the agreement, the nuns would receive one-sixth of the selling price of each lot, less a 10 per cent commission, a perpetual ground rent, and transfer dues (a surtax on any upgrades and increases in land values). They also retained the right to approve the subdivision plans, as well as the right of first refusal on the sale of each property. The deal promised to be a lucrative one for the nuns, although their correspondence would later reveal that their agent often failed to collect the unpopular ground rents and surtaxes in Griffintown, out of fear of the Irish. In the mid-1850s, the nuns managed to recover some £15,000 that had been in arrears.

Mary Griffin sketched out street plans and hired Louis Charland, the city's official surveyor and cartographer, to create a map of the development she called Griffintown. Charland's drawing shows the streets laid out on a grid, a departure from the haphazard growth of suburbs in that era. Griffin paid tribute to the Crown in her choice of street names: King, Queen, Prince. But her proposal for a Trafalgar Square, commemorating Britain's decisive victory over the French and Spanish navies in October 1805, never materialized in Griffintown. Nor did Griffin Street, Mary's new name for old Lachine Road.

McCord finally returned to Montreal, and to some unpleasant realities, in 1805. His former manor had a new occupant. Mary Griffin had leased the Grange des Pauvres to Daniel Sutherland. And she had already sold off several lots on the Nazareth Fief. Small workers' cottages were springing up in the new subdivision and several merchants, a shipyard and slaughterhouses had set up shop on McCord's once bucolic property. McCord made no attempt to regain his land—at first. He settled his family in a rented house in Montreal and started yet another merchant business. After it floundered, in 1807, he took a position as a seigneurial agent at Beauharnois, across the river from the city.

But by 1808, McCord had returned to Montreal and launched a legal battle to regain his property. In his lawsuit, McCord accused Langan and the Griffins of "conspiring to injure him and deprive him of his said estates and property." He also claimed that the Griffins were aware of the fraudulent means that Langan had taken to acquire the land, "The said Mary Griffin having consented to such fraud." The Griffins denied the allegations.

McCord won the initial round in the Court of King's Bench in the same year. But the Griffins contested the decision. A year later, after the Appeal Court decided in McCord's favour, the couple took their case to the Privy Council. Much was at stake as the land had increased significantly in value. At one point in the bitter, protracted fight, the Griffins' lawyer suggested that McCord may have been dishonest during his earlier bankruptcy proceedings and had perhaps been trying to protect his property from creditors in Ireland. "The insinuation was cruel . . . and is hard to bear in addition to the load of misfortune which it has pleased the Almighty to try me," McCord wrote in a letter

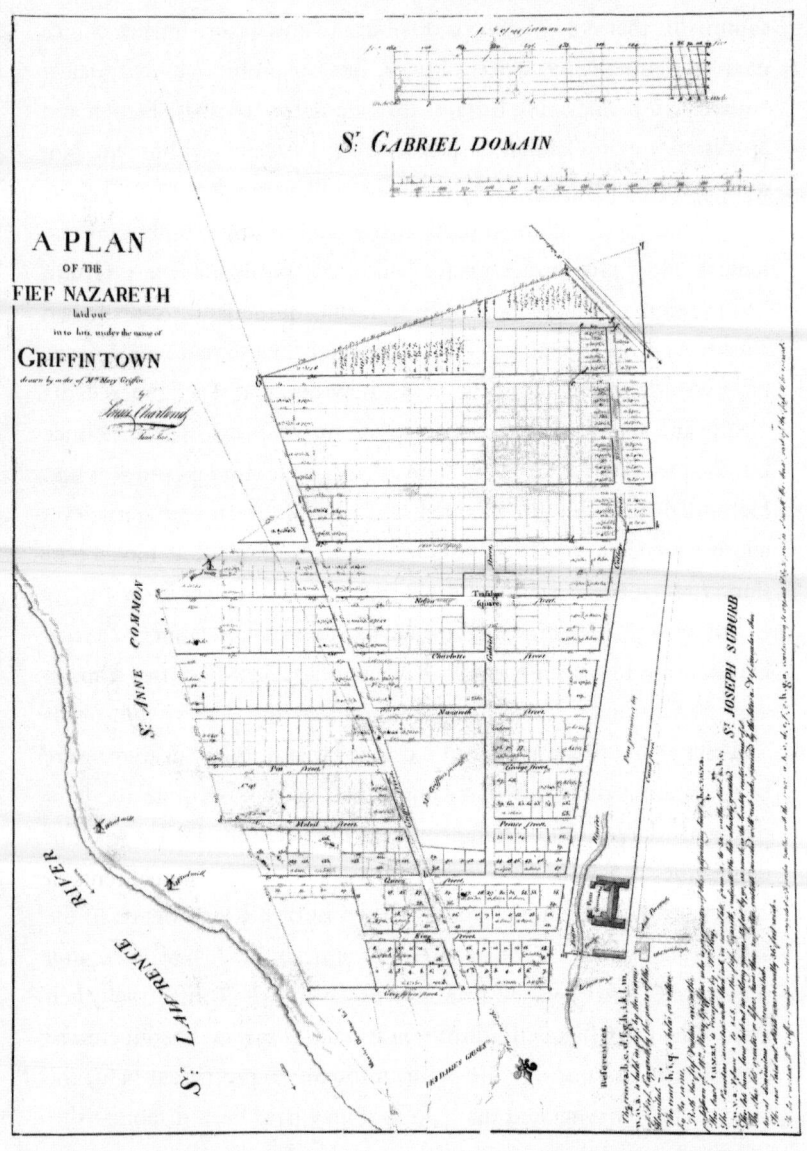

The first map of Griffintown. Mrs. Mary Griffin sketched out street plans and hired Louis Charland, the city's official surveyor and cartographer, to create a map of the suburban development she named after her husband.

to a confidante, adding that he feared the accusation could sway the court and deprive him of "this chance of preserving something out of the wreck started by Mr. Langan's deceit."

Meanwhile, Robert Griffin continued to operate the Griffin Mills soap factory on Lower Lachine Road, now called Wellington Street. The Griffins had made sufficient impact that their name became irrevocably associated with the district. Griffintown would never become an official moniker, but by 1825 newspapers, and even some legal documents and records, were already referring to the fief as the "Griffintown Suburb."

Nor did the legal dispute prevent McCord from entering politics. He ran successfully for the Legislative Assembly, winning one of two seats in Montreal's West Ward in the 1809 election. He withdrew from the riding in the next election the following year, however, after he lost support by backing the governor general's unpopular attempts to weaken the powers of the Assembly. In 1810, the well-connected McCord accepted another appointment as a senior justice of the peace, in addition to becoming a police magistrate.

In 1812, the Privy Council upheld the judgments of the lower courts. But two years would pass before McCord regained full possession of his properties. Finally, in 1814, he moved back to the fief. Thanks to the Griffins' business acumen, McCord now collected annual rents of more than £400, from which he paid £80 in rent to the nuns. He also adopted the Griffins' clever development strategy—one that would transform the fief and bring him great wealth. In 1816, McCord subdivided another section of Griffintown and offered up dozens of new lots—just as the first of a large wave of Irish emigrants had begun to arrive at the port of Montreal.

That same year, McCord and his wife Sarah sat for portraits by French-born artist Louis Dulongpré. The paintings, in a chiaroscuro style reminiscent of Rembrandt, depict the aristocratic couple in tasteful finery: Sarah, plump, delicate and sensitive, holds an open book in

Portraits of Thomas McCord and Sarah (Solomon) McCord.

her lap; a rose adorns her bosom and a feathery cap sits aslant on her greying hair. McCord sits proud, upright, in high collar and cravat; his prominent nose offsetting thin lips and soft, effete features. There is an understandable smugness in the sly eyes that gaze, not quite directly, at the viewer.

McCord was perfectly positioned to profit from the imminent construction of the canal. He had lost his seat as a representative of Montreal's West Ward but he found another entry into the corridors of power. From 1816 to 1820, he sat in the Assembly as a member for Bedford, a position that would make him privy to the government's plans and decisions affecting the Lachine Canal. In March 1821, when a private consortium failed to raise sufficient funds, the Quebec Assembly decided to finance the canal.

The celebration took place at Lachine, the starting point for the nine-mile-long canal that would wend its way to the port of Montreal. On Tuesday, July 17, 1821, two hundred labourers, most of them Irish, stood at the ready, in two parallel lines precisely forty feet apart, the width of the canal they were about to dig. Several hundred spectators—family and friends and curious observers, from the city and nearby villages, including Caughnawaga, on the opposite shore—formed a circle around them on the bank of the St. Lawrence, anticipating the grand event. Minutes before one o'clock, the 60th Regiment's red-coated marching band led the dignitaries—the ten commissioners of the Lachine Canal, the engineer and the contractors—down the aisle formed by the two rows of labourers.

Right on the hour, one of the contractors stepped forward and handed the ceremonial spade, decked out in cheerful ribbons, to Thomas Burnett. The eminent British engineer then turned and presented it to the Hon. John Richardson, chairman of the commissioners. Richardson nudged out the first shovelful of earth from the canal bed. Then, after each of the commissioners and contractors had taken a ritual stab at the turf, Richardson began his brief speech: "Mr. Engineer and Gentlemen Contractors for the Lachine Canal, may the completion of this great undertaking be as auspicious as its commencement."

The solemnities concluded with "God Save the King." Then the military band picked up the pace with "Off She Goes," a sprightly Irish jig, for the labourers' turn at the sod, an enthusiastic display of the much-lauded Irish muscle, cut short by an invitation to a food-laden table.

The promised roasted ox failed to appear. The Montreal *Herald* later explained that the grand idea had been rendered impractical by "the absence of proper materials and the general inexperience in such a wholesale method of cooking." But the substitute—six enormous meat pies, each weighing more than one hundred pounds—appeared to satisfy the five hundred guests. Tall, heavyset Thomas Porteous, one of the commissioners and a merchant with an interest in a local ironworks, carved the pies into wedges, using enormous buckhorn-handled utensils: the knife, "as broad as a scimitar," measured three feet nine inches in length; the fork, three feet. Six immense hams, one hundred loaves of bread and a forty-pound Cheshire cheese rounded out the feast set out on long trestle tables. The labourers quenched their thirst with four hogsheads of beer and covert nips of rum bought at a nearby contractor's store.

Around three o'clock, the commissioners, the engineer, the contractors and their friends slipped away to Connolly's Inn. There the gentlemen partook of a more refined, though no less ample, dinner punctuated by numerous toasts: *The King, God bless him! Our noble Governor! The Lachine Canal, success to it!* Each one greeted with enthusiastic cheers and a tune from the brass band, lively and loud enough to drown out the shouts of the Irish and French Canadians fighting down on the riverbank.

Newspapers struck an indulgent tone in their reports of the incident: "Some spirited Hibernians among them, wishing to give a specimen of their bruising skill to the Canadian portion of the company, introduced knock down arguments . . . they warmly and effectually returned the compliment," the *Canadian Courant* wrote. "No very serious consequences were the result; nor were any, as has been reported, dangerously injured; indeed it could hardly be supposed that such a quantity of exhilarating liquor could be disposed of peaceably."

The dignitaries rode back to Montreal in elegant carriages in the early hours of the morning, basking in the impending glory of the future canal. At dawn, the Irish labourers sank into the dirty daily grind. It would take hundreds of men five years to excavate the length of the channel—eight and a half miles of rock and soil from Lachine to Montreal. The five-foot-deep canal measured forty feet across on the surface and twenty-eight feet at the bottom. Ploughs and horse-shovels helped break the ground, but labourers dug the trench by hand, with pick and shovel, carrying the earth and rock away in wheelbarrows, using gunpowder, and chancing injury and death, to blast through the first three miles of solid rock. The canallers, or navvies as they were called, toiled fourteen hours a day, pressed by hard-driving contractors trying to compensate for a short construction season.

Only desperate men would accept such arduous labour and rough living conditions for wages as low as two shillings a day. And, apart from a few French Canadians, the navvies on the Lachine Canal were almost exclusively Irish. Unskilled tenant farmers—most from southern Ireland, a small number from Ulster—they had landed in Montreal in the surge of emigration that began in 1815, but lacked the funds or inclination to follow the thousands of their compatriots flowing westward to lay claim to wilderness plots in Upper Canada and the United States.

By 1818, local newspapers had taken notice of the growing number of needy Irish congregating in the city. "Give employment to the poor emigrants!" declared the Montreal *Herald* on August 15, 1818, noting the "prodigious" number of emigrants "now swarming among us for employment." The writer included a glowing reference from a small Quebec village. Residents of Maskinongé, he reported, were "astonished at the rapidity which was displayed by about forty Irish labourers in excavating water work trenches of eight feet deep. Double the number of Canadians would not have done the work in the same time." It was the colony's first glimpse of the Irish navvies' legendary prowess with a pick and shovel.

The tradition of the navvy—short for navigator—originated in Britain in the 1790s, in the golden age of canals. Gangs of itinerant labourers, typically unemployed Irish farm workers, would travel to public works across Europe and Asia, digging canals and, later, building railways—by hand. Navvies' reputation for muscle power and their colourful, earthy, brawling ways would follow them, as tens of thousands migrated to North America in the early decades of the nineteenth century, seeking employment on the new canals and railways under construction across the continent. In addition to the hundreds of men employed to dig the Lachine Canal in the 1820s, as many as nine thousand navvies were employed on the Rideau and Welland canals between 1826 and 1832.

A strong sense of camaraderie developed in the freewheeling work camps and the men occasionally united to fight for better wages and working conditions. But feuds often erupted, especially in the winter months, when a surplus of labourers competed for limited employment. Crews tended to form around regional and religious ties, so tensions and rivalries frequently pitted Irish against French and, more often, Irishmen against their own countrymen. The struggle for work, and for the wages that made the difference between subsistence and starvation, aggravated the historic bitterness between Corkmen and Connaughts and between Catholics and Orangemen.

At first, Montreal newspapers dismissed the Irish labourers' alcohol-fuelled sparring as harmless, even amusing, especially in their reports of the brawls that erupted around Orangemen's Day and St. Patrick's Day. But in October 1822, a battle between Orange and Catholic navvies raged for a week. In late 1829, when weather halted construction on the Rideau, four hundred Irish Catholics and Orangemen fought bitterly over the few available winter jobs.

Yet contractors happily quenched the navvies' thirst—for a profit. Stanley Bagg's account books reveal that daymen made almost daily trips to his store on the construction site to purchase food, tobacco and alcohol, rarely leaving with less than half a pint of rum, and often with much more. Along with fish, eggs and other staples, the May 15, 1822, entries on John McCourt's not-untypical account included one gallon of rum, half a pint of whiskey and half a pint of rum. But, over time, as the navvies' drinking and shenanigans got out of hand, and as their numbers increased, the tone of the editorials changed and their reputation took a beating. The St. Lawrence canals continued to expand in the 1830s and '40s. And so did the number—and militancy—of the navvies.

Some canallers boarded with locals, but most lived in bunkhouses, tents and shanties along the construction site. And the transient labourers—often broke and far from stores—irked local residents with their tendency to help themselves to produce from gardens and orchards, and to pluck boards from fences and outbuildings to build shanties and fuel campfires. When the navvies were digging the section of the canal that cut through the pastures of the Sulpicians' St. Gabriel farm, near Griffintown and under the watchful eye of the powerful priests, the commissioners strictly controlled the flow of alcohol.

Shanties and sod huts sprang up in Griffintown as the excavation of the Lachine Canal progressed toward Montreal. McCord's investment began to pay off: he leased seventy-three lots on the Nazareth Fief during the construction of the canal, some of them to poor navvies who struggled to pay the rent. Between 1820 and 1821, five properties were seized by the sheriff and put up for auction after the owners fell into arrears. Still, McCord displayed some flexibility, often accepting payment in the form of labour. One debtor arranged to pay his entire rent in loaves of bread. McCord could afford to be lenient. While Irish navvies earned between two and three pounds a month, sweating out fourteen-hour days on the canal, he was collecting nearly fifty pounds a month in rental income alone.

McCord indulged himself with a new house on his sprawling Griffintown property—a peculiar six-sided, two-storey brick building with Gothic-style arched windows, flanked by two single-storey wings that jutted forward at forty-five degree angles. He didn't skimp on its furnishings. Between 1819 and 1822, McCord lavished nearly £2,000 on his estate. His refined tastes demanded custom furniture—some of his special orders included sideboards, a walnut chest of drawers, cherry shelves, library steps covered with carpet, hat stands, a liquor case with drawers for tumblers, and a special chair for his use at the courthouse. He also spent £200 a year on local and imported food, which he served on the finest imported china, bought in quantity. He ordered dozens of dessert plates, wine glasses, tumblers, compotes and decanters from a London supplier. Some of his more unusual purchases included a mahogany barometer with a thermometer and a camera obscura.

McCord read widely and held subscriptions to the *Canadian Spectator*, the *Boston Athenian*, the *Albion*, the *Canadian Times*, the Montreal *Gazette*, the *Herald* and the Quebec *Gazette*. He also lined his library with hundreds of books: magistrate's manuals, history, poetry and classics like Virgil's *Aeneid* stood on shelves next to French and Latin dictionaries, prayer books and bibles. He must have had a sense of humour, since he also acquired seven volumes of the popular caricature series *Percy Anecdotes*.

Thomas McCord lived long enough to cruise down the first seven miles of the canal—from Lachine to the fourth lock at the edge of St. Ann's Ward—when it opened to commercial traffic in August 1824. But he died of cancer on December 5, 1824, only months before the canallers began to dig the last mile and a half. The following year, the navvies slashed across the southwestern edge of Griffintown and plowed through the St. Ann Common, along the riverbank, taking the canal to the edge of the city. McCord's sons, John Samuel and William King, both of whom became judges of the Superior Court of Lower Canada, inherited their father's sizeable debt and his unrealized fortune. Rental income from their Griffintown properties would quadruple to more than £1,260 over the next fifteen years.

In 1826, after the completion of the wharves and locks on the Lachine Canal, hundreds of navvies, along with new recruits from Ireland, left Montreal and joined the crews on the next major public work, the Rideau Canal. The workers faced particularly difficult conditions on its route through the wilderness between Ottawa and Kingston. Inflated prices at the contractor's store—often the only option in the bush—took up most of their meagre wages. Contractors did not always pay for work completed, leaving labourers stranded and unable to afford food, shelter or a doctor if they were ill.

At least one thousand labourers, the vast majority Irish, lost their lives during the seven-year project. Many Irish, particularly the recent emigrants, died of swamp fever, a malaria-like disease spread by mosquitoes in the marshy terrain between Newboro and Kingston. Accidents killed and maimed many who were untrained in the use of explosives. Some drowned, swept away by the current or mudslides, as they cleared trees from the banks along the route of the canal. The casualties were buried quickly in anonymous graves, no priest and no gravestone to mark their ignominious end.

A large contingent of Irish navvies, however, stayed in Montreal after the completion of the Lachine Canal. Most settled in and around Griffintown, and the sons of Erin soon outnumbered the district's English, Scottish, French-Canadian and American residents. An 1825 census shows that four hundred, or roughly one-third, of the twelve hundred residents in the St. Ann's Ward, the official designation for the area, were born in Ireland. Another 323 Irish lived in Pointe-à-Callière, an adjacent district near the mouth of the canal.

The census paints a picture of a nascent, working-class suburb with a youthful, predominantly male population. One-quarter of income earners were day labourers; almost as many were domestic servants. Most of the others were artisans and skilled tradesmen employed in construction as carpenters and bricklayers, or in local industries as ironworkers, coopers and factory hands.

By 1825, thirteen industries, including a brickyard, a distillery, a tannery, a shipyard and several warehouses and blacksmiths, were operating in the area once dominated by Robert Griffin's soap and candle works.

Griffintown, still largely rural, had taken on apects of an Irish shantytown. Two-thirds of the houses were made of wood, the cheapest available construction material. Crowding was common. Two hundred and twenty-two families lived in 126 houses—an average of nine people per house. One butcher shop, five bakeries, three taverns, five grocers, three inns, two boarding houses, and a handful of shoemakers, haberdashers, hatters and apothecaries rounded out the colourful community.

But the census-taker also counted nearly four dozen houses made of stone and brick—materials well beyond the means of a day labourer. The McCords and the prosperous contractor Abner Bagg made up the Griffintown elite, along with a handful of professionals—two lawyers, three law students, one medical student, two military officers, two teachers—and five self-described "men of independent means."

A tourist visiting Griffintown in 1834 described it as "the most attractive of all the city's suburbs, marked by so many fine wooden cottages surrounded by small plots and gardens, where many of the well-to-do had taken up their residence." But wealthy residents had already begun to abandon the increasingly industrial neighbourhood. In 1831, McCord's sons moved to Temple Grove, a mansion often compared to the Parthenon, on an estate near the top of Mount Royal. A Methodist chapel opened on the McCord property.

THE LACHINE CANAL CHANGED GRIFFINTOWN DRAMATICALLY. Over the next decade, a nail factory, an oil manufacturer, a comb manufacturer, a tannery, four flour mills and a grist and smut mill, as well as numerous small artisan shops, foundries and shipyards set up shop in the district. John Dod Ward's Eagle Foundry, which began building steam engines in a small blacksmith shop on a seventy-by-ninety-foot lot on Queen Street in 1819, grew into one of the largest industrial establishments in British North America. By 1830, Ward had teamed up with two of his brothers to build a much larger foundry across Queen Street. The newly named firm, John D. Ward & Co., employed one hundred full-time workers, and as many as three hundred at peak times.

Montreal may have been booming but few could argue with Benjamin Workman's editorial in the *Canadian Courant* in August 1832, condemning the city as "one of the foulest haunts of men on the American continent." The piles of rotting refuse that filled cellars and yards and lined streets already filthy with animal excrement provided tangible, pungent evidence.

In a letter to her mother on August 21, 1832, Catharine Parr Traill expressed great disappointment in the city that travellers had praised so highly. "Although it may be a little cleaner than Quebec, it is still very dirty," she wrote, saving the worst of her criticism for the "dirty, narrow, ill-paved or unpaved streets of the suburbs" and the "noisome vapour" of the infamous Little River St. Pierre on the eastern edge of Griffintown: "a deep open fosse that ran along the street behind the wharf. This ditch seemed the receptacle for every abomination, and sufficient in itself to infect a whole town with malignant fevers."

A few years later, the newly incorporated city filled in a section of the creek and erected the St. Ann's Market. But it had only begun to implement sanitation measures, and the suburbs remained largely unserviced. Garbage collection was intermittent in Montreal and rare in Griffintown. In 1832, a piped waterworks system was installed in the city but mains were not extended into Griffintown until fifteen years later. Clean drinking water remained a luxury for residents who relied on public pumps or purchased it by the bucketful from carters who rode through the streets with a barrel mounted on a wagon or a sled in winter.

Poor sanitation led to frequent outbreaks of diphtheria and typhoid in the flood-prone district. Inhabitants endured annual inundations so severe they had to retreat to attics, usually with their livestock in tow. Even after waters receded, houses remained cold, damp and airless.

Conditions deteriorated further with Griffintown's seasonal population explosions. Many city residents opened their homes to boarders during the yearly migration. But the hospitable Irish routinely exceeded the legal limit of four persons for every twelve square feet.

And, when epidemics struck, blame tended to fall on the Irish residents and their old-country customs, rather than on the lack of amenities. In Ireland, pigs provided tenant farmers with valuable manure, and their sale provided ready cash to pay the rent. In Griffintown, a day labourer might keep a hog or a pig to supplement his meagre income or feed his family during spells of unemployment. But in 1832, city magistrates used the cholera epidemic in the city as an excuse to place restrictions on pigs and hogs, which were widely viewed as a public nuisance.

On July 28, 1832, in the Court of Special Sessions of the Peace, John Carrol was found guilty on two counts. Not only did he keep hogs at his dwelling, he had also violated another health board regulation: Carrol had lodged more than thirty people in his small house.

Griffintown was acquiring a reputation as a tough district, with its rough-hewn Irish residents and numerous illegal drinking establishments, known as blind pigs. In early 1827, an unknown assailant fired a pistol through the window of a house on Gabriel (later Ottawa) Street in Griffintown, killing the owner, a customs inspector, as he sat in his parlour, talking to his minister. No charges were ever laid in the case and the two prime suspects, George Henderson and John McDonnell, were hanged for other crimes. The apparently random, senseless murder shocked the city.

Another horrific murder took place that summer. On Sunday, August 19, landlord George Henderson and John Shields, one of his lodgers, attacked one Peter Keho, who had refused to leave the blind pig Henderson ran in his boarding house. Henderson and Shields later threw Keho, drunk and bleeding, into the canal. On Friday, September 7, a jury found the two men guilty of murder and the judge sentenced them to death by hanging.

LORD HAVE MERCY ON THEIR SOULS: Griffintown's Irish Catholics found solace in their faith and in their priests.

The legend of the beloved "Father of the Irish" begins in August 1807, when the porter opened the door of the imposing stone Seminary of St. Sulpice on Notre Dame Street to a young American Protestant preacher, politely requesting a meeting with the superior. Rev. John Richard Jackson, a 20-year-old newly ordained Methodist minister, had left his home in Alexandria, Virginia, intent on saving the souls of the Sulpicians in far-off Montreal. The earnest young minister, having learned of the priests' courageous missionary work, was distressed that such selfless men had been misled by the errors of Roman Catholicism.

Father Auguste Roux listened politely to Rev. Jackson. The priest, it is said, contained his amusement, then proceeded to explain his church's doctrines, patiently answering the young minister's queries and, most likely, offering him a catechism. Whatever transpired, on October 31, 1807, Rev. Jackson converted to Catholicism, then spent the next six years studying for the priesthood. After his ordination on July 25, 1813, in Baltimore, he returned to Montreal and joined the Sulpicians.

The story of the priest's first encounter with the Irish, his special flock, has been told and retold with the romantic haziness of a happily married couple remembering their first kiss. In the summer of 1817, Father John Richard Jackson, or Father Richards, as he came to be known, noticed some unfamiliar faces in the congregation at Notre-Dame-de-Bon-Secours church. Perhaps it was the clothes they wore, or their habit of bowing their heads at crucial points in the service, that set them apart from the French Canadians.

One Sunday morning, he made a point of greeting the newcomers after mass, as they descended the wooden steps onto the narrow cobblestone street. They told him, in English spoken with a heavy brogue, that they had recently come from Ireland, about thirty to fifty men and women, and had settled in the vicinity of Jacques Cartier Square. With no English Catholic parishes in the city, they attended mass at the French churches: Notre-Dame-de-Montréal, Notre-Dame-de-Bon-Secours and the old Recollet Chapel. Father Richards invited the newcomers to an afternoon meeting in the church. Few turned out. "They would hardly have covered a good size parlour carpet," or so the story goes. The priest led them to the sacristy where they discussed his plan to hold a weekly service for them in English. Soon, the Irish who had been attending mass at Notre-Dame-de-Montréal and the old Recollet Chapel began to cluster at Bon-Secours for Father Richards' mass. This small group of faithful—Montreal's first English-speaking Catholic congregation—grew in numbers and influence as more and more emigrants landed in the city.

In 1822, at the urging of his flock, Father Richards opened a school for Irish children in the west wing of the old Recollet convent. A year later, the Sulpicians established an orphanage for Irish children in the same building.

Though French Canadians shared a faith with Irish Catholics, they did not necessarily want to share the same building with the foreign newcomers. Frictions soon arose at Bon-Secours, or Old Bosco as the Irish called it. A church historian hints at a fistfight or two. The French Canadians and the Irish were so compatible that they often formed political alliances and intermarried, yet so competitive that they fought over jobs and even mass times. French-speaking worshippers at Bon-Secours grew impatient as the English-speaking Irish filled their small chapel in ever-increasing numbers. At the same time, many of the Irish, concentrated in Griffintown three miles away, found the chapel's location inconvenient.

In 1825, the Sulpicians resolved the dispute by moving the Irish congregation to the old Recollet chapel on Notre Dame Street. A year later, they renovated the building that the Irish called the "Regalec," adding two side aisles to accommodate the growing flock, now numbering about a thousand. Meanwhile Father Richards, the beloved "Father of the Irish," took a study leave in France, and Father Patrick Phelan, a thirty-year-old native of Kilkenny, took over the spiritual—and temporal—care of the city's Irish Catholic congregation, drawn mostly from Griffintown.

The charismatic Father Phelan wielded an influence over his flock that went far beyond the spiritual. The Irish had always revered their

The dynamic Kilkenny-born Sulpician Patrick Phelan served Montreal's Irish Catholics for nearly seventeen years before his appointment as Bishop of Kingston in 1843.

priests and turned to them for every trouble. The most beloved, like Father Phelan, they called *soggarth aroon,* or "dear priest." A hero in the 1832 epidemic—he was one of a very few clergymen who dared enter the cholera sheds—the devoted priest ministered to the sick and dying until he collapsed from exhaustion after more than forty-eight hours without a break. Parishioners would bring their small savings to him for safekeeping. In 1840, he founded the St. Patrick's Total Abstinence Society, the first North American branch of the famed Father Mathew's temperance crusade. Its membership would grow to three thousand.

Father Phelan, like many Irish clergymen, quickly became dismayed at how so many of his parishioners from rural Ireland had drifted into poverty and illness and alcoholism in the city. In the late 1820s, when he learned that the Sulpicians owned a largely unsettled tract of land in the Two Mountains seigneury, forty miles northwest of Montreal, he encouraged the Irish to leave Griffintown and establish farms in the district.

He obtained a land grant from his superiors for a forty-square-mile territory on the North River and led the first group of Irish to the thickly forested district, which he named St. Columban after a sixth-century Irish missionary. The would-be pioneers travelled north by stagecoach, at about five or six miles an hour, through several villages before disembarking at St. Scholastique. A horse-drawn wagon took them the short distance to the North River. A raft carried them across the waterway but they had to walk the last few miles to St. Columban. There, the settlers claimed their wilderness lots, roughly 580 feet wide by 6,000 feet long, at no cost apart from annual taxes due to the Sulpicians. Equipped with only a few primitive implements, they spent the first long, bitterly cold winter in drafty shanties and lean-tos. They faced years of hard labour, clearing the land and establishing homesteads.

The rocky terrain in the foothills of the Laurentians resisted their efforts at cultivation, but their faith flourished. On Sundays, the Irish settlers walked nine miles through the woods to attend mass in St. Scholastique, the nearest village. In bad weather, they gathered at a wayside cross to pray together. In 1831, they built a small, rough-hewn chapel and a priest from St. Scholastique came to conduct services.

Father Naud found the trips into the wilderness to minister to the Irish as appealing as a visit to purgatory. The French-speaking priest disliked celebrating Holy Mass in the crude chapel built by English-speaking foreigners with strange, coarse manners. In a letter to the bishop in Montreal, Father Naud complained about their religious laxity: many of the older children had yet to make their First Communion. Naud also grumbled to his bishop about "confessions à la mode irlandaises," judging the adults' typical list of sins—"I cursit, I sworn, I got in a passion"—too rushed and simplistic.

One hundred Irish families had migrated to St. Columban by late 1835, a sufficient number to form a parish. And the bishop took care to place them in the spiritual care of Irish-born priests. The first pastor, Father Stephen Blyth, ministered to them from St. Jerome, coming in person or sending one of his priests to the mission at St. Columban. Father William Dolan succeeded him in 1838, but was dismissed a year later because of his affinity for the devil drink. The saintly Father John Falvey, born in Limerick, Ireland, on December 11, 1797, became parish priest in St. Columban in 1840. Except for a brief stint as a chaplain to Irish navvies at Beauharnois, he stayed for thirty-nine years, building a rural parish community like the ones they had left behind in Ireland.

Despite the migration to St. Columban, the Irish Catholic population of Montreal continued to grow at an extraordinary rate. In 1829, the Sulpicians had to put an addition on the Recollet church to accommodate the ever-increasing Irish Catholic flock, numbering more than three thousand. By 1833, the faithful had once again outgrown their church. Every Sunday, the overflow crowd spilled out the doors, kneeling on the street, in all kinds of weather, caps in hand, straining to hear the priest. There—according to a petition signed by several hundred parishioners—they were "exposed to the ridicule of the irreligious." Father Phelan, with the support of influential parishioners, began to lobby the Sulpicians for the construction of a new church, one large enough to accommodate the entire congregation.

But political unrest disrupted the Irish Catholics' dream of a new church. French Canadians, long restive under British rule, were pressing for an elected legislative council, and by 1836, an armed rebellion seemed imminent in Lower Canada. To the dismay of the government, the loyalties of Irish Catholics remained in question. Though their numbers were small, as a double minority, they could influence the outcome of an election—or, perhaps, an insurrection—with a shift of allegiance from the English Protestant regime to the French Catholic rebels. Nor were the authorities unaware of the potential threat of a thousand or more Irish Catholics concentrated in Griffintown, many of them labourers and navvies, celebrated for their physical strength and no great love for the British.

By now, the Irish had made a significant impact on Montreal and had infiltrated the ranks of the elite. The shamrock appeared on the city's coat of arms, along with the French fleur-de-lis, the English rose and the Scottish thistle. And Irish Catholics and Protestants had made their mark in the city as politicians, lawyers and businessmen.

Religious differences had not yet tested the unity of the Montreal Irish. They numbered no more than three thousand in 1824, when Michael O'Sullivan, a Catholic lawyer and prominent Tory, organized the city's first St. Patrick's Day parade. Protestants and Catholics from some thirty families joined in the pubic procession and marked the anniversary of Ireland's patron saint together. Later that evening, Wednesday, March 17, a few dozen Irishmen of different faiths convened at a banquet at the posh Mansion House, where they raised their glasses in a toast to the Emerald Isle.

Ten years later, in 1834, their unity seemingly intact, Irish Catholics and Protestants formed the St. Patrick's Society, the city's first national organization, to celebrate their shared heritage and to help less fortunate compatriots. The founders promised in their constitution to welcome "Irishmen and those of Irish descent, of all classes and of all creeds."

But loyalty to the Crown threatened to divide the Irish community as the politically charged atmosphere of Lower Canada heated up in the 1830s. French-Canadian nationalists had been fighting for reform since the early 1800s and now there was talk of a rebellion. Many Irish, particularly Protestants, had naturally aligned themselves with the powerful ruling minority in those turbulent years. Others, especially working-class Irish Catholics, mindful of their own fight for emancipation in Ireland, tended to sympathize with the Quebecers' resistance to British rule. French Canadians' adoption of Irish hero Daniel O'Connell, the "Great Liberator," as their own idol and an inspiration, only deepened the bond.

A number of well-educated Irish Catholic emigrants—lawyers, doctors and other professionals—openly supported Louis-Joseph

Papineau's Patriote Party, formed in 1826 to push for self-government. And three passionate, articulate Irishmen—Jocelyn Waller, Dr. Daniel Tracey and Dr. Edmund Bailey O'Callaghan—jumped headlong into the French-Canadian cause. All three published English-language newspapers that championed the cause of reform. Authorities silenced the outspoken Waller, editor of the *Canadian Spectator,* with an accusation of libel. He died in a Montreal prison in 1828, eight years after he emigrated from Tipperary.

The Patriotes found a particularly ardent proponent in Dr. Daniel Tracey. In 1828—three years after he and a younger brother and sister emigrated to Montreal—the doctor established the *Irish Vindicator* (later called the *Vindicator*), a controversial weekly newspaper that stirred up Irish sympathies for the French Canadians' cause. The government briefly imprisoned Tracey for libel, too, in 1832. They laid the spurious charges after he wrote an editorial that condemned the unelected Legislative Council for killing legislation passed by the House of Assembly.

In the spring of 1832, following his release from prison, Tracey ran against Stanley Bagg, a wealthy canal contractor, for the Montreal West seat in the Legislative Assembly. The infamous election coincided with a cholera epidemic and was cut short after British troops shot and killed three French Canadians, supporters of Tracey. The trouble began when a special "peace-keeping" constable struck one of the Irishman's followers and knocked him unconscious, when he yelled out "Huzza for Tracey" after leaving a poll. The deaths occurred after city magistrates—all Bagg allies and government appointees—called in the military to quell the ensuing scuffle.

A government inquiry later revealed that city magistrates, citing rumours of violence planned by the Irish, had employed more than two hundred special constables for the duration of the election. More than twenty of them, known locally as the Bullies, were paid to use violence to keep Tracey's voters from the hustings. Two had been arrested for attacking the Irishman's supporters and were out on bail when they were hired to keep the peace. Violence only occurred in the presence of the constables. Tracey won by a margin of three or four votes. But he did not live to take his seat. He contracted cholera while treating a patient and died on July 18.

O'Callaghan, who had emigrated to Quebec City in 1823 with his hatred of the British government intact, abandoned his medical practice and moved to Montreal in 1832 to take over as editor of the *Vindicator* after Tracey's death. He won a seat in the Legislative Assembly in 1834 and worked closely with Papineau. The fiery O'Callaghan openly advocated rebellion. "Agitate! Agitate! Agitate! Destroy the revenue, denounce the oppressors. Everything is lawful when fundamental liberties are in danger," he once wrote in the *Vindicator*. The tricolour flag of the new republic of Lower Canada, in fact, had a green stripe to represent the Irish. But pressure from the clergy held most would-be rebels from responding to O'Callaghan's call to arms.

Talk of rebellion alarmed the conservative Seminary of St. Sulpice, which was dependent on the goodwill of the British for its seigneurial rights. The priests used their God-given authority to prevent the insurrection and to discourage their flock from attending protest rallies and boycotting British goods. Respect lawful authority, the priests counselled Catholics—both Irish and French Canadian—from the pulpit.

The charismatic Father Phelan helped sway the Griffintown Irish. A number of Irish Catholics from St. Columban participated in a skirmish north of the city, but the rebellion fizzled in Montreal.

Lord Durham, the governor general, acknowledged the Sulpicians' role in suppressing the uprising. In his 1839 report on the Rebellion, he wrote: "The endowments of the Catholic Church, and the services of its numerous and zealous parochial clergy have been of the greatest benefit to the large body of Catholic emigrants from Ireland, who have relied much on the charitable as well as religious aid which they have received from the priesthood. The priests have an almost unlimited influence over the lower classes of Irish; and this influence is said to have been

Excavation site near the Wellington Bridge in 1876,
during the second expansion of the Lachine Canal.

very vigorously exerted last winter, when it was much needed, to secure the loyalty of a portion of the Irish during the troubles."

News of the rebellion reached Ireland, and emigration to Quebec dived to below three thousand in 1838. But the union of the Upper and Lower Provinces in 1841 brought renewed political stability, and the flow of emigrants into Canada surged to a record high of more than forty-four thousand in 1842. The new government, awash in British funding and blessed with a swelling labour market, decided to revamp the canals along the St. Lawrence.

The most ambitious plans centred on Montreal, widely expected to become the capital of Canada. The massive five-year project would almost double the depth of the Lachine Canal to accommodate the large new ships. But the most dramatic improvement—the one designed to cement Montreal's position as the commercial heart of the young country—came with the decision to install large new basins, equipped with hydraulic power, at the mouth of the canal. A magnet for industry, the modernized canal would transform St. Ann's Ward. And, once again, the Irish would provide cheap muscle power.

On July 7, 1842, Martin Donnelly landed in Montreal with his wife and three young children. Two weeks later, the poor young emigrant from County Mayo found a job on the construction of the Beauharnois Canal, across the river, west of Montreal. Many of the twenty-five hundred navvies sweating and slogging alongside Donnelly had, like him, come right off the boat from Ireland. Thomas Reynolds had emigrated from King's County in 1840; Kilkenny-born Matthew Coogan arrived in March 1842; Francis Dowd came from Queen's County in July 1842. Thousands more Irish navvies migrated from the United States, where the major canal projects were nearing completion, and descended on Montreal in search of jobs.

The navvy's lot had not improved since the 1820s, when Irish labourers first built the Lachine Canal. Donnelly worked from six in the morning to six at night, with two hours for meals. He earned three shillings—about sixty cents—a day, paid twice a month. The Board of Works assigned Donnelly to a team of four men, expected to excavate six or seven square yards of rock and clay each day, an inhuman workload known to have broken down horses, a writer for *La Minerve*, a French-language Montreal newspaper, observed on June 8, 1843.

But the navvies, counting on reasonably steady work for the next five years, had few complaints—at first. The men worked relatively peacefully on the canal project, partly due to the presence of Father John Falvey. Montreal's bishop, Msgr. Bourget, had moved the priest from St. Columban to Beauharnois in the summer of 1842 to serve as chaplain for the two thousand canallers, most of them Irish Catholics. The Board of Works put him on the payroll for £200 a year. On August 29, Bourget wrote a letter to the board, thanking them for their support of Father Falvey.

The Board of Works—like the managers of canal projects across the continent—understood the benefits of providing a priest for Irish Catholic workers. A high-ranking public works official named Begley went to mass at Father Falvey's chapel every Sunday. "I always heard him preach moderation to his flock, respect for their superiors and punctuality at work. He did his best to prevent his men from organizing, encouraged them to return peacefully at their old rates and to present their grievances to the government peacefully and not to try to redress them themselves. He was constantly among them and whenever he heard of an irregularity, he would appear on the site and to resolve the issue," Begley would testify after a violent strike.

The trouble started in January 1843, when the Board of Works turned the canal project over to private contractors. At Beauharnois, the work was divided among thirteen contractors. Across the river, a single private contractor, Henry Mason, took over the expansion of the Lachine Canal. He hired sixteen hundred labourers and put them to work immediately.

The new hires at Lachine expected Mason to pay the same rate as the Board of Works. But on January 24, their first payday, the navvies' wages amounted to only two shillings a day—paid not in cash but in coupons redeemable at his company store. Paydays, they learned, would come once a month. At the same time, Mason increased their hours. The workers put down their shovels and walked off the job, demanding the same conditions and pay offered by the Board of Works—three shillings, six pence, a day.

Less than a week into the strike, Mason claimed that a Corkman offered to return to work for two shillings, six pence. The rumour sparked a feud between two rival Irish factions. Tensions mounted as both sides—the recent emigrants from Cork and the Connaughts, most of whom had migrated from the United States—organized goon squads to intimidate scabs. On February 4, six hundred Corkmen—at least two hundred of them armed—invaded the Connaughts' shanties and boarding houses at Lachine and threatened to kill them if they broke the strike.

Frightened Lachine residents called for protection, and, on February 6, the government posted troops along the works. Influential Montreal Irishmen rode out to Lachine to negotiate an end to the feud. On February 9, the canallers returned to work on the understanding that a new rate, three shillings a day, would come into effect on March 24.

But the contractor rehired only eight hundred workers, leaving five hundred men unemployed and angry. On Thursday, March 2, two people were killed and several injured when the Corkmen attacked the Connaughts, who fled to Montreal with their families.

On Wednesday, March 8, six Corkmen were tried in criminal court for their role in the Lachine riot. But the Irish distrusted the law more than each other. The Connaughts refused to testify against their bitter—but Irish—enemies.

The day of the trial, Father Phelan went to Lachine, accompanied by Benjamin Holmes, a respected banker and member of Parliament, and several members of Montreal's St. Patrick's Society, to reconcile the two groups. Father Phelan held a special mass, during which a collection was taken up for those injured in the riots. After the service, the charismatic priest addressed two thousand workers. Not only did he convince them to end their dispute, he also enrolled ninety Irishmen in the temperance society. Many voluntarily gave up their weapons.

On March 22, after the contractor laid off half the workers, the Irish dropped their shovels and walked off the job again. This time, they heeded Father Phelan's counsel. Five hundred men, lined up with military precision and led by a fifer, calmly marched into Montreal through Griffintown to St. Ann's Market. There, the Irish-born Holmes and members of the St. Patrick's Society listened to their grievances and promised a legal investigation the next day.

The protestors marched back to the construction site the following day, vowing to keep the peace while waiting for a response to their complaints, a promise they kept until they discovered the contractor had filled the ranks with French Canadians. On March 30, the Irish beat up and bullied the replacement workers until they fled the site. Construction resumed. The details of the settlement remain unclear, but the navvies' cooperation suggests they likely won their three shillings a day.

But across the river at Beauharnois, workers' grievances were building. All thirteen contractors had refused to pay more than two shillings a day. One, named John Black, went further and demanded longer hours—from four in the morning till eight at night, six days a week. Like many a hated landlord, the contractors exploited the Irish. Several forced them to purchase food and supplies from company stores stocked with overpriced items. Many ignored contracts with the Board of Works requiring them to provide reasonable accommodation and charged high rents for wretched wooden shanties, crowding as many as a dozen into a twelve-square-foot space. One failed to pay his workers at all for a period of two months, handing out due bills instead. The labourers were reduced to eating boiled herbs to survive.

On May 15, Black's crew decided to strike for higher wages and fewer hours. About one hundred of his men went down into the adjoining pit and demanded that Crawford's 250 employees join them. "We refused to turn out with them on the ground that we had agreed with our contractors for the month at half a dollar a day," Martin Donnelly later told an inquiry into the strike. "They called us cowardly two and three penny men." But the ringleaders talked to navvies along the length of the line, and by the end of the day the entire workforce secretly agreed to strike at the end of the month.

On the evening of May 31, all the labourers on the Beauharnois site laid down their tools and walked off the job. It was an illegal action and Canada's first large-scale labour strike. Despite Father Falvey's repeated advice to respect the law and submit to their superiors, the men still had not returned to work by June 10. They remained quiet in their shanties. But local magistrates, fearing the strike might erupt in violence, had appealed for military protection.

Fifty soldiers of the 74th Regiment, under Major Campbell, arrived on June 10. That same day, some three hundred workers went down the line to announce a mass meeting on the following Monday. On their return, for good measure, the men visited a few contractors to inquire if they planned to meet their demand for three shillings a day. The navvies broke several windows in a company store, dropped some threats and threw a few knockout punches to show their displeasure at the negative responses.

The horns sounded early on Monday, June 12. Donnelly, whose wife had died a few months after landing in Canada, stayed in his shanty with his three young children. "I remained below with my little family. I cannot say what occurred," he later told an inquiry trying to sort out the contradictory accounts of the day's catastrophe. But upwards of one thousand labourers from both ends of the canal responded to the call. The men gathered, forming larger groups as they headed toward Duncan Grant's hotel, the meeting place in St. Timothy, roughly halfway down the line.

On their way to the rendezvous, men from the western end stopped along the route to press the contractors for a raise. Alexander Stewart was asleep in his shanty when a navvy armed with a club ordered him to get up and follow him, declaring, "We are going for higher wages or blood." Stewart eluded them by promising to follow in his raft. But first he watched them force their into the house of another contractor, named G.N. Brown. A few minutes later, they emerged, carrying him aloft on a chair, cheering him for agreeing to three shillings a day.

Local magistrate Jean-Baptiste Laviolette and a party of thirty soldiers stood waiting at the next stop, the home of a man named Larocque. But the navvies, numbering in the hundreds, encircled the soldiers, and the contractor quickly agreed to three shillings a day. The incident boosted the workers' confidence. "I heard them then boast of having surrounded the soldiers, and that there was not a Regiment in Her Majesty's service could do anything with all that were assembled that day," Stewart later testified at a government inquiry.

Meanwhile, the crowd from the east end had gathered near Grant's Hotel, where another contractor, McDonald, lived. He emerged to face the angry strikers but when he refused to consent to a wage increase, they chased him into the building. While the contractor hid in the cellar, the mob broke several windows and ransacked a nearby store, before heading off toward the western end of the canal. "Men did not come to this country to be treated in the manner they were here," Martin Action, one the leaders, told Crawford, the proprietor of the store.

The showdown came at noon, when the two groups of strikers—more than a thousand, by most accounts—assembled near Grant's Hotel. The military, prepared for the encounter, formed a line in front of the gallery: Major Campbell's 74th Regiment stood in the centre, flanked by thirty cavalrymen from the Queen's Light Dragoons. Laviolette ordered the labourers to disperse peacefully. Undeterred, the strikers marched up and down the road, about twenty paces from the troops, waving their clubs and yelling out their demands—three shillings a day, fewer working hours and the right to buy food from local farmers.

The magistrate read the Riot Act. The strikers ignored him. They made no attempt to advance on the troops, but continued to march up and down the road. Four minutes later, Laviolette yelled: "Major Campbell, fire." The officer signalled his troops. The infantry aimed their muskets at the strikers. Shots rang through the air and the canallers scattered in every direction, pursued by the sword-wielding Dragoons and the cavalry. Several navvies leapt into the St. Lawrence to escape their attackers. At least one labourer drowned in the rapids.

Father Falvey arrived at the scene shortly after the attack, to find the ground covered with the blood of the wounded and the dead. Holding one of the dying men in his arms, the mild-mannered priest lashed out at the magistrate: "The blood of these people cry [*sic*] to heaven for vengeance. May my curse and that of the Almighty fall on this French magistrate and the contractors. Coward! Murderer!"

An inquest into the massacre acknowledged the deaths of only five men: William Dowie, Miles Higgins, Thomas McManus, Bernard Gormley and one unnamed worker. It ruled that the strikers had assembled for "illegal purposes"; that Magistrate Laviolette had responded appropriately; and that the result was "justifiable homicide."

A second inquiry undertaken by the government and presented to the Legislative Assembly in October 1843 showed some sympathy for the Irish workers and concluded that at least six protesters were killed by soldiers' muskets. Doctors testified that an examination of the men's wounds showed that four had been shot in the back as they were fleeing. The commission concluded that the navvies had "just grounds for complaint" and questioned the magistrate's use of the military, which had led to the "lamentable catastrophe." Later reports placed the number of casualties as high as twenty.

Small, isolated bands of workers continued the protest at the Beauharnois site for a week after the incident. But the slaughter—and the continuing presence of the military—had silenced the canallers. When the navvies slowly returned to work, some found that their demands for higher pay and reduced hours had been met.

The canal strikes of 1843 were the bloodiest in the history of Canada's labour movement. (One man died and thirty others were injured in the armed intervention that ended the larger, six-week-long Winnipeg Strike of 1919, staged by some thirty thousand workers.) And the law would continue to side with employers until 1872, when the government passed legislation granting workers the right to strike. In the meantime, business continued to profit from a glut of labour. More

*Labourers, angered by a cut in wages, gather in protest
outside a contractor's office in December 1877, during one
of several bitter strikes in the history of the Lachine Canal.*

than a quarter of a million Irish poured into Canada in the remaining
years of the 1840s and, as Lord Elgin, the newly appointed governor
general, predicted in a letter to British Colonial Secretary Lord Grey at
the end of 1847, the large numbers of destitute among them became "a
defenceless and easily exploitable supply of unskilled labour."

IRISH WORKERS FARED NO BETTER in Canada's first railway boom, in the
mid-nineteenth century. "There's an Irishman buried under every tie,"
goes one old saw. There were only sixty-six miles of railroad in British
North America in 1850, but by the end of the decade navvies had laid
2,065 miles of tracks in the Maritimes and Canada. With Montreal as its
hub, the Grand Trunk line ran west to Sarnia, east to Quebec City and
south across the Victoria Bridge—the first to span the St. Lawrence—
to Portland, Maine. The railways cost a staggering $150 million (roughly

$600 billion in current dollars) and at one point employed more than fourteen thousand men. Contractors and promoters made handsome profits but the navvies barely scratched out a living.

The railroad sparked a boom in Montreal, the heart of Canada's vast transportation network. And, Griffintown—the hub of the Lachine Canal and the Grand Trunk Railway—suddenly became the most industrialized area in the country. By 1851, ambitious entrepreneurs had plunked sixty-four factories into the crowded Irish neighbourhood that covered less than five hundred acres. The number of factories, and the population, would triple over the next two decades.

Tough Irish navvies had helped to set the stage for Canada's Industrial Revolution. Now they and their children, along with their compatriots who had landed in the Famine years, would provide the cheap, unskilled labour to keep the factories running. By the end of Black '47, Montreal had the highest concentration of Irish in Quebec and one of the highest concentrations of urban Irish in British North America—with roughly two-thirds of them clustered in Griffintown.

Over the next decade, the growth of the Irish population would outpace that of other ethnic groups in Montreal. While the city's population increased from 57,715 to 90,323 between 1851 and 1861, during the same period the proportion of Irish increased from one-fifth to one-third. And 16,200, or more than half of the roughly 30,000 Irish living in Montreal in 1861, lived in the booming St. Ann's Ward.

While most Irish emigrants in Canada migrated to rural areas, those who stayed in Griffintown traded tiny potato patches in Ireland's emerald fields and rainy valleys for uncertain, often dangerous jobs in dusty factories that paid a dollar a day—and life in a teeming Irish quarter at once notorious and beloved.

PART TWO

Hard Streets

FOUR

⁓

Irish in the City

Many that are red-cheeked now will be pale-cheeked;
many that have been free to walk the hills and the bogs and
the rushes will be sent to walk hard streets in far countries.
—William Butler Yeats, *Cathleen ni Houlihan*

THE FIRE BEGAN BEHIND McNEVIN'S CARPENTRY SHOP at the corner of Nazareth Street and Gabriel (later renamed Ottawa) Street in Griffintown. Some blamed it on little boys playing with lucifer matches in the yard. But no one noticed the spark fly into the wood shavings scattered near the stacks of dry timber on the bright and breezy afternoon of Saturday, June 15, 1850. McNevin's employees were working inside, unaware of the smouldering fire hissing toward them until flames burst through the wooden floorboards. The men shouted a warning to tenants upstairs, then escaped empty-handed as the fire engulfed the building.

Whipped by the wind, the fire quickly swept down the block, consuming a row of frame houses in its path. At the corner, the roaring blaze hurled glowing embers at St. Ann's Episcopal Church, a handsome stone structure topped by a tall wooden spire. The roof caught fire and the gusty westerly tossed burning shingles into neighbouring streets. In Griffintown, a tinderbox of wooden rowhouses standing smack up against warehouses and factories, the fire skipped easily from one block to the next.

Flames were leaping from buildings on both sides of Gabriel Street when the Union Fire Company arrived on the scene, shortly after four o'clock. Determined to save the church, the crew dashed between the walls of fire, a daring run that injured their horse and left some of them with burns. In the heat and blinding smoke, the men rushed to hook up the hose to a water main, an awkward manoeuvre in which they had to remove a wooden plug from a pipe in the ground. They pumped their hand-operated engine with all their might, but the narrow noz-zle—capable of only a modest stream of water—had little effect.

Then, with a sudden swoosh, masses of flames from the church and nearby buildings shot into the air and swept in sheets toward the canal, raining fire on the shingled roofs. Terror and confusion mounted as the conflagration continued its assault on the neighbourhood. Distress smeared the faces of tenants suddenly driven from their burning houses, with little more than the clothes on their back. Mothers called for their children.

Alarms rang and firemen shouted as residents whose homes stood in the path of the fire pushed their way through in an attempt to remove their possessions before the flames overtook them. Piles of furniture, beds, and all kinds of goods mounted in empty lots, only to be moved again as the fire progressed. Wagons, handcarts, every form of wheeled vehicle raced headlong through the chaos, carrying passengers and belongings to safety. One pedestrian died instantly when a speeding carter ran over his head and fractured his skull.

In the furnace-like heat, old men and women, too frail to help, watched as their meagre possessions disappeared in the roaring flames and crackling timber. An elderly widow, Mrs. Livingstone, managed to save her cows from a backyard stable. When she returned to her house to retrieve money and valuables hidden in the cellar, a burning wall collapsed and blocked her exit. Portions of her incinerated corpse were found the next morning in the smouldering ruins.

With nearly a third of Griffintown engulfed in flames, residents watched appalled as the inferno rolled on, unchecked, in every direction. Alarmed by the possibility of an explosion, a team of firemen stood guard at the gasworks, extinguishing the flames that repeatedly broke out in the building, only a few blocks away from McNevin's shop.

Montreal's mayor, Raymond Fabré, directed operations at the scene and encouraged bystanders to help the firemen. He called out the local garrison to back up the men of the Hook, Ladder and Hose Company, who were struggling to create a firebreak by toppling buildings with axes and other hand tools. The Royal Engineers of the 20th Regiment used explosives to blow up a row of buildings, but the tactic failed to stop the fire. After swallowing an old windmill and a lumber yard, the blaze reached Wellington Street. Soon buildings on both sides of the main thoroughfare, many of them large stone and brick houses, sprouted flames. The fire rushed toward the lumber yards, stables and large industrial buildings along the canal. There, workers armed with brooms and buckets of water climbed onto the roofs of warehouses filled with goods imported from Europe and produce from Upper Canada and frantically swept away the fiery embers falling down around them.

It was, up until that time, the worst fire in the history of Montreal. (In 1852, a massive conflagration in the city's east end would leave ten thousand of the city's fifty-seven thousand residents homeless.) By the time it had burnt itself out, the fire had levelled a third of Griffintown. Five hundred families lost their homes and many more, their possessions. Dozens of grocers, blacksmiths, carpenters and other tradesmen who operated small businesses on their properties lost their livelihoods as well as their houses. The authorities opened the fever sheds as a temporary shelter for victims of the fire, many of them Irish emigrants, homeless again.

Traces of soot and ash hung in the air the next morning, as churchgoers tramped along the cobblestone streets of the old city to Sunday mass. Inside Notre Dame Cathedral the whiff of smoke gave way to the scent of incense and beeswax, and the French-Canadian congregation listened as the priest read an open letter from Bishop Ignace Bourget, with yet another appeal to help the Irish:

> Every year brings some new misfortune, one appalling disaster after another. The deplorable events of the last few years brought so many tears and tore at our hearts. And now one of the most disastrous fires to devastate our city has plunged us into a new abyss of misery.
>
> You will learn nothing new if I tell you of the desolation in the heavily populated St. Ann's Ward. You have seen, with your own eyes, the vast ruins and smoking rubble of more than two hundred houses. You have witnessed the great devastation caused in a few hours by a destructive element that nothing could overcome. The sight of heaps of ashes and scorched walls, all that is left of so many buildings, and the thought that now there are hundreds of families without shelter, food and clothing tears at your heart. . . .
>
> In the desolate days of typhus, when thousands of sick, widows and orphans landed in our city—strangers to our country but not to our hearts—you treated them like brothers. . . . Do not be less generous now that fire has destroyed a quarter of your own city and reduced to frightful misery a large part of our population.

Bishop Bourget saw "the hand of God in this lamentable desolation"; the fire, he believed, was divine retribution "for our sins." But John J. Broomfield blamed human neglect and a lack of fire regulations. He had

*Brave members of the Queen Fire Company
on duty at No. 3 Station on Wellington Street.*

expected Griffintown would burn down, sooner or later. The British insurance inspector had arrived in Montreal on September 7, 1845, to assess local conditions for his employer, England's Phoenix Fire Office, one of the world's largest insurers. The stone buildings and metal roofs of the old city met his safety standards. But, as he toured Griffintown, a fire broke out in a cooperage. He rushed to the scene to find the wood-frame building "all in a blaze, the flames darting up through the roof a fearful height." The fire had already spread to wooden lean-tos attached to the shop, and threatened to sweep through the neighbourhood. But the firemen quickly extinguished the fire, leaving him amazed at their skill and heroics.

In his report to the home office, Broomfield expressed relief that his firm had assumed little risk in St. Ann's Ward, one of the most "thickly built" districts of the city and, like the other suburbs, lacking building regulations. "Fires are often occurring there," he wrote. "Houses are crowded together, all sorts of hazardous trades carried on and nearly the whole of the buildings of timber and shingles."

Though his report does not name Griffintown's Queen Engine Company No. 3, manned by Irish volunteers, he does gives them credit for saving the ward from burning down: "Owing to the activity of the fire company, [fires] seldom extend beyond one or two houses, although the district consists wholly of timber and shingled buildings."

Broomfield delayed his departure when another fire erupted in Griffintown the next day. It was, he wrote in a letter to the home office on October 4, "the most alarming and extensive conflagration witnessed here for many years. The fire broke out at three o'clock this morning in a building used for roasting coffee in the St. Ann's suburb and before the arrival of the engines, which were speedily on the spot, the flames had extended to the contiguous buildings and some delay having occurred in procuring water, together with the circumstance of most of the houses in that district being timber and shingled, the firemen were unable for some time to check the progress of the flames." The military blew up two brick houses, a tactic that stopped the fire from crossing Wellington Street. It took four hours to extinguish the blaze, which destroyed more than one hundred houses, a large Methodist chapel and other buildings.

In his letter, Broomfield apologized to his employer for the loss of more than £1,000 on Wragg's nail factory, admitting he should not have insured the steam-powered operation in a wooden structure with a wood-shingle roof.

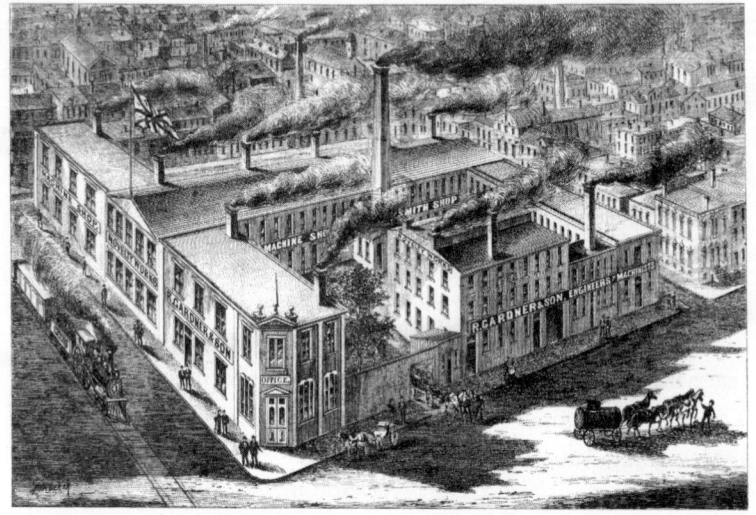

The R. Gardner and Sons factory, one of more than a dozen large foundries based in Griffintown, shipped "every description of machinery" across Canada and the United States and as far away as Prussia.

The hodge-podge of jerry-built housing, stables and cartage companies, carpentry shops, bakers, breweries, brickyards, coopers and blacksmiths, small manufacturers and warehouses that Broomfield surveyed in 1845 grew dramatically in the second half of the nineteenth century. And so did the risks and hazards.

Slightly more than seven thousand people lived in Griffintown in 1851, many in humble homes pressed up against their commercial neighbours. Over the next twenty years, the number would nearly triple, to more than nineteen thousand, as workers poured into St. Ann's Ward while industry expanded.

Thousands of workers streamed into the district's booming foundries, machine shops, sawmills, shipyards, and factories. Machinists, steamfitters and mechanics hailing from the industrialized cities of England and Scotland filled most of the well-paid jobs, producing engines and boilers, stoves and sewing machines. Unskilled Irish emigrants settled for rote work in factories that produced sundry goods: boots and shoes, boxes and brooms, shirts and hats, sashes and doors, drugs and cigars, paint and nails, axes and saws, rope and cotton sacking.

Huge foundries and metal works dominated the east side of the old Nazareth Fief: Gardner and Sons spread over several blocks at the corner of Nazareth and Brennan streets; Clendinneng's Foundry took up an acre, and Ives & Co., Wm. Rodden's Foundry, C.S. Rodier, and several others stood nearby, their smokestacks spewing out noxious black clouds.

In the 1860s, *Montreal Illustrated, or, The Stranger's Guide to Montreal* gave fair warning to tourists venturing down Wellington Street: "All the sights and sounds on this street remind us we are in the vicinity of large manufacturing establishments. Heavy drays laden with machinery or carts conveying goods to the depots or wharves at times block our way, although the smoky atmosphere would hasten us along."

JOHN O'ROURKE HURRIED TO PUNCH THE CLOCK at McLaren's boot factory, on Victoria Square, at seven o'clock. Every morning, from Monday to Saturday, he climbed the stairs of the three-storey building where as many as two hundred men, women and children worked sixty hours a week churning out shoes and boots, in the incessant din of clicking, clattering machines. In the winter, O'Rourke, a shoe cutter by trade, wore an overcoat and mitts as he stood at his work station, stamping out soles and uppers from the leather hide stretched across the chopping block, scanning for flaws in the dim gaslight. The factory's few small windows provided little natural light. The drafty brick building—a firetrap with a single staircase and no fire escape—had no electricity, and the stove on the factory floor remained unlit. O'Rourke would later tell an examiner at the Royal Commission on the Relations of Labour and Capital that the boss had dismissed his complaints about the cold, telling him that "too much heat was injurious to the health of workmen." In the summer, he toiled in the oppressively hot, stagnant factory air, breathing in the fumes of polish and tanning oil.

In 1886, company records listed 125 women employees, eighty-three men and eight boys and girls under the age of sixteen. O'Rourke knew better: "To my personal knowledge, they work from the age of six years up," he told the government inquiry.

Most companies under-reported child labour. A young lad capable of doing a man's job counted as a man, no matter his age. Yet a boy's wages seldom exceeded a quarter of the amount an adult male earned. Charlie Weir, a widow's son, was paid $1.50 a week when he first went to work at a cigar factory at the age of twelve. Five years later, he received nine dollars a week for performing the same task. Ambitious entrepreneurs relied on cheap child labour to build their industries.

When the Quebec government introduced a law prohibiting boys under twelve and girls under fourteen from working, many employers—and needy parents—ignored it. "We have twenty-four boys and girls," stated John James McGill, manager of the Canadian Rubber Company, which employed more than eight hundred workers. "Well, they are not exactly children," he added, claiming that it was difficult to know how old they were. "We simply ask their parents their ages, and if their parents say they are old enough, we employ them." Nor did he see any harm in forcing children to work long days, occasionally as late as midnight. "They are not made to stay-over their ten hours, unless they have work to do," he told the investigator.

In those paternalistic times, some employers had a reputation for treating their employees well. One Montreal directory boasted that William Clendinneng, owner of the aforementioned foundry, set up a "comfortable reading room on the tables of which are the leading papers and manuals," for the use of his employees. In 1888, *Commerce of Montreal and Its Manufactures* declared that the Irish Protestant industrialist, who emigrated to the city in 1847 at the age of fourteen, "takes a deep interest in the welfare of all his employees and exercises a fatherly care over them."

Frequently, employers assumed they had the authority to inflict corporal punishment on their child workers, sometimes, with the assistance of the police. Until the Royal Commission on the Relations of Labour and Capital carried out a nationwide investigation between 1886 and 1889, most abuse went unchecked.

Children in Montreal's cigar and cigarette factories endured the worst treatment, according to the inquiry. "When the children don't behave, they stick them among the coals," a former cigar maker testified. Charlie Weir, he recalled, once spent two hours in the black hole. Another foreman fined or beat young workers: "If a child did anything, that is, if they looked on one side or the other, or spoke, he would say, 'I'm going to make you pay 10 cents fine,' and if the same were repeated three or four times, he would seize a stick or a plank, and beat him with it."

Employers routinely imposed fines on workers as punishment for mistakes and other "infractions" such as running. "If we happened to be cutting our leaf wrong, they would give us a crack across the head with the fist," said one fourteen-year-old boy, who started his apprenticeship as a cigar maker at eleven. He often had to pay fines—as much as twenty-five cents in a single day—for "talking too much."

The commission exposed numerous examples of unhealthy working conditions. Toilets were often unsanitary, or non-existent. Richard Powers, a moulder, testified that at Clendinneng's and Ives', "they are just open troughs . . . located near the furnaces where the iron is melted. There is an awful smell there sometimes."

Many complained that employers frequently reduced employees' wages during the winter months when workers were plentiful. Still, Powers felt fortunate to have a steady job after spending seventeen years in part-time work at Clendinneng's and other foundries. "Nothing but slow suicide for a moulder," Richard Powers told a government investigator. "The moulder continuing to work piecework in machinery is either in his grave at 45 or otherwise a broken down man. He is supposed to do about two days' work in one day."

Workers at Clendinneng's Foundry complained of long hours, low pay and unhealthy working conditions in this massive establishment that produced stoves, bed frames, machinery, agricultural and railway castings, ornamental railings and sinks.

And day labourers often sought factory jobs despite the twelve-hour shifts and appalling conditions because they offered indoor work and reliable hours. Many unskilled Irish worked on the docks, loading and unloading ships, back-breaking labour, with long, irregular hours. At least once a week, longshoreman Patrick J. Dalton toiled thirty-five hours at a stretch without a rest. "I have not been able to drag myself home, or scarcely able," he told the inquiry. If a worker refused or asked for a break, he risked losing out on future work. "His services were not required any longer there—if he was not man enough to come back after working thirty hours," Dalton reported.

Grain trimming—the task of loading bulk grain to avoid shifting—was particularly gruelling since it confined the men to the dusty, airless ship's hold. "After a man has been grain trimming five, six or seven hours there is a feeling akin to fever comes on, which is very depressing and injurious to the constitution, and this is more so from wearing a sponge to cover the mouth and nose while you are at work . . . [Men keep themselves awake] very often by artificial means. That is by running to the tap and sprinkling water on the face and eyes, and what is more injurious, to the grog shop for liquor to keep themselves awake as a stimulant."

Taverns offered more than a chance to quaff a pint. They also served as gathering places, where Irish workers shared news, talked politics and aired their grievances. Charles "Joe Beef" McKiernan, the hard-bitten owner of the Crown & Sceptre Tavern, notorious for keeping a bear chained up on the premises of his waterfront establishment, had a heart soft enough to give strapped workers a meal and a bed in exchange for a couple of hours' work. The ex-military man from County Cavan also doled out bread and soup—and advice—to strikers. In January 1878, following a strike on the Lachine Canal, he sent two workers' delegates to Ottawa to present their case to the prime minister. A few years later, during a strike at the Hochelaga cotton mills, he urged workers to hold out for reduced hours.

But strikers risked fines and even prison sentences for "infringing on an employer's freedom of contract." Employers came down hard on labour sympathizers. "On several occasions there have been one or two cases where union men have been thrown out of work and had to walk the streets a number of days before they could procure employment," said Powers.

Still, workers often banded together to press their case with an employer. Contractors faced a severe shortage of labour during the construction of the Victoria Bridge that linked Montreal, from Windmill Point, near the fever sheds, to the south shore. In 1854 and 1855, labourers and carters, many of them Irish, staged walkouts and forced the Grand Trunk to raise their pay to match the rates offered by outside agents. And when the company gave an exclusive contract to Sheddon Cartage in 1863–64, independent carters organized two major demonstrations

A carter at Meldrum Bros., a Griffintown coal yard.

that led to general strikes, paralyzing the city. "It is almost a custom in Canada for mechanics and labourers to strike twice a year," James Hodges, the celebrated engineer, wrote in *The Construction of the Great Victoria Bridge*.

The iron railway bridge, the first to span the St. Lawrence, had a three-mile-long enclosed tunnel, supported by twenty-four immense limestone pillars—an engineering feat touted as one of the eight wonders of the world. But the construction often put workers in dangerous positions, in brutally cold weather, a fact that bestowed a certain prestige on the humblest of labourers. "As children we looked reverently on stooped, bearded figures, about whom it was said in awe, 'He worked on the building of Victoria Bridge,'" wrote John Loye, an amateur historian and long-time president of the United Irish Societies.

Boys as young as eight years old worked with the riveting crews who assembled the bridge's heavy iron panels. They stood on narrow boards, seventy-five feet above the river, without safety belts or guard rails, heating rivets in a portable forge. Twenty-six workers were killed during the construction of the Victoria Bridge between 1854 and 1859. Most of them, like James McLeary, a Griffintown labourer who fell from the bridge in July 1856, drowned. Edward Burke died instantly on May 16, 1859, when a beam fell and crushed his head.

On construction sites or in factories, accidents happened frequently, often causing workers to lose time and wages. Or worse. Foreman James Hayes lost his eyesight in an accident caused by "the carelessness of one of the boys" at B.P. Paige & Co., a Wellington Street foundry, the *Gazette* reported on November 21, 1853. "Mr. Hayes was a most deserving, industrious man, with a family, and is thus deprived of ability to earn a livelihood."

Sometimes, an industrial accident imperiled the entire neighbourhood. Shortly before three a.m. on Sunday, April 6, 1856, the gasworks on Dalhousie Street blew up. The accident, caused by a spark from an open lamp carried by an employee investigating a leak, killed one man and severely injured several others. Alfred Sandham, who lived a few blocks from the scene, described the impact of the explosion in his 1870 book *Ville Marie: Or, Sketches of Montreal, Past and Present:* "The building was torn in pieces and a column of fire shot towards the sky; then came a hail of timbers, rafters and bricks. The destruction was complete, from the foundation up not one brick remained on another and roofing and beams were shattered to atoms. A building directly opposite was also destroyed and the windows and sashes in the neighborhood were much injured."

The consequences of unemployment led many to put up with appalling conditions on the job. A man without work might be driven into the ranks of the homeless, forced to seek temporary lodging at St. Bridget's Refuge or line up for soup with the city's hundreds of vagrants. Day labourers in long stretches of unemployment faced dire poverty. In

January 1872, when the price of firewood soared from three dollars a cord to twelve dollars, beyond the means of a dollar-a-day worker, two small children froze to death in a house on Kempt (later Young) Street.

Excessive toil in grimy, poorly ventilated factories also took its toll. "I have often heard parish priests of my diocese say that the majority of persons and specially of girls who leave their families to go and work in factories, return broken down by work, and consumptive, for the want of ventilation in factories," the Archbishop of Quebec told the inquiry. But "most painful," the report stated, were the consequences for the boys and girls employed in the cigar and tobacco factories. "The tobacco had stunted the growth of the witnesses and poisoned their blood. They were undersized, sallow and listless, wholly without the bright vivacity and rosy hue of health which should animate and adorn children."

THE BOOMING INDUSTRIES ALONG THE LACHINE CANAL generated vast fortunes for their capitalist owners. And although a few factory owners and managers lived nearby, in the evenings elegant carriages transported wealthy manufacturers, financiers and merchant princes to leafy estates on the slopes of Mount Royal, up and away from the grimy, fire- and flood-prone industrial district.

Unless they landed jobs as servants or coachmen, Griffintown residents rarely caught a glimpse of the mansions that stood amid the trees on the mountain, overlooking their dreary neighbourhood below. A ride in a fine carriage along the avenues that traversed the mountain impressed Rev. Michael Buckley, an Irish priest from County Cork, during his stay in the city. "The mountain is wooded to the top, and here and there, as you pass, splendid mansions, all of cut stone, and many of elegant design, peep out from the foliage, or stand in bold relief with the mountain for a background," he wrote in his 1870 *Diary of a Tour in America.* "In no place have I seen finer suburban residences."

Montreal's lawyers, notaries and doctors, administrators, accountants—typically English or Scottish Protestants—shared in the prosperity. To meet their demand for fine homes, in the late 1850s the Sulpicians developed a parcel of land adjacent to their seminary property on the slopes of Mount Royal. Affluent middle-class buyers built elegant single-family dwellings on avenues along Dorchester, St. Catherine and Sherbrooke streets. Removed from the smokestacks of St. Ann's Ward, residents enjoyed paved roads, water and other amenities. The Sulpicians' sales agreement placed numerous restrictions on the lots, requiring owners to build private residences of stone or brick at least twelve feet back from the street, and to plant trees in front of their homes. The contract also banned brickyards, butchers and any other type of "nuisance" enterprise that might detract from the neighbourhood's residential ambiance.

No such rules protected residents of Griffintown, where streets remained unpaved, without sewers or street lighting, and where tap water was dubious and garbage collection sporadic. Beginning in the 1850s, expanding industries took over large lots, pushing into the neighbourhood southwest from McGill Street. Factories and foundries, even a gasworks, set up shop next to wooden cottages and rowhouses. Nearby, crates and barrels of tallow, dyes, pitch oils, gunpowder and other hazardous stores, along with flammable paper, rope, shingles and sundry other goods, sat waiting shipment in massive new warehouses, clustered along Wellington Street, blocking off the canal and the river.

In the mid-nineteenth century many of Griffintown's cottages gave way to brick rowhouses, some of them solidly built and boasting stained glass windows, decorative stonework and other architectural flourishes. However, in the more typical two- or three-storey rowhouses, developers cut corners, constructing narrow flats—one up, one down, with shared inside staircases and dirt cellars. Few were equipped with baths or toilets. Tenants shared privies in the backyard, often near stables where residents—many of whom earned their living as carters—kept horses, maybe a cow, goats and chickens. Stray goats ran wild, chewing on garbage, laundry and sparse vegetation.

The teeming Irish precinct faced a housing shortage as warehouses and factories crowded out workers' dwellings in the older section. The problem became so acute in the 1850s, that when Grand Trunk erected its vast sheds across the Wellington Street Bridge in Point St. Charles, they had to convert the old emigrant sheds at Windmill Point into living quarters for workers and their families.

Such was the demand that some Griffintown landlords constructed additional housing in the backyards of their small lots. The rear dwellings, typically two-storey brick or wooden structures, were tucked into small spaces next to communal privies, stables and woodsheds, and were accessible through the arched laneways that punctuated the long blocks of brick rowhouses.

A century later, in *Montreal: Seaport and City*, author Stephen Leacock would describe old Griffintown as "a wretched area, whose tumbled, shabby houses mock at the wealth of Montreal." He bestowed a dubious distinction, calling it "the first of our industrial 'slums,' the gift of the machine age to replace the bush farm of the settler."

In the first decade after the '47 Famine, both Montreal and Quebec City continued to experience outbreaks of cholera. And because Griffintown, still a popular stopover for newly landed Irish, often suffered the brunt of the epidemics, many assumed that the disease entered the country on emigrant ships. But by the 1850s, doctors and social reformers had begun to place the blame for the city's high incidence of illness and premature death on poor sanitation and unsafe water in vulnerable, neglected districts.

In a controversial paper published in the *Canadian Naturalist* in May 1859, Philip Carpenter, an outspoken Presbyterian minister and amateur scientist, calculated that Montreal had a mortality rate higher than any other city in British North America, and closely matching that of the notorious English port city of Liverpool. Carpenter urged city politicians to clamp down on landlords: "It is the duty of the Council to see that wages of death are no longer wrung from the hard [won] earnings of the poor, but that all who undertake to let homes shall be compelled to put them and their surroundings into a condition favorable to health and life."

Decades later, apart from a sharp increase in rents, not much had changed in Griffintown, still one of the most neglected neighbourhoods in the city. In 1888, the Royal Commission on the Relations of Labour and Capital investigated workers' living conditions in Montreal, and found some of the worst cases in Griffintown. One witness, Montreal journalist Arthur Short, testified that he was pressured to drop a series of articles on the sanitary condition of the city after the first one, on Griffintown, led to the threat of a $10,000 libel suit. Short described some of the "nests of contagion" he had found in the district. In yards on Ottawa, McCord and Eleanor streets, "three rows of houses, rickety, propped up facing dirty sheds and germ-breeding closets, and in many of these houses sickness reigned supreme." In a house on Eleanor Street, "bricks have been taken from the walls and replaced by wood, through the cracks in which the wind of winter must whistle cruelly." And in yet another house, an open cellar door revealed the source of a bad smell and dampness that permeated the building: "The floods had been there; it is said it is one of the first houses to be flooded when the flood comes. There is no drainage whatever. The rental of these houses is six dollars per month for the lower flats, and seven for the upper flats. Every family in this row has had a case of sickness during the past year."

Others found it more convenient to blame the luckless tenants for their own plight. In 1889, the anonymous author of *Montreal by Gaslight*, oozing prejudice against Irish Catholics, offers up a voyeuristic look at Griffintown as the home of filthy, godless alcoholics:

> Upon a narrow and unfrequented street in the vicinity of McCord St., and adjoining the Lachine Canal, stands a row of tenement

houses. To the passerby, their neat and clean appearance without
would attract attention in so squalid and poor a district. . . . What
secret is hidden behind those brick walls? . . . Come with me and
see. Upon the ground floor of No. 127, the first in the row, live
in three rooms two families. Eleven human beings—created in
the image of their Maker—eat, drink, sleep and perhaps wash in
these three rooms. In a Christian city is this right? . . .

Certain it is that, with few exceptions, the advanced workers, the
promoters, the pioneers in Lower Canada have been the English.

Rev. Augustus J. Thébaud, the eminent French-born Jesuit scholar,
also appeared to harbour prejudice against his co-religionists. Thébaud
visited Griffintown in 1869, and, several years later, recorded his impressions—tinged with anti-Irish attitudes—in a book, *Forty Years in the
United States of America:* "The Irishwomen of the lower class, it is well
known, form two distinct species, having absolutely nothing in common. Some of them cannot be equaled by any other women, except the
French, in motherly attention. Spotless cleanliness, sweet smiles and
words, devotedness to duty, everything which entitles women to the
name of angels, belong above all to many Irishwomen. But the others?
Let us not speak of them."

Many members of the clergy encouraged Irish emigrants to leave
the soul-destroying city, with all its temptations, and to settle on the
soil. Two decades after Father Phelan lured hundreds of new arrivals
away from rough-and-tumble Griffintown to St. Columban, north of
Montreal, Bishop John Sweeny of Saint John helped hundreds of Irish
families leave that city and carve new farms out of the woods in rural
New Brunswick, in a small community named Johnville, in his honour.
In 1859, he applied to the New Brunswick government for a tract of
wilderness to be parcelled out free, on condition that the settler clear
five acres, build a house of at least sixteen square feet, live on the land
and help build a public road in front of the property.

On Thursday, October 25, 1866, Irish journalist John Francis Maguire, on a quest to see how his former countrymen had fared in North America, set out with Bishop Sweeny to visit some of the settlers, about one hundred and fifty miles from Saint John. Bishop Sweeny, Maguire wrote in *The Irish in America* in 1868, deplored "the ruinous tendency of his countrymen, to congregate in cities, or to 'hang about town,'" where they worked as common labourers and fell into drinking during the idle, off seasons. On the third day of their journey, their carriage "jolting and jumping" over the last thirty-five-mile stretch, a picturesque but deeply rutted, rough road, they reached Johnville.

The first settlers, Hugh M'Cann, who spoke only Irish, and his wife Mary Jane, who knew some English, had travelled into the forest to claim their one hundred acres in the fall of 1861. Five years later, some six hundred Irish souls lived in the community, bordered "by a range of mountains as beautiful in their outline as those that are mirrored in the sweet waters of Killarney." And the M'Canns, having harvested their fourth crop of potatoes, oats and buckwheat, could laugh at their early hardships, with Mrs. M'Cann telling her visitors "how 'it was as good as any theaytre' to see Hugh and herself tramping after the lumbering oxen, and all their cherished property nodding and shaking on the jolting waggon" that took them into the wilderness. Another settler, the "dark-haired, sharp-eyed" Mrs. Crehan, told Maguire if he ever happened to go to Galway, she had a message for the landlord who had evicted her: "You may tell him from me, that I'm better off than himself, and more indipindent in my mind; and tell him, sir, all the harm I wish him is for him to know that much."

But the Irish at St. Columban near Montreal did not fare as well as their compatriots in the fertile Saint John River Valley. The rugged, rocky terrain of the lower Laurentians resisted attempts at cultivation. After reaching a peak of 983 souls, or some two hundred Irish Catholic families, the rural parish went into decline. By 1860, the sons and daughters of the Irish settlers in St. Columban had begun to drift back to the city, lured by well-paying jobs in Montreal and other urban centres in Ontario and the United States.

Still, John Francis Maguire found reason for optimism in Montreal's much-maligned Irish working-class neighbourhood: "Griffintown, the principal Irish quarter, is almost entirely owned by the working classes; and here, as in Quebec, not a single house of ill-fame is to be found in the entire district. In Griffintown, poverty and wretchedness, miserably clad children and slatternly women are occasionally to be seen, but they are comparatively rare, a dark contrast to the prevailing sobriety, thrift, and good conduct distinguishing the Irish Catholic of Montreal."

Nowhere in British North America, Maguire writes, "does the Catholic Irishman feel so thoroughly at home" as in Montreal, "where his religion is respected and his church is surrounded with dignity and splendor." No longer relegated to the old Recollet Chapel, Irish Catholics from across the city now gathered for Sunday mass at St. Patrick's Church, bordering on fashionable Dorchester Street, on the southern edge of the Golden Square Mile.

In 1848, at the request of the bishop, the Jesuits had opened a mission in Griffintown for the burst of Famine emigrants who had settled in St. Ann's Ward. The priests set up a temporary chapel in a rented brick building on the southwest corner of Murray and Ottawa streets, later converted into a grocery store. Soon, a church history notes, "The overflow of the faithful were out on Ottawa and Murray streets striving . . . to hear the voice of the priest they couldn't see." In 1851, the bishop laid the cornerstone for Montreal's second church built specifically for the Irish, on a triangle of land next to the canal.

St. Ann's massive wooden doors opened to the faithful for the first time on Friday, December 8, 1854. A stream of Irish Catholics stepped reverently down two long, green slate aisles lined with marble pillars, and slipped into the dark wooden pews of their new parish church.

St. Ann's Church, built in 1854,
became the social and spiritual heart of the community.

St. Ann's lacked the splendour of St. Patrick's, the grand structure on the hill that rivalled Notre Dame in size and ornamentation. The modest greystone building at the corner of McCord and Wellington streets could seat three thousand worshippers, half as many as St. Patrick's. John Ostell, a leading Montreal architect, surveyor and door and sash manufacturer, had kept costs to a minimum in the design and decoration of the church on the edge of the canal. Still, it would take the impoverished parish forty years to pay their debt to the Sulpicians for the construction of the $44,600 building.

The bishop named the new church St. Ann's, after the historic seventeenth-century chapel that once stood nearby on the well-travelled road between Montreal and Lachine. A church historian would later gently question the decision to name a church for the Irish after a saint revered by French Canadians, a name long taken by local Irish Protestants, first for their chapel on Wellington Street, and then in 1848 for their new church, St. Ann's (Anglican), on the corner of Ottawa and Dalhousie streets.

But the humble parishioners of St. Ann's Catholic Church took great pride in their place of worship. And Alfred Sandham praised the "fine specimen of ecclesiastical architecture" in his *Sketches of Montreal, Past and Present,* calling it "the most striking edifice in this quarter of the city."

And, blessed be to God, St. Ann's first pastor, Father Michael O'Brien, was one of their own. The distinguished priest, standing in the grand, carved wooden pulpit of the new church, understood the history, the sufferings, the frailties, of the Irish faces looking up at him. Born in Aughnagar, County Tyrone, he had served as a parish priest in

St. Ann's Academy, Montreal's first school for English-speaking Catholic girls, opened in September 1857, under the direction of the sisters of the Congregation de Notre-Dame.

Ireland for fifteen years before landing at St. Patrick's in Montreal on October 10, 1849. He had first worked arduously for the destitute in his sprawling parish of Aughnacloy, County Tyrone, during the Famine, then responded to the Canadian Sulpicians' call for Irish priests and followed his people to Montreal. Now he would become their priest and counsellor, friend and advocate, in the New World.

Father O'Brien became known as the "Father of the Orphans" for his efforts to place the hundreds of emigrant children left homeless in the parish after their parents died in the fever sheds. Many had to be placed in St. Patrick's Orphan Asylum, an institution that had its beginnings in a temporary shelter in Griffintown. Appointed director of the orphanage in 1859, the saintly priest worked constantly to raise funds for the children. He established St. Ann's Academy, the city's first school for English-speaking Catholic girls. The superior, Mother St. Agnes, of the Congrégation de Notre-Dame, welcomed 125 pupils to the brand new parish school next to the church on McCord Street on September 6, 1857. When construction delayed its opening, Father O'Brien rented a little brick house on St. Augustin (now Rioux) Street and set up temporary classrooms.

The boys of the parish, at least those whose parents could afford to educate them, attended a Christian Brothers school established in 1843, with three classes in a small building on the grounds of the Sulpicians' Collège de Montréal, an elite private French school on the northeast edge of the district.

A century later, a St. Ann's Parish chronicle dared to call the 1850s "the brightest days of Griffintown's history," a time when "its people had become self-conscious and independent and began to make themselves a power of influence to be felt in the general community at large. In a parochial sense too, their aspirations took flower, and ere long they could boast themselves to be on a par with St. Patrick's and some went so far as to declare St. Ann's to be even superior to the proud and dominating edifice that crowned De Rochebleve Hill."

THE PARISH GREW OVER THE NEXT THREE DECADES, as the population of Griffintown swelled from seven thousand in 1851 to 23,003 in 1891. At the same time, the district gradually became more Catholic. By 1865, there were more than seven hundred Catholic families in Griffintown, nearly double the 432 Protestants families. This trend became more pronounced as large numbers of residents—more Protestants than Catholics—found the means to move up to better neighbourhoods.

In 1864, a large number of well-to-do members of St. Stephen's Anglican, led by their pastor, Rev. Canon Jacob Ellegood, formed a new parish, St. James the Apostle, on the northwest corner of St. Catherine and Bishop streets, then on the outskirts of the city. Other Protestant congregations from Griffintown followed as their members became more prosperous: In 1866, the American Presbyterian Church moved to a new church on Dorchester. Two years later St. Paul's Presbyterian (Church of Scotland) vacated its old church on St. Helen Street, and relocated on Dorchester.

St. Stephen's survived the loss. And St. Paul's departing members contributed to the building of a new church, St. Mark's, for the less well-off members of the Church of Scotland they left behind. But since nearly half of Griffintown's nominal Protestant families never attended religious services, some of their wealthier brethren decided to replace their churches with missions, reaching out to the poor they left behind with religious tracts and Sunday schools, soup tickets and charity. In the eyes of the Protestant establishment, Griffintown was deteriorating into a neighbourhood of the derelict and ungodly.

While there were no ghettos in mid-nineteenth-century Montreal, different nationalities, different faiths, different classes tended to live apart. The English, French and Irish, one Jesuit observed, "formed compact, often hostile, blocks." Working-class Irish Catholics staked an unofficial claim on Griffintown. St. Ann's Church stood at the heart of the community. On Sundays, parishioners lingered on the broad stone steps at its entrance to chat and gossip. Men congregated on the corners; children played about in its bustling streets and laneways. The neighbourhood hummed on Saturdays, at the end of a hard week's work. Women browsed the stalls at the St. Ann's Market, the gaslit shops on McGill Street. And in the evenings, the Irish, in their best garb, strolled along busy St. Joseph Street. In the teeming streets, the Irish found camaraderie and notoriety. Griffintown harboured all the contradictions of the Irish: a strong faith tempered by an outlaw attitude.

In his entertaining 1881 memoir, *Fighting the Flames! Twenty-seven Years in the Montreal Fire Brigade,* the renowned firefighter William Orme McRobie tells how he found himself "running the gauntlet" past a gang of toughs on a Griffintown street corner in 1853. Then fifteen, the plucky lad had landed a job as an engine torch-boy with the Queen Engine Company No. 5, three years after he landed in Griffintown from Perth, Scotland, with his family. The diminutive firefighter recalled the attention he drew in his uniform—his oversized red garibaldi coat, his too-big leather helmet padded with flannel so it would fit, and his wide leather belt painted with the "Queen" insignia. One night, en route to the station, dressed in fireman's attire for a monthly drill, McRobie considered crossing the street to avoid "a corner frequented by one of the worst of many gangs who nightly congregated to insult passersby." He marched past the ruffians, and came out unscathed on the other side. They didn't trip him or spit on him, or squirt a shower of tobacco juice at him, as he had feared. But he had not gone far when one of the fellows insulted him. Not wanting to bring disgrace to the uniform, McRobie turned back and challenged his tormentor to a boxing match in a nearby vacant lot. The bully walked away, and the rest of the gang cheered the little fireman. The crew at the engine house had heard about the incident by the time McRobie reached the fire station. Not long after, the captain promoted the sixteen-year-old McRobie to branch torch-boy and made him a full member—two years under the age required by the Montreal Fire Department.

IN SPITE OF ITS ROUGH-AND-TUMBLE REPUTATION, violent crime was rare in Griffintown. One sensational exception was the infamous murder, in 1879, of Mary Gallagher—axed to death by Susan Kennedy, who chopped off her friend's head and threw it into a bucket, in a William Street flat.

On the day before she was murdered, Mary Gallagher made the acquaintance of Michael Flanagan, an Irish-born labourer, at Bonsecours Market. After an afternoon of drinking, the pair spent the night at a nearby hotel. Around seven o'clock the next morning, Gallagher invited Flanagan back to her friend Susan Kennedy's house in Griffintown. There, they spent the morning drinking two or three bottles of whiskey with Kennedy. Kennedy's husband, Jacob Myers (whose name was sometimes spelled Meyers or Mears in the press), refused to drink with them; he left the house soon after their arrival, returning at various times during the day. At one point, he found his wife in bed with Flanagan. "Shut up," she told him, "we're only talking."

Neighbours never expected any good to come out of the Myers' flat at 242 William Street. During a coroner's inquest, held at a police station on Young Street, a witness described the couple, who had moved into the house on May 1, as "dissipated characters . . . in the habit of having friends in to see them and carrying on the most disgusting orgies." Gallagher and Kennedy had met on one of the many occasions they had been in jail. Gallagher, separated from her husband, James Connolly, for two years, often stayed with the Myers while looking for work as a servant.

Around noon on Friday, June 26, 1879, Ellen Burke, the tenant in the flat below the Myers', heard "an awful stumble upstairs, as if something had fallen; it shook the house and knocked the plaster off the ceiling in two places." Then came the sound of "a person chopping, and the blows were very heavy, as they shook the house; the chopping lasted fully ten minutes," she later told a jury.

That afternoon, Jacob Myers—a pathetic figure frequently subject to teasing by the neighbourhood children—told them, "Let me alone. I have trouble enough; there is a woman upstairs with her head cut off." But no one thought anything was amiss in the Myers' turbulent household, until ten o'clock that night when Kennedy stuck her head out of her back window and screamed, "Murder." Burke sent her thirteen-year-old son upstairs to investigate. The boy saw a woman's barely dressed body lying on her back on the kitchen floor. Her head and right hand were in a tub next to the stove.

Police arrived at the scene and, after questioning the Myers, arrested Kennedy in connection with the murder. Before they took her into custody, she told the officers she was hungry. Cool and calm, Kennedy sat down and ate bread and butter next to the headless corpse. Flanagan, who lived a few blocks away with his mother, was arrested the following day.

Sixteen jurors heard the evidence at a coroner's inquest. Flanagan, they determined, was "intelligent-looking" and "truthful." The thirty-two-year-old labourer admitted that he was present in the house at the time of murder but claimed he was "boosey" and had slept through the crime. He also stated that he saw the dead woman lying on the floor as he left the house at two o'clock, but her head had not yet been removed. The jury concluded that Myers, who frequently contradicted himself, was "slightly demented" and "very much afraid of his wife who seems to have been a terror to the police as well as anyone who had anything to do with her."

Kennedy, whose age was given variously as twenty or twenty-six, claimed that a strange man had entered the house and killed Gallagher. But the details of her alibi kept changing. Once she stated that she had been in a drunken stupor and slept through the murder; another time she said that the man who killed her friend was good-looking, so she gave him time to get away. But the evidence—her blood-encrusted clothing and the discovery of the murder weapon in a trunk in her bedroom—weighed heavily against Kennedy. So did her history of violence. Constable William Craig testified that he had arrested Kennedy on numerous occasions and sometimes "she was so violent with drink that it took two men to hold her."

The jury absolved Flanagan and found Kennedy guilty, with a recommendation of mercy. But the judge ignored the plea for leniency and sentenced her to hang on December 5, 1879. "You and only you butchered and mutilated your friend on the very spot where you had been carousing up to the moment of the murder," he told Kennedy, who appeared indifferent throughout the trial.

Prime Minister John A. Macdonald later commuted the sentence. Kennedy served sixteen years in prison; she died in 1890. But the ghost of her victim, Mary Gallagher, would continue to haunt Griffintown. And the lurid crime reflected poorly on a neighbourhood already bearing the brunt of prejudice. One reporter complained that he "could hardly write his notes for the jostling of the people to get a look at the body." Although police had barred women and children from the premises, "some ugly-looking hags . . . forced themselves to the door of the room."

In 1888, the *Post* offered a rare defence of the district's inhabitants, pointing out that "Griffintown was never notorious for violence. . . . More crimes of violence and murder have been committed uptown than in Griffintown." In fact, local residents occasionally took the law into their own hands. On June 24, 1857, the *Gazette* reported that after police were unable to shut down "one of the most infamous houses in the city, kept by a woman named Mother Fox." Sub-Chief Flynn and his team arrived at the scene the next day to investigate, only to find that "the house was nearly torn down and no person was seen near it. All the information they could get was, that all the respectable neighbours were determined to hunt Mother Fox from the neighbourhood."

Brothels were a rarity in Griffintown. Police reports of the era show that in most years fewer than 10 per cent of the city's dozens of "houses of ill fame" operated in St. Ann's Ward. In most years, there were none. Still, the Montreal Irish faced arrest more often than any other nationality. In 1865, police reported that nearly half, or 5,942, of the 12,810 persons confined in the city's stations had Irish origins. By far their most common offence was drunkenness, followed by drunk and disorderly behaviour and disturbing the peace.

The more numerous French Canadians stole the lead in the number of arrests in the early 1870s, when charges of drunkenness began to slide, a decrease that police chief W.F.L. Penton linked to a downturn in the economy. In 1885, the number of Irish taken into custody shrank even more dramatically, falling to 16 per cent. "The number of arrests this year is the smallest in the last seven years," then-chief Hercule Paradis stated in the annual police report. "To the spring floods, the epidemic and the general stagnation in business may be attributed this decrease, also to the fact that many persons found under the influence of liquor in the streets have been assisted home by the police."

A strong sense of solidarity prompted Irishmen to intervene when police tried to arrest an intoxicated friend or neighbour, leading to many a brawl. "It is always the offender who receives the sympathies and the policeman the disfavour and often the blows of the bystander," police chief Guillaume Lamothe wrote in his 1863 annual report, complaining about the difficulty his constables faced in apprehending drunks. "Should the prisoner attack the policeman, seek to throw him, tear his clothes or face, the crowd applauds and laughs. But should the policeman strike back so as not to lose his prisoner and throw him, the crowd cry out 'brutality,' and sometimes seek to rescue the offender!"

History had given Irish Catholics little reason to trust or respect authority. Deprived of basic rights under Ireland's Penal Laws, the poor and powerless relied on the rough justice of outlaw tradition. And so the Griffintown Irish stood together, faithfully defending each other against authorities.

"I am teetotaler myself," James Dougherty, of Irishtown, New Brunswick, wrote to his brother in Ireland on April 25, 1859. Like many of his Irish neighbours, the country schoolmaster had joined the temperance society established by his parish priest. "Rum drinking and all grog shops are totally demolished in the district, and it is also the wish of the said Rev. gentleman that none of his hearers go to other places to get drunk. I have known districts myself in the country where there were not more than sixty families living in [it] and at the same time there were five grog holes in each district so do you think the priest was wrong or right in putting a stop to this demoralizing practice, this Hell's best did this devil engendered rum. I should say he was right, and if all others would do the same as he has done, there would not be so many going to prison yearly. . . . Nor so many . . . hungry victims."

Griffintown, naturally, offered numerous temptations. Gregarious, hardworking Irish labourers turned to pubs and saloons for a chance to socialize and solve Ireland's, and their own, problems over a pint. And St. Ann's Ward invariably topped the list for the numbers of licensed and unlicensed drinking establishments in the city. In 1866, the police found 91 of the city's 247 illegal taverns in the area and, in his report that year, police chief W.F.L. Penton suggested that there were many more: "There are places which may be more properly called shebeens—low drinking shops without the outward evidence afforded by the existence of a bar and therefore, more difficult of detection."

Critics everywhere, of course, took delight in exposing—and exaggerating—the Irish predilection for liquor. But the Irish had a few eminent advocates. The influential Archbishop Martin John Spalding of Baltimore, Maryland, came to their defence. "They have their faults, which are paraded and greatly exaggerated by the public press; but they also have their virtues which are studiously kept of view," he wrote in his 1875 book, *Miscellanea,* quoted by Maguire in *The Irish in America.* Nevertheless, Father Michael O'Brien, like most Irish pastors, directed his parishioners to stay out of the saloons. And in 1863 he founded the St. Ann's Total Abstinence Society.

Father O'Brien worked day and night to ease the troubles of his Griffintown congregation, through epidemics, fires and floods, unemployment, the strife between Catholics and Protestants, and even domestic disputes. In 1860, the priest was called as a witness in a controversial murder trial of a parishioner accused of beating his pregnant wife to death. The heavy demands of his struggling, impoverished parishioners eventually took their toll on the once sturdy priest. In 1862, he asked his superior to relieve him of his duties. Father O'Brien spent his final years as an assistant at St. Patrick's. He died on March 30, 1870.

In 1863, Rev. Michael O'Farrell, another Irish Sulpician, took over from Father O'Brien as pastor of St. Ann's. Only thirty-one at the time of his appointment, the Limerick native became a close friend of D'Arcy McGee, a Montreal member of Parliament whose West Ward riding encompassed Griffintown.

The scholarly young priest took a strong interest in the education of the children of the parish. When the nuns turned girls away from St. Ann's Academy because of overcrowding, he personally paid for an extension to the school to accommodate three extra classes. (In 1865, the original girls' school was demolished and replaced with a much larger two-storey greystone building, with ten classrooms, a reception hall, music room and a sewing room.)

In September 1866, St. Ann's Boys' School—which had changed locations three times, twice to accommodate the expanding Irish population, a third time to relinquish their classrooms to the British for a barracks—started the academic year in a new building. Although the conditions remained Spartan. Brother Andaine, the director, often remarked that he had every opportunity "to practise his favourite virtue of poverty."

Still, the handsome three-storey greystone structure, on the corner of Young and Ottawa streets, had eight classrooms and, on the top floor, a public meeting hall. The Christian Brothers, many of them Irish-born, instilled in their young charges a love of Ireland, its history and legends, poetry and music. More than once did the stirring beat of the "March of Brian Boru" fill St. Ann's Hall—its stage transformed into the battlefield of Clontarf, overlooking Dublin Bay, so the sons of emigrants could re-enact one of the greatest victories of medieval Ireland. Most fortunate was the student chosen to play the noble Brian Boru, the "last great King of Ireland," dying a tragic death in his tent, after being stabbed by a fleeing Viking.

Strict disciplinarians, the Christian Brothers set high academic standards for their underprivileged charges. At the end of each academic year, the Brothers held public oral examinations. The director would grill the students in front of the pastor, Father O'Farrell, prominent Irish politicians and invited guests (D'Arcy McGee among them on at least one occasion), to demonstrate their skills in grammar and mental arithmetic. "The pupils of St. Ann's excelled in mathematics; they were second to none in patriotism and in dramatics, they were not deficient. The exercise always ended with a hearty 'God Save Ireland,'" noted the school's historian, Brother Mactilius.

Rev. James Hogan took over as pastor of St. Ann's in 1867, after serving thirteen years as an assistant at St. Patrick's. His tall, athletic build gave Hogan "a fine commanding presence," one close friend would later remark. A real *soggarth aroon,* he quickly endeared himself to his parishioners with his warm, outgoing nature. A profile in the *Saint Anne's Fair Journal* of 1891 noted that Hogan, like many a native of Tipperary, could be counted on to defend "the Irish cause against foreign oppression"—even if it presented itself in the form of Montreal's French-Canadian bishop.

Father Hogan may have been too preoccupied by a dispute with the bishop to heed the Christian Brothers' requests for a teachers' residence. By March 1876, Brother Andaine and the seven Christian Brothers teaching at St. Ann's, tired of walking several miles to school each day from their community's residence on St. Lawrence Street, decided to move into the school. They installed an oratory, refectory, kitchen, parlour and dormitory on the second floor, shifting four classrooms to the third storey. They also built a separate entrance on Young Street.

The following September, the Brothers had to turn away twenty children applying for the junior class, for lack of space. By December, when the waiting list reached one hundred, Father Hogan pressured the Brothers to open an additional class. Enrollment in St. Ann's Boys' School reached four hundred, a tight fit in eight classes.

The teachers' makeshift living quarters appalled Brother Arnold of Jesus when he took over as principal at St. Ann's Boys' School in January 1877. "The sanitary conditions were shameful. The closets were in the yard and every other hygienic (I should rather say unhygienic) requirement was in keeping," he wrote in a letter to a confrere. "Seeing how other communities were so nicely kept with proper departments for the Brothers, I was forced to say to the Provincial that 'no Irish need apply for anything in Montreal.'"

Brother Arnold of Jesus came ready to champion the Griffintown Irish. The Tipperary man remained an outspoken patriot after he emigrated, first to New York, then to Montreal in 1855. He had acquired legendary status as an educator and temperance worker after stints as a director of schools in Montreal, Kingston and Toronto. Now he was determined to push the students of humble St. Ann's to academic excellence, to outshine every other school in the city, no less.

Brother Arnold immediately set out to convince Father Hogan to build a separate house for the Brothers and to repair the rundown school, a huge undertaking he described in a letter to Brother Prudent: "The first thing undertaken was to supply two classes with new writing desks which cost $15 each. Next was to get the fence . . . in proper shape and painted. I had one hundred loads of stuff drawn from the gas house to the yard. The floor of the first class was so worn out that I had to get nearly all replaced by three-inch flooring."

By 1879, with five hundred boys squeezed into St. Ann's Boys' School, and several hundred more applicants having to be turned away, Father Hogan agreed to build a separate house for the Brothers to free up space for more classrooms. Construction began in November. But Brother Arnold had to seek the funding for the $7,000 residence from the community. More than half the money, $4,500, came from parish bazaars organized by the ladies of St. Ann's and St. Patrick's. The Sulpicians provided $1,000. Interest-free loans from more than two dozen prominent Montreal Irishmen financed the remainder. "The priests of St. Ann's did nothing and gave not a dollar towards it," he complained to another Brother many years later.

On Friday, March 19, 1880, the Brothers moved into their new home adjacent to the school.

A LACROSSE CRAZE SWEPT ACROSS NORTH AMERICA in the last decades of the nineteenth century, and the Shamrocks, a team of Irish Catholics from Griffintown, excelled at the sport. Father Hogan was one of their most ardent boosters. The pastor rarely missed a game and a chance to support the players, all of whom were members of his parish. The priest took delight in the sport that allowed the underdog Irish Catholics to defend their national honour.

The Shamrocks had opened their fourth season in 1870 by winning a championship challenge against their chief rivals, the Montreal Lacrosse Club. The humiliating defeat of the team of well-to-do young Protestants had delighted the Shamrocks' Irish Catholic fans, who cheered their working-class heroes on to victory in three more matches. Determined to defend their first-place position, the Shamrocks, factory workers and artisans who worked twelve-hour days, had practised as much as they could for their upcoming match against the Caughnawauga Indians.

The dark cloud that descended over Mount Royal shortly before three o'clock, on Wednesday, July 13, 1870, pushed Father James Hogan near the edge of despair. In less than half an hour, on a playing field at the foot of that mountain, the priest's beloved Shamrocks were scheduled to meet the Caughnawauga Indians in a much-anticipated match. Rev. Michael Buckley had accepted Father Hogan's invitation to dine at the rectory at noon. Now, just as the priests prepared to drive up the hill to the grounds, thunder rumbled in the distance between flashes of lightning and it began to rain. "It will clear up," Hogan promised his guest. "It will clear up."

At the grounds, the priests found the players and a scattering of enthusiasts contemplating the sloppy turf. Members of the St. Patrick's Society, organizers of the match—the main feature of their annual picnic in aid of the St. Patrick's Orphan Asylum—postponed the event to Monday. Not long after Hogan returned to the rectory, a tornado tore over the city, lifting roofs, blowing out windows and damaging the spire of St. Ann's Church.

Monday, July 18, brought a cloudless sky and scorching heat. The black-cassocked clerics entered the Montreal Lacrosse Grounds, ignoring the hawkers along Sherbrooke Street trying to catch fans streaming through the gates: "Buy a three copper cigar before you go in, sir," they cajoled. Some seven thousand spectators shelled out fifty cents for a ticket. Inside, the grounds took on a carnival air; under a large, cheery awning, dancers stepped lively to a quadrille band, and high-spirited fans put down pennies for ginger beer at well-stocked refreshment stands.

The next day, the *Evening Star* commended the Irish Catholic fans for their sobriety: "Not one drop of intoxicating liquor was to be found on the grounds. Nor did a single case of drunkenness, as far as could be judged or learned, mar the pleasure of the occasion." The paper also praised the "almost perfect" security arrangements at the game. "Policemen were stationed both outside and inside the fence," the paper reported. "So during the games the utmost order was secured, and the fences kept free from idlers and rowdies."

Members of the Shamrock lacrosse team, Montreal, 1887.

The boisterous enthusiasm of the team's followers—most of whom, like the players, hailed from Griffintown—provided a stark contrast to the gentlemanly restraint displayed by Montreal's Protestant fans. Shamrock lacrosse matches drew immense numbers—as many as nine thousand, in a city with a population of ninety thousand (enough for historians to call Griffintown fans the first mass sports audience). The antics and cheers of the partisan Irish crowd attracted almost as much press attention—and criticism—as the players' worst gaffes. "There is a certain element of the Irish population which is so antagonistic to and irreconcilable with the English element of the city, that they find it impossible to avoid continual collision," the *Evening Star* commented on June 22, 1870. "Large bodies of persons follow the players to the grounds . . . and taunt their adversaries. . . . If one of the opponents commits a blunder . . . insulting cries of triumph and contempt are raised. When a game is won, too, yells of satisfaction are raised in a manner altogether beyond the common rules of courtesy to the vanquished. . . . insolent shouts and gross impertinences on the occasion of every mistake."

Father Buckley did observe a small skirmish—later included in his *Diary of a Tour in America*—when some young females, Shamrock fans, edged on to the playing field to get a better view.

"Come now, girls, keep back, if you plaze," Constable Falvey asked amiably, with the authentic brogue of a Cork man, Buckley decided.

But the girls ignored him.

"Ah! Begor, ladies, ye must push back, if ye were twice as handsome," Falvey urged the non-compliant fans, softening his command with a compliment.

Such impudence, Buckley thought, would not have been tolerated at home, where the Royal Irish Constabulary, with "a stern face and a still more stern baton would have pushed the fair daughters of the Emerald Isle outside the ring." Still, he delighted in the brogues he heard in the largely Irish crowd. "Everywhere the sweet Irish accent salutes my ears, and now and then, some Irish pleasantry, until I fancy I am at home amongst my own people."

By three o'clock, cheering spectators filled the bleachers, the overflow spilling into the spaces around the roped-off playing field. The children in the St. Patrick's Orphan Asylum band played swelling Irish melodies as the Reverends Buckley and Hogan took their seats under a canopy on a small stand, set up especially for the clergy, with a prime view of the field. At four o'clock, the athletes appeared on the field, each armed with a lacrosse stick. The Shamrocks wore green tights; the Indians, red. Buckley noticed an exception: "One little Indian who insisted on the style known as sans culotte." The Shamrock twelve included J. Burns, goalkeeper, J.R. Flannery, point, J. Hoobin, cover-point, J. Brown, P. Bentley, E. Giroux, P. McKeown, A. Moffatt, J. Hyland and G. Garrett, fielders, and J. Madigan and H. O'Rourke, home.

The play began, and the crowd cheered and shouted as players strove to capture the ball in their lacrosse stick, or fling it, or run it through their opponents' poles, or try to dislodge it and block the goals. Buckley glanced at Father Hogan and saw that he was "trembling all over with the excitement of fear and suspense for the success of his protégés."

In the eyes of the Irish visitor, lacrosse resembled the Celtic game of "hurling." By the end of the afternoon, Father Buckley had absorbed the essentials of the sport, invented by Canada's native people. The Indians scored after nine minutes and took the first game in the best-of-five match. Nobody cheered. The orphanage band played a solemn refrain.

The Irish won the next game in twelve minutes. The crowd roared and the band picked up the tempo. The third game lasted forty minutes. The Shamrocks emerged victorious. Jubilant fans shouted and threw their hats in the air. The band played a triumphant melody. By the fourth game, the rivals were tied. In the fifth and final game, Moffatt tipped the ball through the Indians' goal, after six minutes.

Ecstatic Irish fans rushed onto the field to embrace their heroes. While Buckley felt sorry for the defeated Indians, the priest from Cork watched an elated Father Hogan make his way through the crowd, to shake hands with all of his boys. The Shamrock Lacrosse Club's winning streak would continue for the rest of the season, one of the best in its remarkable history. Over the next three decades, the team would tour the United States and Canada, racking up numerous championships, including one at the Chicago World's Fair in 1893. Despite the club's success however, opponents continued to snub the Griffintown team: In 1883, organizers failed to invite any of the top-ranking Shamrock players on a prestigious European tour.

But in July 1870, after the Shamrocks defeated the Indians, the team could bask in the glow of immediate victory. A few nights after the game, Father Hogan entertained the whole Shamrock club at a supper in the rectory. Reverend Buckley attended and recorded the celebratory dinner in his diary, although he may have made a tactful error in naming the beverage: "We spent a very pleasant evening; we had toasts and songs and plentiful draughts of ginger beer, a great deal of talk about old Ireland, and strong expression of hope for her future prosperity."

FIVE

An Unlikely Venice

In the centre of a room is a punt, in which the lady of the house
navigates the first floor. In the kitchen the scene is indescribable
and heartrending. Tin pots, a wooden table and chairs are floating.
The teakettle sails helplessly about with the coffee pot. And lo!
Afloat in a soup tureen, drenched, its long hair draggling,
an object of abject misery, whining piteously, is the family poodle.
—Excerpt from a report by a Montreal journalist who
rowed a boat into a flooded Griffintown flat in April 1861

THE DELUGE CAME WITHOUT WARNING. On Sunday, April 14, 1861, while the faithful attended vespers at St. Stephen's Episcopal Church, an act of God sent a wall of water rushing into Griffintown, engulfing the sturdy stone church on Dalhousie Street, along with hundreds of other buildings in the crowded Irish quarter. Rev. Canon Jacob Ellegood stood fast on the altar, immersed in his sermon, until—as he wrote in an article several decades later—the sexton quietly approached him and whispered that "the church was surrounded by a flood; that the water was rising; and what were we to do."

Griffintowners try to stay afloat outside St. Stephen's Church
near Haymarket Square during the flood of 1887.

Water pooled around the bottom of St. Stephen's heavy oak doors and covered the eight steps leading down to the wooden sidewalk. But Ellegood, determined to find help for his stranded flock, waded into the dark, flooded streets. His friend Rev. John Torrance accompanied him, carrying his little son George on his shoulders. Tall and reasonably strong, both men had to struggle to stay upright against the strong currents in the frigid, waist-deep water that surged through the neighbourhood, bringing planks and tree branches and other debris from the St. Lawrence. "Sometimes we were up to the neck," Ellegood recounted. "The ice struck against our legs."

Heading up toward Mount Royal, they finally reached dry ground five blocks away. At St. Antoine Street, Ellegood ran straight to Mayor Charles-Séraphin Rodier's house and rang the doorbell until his unadorned head appeared in an upstairs window. "His Worship wore a wig and I shouted for him not to mind the wig, but to come down wigless—in any way—as the matter was urgent," the pastor wrote. Ellegood explained his congregation's predicament and asked the mayor to send out a rescue crew, then went home to soak in a hot bath. In time, the police arrived at the church and by 1 a.m., they had evacuated most of the congregation by boat.

Meanwhile, Mayor Rodier and several members of the municipal corporation toured the district on a skiff, surveying the damage. The flood had created islands of anxiety all over Griffintown. A few blocks from St. Stephen's, firemen equipped with torches arrived in boats to rescue members of the Wesleyan Chapel on Ottawa Street. But a shortage of vessels meant many were marooned overnight in the darkened church, dangling over the submerged pews.

Griffintown residents who had been out of the district when the St. Lawrence spewed over its banks stood on the edge of the flood zone, pondering their next move. Not even an exorbitant offer could tempt a cab driver to risk a trip into Griffintown where, in most places, the water was too deep for a carriage.

Not everyone was caught unprepared. At the first sign of a trickle on the streets that morning, a few cautious veterans of earlier floods had moved furniture and belongings to upper floors and attics and led their horses, cows and pigs to higher ground. Storekeepers and owners of warehouses south of Wellington Street, close to the riverbank, where water had begun to pour in, transferred stock or hired carters to transport goods to safer locations.

Most old hands, expecting the river to swell slowly—as it did almost every year—laughed at the efforts of their nervous neighbours. But when the flood hit that evening, it came like a tsunami, taking only minutes to fill cellars and burble up into ground-floor flats. It sent occupants scurrying upstairs to sympathetic neighbours. Some rushed back down to retrieve their possessions and furniture, only to be chased back up by the rising water.

Trapped in the cold and dark, with water nipping at their windowsills, residents in a row of flats near the canal fired pistol shots into the wind, panicky calls for rescue from the renegade river.

The flood of 1861 set a new record for disaster-prone Griffintown. But the mighty St. Lawrence had been spilling over its banks into the low-lying area of Montreal at least once a year since the earliest days of the colony. The first record of a flood in the area occurred over two centuries earlier, in the winter after the arrival of Montreal's founder, Paul de Chomedey de Maisonneuve. In December 1642, the St. Lawrence suddenly overflowed, threatening to swamp their outpost on the edge of the district that would become Griffintown. When water filled the ditch at the base of the log palisade, Maisonneuve led his party of some sixty men and women to higher ground and prayed to the Blessed Virgin Mary, namesake of the settlement of Ville-Marie de Montréal. A devout Catholic, he placed a small cross at the shore and vowed, if they survived, to install a much larger, permanent one at the top of Mount Royal.

On January 6, the feast of the Epiphany, one of the Jesuits in the party led the procession of thanksgiving. Maisonneuve, one witness reported, trudged through the snow, "bearing a cross so heavy that he could scarcely ascend the mountain." Just below the summit, he and his men erected the cross, knelt in a prayer of gratitude, then gathered around a crude altar for mass.

God saved the colony, but the floods would return again and again. At least once and sometimes twice a year, the St. Lawrence overflowed its banks at Montreal. And the low-lying St. Ann's Ward always suffered the most.

By 1841, the perennial flooding had become so acute that the British colonial government appointed a Royal Commission to investigate its causes and seek a solution. Major P. Cole, the chief engineer, invited public comment, and dozens of citizens responded. Many displayed a scientific bent in their submissions, with careful observations on flood levels in different parts of the city, the force and direction of the river currents, ice formations, and the impact of the creeks that ran through the city. A few skeptics doubted that engineers could control the inundations. "It is beyond the power of men to check in any way the rising of the water in front of the town," stated the long-suffering Henry Corse, who had lived in the St. Ann Suburb for forty years. "When the water is very high, my buildings are completely surrounded with it."

Others, like Colin Campbell, described their attempts to protect their properties. "In the construction of my drains as also the foundation walls of my buildings I had been at considerable pains and expense in puddling, hoping by this means I have kept the water out," wrote the owner of a commercial house on Wellington Street. Still, he added, "Water came in the cellar doors and penetrated nearly as fast as it rose outside."

Another proprietor, John Try, had made "careful inquiry" of longtime residents before choosing a site on Commissioners Street in the lower town. "But in the winter of '38 and '40, water rose up through the drains . . . through the ground under the cellar floors . . . filling the cellars and rising to a level with the waters of the river." Try blamed the nearby wharves that reached out into the river, blocking the flow of ice. In one instance, he reported, so much ice had collected around a pier that it mounted "up to the roof of a three-storey building in its vicinity, entering the windows and filling the attic rooms."

Mr. O. Bostwick, too, had "sustained damage and inconvenience" during his sixteen years in the St. Ann Suburb. Still, the grocer remained optimistic about his latest plan—raising his buildings out of the reach of the water. "I expect an architect here from New York to examine my buildings and others, sometime in the next month," he reported. He had been advised in a letter that "it can readily be done and the expense will not be quite so [high] as to deter those proprietors whose buildings are valuable." Thomas McGinn, a one-time Griffintown resident, dismissed this idea as "too expensive." Like most respondents, he favoured the construction of an embankment and the redirection of creeks and rivers to relieve the "heart-rending scenes of wretchedness among the working classes of the community" that he had witnessed during the nine years he had lived there.

In his long, rambling letter to Major Cole, sixty-seven-year-old Dr. Daniel Arnoldi looked back on the great flood of 1789 and others he had witnessed with a survivor's pride. "I remember having been in the batteau that went over the wall to the succour of the Grey Nuns, whose cattle were removed upstairs," he wrote. "In 1809 or '10, the waters were so high that the timber in Mr. Munn's shipyard floated along Grey Nuns Street." He marvelled at the masses of ice hurled onto the shore as the frozen river burst at the seams and the occasion when the ice rose so high next to one building, "I saw the majestic site and was the first person that got into the house in their third-storey window."

His missive also took a nostalgic turn: "The Canadians had a saying that the winter was never truly done until the meadows were overflown," he told Major Cole. The Montreal native harked back to the years when the floodwaters froze over and locals delighted in skating on the vast natural rinks formed by the inundation. "Formerly these fields were the theatre of the most splendid performances of skaters of all classes," he recalled.

Arnoldi, of course, had moved to the upper town, out of the reach of the river, but he told Major Cole: "I am truly sympathetic to the

Gigantic ice formations, some reaching three storeys high, would rise along the shore of Montreal in the massive ice jams on the St. Lawrence that often preceded floods.

sufferers. Were I an inhabitant of Griffintown, I should earnestly entreat that every street should be saved at least a foot above the highest watermark. The cellars, of course, will have to be sacrificed in the winter. As for keeping the waters out, I can really see no prospects within the bounds of rational economy."

Arnoldi and others concerned about the expense may have swayed Major Cole. The government subsequently erected a stone revetment wall along the harbour in front of the old town, but despite the recommendations of many citizens, it stopped short of the St. Ann Suburb. Half a century would pass before the authorities moved to protect the low-lying district on the edge of the river. In the meantime, Griffintown endured dozens of floods.

The monumental ice jams that caused the floods held a certain fascination for those who lived out of their reach, on the slopes of the mountain. In the spring, when the first ice floes began to sail downstream from a milder stretch of the St. Lawrence, curious crowds would collect at the harbour, enthralled by the gigantic ice formations. Tension would build in the city as the ice grew to menacing proportions, sometimes to a height of over twenty feet, in the stubbornly frozen river. The watch for the big shove—an ice collision strong enough to force the river up and over its banks—could last days or weeks.

On April 21, 1847, Maximilian Montagu Hammond, a British soldier stationed at the Montreal garrison, wrote home to England, describing his excitement at the prospect of witnessing the powerful natural phenomenon:

My dear Mother,
I am very anxious to witness the breaking up of the ice in the river. I believe it is a magnificent sight. You can fancy what the effect would be, when you know that the St. Lawrence is very narrow just opposite Montreal, with a stream running six or seven knots an hour. When the ice above has broken away, it is carried on by the current, until it receives a check in the narrow part opposite the town. When it reaches this it gets jammed up, so as to form a complete barrier, and all the ice continues to push on until it meets the barrier; it is then thrown up into all sorts of shapes in large masses, until the weight behind forces all before it, and it floats away towards the sea.

Some years ago an event occurred, which gives some idea of the strength and weight of this moving ice. A house had been built too near the edge of the river, the water rose rapidly, and the ice too: the poor inmates were sitting at dinner, but before they had time to escape, the whole house was carried down with the torrent, and every soul perished.

Ever your affectionate son, MMH

A few months after writing that letter, Hammond spent several weeks in the fever sheds as a volunteer, caring for Irish emigrants during the typhus epidemic. The young officer transferred to Toronto in August, but he would have been distressed to learn that the flood of 1848, one of the meanest and most severe, inflicted yet another cruelty on the long-suffering Famine emigrants.

Rescuers waded through knee-deep water to save the sick and the dying as the rushing waters rose and penetrated the sheds. "We could only approach from one side and across a field," Father Rem. Jos. Tellier recalled in a letter to a confrere that summer. The Jesuit missionary and a few others hazarded an approach on horseback, while others paddled across in canoes as enormous ice floes were thrown up onto the shore, where they slammed into buildings, moving the police quarters and overturning a kitchen. The crashing of the ice and the darkness frightened the emigrants unaccustomed to Montreal's annual floods. "It was easy to understand the fears of the poor patients," he wrote. "And impossible to describe the warmth and enthusiasm with which they greeted him, asking, 'We're not going to drown, are we, Father?'"

The flood of 1848 made a strong impression on then eighteen-year-old Alfred Sandham. In his 1870 book, *Sketches of Montreal, Past and Present,* the historian, born in Griffintown to British parents, wrote: "The streets and dwellings in the lower parts of the city presented a piteous spectacle, showing an almost unbroken sheet of water. The condition of the families was sad in the extreme. In some houses the furniture was completely destroyed. In parts of Griffintown the inhabitants had to take refuge in the attics."

By 1853, the city had installed a new sewer system designed to minimize the flooding in the old town, the commercial heart of Montreal. But St. Ann's Ward—most affected by the annual inundations—would have to wait three more decades for relief. "Proper drainage would make a great change in Griffintown and that suburb now growing up around the canal factories," argued an editorial in the *Gazette* on August 18, 1853. "Instead of a half reclaimed swamp subject to inundation every spring and fall and to the influence of noxious exhalations during the summer months, it would become one of the most pleasant and healthy portions of the city."

But the largely Irish population of Griffintown continued to endure the squalor and misery of annual inundations that occasionally stretched to catastrophic proportions. The flood that interrupted Rev. Ellegood's sermon and sent his congregation home in boats, in fact, broke all previous records. After a bitter, unseasonably cold night, Montrealers woke up the next morning, Monday, April 15, 1861, to an appalling scene. The St. Lawrence had risen twenty-four feet above its normal level, submerging most of Griffintown in ten to twelve feet of water. And the flood extended well beyond that forlorn district—forming one vast lake that stretched as far as Bonsecours Market to the east, into Point St. Charles to the west, and up the lower slopes of Mount Royal, as far as St. Antoine and Craig streets. Hundreds of acres—more than a quarter of the city—were covered in three or more feet of water.

In Griffintown, worried faces peered out of upper-storey windows at the watery landscape. With their staircases submerged, many wondered how they could get out of their houses to buy food and, with firewood soaking under water in backyards and cellars, how they might cook it.

A navy of clergymen, politicians, police and other volunteers set out in boats on Monday morning to deliver food to stranded residents. Placing loaves of bread into hands reaching out from second-storey windows, or into baskets lowered from attics, they caught glimpses of water-filled rooms where beds, chairs, assorted household articles—and in one place a large, drowned cat—floated about.

At one end of Catherine Street (later renamed Shannon Street), a man sat disconsolately astride a shed; his cattle drowned, his hay and grain lost, he faced financial ruin. His neighbours, in a row of wooden houses on the same street, had lost cattle, pigs, grain and firewood. Now they stood on their galleries, their furniture and possessions floating on a cluster of rafts in case their homes' shaky foundations gave way.

Meanwhile, the sound of hammers rang through the watery district as residents cobbled together rafts out of stray sidewalks and scrap wood. By the second day of the flood, a raft floated outside nearly every house.

Frantic residents, on urgent missions to find food, fuel and drinking water, launched boats, canoes, scows, hastily assembled rafts, tables— anything that would float. Griffintown soon took on the appearance of a sad, improbable Venice, with a bizarre assortment of craft scudding about on its busy, watery streets, mingling with horses, carts and cabs. Inexperienced boatmen strained to manoeuvre through the odd traffic: one paddler dumped his canoe in four feet of water in Chaboillez Square and surfaced to a round of jeers and heckling. Stray dogs paddled about in the melee. Currents and eddies sent the hairy carcasses of drowned animals, chunks of ice, timber and other debris bobbing to the surface.

On Monday morning, a cow chewed contentedly on a gallery over-looking Chaboillez Square, oblivious to the chaotic scene below. A lack of convenient grazing spots forced most animal owners to devise inge-nious modes of transporting their horses, cows and pigs to dry ground. One sad-faced fellow poled down a street with his cow mounted on a raft fashioned from two tables and a few planks. A few men rowed down Wellington Street, leading a herd of forty or fifty cattle, swim-mingly submissively behind their boat.

Fire, a constant threat in Griffintown, seemed remote in the deluge. But at the Potash Inspection Stores on College Street water had been trickling in, unnoticed, through the roof and into barrels of unslacked lime, a substance that ignites spontaneously when wet. Shortly after noon on Monday, the barrels exploded into flames. By the time the alarm was sounded, the fire raged out of control. Hundreds of onlook-ers moored their rafts and boats to watch the firefighters.

Unable to ride their horse-drawn wagons through the deep water that surrounded the building, the firefighters had to load their hose reels onto boats and paddle up to the blaze. William Orme McRobie, a member of the Protector Engine Company, dared to push ahead. "I put the whip to my horse and dashed into the water. He took to it like

WILLIAM McROBIE

William Orme McRobie, appointed as Winnipeg's first fire chief in 1882, started out as a lowly torch-boy for the Queen Engine Company in Griffintown.

a duck," he explained in *Fighting the Flames!* "There were plenty of rafts all around—public and private—so that as soon as I got my hose off the reel, and into a good position on one of the largest, I left my horse." But the horse bolted, and after catching a wheel on a lamppost, fell into the water. McRobie nearly drowned trying to extricate him.

The firemen spent a gruelling day battling the flames. "All the hydrants in the vicinity were under water, so that we had to duck under water to take the cap off of the hydrant. Come up to take breath and duck down again to couple the hose," McRobie explained. The crew erected a bridge to the Temperance Hotel on the opposite side of the street, where they broke for meals. Still, the dedicated firemen stood for hours in ice-cold water up to their armpits. Some developed cramps and had to be floated away from the scene.

The heavy slate roof collapsed as the rafters burned. And by the time the flames were extinguished, only the walls of the building remained. But the firemen managed to keep the fire from spreading into nearby buildings.

After forty-eight hours at the scene, without a change of clothes, McRobie suffered from exposure and fatigue. The chief sent him to the country to recuperate, and after a short stint McRobie was back in action. Sadly, his horse died of exposure.

The flood receded noticeably on Tuesday, though six feet of water remained in some parts of Griffintown. But the temperature plunged, the wind picked up and overnight a fierce snowstorm pelted the damp, freezing houses where beleaguered residents huddled in the upper storeys without food or fire. By morning, a foot of snow covered the rooftops and thickened the water in the flooded streets.

By Thursday, the flood was over, leaving a wilted populace shivering in dank houses. Foul air hung over the bleak streets strewn with chunks of muddy ice, broken sidewalks, the remains of rotting animals and other debris. Now began the heart-rending task of salvaging meagre belongings damaged in the flood. A few desperate souls could be seen skinning the slimy carcasses of drowned cattle abandoned on the street.

In 1869, THE RIVER WOULD SURPASS the record-breaking flood of 1861 but this time, instead of slamming Griffintown with a single, overwhelming hit of water, it turned torturer, climbing slowly to catastrophic levels. The assault began on Saturday, April 17. By Wednesday, the river had matched its previous high—and kept going, reaching a new peak on Thursday evening, when the flood shut down the gasworks, plunging the city into darkness.

The devastation in Griffintown was heartbreaking. After days steeping in several feet of water, some houses, as well as rear buildings, stables and privies, had loosened from their foundations. On Murray Street, a small clapboard cottage tilted to one side, as if ready to float away.

The desperate and the daring launched makeshift rafts, planks, and tubs into the canal-like streets to search for provisions. On Wednesday afternoon, with the flood waters still rising, sixteen energetic youth propelled a length of wooden sidewalk carrying several cows through busy Chaboillez Square. "Be careful! Be careful!" shouted a nervous old gent rowing a punt. Nearby, a father and son shared a plank; the man steering with a pole, the boy, his legs dangling in the water, his hands holding down a loaf of bread on the dirty board.

Doctors kept up their rounds, although one MD, after visiting a patient in Chaboillez Square, had to lower himself from a second-storey window into a scow propelled by a youth who charged fifteen cents a crossing.

Police worked around the clock, dealing with the inevitable collisions and offences. While making his rounds that afternoon, a police officer, with the help of Councillor Jimmy McShane, saved two women from drowning on Kempt Street. But the flood prevented another constable from making an arrest. One lad who was caught in some mischief on Colborne Street managed to escape arrest by clambering out a window and down a ladder to a raft; as he shoved off, he yelled out to the housebound policeman that he would have to swim after him.

Tempers flared, but, more remarkably, wit and goodwill flourished. "The real sufferers are to be found in Griffintown and to the credit of the Irish in that locality it must be said they take the calamitous rising of the waters with grace and humour hardly to be expected under the circumstances," wrote one reporter after a tour of the inundated area.

In one Colborne Street saloon, at the height of the flood, a local man with sense of humour swam up to the bar and asked for a whiskey.

"Will you take water in it?" asked the landlord, from his perch on a ladder high up among the shelves.

"Not much," said the man. He downed his drink and swam away.

Suddenly, late Thursday night, the mountains of ice that had blocked the harbour slid silently down the river in the moonlight. By Saturday, the great volume of water that had filled Griffintown had drained away, leaving rafts and boats high and dry. In damp, dreary houses, women cleaned and arranged furniture and other domestic items that had been floating about for most of a week. Outdoors, men and boys replaced and repaired doorsteps and fences and cleaned out water-logged stables for the surviving livestock.

A few days later, a newspaper editorial called on the municipal surveyor to paint a blue line, "a few inches long, with the letter F above it," to mark the height of the flood on lampposts, buildings and other objects. Then, the editorial explained, owners could construct new buildings above the flood levels; some streets and sidewalks might also be raised out of harm's way.

After decades of advocating flood protection for Griffintown, one editorial writer seemed to have given it up as a hopeless cause. "That the Corporation should abandon the projected [Mount Royal] park, and spend the money in raising Griffintown to a proper level is not to be expected; the grandeur of the city has been progressing and will progress, with pestilence and degradation alongside."

The annual floods persisted. And the worst was yet to come.

ON SUNDAY, JANUARY 10, 1886, the St. Lawrence suddenly spewed a pile of ice over a new wooden flood barrier, flattening sheds and shanties along the edge of the canal. In its wake, icy water gushed into Griffintown.

By Monday morning, the river height measured thirty-nine feet, seven inches—twenty-two feet higher than the average low-water mark. And the water kept rising.

In winter, freezing temperatures intensified the familiar miseries of a flood. The water that filled cellars on Sunday froze into a solid block of ice by Monday. Shivering and hungry, residents confined to the upper stories without fire or fuel could not escape the bone-chilling cold. Churches, schools and factories closed, unable to heat their inundated buildings. Food became scarce as local grocers and butchers shut down. And bakeries had trouble supplying bread for customers.

Streets were impassable, hampering the distribution of relief. The water stood at two feet in most streets—low compared to most floods, but too shallow for most boats and too high for vehicles. As the temperature dropped, an icy crust formed atop the floodwaters, but it was not strong enough to bear the weight of a pedestrian. By Tuesday, below-zero weather had frozen the water to a depth of eight or nine inches, making walking a little easier. Small consolation for mourners wending their way to St. Ann's Church for the funerals of Mr. McCarthy and Mr. McGarrity.

The walls and cellars of Griffintown barely had time to dry out before the next flood arrived several months later. On Friday, April 16, a massive icefield sailed down the river and smashed into an ice jam across from the city. The river surged five feet in five minutes, throwing a tidal wave over Griffintown and Point St. Charles. Water rushed in torrents all the way up to Chaboillez Square. A massive lake formed over the streets near the river, covering more than one hundred houses.

At six the following evening, a second surge of icy water crashed over the revetment wall along the harbour. Without warning, shoppers and clerks in the shops and warehouses in the old city suddenly found themselves standing in ice-cold water past their knees, with merchandise swirling around them. The water continued to climb, and the entire city fell into total darkness when the flood shut down the electric and gas companies, located in Griffintown.

On Saturday night, the river swelled to the unprecedented height of forty-one feet nine inches. It was the worst flood in Montreal's history. A vast sheet of water covered Griffintown. Near the river's edge, smokestacks, chimneys and rooftops poked up like buoys on an inland sea. On Monday, the municipal surveyor measured the water levels across the flooded area; Griffintown's narrow streets recorded the deepest: eight feet in Wellington Street; eight feet, six inches in Ottawa

Street; from three to nine feet in Dupré Lane. The water reached far up the sides of factories, houses and shops, and ran at a dangerous pace through streets and lanes, hurling logs and boards, barrels and chunks of ice. One man who was navigating his way down Young Street in a scow got tangled up in the horns of a drowned cow.

On Sunday, April 18, the sun shone with incongruous cheer over the record-breaking deluge. Hundreds of people set out in rowboats, rafts and canoes; some trusted wooden sidewalks, planks, washtubs, doors or even tables to carry them across the hazardous expanse in the search for food and fuel. Or burial—Mrs. Martin O'Laughlin died that morning and two police constables came to her residence, near the corner of Prince and Ottawa streets, to remove her body. They placed her corpse in their canoe and paddled several blocks to McGill Street, where a hearse waited to take the body to the cemetery.

The flood forced another mourning family to adapt an old Irish custom. On Basin Street, black crepe—traditionally placed on the front door as the sign of a death in the family and an invitation to the wake within—fluttered from an attic window.

At three on Sunday morning, at the height of the flood, a fire broke out in a row of houses on Duke Street. More than a dozen tenants took refuge in wooden sheds at the rear. But one woman—too terrified to make the leap—stood screaming on the steps of a wooden staircase, caught with a child in her arms between the approaching flames and the six feet of water that filled the yard. Firemen appeared on the scene, paddled behind the burning building, lifted the woman and child, along with several others who found themselves trapped, into boats and transported them to safety.

The misery and ruin of the flood so overwhelmed John Doyle, a stonecutter, that he decided to end his life. On Sunday night, the respected fifty-year-old father of two sons took a rope and slipped away to another room, unnoticed by his family. An hour later his wife found him hanging by a hook from the ceiling in their inundated house.

The epic flood of 1886 subsided the following night, oblivious to the monumental damage left in its wake. By Tuesday morning, April 20, two feet of water remained in the low-lying areas of Griffintown, but most residents could abandon their rafts and boats and trudge out into muddy streets. The clean-up began for the twelve thousand families—as many forty-five thousand individuals—in the flooded districts of the city, as they sorted through their soggy and largely unsalvageable belongings: soaking beds, sodden clothing and furniture. The loss of their household effects would exceed $600,000.

Days, even weeks, would pass before many of the damp dwellings in Griffintown would be habitable. Hundreds of small grocers, shoe-makers, saloon keepers, blacksmiths and other artisans, trying to stave off financial ruin, put their sodden stock and wares—their fortune, their livelihood—out to dry.

The mayor's relief committee, recognizing the exceptional suffering in the neighbourhood, gave twenty-five tons of coal and twenty-five cords of wood to the Redemptorist priests at St. Ann's, to be distributed to destitute parishioners. The same day, Arthur Lawrence, a neighbour-hood youth caught stacking broken sidewalks in his cellar for firewood, was arrested and charged with stealing. The sentence: a two-dollar fine or eight days in jail.

The flood of 1886 showed no respect for the prosperous elite. It intruded on the property of seven hundred businesses, inflicting $2 million in damages to buildings and equipment alone. The powerful Grand Trunk Railway faced enormous losses. The flood washed out several miles of track; wrecked expensive first-class cars and new Pullmans that stood in seven feet of water at Bonaventure Station, and inundated the company's vast workshops and general offices, putting fifteen hundred employees out of work. At the St. Lawrence Sugar Refinery, twenty thousand barrels of sugar sat under water. The city's transportation companies had to move hundreds of horses out of flooded stables.

Surely, the authorities could no longer ignore the floods that had

A record flood in January 1886 stretched beyond Griffintown
and poured more than three metres of water into the Grand Trunk
Railway depot, inundating the workshops, ruining expensive sleeper cars,
damaging tracks and disrupting train traffic for several days.

plagued Griffintown. So the *True Witness* reasoned, in an editorial on April 21: "Year after year the city has been a victim to these floods, with a varying measure of damage to property, of distress and disease to the working classes, whose misfortune it is to be obliged to inhabit the low levels of the city. Now that many of the rich as well as the poor have suffered, that traffic was largely suspended for days, that trade and commerce were brought to a standstill, there is no further question as to the necessity of taking adequate steps to prevent the recurrence of such disastrous visitations."

In fact, the city's inundation committee had met the previous day, in boats, at the corner of Ottawa and Ann streets. After much discussion, its members decided unanimously to call for tenders for an unlimited supply of centrifugal pumps. Minutes after they reached that decision, a large raft rammed into the chairman's boat, tossing him and two other members into six feet of water. The chairman swam to a nearby fireplug and hung on, waiting for rescue.

CITY OFFICIALS HAD YET TO TAKE ANY ACTION when masses of ice began to clog the St. Lawrence in March 1887, setting the stage for yet another spring flood. "The apathy of city authorities with regard to these annual inundations is incomprehensible," the *Montreal Star* stated in exasperation. "I do not think there is another city of the magnitude and importance of Montreal that would quietly sit down and allow fully one-fourth of it to be periodically inundated without adopting some preventive measures," foundry owner William Clendinneng wrote in a letter to the editor.

The federal government in Ottawa, responsible for maintaining navigable rivers, had, in May 1886, appointed a Royal Commission to investigate the causes of floods at Montreal. The following spring, a team of engineers tested one of several flood prevention schemes. For six weeks, beginning March 23, 1887, they blasted a series of holes in the river ice, for several miles below the city, expecting that it would clear a path for the ice. Roman Catholic Archbishop Fabre looked for another solution—with equally dismal results. On March 27, he made a solemn procession in the cathedral, asking for heaven's protection against a flood.

Shortly after eleven on the morning of April 22, 1887, the river suddenly jumped several feet, catching residents by surprise. The flood triggered the familiar stampede. Tenants on the first floor clambered upstairs with furniture and belongings and prepared for a siege. While falling short of the unprecedented levels of the previous year by one foot and seven inches, the flood of 1887 ranked among the five worst in the history of the city, high enough to spread a sheet of water across Griffintown and into neighbouring districts and high enough to put twenty-six miles of streets under water.

Bitter experience had prompted residents in the most vulnerable areas to stock up on provisions, but by the second day of the flood, supplies were beginning to run out. For five days, police and priests rowed through the streets of Griffintown in a fleet of ten heavily laden boats, delivering bread, tea, sugar, cheese and milk supplied by the city for marooned residents, though boats could not enter some streets blocked by lingering mounds of ice and snow. On Saturday, rain fell so heavily that boats needed frequent bailing.

On April 26, the water slowly started to slip away. That summer, the municipal government installed temporary dikes and retaining walls. But political wrangling continued to delay a permanent solution to the floods, an issue that overlapped jurisdictions. Even within Montreal, aldermen from districts untouched by the inundations continued to resist the expenditure of tax dollars on a project that would not benefit their own wards. But by 1901, a wide, solid stone wall formed an impregnable barricade against the might of the St. Lawrence. Griffintown would never again suffer from a severe flood.

six

The Orange and the Green

The priests, my dear brothers, are the very devil, men of blood and slaughter. . . . Destroy the nunneries, my dear ladies. Very nasty things are done in nunneries. . . . and the Jesuits are the soul of the devil.
—Italian patriot and ex-priest Alessandro Gavazzi, 1853

ALESSANDRO GAVAZZI'S BOOMING VOICE REVERBERATED around the small Zion Congregational Church in the centre of Montreal and out through its windows on the balmy spring evening of June 9, 1853. Inside, hundreds of Protestants clapped and stamped their feet in approval as the ex-priest attacked the Roman Catholic Church. Outside, hundreds of Irish Catholics stood in protest, waiting for a chance to confront Gavazzi and his sympathizers. Seventy police officers armed with batons kept watch, one contingent opposite the church, another in the nearby Victoria Square. Tension mounted as crowds continued to flow up McGill Street from Griffintown.

Gavazzi, a tall, commanding Italian dressed in a black soutane, had embarked on a controversial lecture tour of North America, a one-man crusade to liberate Roman Catholics from what he called the "tyranny" of their church. He had found a receptive audience for his brazen anti-Catholic rhetoric in Toronto. But the former cleric had barely escaped with his life after his last speech, in Quebec City three days earlier, when he delivered a talk on the Inquisition that so enraged his Irish Catholic listeners that they rushed up the pulpit to attack him. The one-time military man fought off sixteen assailants with a stool before one finally overpowered him and tossed him into the crowd below. A quick response from the military probably saved his life.

Gavazzi had arrived in Montreal by steamer that morning, accompanied by fifty armed Orangemen—members of the staunchly Protestant and monarchist Orange Order—who had volunteered to serve as his bodyguards. Apart from a bruised face, he appeared unperturbed by the incident and had apparently slept soundly in his cabin while his escorts spent the night drinking and plotting revenge on Irish papists. Gavazzi's guards planned to return to Quebec City that night but they intended to spend the next eight hours walking the streets of Montreal, taunting Irish Catholics.

The Italian's powerful, heavily accented voice travelled far on the evening's gentle breezes. A local doctor claimed he could hear him in his office six hundred feet away. Those who listened beyond the walls grew more restless as Gavazzi continued his inflammatory tirade: "Why are a people so favored by nature, with an ardent heart and spirit, why are they so ignorant, so coarse, so savage?" he asked his Protestant listeners. "Simply because they are subservient to their priests. . . . The Catholic clergy prefer ignorance, grossness and brutality in their faithful rather than the civilized enlightenment of the Protestant working class."

A wave of protesters tried to force their way into the church. Montreal's mayor, Charles Wilson, a Roman Catholic, implored them to stay back. He had feared Gavazzi's visit would end in violence. He also worried that the city's small, lamentable police force would be unable to maintain order. Around seven o'clock, when the police began to lose control, Wilson went to summon the backup, a small Scottish

Haymarket Square, the scene of a riot that erupted in June 1853 when Irish Catholics gathered outside the Zion Congregational Church to protest a speech by the rabble-rousing Alessandro Gavazzi. Ten people died.

military unit made up of one hundred soldiers of the 26th Regiment Cameronians, only recently posted to Montreal and concealed in a house a few streets away.

Around 7:30, one of Gavazzi's escorts tried to leave the church to catch the eight o'clock steamer back to Quebec City. But he quickly retreated after angry demonstrators pelted him with stones and fired at him, putting two bullet holes in his hat. The sound of gunshots and the sight of blood pouring down the Orangeman's face set off a panic inside the church. Gavazzi quickly concluded his lecture and yelled out three cheers for the Queen, for freedom of speech and for his listeners as they poured out of the church into the hostile assembly. The men in the audience carried pistols; they had come prepared to defend themselves.

The protesters made a rush toward the church but the troops tried to hold them back. The crowd resisted and, as they made another push toward the doors, one protester pulled the trigger on his gun. A

Protestant returned fire, shooting him down. Fighting broke out and the screaming, panicked crowd ran for their lives. Two women were nearly trampled to death and dozens were injured in a melee of stone throwing. Amid the confusion, the mayor read the Riot Act. Suddenly, a voice in the crowd—never identified—called out "Fire!" The military began to shoot at the fleeing masses.

At least six people died that night, one of them, James Walsh, a twenty-two-year-old coppersmith from Griffintown. Four others later succumbed to bullet wounds and injuries suffered in the riot. The last victim, Michael Donnelly, died a month later, on July 11.

Gavazzi managed to escape the riot scene, sandwiched between two clergymen and a military escort. Later than evening, he rode to the wharf in an enclosed cab, crossed the river on a steamer and fled to the United States.

Shock and mourning brought Montreal to a near standstill the next day. Most of the victims were Protestant, although at least two Irish Catholics had died at the scene and many others had been pursued and beaten in the streets of Griffintown.

Dozens of witnesses testified at the five-week-long inquest that followed the riot. But the divided jury, nine Protestants and ten Catholics, produced no clear verdict. They failed to assign responsibility for the deaths. Nor did they comment on the crucial question: Who had commanded the military to fire on the crowd? Many suspected the mayor but he denied it. So did Colonel Hogarth, of the 26th Cameronian Rifles. A military inquiry accused the regiment of "a want of discipline" and removed them to Bermuda. In the end, there were no arrests, no official laying of blame.

But public opinion went against the Irish Catholics. One commentator, Émile Chevalier, wrote an article for a French newspaper denouncing them as "intolerant fanatics" and "a disgrace to the Catholic religion." No friend to Griffintown, the French-born intellectual later described the district in a novel as "a foul slough, a leper house, where swarms a sordid Irish population, tattered, fanatic, prone to crime of every sort, the shame and dread of the French Canadian metropolis."

In the aftermath of the Gavazzi riot, Griffintown became a hot spot for clashes between Protestants and Irish Catholics. On the night of June 12, vandals broke dozens of windows in St. Stephen's Anglican Church and the Wesleyan Chapel. A few shots were fired in the streets. Exactly one month later, gangs inflicted beatings on a few suspected Orangemen. Protestants retaliated with further assaults on Catholics in the neighbourhood. Although these were minor incidents, the undercurrent of religious and racial prejudice would persist for decades.

The violence never reached the levels it did in New York, where American-born "Know-Nothings" terrorized Irish Catholic emigrants, or in Toronto, which was plagued by Orange–Green riots. Goodwill more often prevailed in Montreal. Yet the antipathy between Catholics and Protestants in that city could still shock outsiders. "There is as much religious bigotry here as in Belfast," Rev. Michael Buckley would write, decades later. "It is worse in Toronto but it is more remarkable in a city where the majority is Catholic, in a city which some have rather inconsiderately designated as the 'Rome of North America.'"

IRISH CATHOLICS' PASSIONATE DEFENSE of their faith against Gavazzi and other perceived enemies followed centuries of religious persecution in Ireland, and, for a time, in North America. For most of the eighteenth century, the British had enforced the Penal Laws in some of its colonies. Catholics suffered discrimination under harsh legislation that, among other restrictions, made it illegal for them to practise their religion, to establish schools, to vote or to own land or even a horse worth more than five dollars. In 1758, Nova Scotia's first Assembly enacted its own version of the Penal Laws, including the stipulation that a Catholic could not act as the guardian of a minor if the child had a Protestant relative. But the laws were never applied as rigorously there as in Newfoundland. In 1755, authorities in Harbour Main found Michael Keating guilty of permitting a priest to celebrate mass in his store, deemed a public place. The Catholic merchant faced stiff punishment for his crime. The government imposed a fifty-dollar fine, seized his property, tore down his house and expelled him from the colony.

To circumvent the Penal Laws, Irish Catholics would travel to Louisbourg (the Cape Breton Island fortress held by France until 1858), or cross the Atlantic to Ireland to marry and to have their children baptized by a priest. In 1784, Newfoundland followed England's lead and passed a law granting religious freedom to Catholics. Still, change came gradually. The Nova Scotia Assembly withheld Catholics' right to establish schools until 1786, the right to vote until 1789.

Catholics faced bigotry and violence in the New England colonies too. In the late seventeenth century, New Jersey laws prevented Catholics from holding public office and practising their faith, going so far as to prohibit priests from entering the colony, a crime that was punishable by life imprisonment.

Yet Irish Catholics had long found a safe haven in Quebec. Even after France lost the colony to Britain, the new British governor tolerated the practice of the Catholic faith, partly out of fear of a rebellion, but still a major concession to French Canadians, given the official oppression of the religion in other parts of North America.

Such was the goodwill between the Catholics and Protestants in Montreal that the Recollet monks cordially shared their chapel, first with the Anglicans, then in 1791 with the Presbyterians, during the construction of the St. Gabriel Street church, the city's first Protestant church. For nearly a year, on Sunday mornings, after the French-speaking priests offered mass in Latin, Rev. John Young and his congregation would fill the chapel at the southeast corner of Notre Dame and St. Helen streets—a short distance from the site where the Gavazzi riot would erupt sixty years later.

The Recollets kindly declined payment. To express their gratitude, the Presbyterians gave the priests two hogsheads of Spanish wine, each containing sixty gallons, and a box of candles—a gift valued at more than fourteen pounds. The Catholic monks welcomed the Presbyterians again in 1809, when their church needed a new roof.

Beneath the civility lay a complex political reality. After the British conquest of North America, ownership of the Recollets' property had reverted to the Crown. However, the monks, prohibited from accepting new recruits, continued to occupy the monastery and worship in the chapel. It was a delicate balance of the interests of the ruling Anglo Protestants and their far more numerous French-Canadian subjects, a compromise that would be shaken by the arrival of large numbers of Irish in the coming decades.

Patterns of faith shifted as the tide of Irish emigration washed over the country in the first half of the nineteenth century. More than half a million Irish emigrants landed in British North America between 1815 and 1845, and almost 50 per cent were Catholic. While Irish Protestants, a minority in Ireland, continued to dominate in Ontario and much of New Brunswick, Newfoundland remained predominantly Catholic. So did New Brunswick's Miramichi Valley. And the sons and daughters of Erin bolstered the Catholic population of Quebec and the emerging urban centres of Saint John, Quebec City, Montreal and Toronto.

The vast majority of the newcomers scattered into the countryside, burying Ireland's ancient animosities as they struggled to clear their corner of the wilderness in the New World. While the Orange Order flourished in Ontario and New Brunswick, gregarious Hibernian exiles formed numerous nationalist associations, many of them non-sectarian. St. Patrick's Societies in Montreal, Kingston, Halifax and other centres included Catholics and Protestants, typically middle- and upper-class Irish—merchants, lawyers, teachers, doctors and craftsmen—looking to share their common heritage. But religious differences gradually became more obvious as the number of new emigrants grew, especially in the towns and cities.

The Irish in North America attached great significance to their parades, rousing spectacles intended to demonstrate their solidarity. The worst of weather rarely deterred Irishmen intent on celebrating St. Patrick's Day. The Irish of Montreal had staged their first annual procession in 1824. From that date on, they took to the main thoroughfares each March 17: troops of marchers decked out in green sashes, strutting in lockstep (or "trying to control nervous horses," as one wag remarked), with brass bands blaring and ancestral banners held high. And by the mid-nineteenth century, parades had become an annual ritual in dozens of communities. In northern New Brunswick, hundreds of enthusiastic Irishmen turned out for a three-day trek across the frozen Miramichi River. But the clannish displays occasionally aggravated old rivalries. By the 1850s and 1860s, serious disturbances, vandalism and arson would mark almost every March 17, as well as July 12, the "Glorious Twelfth," when Orangemen celebrated the humiliating defeat of the Irish Catholics at the Battle of the Boyne in 1690.

OLD FEUDS, AND FRESH ONES, had first surfaced in Montreal in the early decades of the century among the working-class Irish emigrants. But Montreal newspapers did not then treat their conflicts, which typically erupted around Orangemen's Day and St. Patrick's Day, at all seriously:

> *They were friends for sartin;*
> *They had a drink as soon's they met,*
> *And had a fight at partin.*

So opened the *Gazette*'s report of a waterfront brawl on Orangemen's Day, 1825. The jaunty account explained that the "King William boys," and "a number of Irish in this City celebrated the day" with a fight near the port, "and with stones, sticks and other missiles, left undeniable proofs on the bodies of each other. Some were severely treated." Almost as an afterthought, the writer concluded with the news that one man was believed to have died from his injuries.

Some Irish labourers employed on public works bound themselves together in secret societies for mutual protection. D'Arcy McGee acknowledged their existence in the United States, and by inference in Canada, in a three-part series in the *Gazette* in August 1867. "The Shamrock, and similar societies, though sometimes used for American electioneering purposes, resembled rather trades' unions," he wrote. "They were generally imitations of the agrarian secret societies such as the Ribbonmen in Ireland." He added that "the Shamrock Society, which excluded natives of Cork and Connaught, King's and Queen's Counties" was one of the best known in the United States. The initiated recognized each other with passwords and peace words. McGee revealed one used in 1853:

Q. Shall we quarrel for nothing?

A. No: friendship now prevents us.

Finding strength in their solidarity, the Irish quickly realized that they could play an active role in politics. Through most of the nineteenth century, only men could vote or run for office, and only if they owned property. In the early 1830s, barely 250 Irish Catholics were eligible to vote in Montreal's West Ward, the riding that encompassed Griffintown. Still, they could help determine the outcome of an election.

Voting requirements pushed large numbers of Irish Catholics in the labouring class to the periphery of power. But in the rough-and-tumble politics of the era, when elections were frequently settled with fists, the Irish navvies' solidarity and physical might gave them a measure of influence—and notoriety.

Open polls, common in the nineteenth century, placed considerable pressure on voters who had to mount an open platform and make a public declaration to a returning officer while the candidates harangued them, and their opponents, from the nearby hustings.

Fights frequently broke out at polling stations. As voters tried to make their way through the crowds to vote, party heavies would try to move their candidate's supporters forward and block those they thought would vote for the opposition.

Elections often lasted for weeks, giving the government, the candidates and their supporters plenty of time to bribe, threaten and manipulate the voters, the returning officers and even the special constables hired to keep the peace. Campaigns rarely passed without violence, and, in Montreal, they almost always involved the Irish.

Churches often became targets as politics began to break down along religious lines. Griffintown's first Protestant church, the small stone Wesleyan Chapel, built in 1833 and known as the "Ottawa Street Church," was "the scene of many acts of outrage," writes Alfred Sandham in *Sketches of Montreal, Past and Present*. "On two or three occasions, during riots which were so common during elections, the windows were completely destroyed and on one occasion some soldiers were in occupation and the marks of the nails of their boots were easily discerned on the seats and backs of pews."

A much worse fate awaited the recently created Canadian Parliament after it moved from Kingston to Montreal in October 1843. In early 1844, the new site in St. Ann's Market, on the very border of Griffintown, appeared to provide a convenient, central location for the new country forged by the Act of Union in 1840.[4] The government forced butchers, fishmongers and other vendors out of the three-storey limestone building at the foot of McGill Street and remodelled it to accommodate the Legislative Council and Legislative Assembly.

But the government—an uneasy marriage of French and English, Tories and Reformers, Catholics and Protestants from Upper and Lower Canada—faced a crisis almost as soon as it moved into its new quarters. The rift began in November 1843, when Governor General Sir Charles Metcalfe failed to consult the Legislative Council before making a flurry of political appointments. Disturbed by their exclusion from power, the councillors, with the exception of the Galway-born provincial secretary, Dominick Daly, resigned en masse. The issue caused a serious split among French-Canadian leaders. While moderates sided with Metcalfe, a generous benefactor, others, more suspicious of British institutions, accused him of eroding the principle of responsible government. After months of rancorous debate, with no resolution in sight, on February 5, 1844, Legislative Assembly member Benjamin Holmes agreed to resign his Montreal seat. A by-election would test the political waters. And the Irish would play a crucial role in its outcome.

The vicious battle pitted the reform candidate, Liberal Lewis Thomas Drummond, an eloquent, bilingual Irish Catholic lawyer, against the establishment brewery owner William Molson, an English-speaking Tory. But it was another Irishman, Francis Hincks, editor of the *Pilot*, and mastermind of Drummond's campaign, who set the tone of the election. His improbable strategy: to woo the support of two competing camps—French-Canadian labourers and Irish navvies. The handsome, bilingual journalist enticed the traditional rivals to mass rallies and torchlight parades and encouraged them to mingle with the help of lively brass bands and flowing liquor. He persuaded the French Canadians that their Tory employers had no sympathy for their rights—a prophetic statement given that Molson would later fire those of his employees who did not vote for him—and played to the fears of the Irish Catholics by reminding them of Molson's membership in the Freemasons, a fraternity condemned by the Pope and loosely linked to the Orange Order. The pro-Tory *Gazette* described the bilingual meetings as "nightly assemblages of mobs of ruffians to listen to incendiary harangues."

On March 27, 1844, Hincks organized one of the largest political meetings ever held in Montreal. More than six thousand flag-waving, cheering supporters turned out to hear Drummond, Louis-Hippolyte

LaFontaine, the first prime minister of the Canadas, and George-Étienne Cartier, a future Father of Confederation, make rousing speeches. Tory thugs tried to disrupt the meeting but the Griffintown Irish arrived in force to take care of them.

But on election day, April 11, Molson's faction appeared to have the upper hand. Tory supporters flooded the polling station at Place d'Armes and chalked up nearly one thousand votes in the first fifteen minutes after the poll opened. A fight broke out when Irish enforcers arrived to take control of the square, occupied by two or three thousand people. "We think the Drummondites began it, but we must admit the Molsonites showed the most sticks, though their number on both sides did not exceed a couple of dozens," the *Gazette* reported.

Unable to contain the riot, the returning officer, Alexandre-Maurice Delisle, adjourned the election until April 16. Then he jumped down from the platform, drew his sword and made his way through the melee, followed by the chief of police and the two candidates, with Drummond waving a white linen handkerchief as a sign of peace. The Irish stayed to finish the fight.

Griffintown navvies turned out en masse when the voting resumed on April 16, this time backed up by additional recruits from the works at Lachine and from as far away as Malone, New York. More than fifteen hundred canallers gathered in Montreal to help Drummond win the election. The *Gazette* accused Hincks of masterminding the "invasion": "They were met by agents, who distributed detachments at different polling places, and marched a main body through the streets, regularly relieving the posts, who were billeted and victualled in the most orderly manner. Leaders of 'Mr. Drummond's military junta' concerted with them in signs and passwords and they formed a dense body around the hustings, with outposts along the footpaths and they hustled, and, if any more were necessary, beat and knocked down any person pointed out to them as a voter for Molson."

Hundreds of Irish navvies occupied polling stations around the city. The sight of gangs of tough canallers intimidated returning officers as well as Tory voters. By noon, most of the polls had closed, although one reopened after Molson's supporters disappeared.

That night, at 10 p.m., Delisle wrote a private letter to the provincial secretary Dominick Daly, describing the day's events:

> The canallers were, I understand, (& I fully believe it, though I could not distinguish them) all in town & took possession of all the polls, but were not armed. Their numbers, however, supplied this. . . .
>
> It is strange that the Canallers were not armed, their chief missiles being stones which as you know abound on our Macadamized roads. . . . One of my deputies, Larocque (Centre Ward) was struck by the mob and was forcibly dispossessed of his sword. Such was the violence there that instead of adjourning he *closed,* which I believe invalidates the election. He had, moreover, the folly, on being summoned by Drummond to resume, to continue after this faux pas—and again adjourned for violence.
>
> PS. . . . Hincks has brewed all this mischief and would do more if he could. He is a designing villain.

Delisle wrote a second letter to Daly before the second day of voting began on April 17:

> The most desperate preparations are making by the Irish this morning. They have compelled several large establishments where their people were at work to close and they will be again in possession of the polls at the opening, but my Deputies have all promised to ask aid of the troops. There are troops now at Queen's, St. Ann's and St. Lawrence Wards,
>
> Yours in haste, (signed) AMD

But the presence of the military on the second day did not deter the canalmen. Again, their sheer numbers empowered them. In Centre Ward, they seized the deputy returning officer's sword and broke it. In another ward, the returning officer abandoned his station when they appeared.

And they added a new twist to their punishment of Tory voters. Angered by newspapers' criticism of their ragged garb and praise of Molson's well-dressed followers, Drummond's supporters decided to inflict "tatters" on the fine gentlemen. "As soon as a vote was polled for Molson, the voter was literally stripped by the mob, the clothes torn from his back, while the troops stood by without power to interfere," the *Montreal Times* reported.

Voting was suspended as early as twelve o'clock in several polls. Molson resigned from the race early, while Drummond supporters continued to cast votes until five in the evening.

In a letter to Lord Stanley, a British official, on April 26, Lord Metcalfe talks of reprisals against the Irish:

The canal gentry, it appears, did not find work on their return from their vile mission, and already begin to express dissatisfaction with their political employers. They behaved like devils and I really think it will be a good lesson to them if you would cause [superintendent Hamilton Hartley] Killaly to stop the [canal] work for six months. The outrage has been felt severely and is bitterly resented. Numbers of gentlemen have this day turned off their Irish Roman Catholic servants and I have heard several express their determination never again to employ them.

To the residents of Montreal who witnessed the election, all is well understood and Drummond is regarded only as the representative of the laborers on the Lachine Canal, but I fear it will not be understood throughout the Country and that the effect will be damaging in the extreme. . . .

Hincks would later justify his and the Irish navvies' tactics. "A great principle was at stake," he told the St. Patrick's Society in a speech in 1877, before going on to damn Metcalfe with his own words, quoting a letter the former governor general wrote, acknowledging the unfairness of the electoral rules and stating "that if all the electors could have voted there would have been a majority in favor of the Opposition candidates, owing to the great bulk of the French Canadian and Irish Roman Catholic voters being on their side." Indeed, Montreal would see several more wild elections and political plots. And by May 1848, Lord Elgin was warning, in a letter posted to Lord Grey in England: "It is the Irish not the French from whom we have most to dread at present."

By July 1844, Orange supporters, emboldened by the tacit support of Governor General Metcalfe, were flaunting their colours as never before in Montreal. The provocative Orange flags and emblems that dominated the site of a new Protestant church on Dalhousie Street in Griffintown achieved their intended effect. A fight broke out when Metcalfe came to the predominantly Catholic district to lay the foundation stone of St. Ann's Anglican Church on July 9, three days before the Orangemen celebrated the "Glorious Twelfth."

But, as an editorial in the *Pilot* pointed out on July 17, it was so "very extraordinary that so many Orange Lilies happened to be carried about accidentally on the 12th of July and that so many people were in utter ignorance that this flower has long been an emblem of a faction." One young woman entered a store and boldly asked the Catholic owner if she could leave a bunch of orange lilies on the counter.

The Catholic clergy had encouraged their flock to stay home on Orangemen's Day. The priest at the Recollet Church warned his parishioners that if they retaliated they would only harm themselves and give the impression that the Irish were "a nation of devils." But the more volatile Catholics created several disturbances, by annoying women carrying orange flowers or wearing orange-trimmed garments. Around ten p.m., some two hundred labourers pitched stones at a tavern where heavily armed Orangemen celebrated with drinking and belting out anti-papist tunes.

Ogle Gowan founded the first Grand Lodge of British North America in Brockville on January 1, 1830. A journalist and scion of a prominent Orange family, Gowan had just emigrated from Ireland, where the order had taken on a new militancy in reaction to the Catholic Emancipation Act passed by the British Parliament in 1829. Alarmed at the prospect of Catholics gaining political power, Ireland's Protestants brought new fervour to the ranks of the institution. Gowan, meanwhile, galvanized the fraternal society in the colonies, where it had been a source of mutual support and conviviality for Protestant soldiers and settlers since the early nineteenth century. Under Gowan's leadership, the membership and the political activities of the order expanded dramatically, especially in Ontario and New Brunswick. More than one hundred and fifty Orange Lodges were operating in British North America by 1835. By the 1860s, the organization boasted more than 150,000 members nation-wide. In 1866, Irish journalist John Francis Maguire described Toronto, the Orange stronghold with seventeen lodges, as the "Belfast of Canada."

The Orange Order in Quebec never rivalled the numbers and influence of their counterparts in Ontario and New Brunswick. But in 1849, they opened the new provincial Grand Lodge of Canada East in Montreal, and conflict between Orangemen and Roman Catholics in the city intensified, heightened there and across the country by hostility toward the influx of needy Famine refugees. On July 12, a sword-carrying marcher in an Orange procession seriously wounded a bystander. Two days later, Thomas Fleming, an Orangeman and the keeper of an eating house near St. Ann's Market, was standing in his doorway when a young Catholic, T. Clunen, came by and the two exchanged religious insults. Fleming stepped into his house to get his

In Toronto, dubbed the "Belfast of North America," thousands of Protestants march in the Orange Order's traditional July 12 procession in 1874.

gun, then shot the seventeen-year-old journeyman shoemaker several times in the head, at close range.

That same day, elaborate Orange celebrations provoked some of the bloodiest Catholic–Protestant confrontations in the history of the country. In Ontario, two or three hundred Irish Catholic canallers marched nearly two miles to Hamilton's Slabtown and surrounded Duffin's Tavern, where members of an Orange Lodge had gathered to mark the Glorious Twelfth. "No attack was made on the house—but three cheers were given for the Queen and Prince Albert and three more for the Pope; ere the huzzaing ceased, the Orangemen opened fire upon them, killing two on the spot, and wounding many others, some of them fatally," according to an account in the *Globe* on July 21.

The pro-Tory *Hamilton Spectator* claimed the Catholics initiated the violence: "Two or three of the madmen then deliberately fired at the house, wounding one of the party inside, upon which they came to the windows and fired a volley at their assailants."

Both sides agreed on the casualty count: four men dead and six seriously wounded.

In Saint John, resentment flared into violence on July 12, 1849, when hundreds of Orangemen marched through a Catholic neighbourhood. The senior deputy grand master of the Grand Lodge, outfitted as King William, rode a white horse at the front of a procession of flag-waving stalwarts, armed with guns and swords and chanting offensive songs and slogans, through York Point.

But the Catholics, anticipating the interlopers, had erected a symbolic green arch along the route. They then jeered and threw stones as the Orangemen were forced to dip their flags to pass under it. The Protestants returned, six hundred strong, most of them armed and determined to redress their humiliation. No one knows who fired the first shot. But more than a dozen—mostly Catholics—died and more than one hundred were seriously wounded in the riot that came to be called the Battle of York Point.

Fierce Protestant–Catholic rivalry also surfaced in Montreal's fire companies. The mid-nineteenth century was the heyday of the volunteer fireman, and at times as many as a dozen independent companies vied for supremacy in the city: besides the Irish Queen Fire Company, they included the French Voltigeurs and Héros and the English Protestant Neptune, Montreal, Union and Protector engine companies, as well as a Hook and Ladder Company. To encourage a speedy response, Montreal, like most cities across North America, paid a premium to the first engine company to deliver a stream of water on a fire. Competition between the volunteer fire companies helped keep buildings from burning down, but rival squads often resorted to bribes, fistfights and dirty tricks, like slashing the competition's hose to get "first water." And since members generally reflected the population of the ward in which they were located—British, French Canadian,

Irish Protestant and Irish Catholic—the rivalry often became a test of national and religious pride as well as of virility. Language differences led to friction between the French Voltigeurs and the English companies, but it was most intense between the Orange and Green companies.

A militant fireman led one of the most infamous riots in the history of Canada on April 25, 1849. The battle began on the floor of the Canadian Parliament, still located in St. Ann's Market on the eastern boundary of Griffintown. The Reformers, now calling themselves Liberals, had wrested power from the Tories in 1846. And in February 1849, the government under Robert Baldwin and Louis-Hippolyte LaFontaine introduced legislation to compensate citizens for property damaged during the Rebellions of 1837 and '38. The opposition Tories furiously opposed the Rebellion Losses Bill, which in their view would, at great cost to taxpayers and innocent victims, benefit treasonous radicals who had inflicted the damage.

On the afternoon of April 25, when Governor General Lord Elgin rode to the Parliament Building in St. Ann's Market to sign the legislation, angry spectators watched the ceremony from the galleries. Afterwards, they threw eggs at Elgin and his aides as they boarded a waiting carriage, in plain view of the vendors and shoppers at the busy market stalls on the ground floor.

News of the passage of the bill spread rapidly through the city. And so did the rallying cry "To the Champ-de-Mars!" That night thousands gathered at Montreal's promenade grounds, where impassioned critics demanded the recall of the governor general. To heighten the protest, the firemen sounded an alarm, and church bells began to peal across the city, summoning the city's fire brigades. Alfred Perry, captain of the Hook and Ladder Company, addressed the crowd and led the swirling raging mob, torches in hand, to the Parliament Building, where members were sitting in an evening session. Perry confessed, in a memoir written many years later, that he had led the rampage and had

Rioters cheer while the Canadian Parliament Building, then located in Montreal on the edge of Griffintown, burns to the ground on April 25, 1849.

accidentally struck a gas chandelier, sparking the fire that destroyed the three-storey limestone structure.

Members of the Queen, Protector, Hose, Neptune and Montreal fire companies arrived at the scene, but not a drop of water was aimed at the Parliament Building or its contents. The French Canadian Héros and Voltigeurs held back, waiting for reassurance that they would not be attacked. Firemen did work, however, to save the surrounding buildings. And, in a letter to a confrere later that summer, one Jesuit priest credited the Irish Queen company for saving the Grey Nuns' convent when flames spread from the burning Parliament Building: "The brave Irish ran to their help and managed, after incredible efforts, to contain the fire. For several days they set up a guard around the buildings of the nuns, who they regarded as mothers." They also offered to protect the Jesuits, he added. "One night, during a riot, friends came to alert us that they had heard of several threats against us in particular; though they never materialized. The Irish, who kept a constant vigil around their church, promised to defend us against any attackers. These good people, with their strongly expressed resolution to defend all that belonged to their religion, is without doubt a barrier that the most fervent revolutionary would dare not cross."

Thousands participated in two days of rioting. Within the month, the government decided to relocate Parliament, alternating it between Quebec City and Toronto before settling on Ottawa as its final location in 1857.

Nearly a decade after Black '47, religious strife showed no signs of abating, on the streets or in the press. The city's English newspapers, all Protestant-controlled, with the exception of the *True Witness,* a Catholic newspaper that reflected the views of the ultra-conservative Bishop Ignace Bourget, attacked Irish Catholics almost daily. And, in 1856, Protestants split away from the St. Patrick's Society, partly in reaction to its Catholic members' increasing nationalism. Fiercely loyal to the Crown, they formed their own organization, the Irish Protestant Benevolent Society, to focus on serving their own needy. Relations between the two groups would remain polite but distant for more than a half a century, as the Protestants tried to dissociate themselves from the Catholics' increasing agitation for a free and independent Ireland.

Leaders of the city's close-knit Irish Catholic community began to cast about for a champion to take up their cause. They wanted a strong voice, someone as eloquent and patriotic as Thomas D'Arcy McGee, a prolific journalist and orator who was making such a name for himself promoting the interests of Irish emigrants in the United States. And they wanted a Canadian version of his popular, respected newspaper, the *American Celt,* which took a strong pro-Irish stance on political issues.

The deal was made in November 1856 in Griffintown, at the Franklin House at the corner of William and King streets. Several prominent Irish Catholics invited McGee, then in the city on a lecture tour, to a meeting at the inn and made their proposal. They offered him financial backing, the prospect of a political career and the support of the Irish clergy, in the belief that McGee, the one-time rebel, would fight for the rights of Canada's Irish Catholics.

THOMAS D'ARCY MCGEE HAD FIRST SAILED out of Ireland in 1842, at the age of seventeen, on a timber ship to Quebec. But the brilliant young emigrant did not tarry long in Canada. Like many Irish Catholics, he wanted to escape the shadow of the Union Jack. He quickly travelled on to Boston where he found work and acclaim as a journalist for the *Boston Pilot,* writing and lecturing about Ireland and the Irish.

In 1845, McGee returned to Dublin to write for the venerable *Freeman's Journal,* and later joined the staff of *The Nation.* But the Great Famine soon inflamed his Irish nationalism. He became involved with the radical intellectuals of the Young Ireland movement and, in 1848, fled to the United States, disguised as a priest, to avoid arrest for his involvement in a failed insurrection.

Like many Irishmen, the young McGee idealized the American republic and yearned for the day his beloved Ireland would enjoy the freedom and independence of the United States. In 1849, the outspoken nationalist went so far as to argue in an article that Canada should slip out of the grasp of Britain and join the United States, a viewpoint that his enemies would later use to taunt him.

But McGee gradually became disillusioned as he witnessed the prejudice and hostility suffered by Irish Catholics pouring into the United States after the Famine. In New York, tens of thousands had settled in the Fourth and Sixth Wards in Manhattan, where they faced discrimination and physical violence at the hands of gangs of American-born Protestants known as "nativists." The Bowery Boys, the most notorious, had links to the Know-Nothings, an anti–Irish Catholic political movement that swept through many states. McGee became an outspoken advocate for his countrymen. He wrote about their poverty and degradation and their "miserable town tenantry," and worked for their welfare, helping to organize night schools, and later, a scheme to help them settle in the rural West. He also began to think that the Irish enjoyed greater liberty in Canada under British rule. By late 1856, McGee was ready to move to Montreal.

Within weeks of his arrival in Montreal in January 1857, McGee launched the *New Era* and fed the hopes of Montreal's Irish Catholics with his fearless, outspoken editorials. McGee championed the devout, hard-working residents of Griffintown. "St. Ann's Ward contains 10,000 stationary inhabitants. But it also, unfortunately for its peace, includes the Canal basin. And the low resorts of the floating population who daily come down the Canal," he wrote on September 12, 1857. He asserted that the district's reputation for rowdiness was "undeserved" and that the "lawless element was provided mainly by transients in the area supplied by the Lachine Canal." He also protested the police practice of keeping a record of crime by nationality.

He lashed out at the Orange Order in the summer of 1857, slamming their cherished tradition of celebrating the anniversary of the Battle of the Boyne. "It has been said by the unreflecting, 'You have your 17th of March—why not they their 12th of July?' We answer, there is no possible parallel between a conversion and a conquest—a missionary and a military victory." At the same time, he condemned the use of violence against Orangemen—a reflex of certain "unreflecting" Irish Catholics.

At one in the morning on July 13, 1857, after a particularly troubled Orangemen's Day, a fire, believed to be the work of arsonists, broke out in a sawmill on McCord Street. Several fire companies responded to the blaze, but members of the Irish Protestant Union Engine Company and two other squads deserted their posts when Griffintown youths attacked them. "Several were severely beaten, so much so that some had to take refuge in the Station House," the *Pilot* reported the next day. One of the Union firemen, James Sadler, was shot in the head.

The future Father of Confederation Thomas D'Arcy McGee (shown here in 1862 at age thirty-seven) launched his political career in Montreal with the support of Griffintown voters.

McGee's editorial in the *New Era* on July 16 showed no sympathy for the Catholic ruffians who threw rocks at Protestant firemen: "The attack on the firemen at the burning of Mr. Douglas' mill in Griffintown, on Monday night was a wanton outrage, the perpetrators of which ought to be severely punished. . . . They were chiefly a lot of lads; but all had pistols. . . . If it had not been for the courageous resistance offered the rowdies by Mr. Patrick Brennan, one of the oldest inhabitants of that part of the city, Mr. Councillor Ryan and others, their friends, and the prompt measures subsequently taken by Capt. McLaughlin of the police, many lives would have been lost. As it is, Mr. Sadler, bricklayer, wounded at the fire, lies in a very critical condition."

But McGee's vision went far beyond the narrow interests of his own people. While his wide-ranging editorials defended the rights of the Irish to representation in the Assembly, in a series of articles that first summer after his arrival, Canada's great statesman-to-be became the first to talk of a "new nationality," a federation of the provinces of British North America that would stretch coast to coast.

McGee launched his political career in the late fall of 1857. Shortly after the call for a general election, a petition circulated in the city: "The Irish population constitutes one-third of the whole population of Montreal," it stated. "It would be an injustice if we are not represented." Two thousand electors signed the document. And on Tuesday, December 1, at a mass meeting in Bonaventure Hall on Haymarket Square, the president of the St. Patrick's Society proposed McGee as the Irish candidate in the upcoming election. McGee's gracious, witty acceptance speech was met with wild cheering.

The homely, five-foot-three-inch Irishman with unruly black curls, merry eyes and a keen sense of humour became a familiar figure in the neighbourhood. The pro-Irish views of their new champion easily won over its residents. "We are fighting in Griffintown the battle for Irish equality," he told the enthusiastic crowds that turned out to the hustings. The eloquent politician promised to push for better education—the hope of many voters who, like him, had been tutored, if at all, in Ireland's "hedge schools," and who remembered the clandestine classes taught in huts and barns and out-of-doors by itinerant masters, when Penal Laws prohibited Catholic schools. McGee spoke ardently for the persecuted Irish and castigated the despised Orange Order. But the future Father of Confederation spoke, too, of a grander vision, of united provinces and an independent Canada.

McGee faced a tough contest as one of six candidates vying for the Montreal riding's three seats in the December election. (The city was not divided into electoral districts. The three candidates with the highest vote count would become members of Parliament.)

The campaign had barely begun when the government promised to reward McGee and find him a safe seat in the country if he would pull out just before the vote—a deal that would favour Henry Starnes, a Conservative banker and close friend of the president of the St. Patrick's Society. McGee publicized the bribe and formed a loose coalition with Liberal candidates Antoine-Aimé Dorion and Luther Hamilton Holton, a wealthy Protestant-backed businessman.

The anti-Catholic press turned against McGee and hurled a barrage of criticism and insults at the threatening newcomer: "A mere adventurer," they called him, "a fomenter of strife" and "the leader of a crusade against Protestants."

The results of the election, held on December 21 and 22, were extremely close. A spread of only 598 votes separated McGee, Dorion and John Rose from the lowest. Starnes, Holton and Cartier went down to defeat. Dorion and McGee drew most of their votes from the Irish in St. Ann's Ward.

Critics claimed that Irish Catholics "forced" McGee on Montreal voters. "These crashing majorities from Griffintown elected Dorion and McGee and both these gentlemen are virtually members for Griffintown, rather than Montreal," the *Gazette* declared on December 26. "Griffintown does not exactly reflect the public opinion of Montreal." Editorials dug up McGee's rebel past and called him a hypocrite. How could the former revolutionary pledge allegiance to the British sovereign, "the very power which he has vowed to ruin"?

The *Gazette* also accused Griffintown residents of rigging the election. "How many of their votes are bad; or how many are treacherous plumpers for D'Arcy McGee we are unable to say." In its extensive, partisan reportage, the pro-Tory newspaper asserted that the results would have been different "had there been peace and the polls not been taken possession of by the Griffintown gentry—there is reason to believe by direction of their leaders, apart from the obvious fact which these people well knew—that the voters in this Ward would stay at home rather than push their way to the polls at the risk of being jostled or beaten. . . . We scarcely believe so many Irish Roman Catholic voters could have been secured for Mr. Dorion. We find, however, that the treachery came from the Griffintown side."

McGee's election came at a critical point in the history of Canada. Parliament had reached an impasse in the debate about the union of the Canadas imposed in 1840 by Britain. At the same time, there was talk that the British colonies of New Brunswick, Nova Scotia and Prince Edward Island would form a Maritime Union. The future of the country seemed to hang in the balance. And the "representative for Griffintown" spoke eloquently in Parliament of his vision for his adopted land; his dream of "one great nationality, bound, like the shield of Achilles, by the blue rim of ocean." A political realist, he also understood that it would take compromise to reconcile the competing interests of Catholics and Protestants, English and French, Upper and Lower Canada. And so McGee spent considerable time away from his constituency, endeavouring to find an alternative to the unworkable Act of Union.

His lofty political ambitions may not have inspired his constituents, but McGee enjoyed enormous personal popularity among the Griffintown Irish. The convivial politician in the ill-fitting suits bore none of the pretensions of a wealthy gentleman. He enjoyed spending hours in a tavern and he entranced his listeners with Irish tales and history and recitations of poetry and ballads, often his own.

McGee received a hero's welcome when he returned to Montreal after his first session in Parliament, now in Toronto. An immense crowd, as many as ten thousand, met him at the train station on the night of March 23, 1858, with a brass band. Strong Irish muscles lifted the diminutive politician onto their shoulders and carried him to a sleigh at the head of a parade. Torchbearers, followed by a long procession, escorted McGee home through streets lit by lanterns and fireworks.

The Montreal Irish were proud of their plucky MP's impressive debut and relieved that he had survived an attack in Toronto, the same day Orangemen had shot a young Irish Catholic in the St. Patrick's Day parade. That evening, a mob threw stones at McGee's carriage as he left a dinner in honour of Ireland's patron saint. After he escaped, they vandalized the building and later surrounded his hotel, pitching bricks and breaking windows, yelling "Get McGee!" "Griffintown papist!"

McGee's efforts to reach a consensus, to achieve the goal of a united Canada, drew wide admiration across the country. But his willingness to compromise cost him the support of the Catholic press and Montreal's Bishop Bourget. McGee scandalized George Clerk, editor of the *True Witness,* the city's English Catholic newspaper, when he supported the principle of representation by population, a policy that, in the complex politics of the time, aligned him with Louis-Joseph Papineau, a fierce supporter of French-Canadian rights, and with Toronto MP George Brown, a Protestant and fierce opponent of separate schools for Catholics in Canada West. Clerk denounced McGee, whom he perceived as a rival for Montreal's English-speaking Catholic readers, as "a traitor to his religion." And on Sunday, August 14, 1858, Bishop Bourget instructed the pastors of Montreal's three Irish parishes to read a letter he had written denouncing "politicians, whosoever they may be, who through imprudence or malice foment prejudice of race."

Although the bishop did not name him, the parishioners of St. Ann's, listening as their pastor, Father O'Brien, a McGee supporter, read the letter from the pulpit, understood that he was condemning their popular MP.

Many expected McGee to face stiff opposition in the 1861 election, and he had even considered dropping out of politics. But his supporters convinced him to run again, and according to an account in the *Gazette,* Griffintown goons allowed no candidate to oppose him. The open-air nomination meeting for Montreal's West Ward began smoothly on June 26. McGee and Holton, both duly proposed and seconded, stood on the platform at Haymarket Square, surrounded by a partisan crowd. The trouble started when Alexander Walker Ogilvie, owner of a local flour mill, tried to nominate another candidate, Thomas Ryan, an Irish-born Catholic and a member of the city's commercial elite. The next day the *Gazette* described the ensuing riot:

> Scarcely had the words come out of his mouth when some of the rabble present forcing themselves on the platform commenced to hustle him and despite the ineffective and altogether inefficient efforts of a couple of policemen, they pushed him off, throwing him headlong down the steps—they then threw him down, kicking and beating him. He was rescued with difficulty, placed in a carriage in a state of insensibility and driven off. As he was leaving, some scoundrel threw a large stone after him, which went through the back of the vehicle, just grazing Ogilvie.
>
> The Returning Officer called for a show of hands, which was declared in favor of McGee. Nobody demanding a poll for Mr. Ryan. None apparently daring to speak, McGee was declared duly elected. He then addressed the assemblage for a few minutes. McGee's qualification was demanded and a protest lodged against his election on the ground of violence.

James Maguire, driver of the carriage that took Ogilvie away from the scene, denied that a stone was thrown at his vehicle. He said the missile had been thrown at another carriage.

But by 1861 McGee's enemies had already begun to plot against him. The member of Parliament for Montreal's West Ward, elected by Irish Catholics as their representative, had begun to think of himself as a Canadian. As McGee concentrated on the future of his adopted country, and his vision for a united Canada under a constitutional monarchy, he alienated those constituents who could not let go of their resentment of the British. Most shocking to Irish nationalists, McGee declared that he no longer believed in the fight for an independent Ireland. When he proposed that Ireland should follow the "Canadian model of self-government" within a constitutional monarchy, nationalists began to view him as a turncoat, a traitor to the Irish cause.

At the same time, the Fenians had begun to infiltrate Montreal's Irish community. The revolutionary movement—founded in Dublin on St. Patrick's Day in 1858, with an American wing formed later in New York—was committed to independence for Ireland, by force if necessary. By the mid-1860s, some of the more impatient members had hatched a back-up plan, one that seemed more feasible than their primary goal of staging a rising in Ireland: the Fenians would invade Canada from the United States. (Their strategy assumed the sympathy, or at least the neutrality, of American authorities.) British North America would then serve as a base from which they would force Britain to free Ireland.

A wild-eyed notion, perhaps, but the Fenians mustered significant support among Irish emigrants across North America, particularly the bitter, impoverished victims of the Great Famine. "These people and their children swell up the ranks of Fenians. All acquainted with the sacred ministry know the difficulties to induce these poor people to forgive their landlords," Bishop John Lynch of Toronto wrote in a letter to a fellow cleric. Almost all of McGee's Griffintown constituents sympathized with the Fenians' goal of independence for Ireland—if not their use of force.

McGee first confronted the Fenians in Montreal in late 1861, at a time of crisis. War between Britain and the United States appeared to be imminent after an American ship intercepted the *Trent,* a British mail packet, and captured two prisoners. Loyal citizens were forming regiments to defend Canada against a possible invasion from the south. But when McGee called a meeting to organize an Irish battalion in Montreal, a small group of Fenians vehemently opposed the idea. The Irish did form a regiment but McGee, determined to eradicate the secret society, launched an open attack on the Fenians.

Using an assumed name, Civis Canadensis, McGee published a warning letter in the Montreal *Herald,* making clear that Fenianism was illegal in Canada and that members could face imprisonment for joining a secret seditious society. But the revolutionary movement continued to make inroads in the city, and McGee became their strongest enemy.

By 1861, the Fenians had also infiltrated the St. Patrick's Society and were attempting to use it as a front for their activities. McGee attempted to expose them by calling on members to take an oath of loyalty, but the Fenians pleaded allegiance and remained undercover.

The Fenian threat caused great alarm throughout the country, but especially in Montreal. Anticipating an attack, citizens formed militias to defend the city and the country. In Griffintown, Rev. Jacob Ellegood, rector of St. Stephen's Anglican Church, became chaplain of the 3rd Victoria Rifles, joining the militia along with many of his parishioners. The British sent troops to Montreal. So many that, in 1862, St. Ann's Boys' School had to move from the grounds of the Collège de Montreal to a cramped space on Dalhousie Street, after the military turned their building into barracks.

Orangemen argued the need for arms, as every Irish Catholic became suspect. To counter the growing backlash, McGee not only denounced the Fenians, he challenged the Irish in Canada to prove their loyalty to their new country. Still, the Fenian movement gained momentum. And some of the most militant revolutionaries were operating right in McGee's riding.

McGee challenged the Fenians head on in the 1863 election. "The slanderer has been busily abroad at all the street corners during the week," he told the large and enthusiastic crowd that turned out at the Haymarket on Saturday, June 6. "I am told that I am opposed among our citizens of American birth and origin, on account of the part I took at the time of the *Trent* Affair. Well, I can't help that. Though I sympathized with their country, and do so still, my sympathy never included an invasion of Canada." He stood ready to face the consequences "in a British colony, under a British constitution, for standing by the British flag, as a British subject."

Fearing an outbreak of violence during the election, the authorities hired two hundred special police. McGee begged his supporters to preserve the peace. "Irritations and disputes may arise," he warned in one speech, predicting that his opponent's supporters might attempt to obstruct the voting process by causing delays at the polling station. "We can beat our opponents. . . . Whoever endangers that success by violence, is an enemy rather than a friend."

At the end of the first day of voting, it was clear that McGee's opponent, John Young, a popular merchant, had no hope of winning.

Late in 1865, the Canadian government learned of a Fenian plot to invade British North America after an informer gave police a note that a Fenian in New York had sent to his wife in Montreal: "Tell Frank I am an out and out Fenian. Advise him to draw all of his money out of the Bank and hide it, for that one of these fine days, we intend crossing over to Canada and taking the contents of every Bank in the province. The traitor McGee will come in for a roasting."

The message put the city on high alert. And the clergy acted to defuse the threat. Father Michael O'Farrell condemned the Fenians from the pulpit of St. Ann's. Father Patrick Dowd denounced those Catholics who had removed their savings from the bank. The clergy organized a special three-week mission for the Irish community at St. Patrick's Church. From December 10, 1865, until January 2, 1866, a team of ten Redemptorist priests from the United States delivered a series of fiery sermons to overflow crowds. The Redemptorists' mission produced measurable results: more than fifteen thousand penitents made confessions; nearly one thousand stood up for confirmations; two thousand took the temperance pledge and—at the height of the Fenian threat—denounced secret societies. And twenty-five Protestants converted to Catholicism.

"We are in a full mess here with Fenianism," said Francis Bernard McNamee, a wealthy contractor who had founded Montreal's Fenian circle (and who was later suspected to be a double agent) in a report to New York. "In fact, nothing else is talked of, from the pulpit to the stable."

By 1865, roughly 350 Montreal Irish had taken the Fenian oath. The secret society counted on the support of another twenty-five hundred of the city's twelve thousand Irish residents. The revolutionaries and their sympathizers had gradually infiltrated St. Patrick's Society meetings, where they now boldly displayed Fenian mottos and sang Fenian anthems.

The Fenians' grand plans called for a series of local uprisings along the border, from New Brunswick to Vancouver Island, to undermine Canada's defences by blowing up bridges and cutting telegraph lines. And, in one foray across the border, the revolutionaries did gain at least a temporary foothold on British territory. A party of Fenians crossed the Niagara River from Buffalo after midnight on May 31, 1866, and occupied the village of Fort Erie.

The American administration foiled the invasion by blocking the movement of the Fenian reinforcements from Chicago and Milwaukee. Yet Colonel John O'Neill and his small troop, outnumbered and low on ammunition, defeated the Canadian militia in the Battle of Ridgeway on June 2. The mission ultimately failed—U.S. authorities arrested O'Neill's soldiers as they withdrew across the river—but it gave the Fenians a taste of victory.

In a second attack, southwest of Montreal, on June 7, a thousand Fenians crossed the border and occupied the village of Pigeon Hill. By the following day they had seized three more villages, but the poorly equipped soldiers fled at the approach of the well-armed militia from Montreal.

Despite the failure of the 1866 invasion, the Montreal Fenians remained committed to their cause and determined to cut down McGee, their most powerful enemy, in the September 1867 election. It was the first election after Confederation, but despite the key role he had played in uniting the country, McGee faced the toughest battle of his political career. Against all advice and in spite of his poor health, he decided to run simultaneously in an Ontario provincial election, for a seat in

Prescott, hoping to increase English Catholic representation in that province—a double feat permissible at that time. In Montreal's West Ward, he faced a formidable opponent in Bernard Devlin, the president of the St. Patrick's Society.

Hundreds had to be turned away from a packed meeting, on July 16, one of the first in McGee's troubled campaign. Fresh from the triumph of Confederation, he told his constituents that, if returned to the House of Commons, he would go "as one of the members for the whole country." McGee talked of Canadian ideals, of civil and religious liberty and guarantees of minority rights: "I look forward to the day when the people of this country will go to the polls, not as British or Irish or French, but as Canadian subjects and fellow citizens." But McGee's lofty principles only antagonized voters expecting him to represent the interests of the Irish.

Devlin focused on local issues, a weak point for McGee. And in a riding where many sympathized with the Fenians' goal of independence for Ireland, if not their means, Devlin did his best to remind voters of McGee's opposition to the movement. At one open-air meeting in Chaboillez Square on July 22, attended by three thousand people, he went so far as to blame McGee for the rise of Fenianism in Montreal, arguing that it was a natural response to his provocation of his own people.

The fiery lawyer from Roscommon took a strong stand as an Irish nationalist, and known Fenians worked on his election campaign. Yet Devlin would deny that he himself was a Fenian. Indeed, he pointed to his role in the Canadian militia during the Fenian raids as proof of his loyalty—although critics would later remark on a certain lack of enthusiasm for the battle when Devlin, as Lieutenant Colonel of the 1st Prince of Wales Rifles, a largely Irish volunteer regiment, was sent to defend the border against the Irish revolutionaries. The following summer, he would give up his command of the regiment and his commission.

McGee's enemies began to issue death threats and the campaign grew violent. On August 2, hecklers threw eggs and shouted McGee down for half an hour, preventing him from delivering a speech. "I have been told that if I would let the Fenians alone, I would be let alone," he told a massive assembly in Point St. Charles the next day. But a defiant McGee shocked the unruly crowd with his claim that he had secret documents about Montreal Fenians and that he planned to publish the details. Despite a heavy police presence, the *Gazette* reported, "the meeting broke up in wild disorder."

McGee's lengthy exposé, published as a series of three articles in the *Gazette* beginning on August 17, caused a sensation. The audacious politician provided a detailed history of the Fenian movement, from its origins in the romantic vision of Young Ireland rebels to its formation in Montreal, with information gathered from his informers as well as from intelligence gleaned as a member of the government. The articles identified numerous well-known Irishmen and incriminated Devlin by association. In publishing these names, McGee defied what he himself called "the hereditary Irish fear of the nickname 'informer.'"

Illness derailed McGee for a week and forced him to rely on a cane. But on August 14, as he shuffled along to one of his committee rooms at the corner of Ottawa and Duke streets in Griffintown, thugs pelted him with stones. On August 26, he received a letter illustrated with a gallows and a coffin, warning that he would be assassinated if he talked about the Fenians.

Many of McGee's supporters were severely beaten when they went to the polls on September 5 and 6, but loyal voters braved the violence. Two Griffintown men carried one eighty-two-year-old Irishman who had been confined to bed for several months to the polling station. "I voted for McGee," he declared.

McGee won by a slim margin of 197 votes. But he had lost the support of the Irish. Devlin beat him in St. Ann's Ward. A short riot broke out after the polls closed, when several hundred Devlin supporters, armed with bludgeons, slingshots and revolvers, descended on McGee's empty committee room, where they hoped to find the candidate. The next day, McGee decided to leave politics. But the Fenians had not finished punishing Canada's great statesman poet. In 1868, Montreal's St. Patrick's Society voted to expel McGee.

Meanwhile, the government learned that Fenians in the United States were masterminding an attack on Montreal, to be carried out by local conspirators. In February 1868, "James Rooney," the pseudonym for an American informer, learned that a gang of Montreal Fenians planned to take control of the arsenal at the St. Helen's Island military installation on the night of March 17, then attack barracks and officers' quarters in other parts of the city, using the St. Patrick's Day celebrations as a cover.

The following month, Rooney delivered four crates of arms, labelled as dry goods, to six Canadian Fenians, at a rendezvous in St. Alban's, just south of the border. On his return, the informer gave the authorities four names. At least two of them—John Ward, a moulder from Kempt (later Young) Street, and Patrick Gushon of Gabriel (Ottawa) Street—gave Griffintown addresses.

But the Fenians cancelled their plans at the last minute after one of their members learned that the government knew about the scheme and were preparing a trap. Yet another Fenian plot had disintegrated.

A few weeks later, in the early morning hours of April 7, 1868, after a late-night session of the House of Commons, McGee walked the few short blocks from Parliament Hill to his lodgings on Sparks Street. Key in hand, he was just about to enter the locked boarding house door when an unknown assassin shot him in the back. The representative for Griffintown fell back onto the street, blood oozing from his mouth, dead at the age of forty-two. Patrick J. Whelan, a suspected Fenian sympathizer, was hanged for the crime.

On April 6, 1868, the day before his death, in his last speech to the House of Commons, McGee described himself as "thoroughly and emphatically a Canadian." Decades would pass before Griffintown's Irish Catholics would wholeheartedly share the sentiments of the man they had sent to represent them.

ONE HUNDRED THOUSAND PEOPLE LINED THE STREETS for McGee's funeral procession, the largest in the history of Canada. Father Michael O'Farrell, a close friend and the former pastor of St. Ann's Church in Griffintown, delivered one of several eulogies at the funeral at St. Patrick's Church on Monday, April 13. "He preached an eloquent, impressive funeral oration before a distinguished packed congregation from all walks of life," *The Centenary* of old St. Ann's notes. "The entire Canadian cabinet was present."

In death, McGee had become a hero. But the Fenian threat did not disappear, although government forces easily quelled their small, abortive risings in 1870 and 1871. Nor did the acrimony between Montreal's Irish Catholics and Protestants soon fade. Almost twenty-five years after the Gavazzi riot, plans for an Orange march caused an uproar in the city.

There was a certain disingenuousness in the Montreal Orange Lodges' announcement, in the summer of 1877, that they planned to celebrate July 12 with a peaceful public walk. Their timing could not have been more provocative. Earlier that year, Toronto Catholics had cancelled their St. Patrick's Day parade, largely to appease that city's Protestants. An Orange procession in Montreal would have been an insult to Catholics. Radicals were determined to prevent it, and it was rumoured they were stocking up on arms and ammunition. Fearing the procession would provoke a riot, leaders of the city's national, religious and benevolent societies urged organizers to call it off. At the same time, the French-Canadian mayor, Jean-Louis Beaudry, warned that he could offer no special police protection. But the Orangemen persisted, asserting their right to parade to their place of worship in full

Thomas Lett Hackett, a member of the Boyne Loyal Orange Lodge, lost his life in a skirmish with young Irish Catholics at the entrance to a shop on Victoria Square on July 12, 1877. Artist A. Leroux witnessed his murder.

regalia, under their banner. Only at the last minute did more cautious Protestant leaders convince lodge members to cancel the walk.

Still, the streets of Montreal were thick with tension on July 12, a Thursday morning, as Orangemen headed to church, in small groups, for a religious service. Gangs of Irish Catholics collected on the streets, riled at the sight of Protestants flaunting their colours, waiting to see if they might hold a procession after all.

Shortly after one o'clock that afternoon, as Thomas Lett Hackett crossed Victoria Square, he noticed some young Catholics harassing one or two Protestant girls sporting orange ribbons. Or perhaps they wore orange lilies: witnesses would differ on the details of the incident, though not on its tragic outcome. The proud member of the Boyne Loyal Orange Lodge had slipped a pistol into his pocket before he attended the morning's church service. He stepped forward to defend the girls. The gang turned on Hackett and he attempted to escape to Messrs. Dunn & Co.'s nearby store. But the doors were closed to him, and his pursuers cornered him on the stone porch and attacked him. Wild with panic, Hackett pulled out his revolver and fired. His shots hit low on the stone steps. His assailants fired back. A bullet penetrated Hackett's head. The gang disappeared, leaving Hackett's dead body lying on the sidewalk.

Trainloads of Orangemen poured into Montreal from Ontario and Quebec's Eastern Townships for Hackett's funeral. "We have come to protect the Orangemen of Montreal on this occasion and woe betide this city if we have to come again," declared the Grand Master of the Kingston Lodge as he sat astride his horse, waving a banner, outside the Orange Hall. Orangemen mounted an impressive display of strength and solidarity: 1,804 members walked in Hackett's funeral procession on July 16, their ranks swelled with another 2,041 mourners from Montreal's Protestant societies. In all, nearly four thousand Protestants assembled on the Champ-de-Mars under a clear blue sky and moved in procession, four abreast, to Christ Church Cathedral on St. Catherine Street.

The military posted troops along the route. And the police chief and fifty constables walked with the mourners, as a further deterrent. Still, there was a moment of panic when a fight erupted as the hearse reached the corner of St. James and McGill streets and a shot rang out. "Right hands found breast pockets, many of them drawing revolvers," the *Gazette* reported, noting that the cavalry responded with impressive speed and force. "As if by magic, the Montreal Garrison Artillery wheeled into line . . . the cortege went on."

Hackett's death inspired "The Twelfth of July," a defiant Orange ballad that ends with a promise of vengeance:

> *But this year will quickly pass,*
> *And another Twelfth will come,*
> *When with Orange banners flying,*

*Police escort Orangemen away from an angry mob after the arrest of their leaders,
who defied city officials and organized an illegal procession on July 12, 1878.*

*Brass bands and fife and drum
All heart and hand together
Down to Montreal we'll go
We'll show these Popish minions
That we're no beaten foe.*

The threat embedded in the martyr's song never materialized. But authorities took the warning seriously. The federal government sent three thousand troops to Montreal to keep the peace on July 12, 1878. Mayor Beaudry took an even stronger stand. His city council proclaimed a ban on all public gatherings in the streets of the city on that day. He also hired five hundred special constables to enforce the ban.

The defiant Orangemen proceeded with their walk, although—much to the embarrassment of the Quebec Lodge—the Ontario Orangemen failed to appear. Around 10 a.m. on the Twelfth, just after the procession emerged from the hall, police moved in and arrested several of the leaders. Constables escorted the remaining members to safety in cabs, away from a mob of angry Catholics.

In 1881, a Quebec court declared that the Orange Order was an illegal society. The Orange movement in the province—never as strong as in Ontario and New Brunswick—gradually declined.

But in Griffintown the embers of Irish nationalism continued to burn, stoked by the threat of another famine in Ireland. Barely thirty years after Black '47, once again, on the street corners, on the steps of St. Ann's Church, in the district's pubs and factories, talk had turned to the failure of a potato crop in western Ireland. Rain had also drenched the hay and corn crops in 1879. Tenants faced ruinous rents. The number of evictions was rising. The economy was failing.

There was talk of Charles Stewart Parnell, an unlikely hero—a rich Protestant—championing the cause of poor tenant farmers. "You must not allow yourselves to be dispossessed as you were dispossessed in 1847," he famously urged at a mass rally in Westport, Ireland, in June 1879. The son of a wealthy Wicklow landlord, Parnell entered politics in 1875, at the age of twenty-seven. He won a seat in the British Parliament and introduced a series of Land Acts that improved conditions for the rural population. In 1877, Parnell was elected president of the Home Rule Federation. The angry young man wanted nothing less than independence for Ireland through peaceful constitutional means.

Hopes soared in October 1879 when Parnell and his Home Rulers joined forces with two other Irish nationalist parties, one of them the revolutionary Clan na Gael. Parnell became head of the historic coalition, known as the Land League. The charismatic leader organized mass rallies and urged the rural workers to agitate for change. The push for land reform and independence took on momentum. Irish nationalism exploded in Ireland and America.

The Land League decided to appeal for help to the millions of sympathetic Irish exiles living in North America. On December 27, 1879, Parnell and barrister John Blake Dillon set sail from Cove for New York City. Requests for Parnell to speak poured in from across the continent. In a little more than two months, he travelled sixteen thousand miles in the United States and Canada, raising £60,000 for famine relief and £12,000 for the Land League. He visited sixty-two cities, including New York, St. Louis, Toronto and Chicago, the last reported to have given him one of his most magnificent receptions. Montreal, the last stop on the tour, gave the revered Irish hero a rousing welcome. Parnell's companion, J. Healy, wrote in a memoir, many years later: "I doubt whether in the 48 years which have since elapsed such a reception was accorded there to any other man. Before stepping from the train we were invested with enormous fur-coats to protect us against the March frost."

Charles Stewart Parnell, MP and leader of the Home Rule Party in the British House of Commons, stood on the rear platform of the Pullman car as his train rolled into Montreal's Bonaventure Station on March 3, 1880, at exactly 9:15 p.m. Thousands were waiting to catch a glimpse of the Irish politician described by the *Gazette* as "a tall, fair, handsome man, with large blue eyes, an earnest intellectual countenance, apparently somewhat nervous and with a wearied look on his face."

Wild cheers, foghorns and brass bands blared as members of the St. Patrick's Society and the Shamrock Lacrosse Club greeted Parnell and escorted him through the crush of well-wishers to a "gaily decorated" sleigh drawn by four white horses. Then, "as if by magic, thousands of torches were lit at once, and lent their brilliance to the scene," the *Gazette* reported.

Six thousand men formed a procession behind Parnell's sleigh, where Brother Arnold, principal of St. Ann's Boys' School, and Francis Bernard McNamee (not yet exposed as a suspected Fenian ringleader) had found a place of honour. Seventy-five torchbearers on horseback led the parade, followed by a genuine Irish jaunting car (a two-wheeled open carriage in which passengers sat on side benches, often back-to-back) and more than a dozen Irish societies, each with their own band and a guard of honour.

More than twenty thousand people lined the streets to catch a glimpse of Parnell. Before heading north to his hotel, the parade took a detour into Griffintown. Chinese lanterns lit up the normally dark streets and a massive bonfire blazed. As the parade continued, the *Gazette* reported, "The enthusiasm of the excited multitude became so great that the horses were detached from the sleigh in which Parnell sat, and the crowd, fastening ropes to the vehicle, dragged it throughout the remainder of the journey."

The next day, Brother Arnold arranged for Parnell to meet some of his Griffintown students at a special reception in their new residence on Young Street. "These were trying days in the 'old sod.' A love of their native country was instilled in the minds and hearts of the pupils of St. Ann's School. It is not surprising for them to give a hearty welcome to the Irish representatives, Parnell, Healy [of the Dublin *Nation*] and O'Brien," a school historian would write. "There was a patriotic address read to which Parnell responded with deep emotion."

That evening seventy boys from St. Ann's stood on the stage of the crowded Theatre Royal to greet Parnell with yet another *céad mile fáilte*—the traditional Irish greeting of "a hundred thousand welcomes." Brother Arnold directed the choir as they sang "Hurrah for Parnell," a new song he had written set to the air of "O'Donnell Aboo."

Parnell spoke fervently to his rapt audience about the recent famine caused by "land sharks." He told them of his attempts "to overthrow the feudal land system in Ireland" by transferring the land to the tenants "voluntarily—but forcibly if necessary." Healy wound up the meeting, declaring Parnell "the uncrowned king of Ireland," a title reserved until then for Daniel O'Connell, the political hero who had led the successful fight for Catholic emancipation in 1829. The St. Ann's boys' choir concluded the patriotic evening with "God Save Ireland."

Collection and door-money at Parnell's meetings across North America had "averaged £500 a night; but in the six or seven I was at this figure was only exceeded in St. Louis and Montreal," Healy reported. In a single night, the Montreal Irish contributed $2,175 to the cause.

But on returning to his hotel Parnell received a cablegram: "Parliament dissolved. Return at once." He decided to cut short his visit to North America. "A farewell supper was given him that night and at Montreal in March we had strawberries," Healy later recalled.

Parnell left Montreal in pitch darkness early on the morning of March 10, 1880. The train rumbled over the Victoria Bridge, hurtling south to New York, where the gloomy hero would board a boat back to Ireland—and an uncertain future. In the 1890s, Parnell would face a sudden fall from grace following revelations of his affair with Mrs. Katharine O'Shea. The "uncrowned king of Ireland" would refuse to give up his position as leader of the Irish National League and the political party would split, as members, shocked at the scandal, drifted away.

SEVEN

Sinners, Saints and Priests

*The Irish are never content with any priest except one of
their own, and they go so far in this desire that they prefer
a priest from their own part of the country to any other.*
—Rev. Michael Buckley, *Diary of a Tour in America*

BISHOP CHARLES-ÉDOUARD FABRE harboured a secret as he walked
in solemn procession down the aisle of the imposing St. Patrick's
Church on March 17, 1884. The scheme he was mulling over, he knew,
would anger the thousands of shamrock-wearing Irish Catholics standing proudly in their pews as soul-stirring Celtic airs filled the grand
church, resplendent in the green banners and emblems of Ireland's
patron saint.

The bishop had confided his controversial plan in a letter to his friend,
l'abbé Marois, at the Episcopal Palace in Quebec City, that morning.
Before going to St. Patrick's to celebrate high mass, he wrote: "The Irish
priests of the diocese are few, but, between you and me, those who came
from Ireland officiate in a very unsatisfactory manner. I would like to
place St. Ann's Parish in charge of a community. With this idea in mind

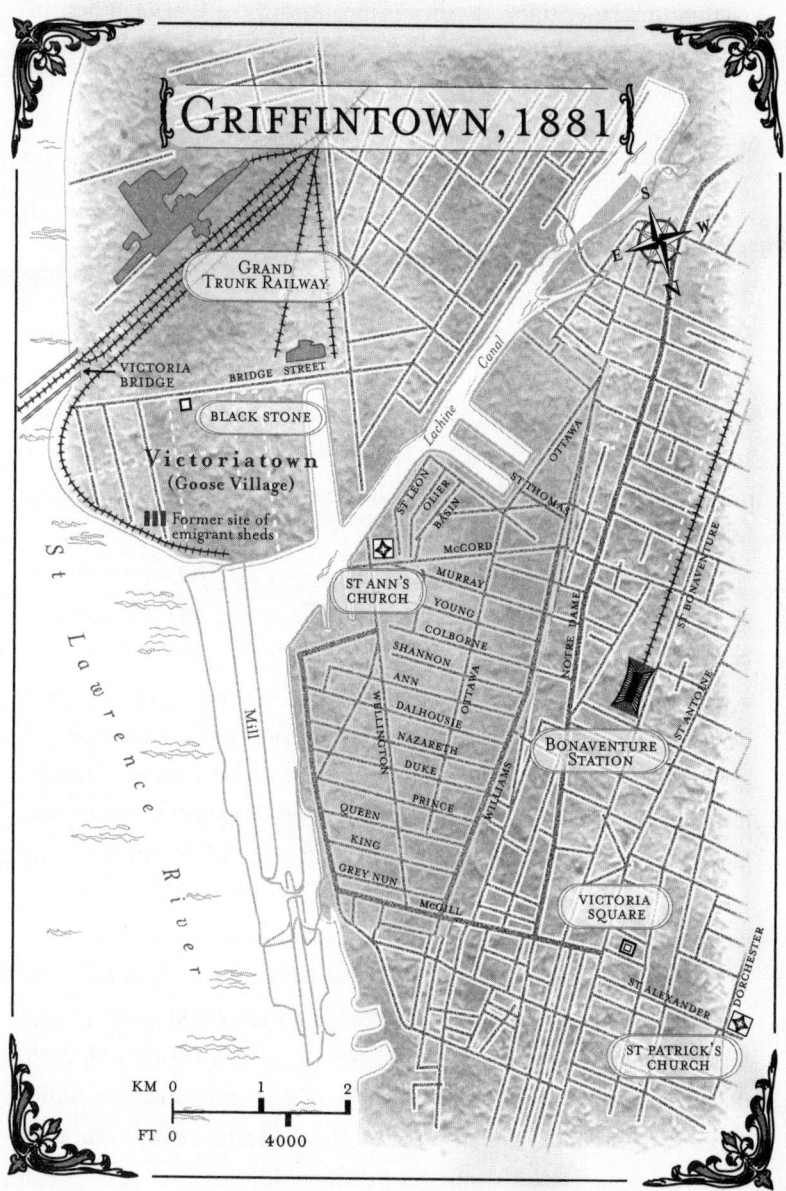

GRIFFINTOWN, 1881

GRAND TRUNK RAILWAY

VICTORIA BRIDGE

BRIDGE STREET

BLACK STONE

Victoriatown
(Goose Village)

Former site of emigrant sheds

Lachine Canal

ST LEON

OTTER

BASIN

ST THOMAS

McCORD

OTTAWA

MURRAY

ST ANN'S CHURCH

YOUNG

COLBORNE

NOTRE DAME

SHANNON

ANN

OTTAWA

ST ANTOINE

DALHOUSIE

WELLINGTON

NAZARETH

BONAVENTURE STATION

DUKE

WILLIAMS

PRINCE

QUEEN

KING

GREY NUN

McGILL

VICTORIA SQUARE

ST ALEXANDER

DORCHESTER

ST PATRICK'S CHURCH

Mill

St Lawrence River

KM 0 — 1 — 2

FT 0 — 4000

would you let me know how the Redemptorists stand in Quebec in relation to salaries? How do they compare with the Oblate fathers in regards to the establishment of congregations, societies and devotions? Tell me what you know of them without seeking information from others, for I wish for the time being to keep the matter a secret."

Marois replied the very next day, highly praising the Redemptorists' work in an Irish parish in Quebec City: "During the short time that they have been here they have brought about such a radical transformation in their parish, that their church has become too small to contain them. As for temporal matters, they have not only paid all necessary expenses connected with improvements, etc, which they themselves have made, they had also paid much off the church debt. . . . They are excellent administrators. . . . They also have the veneration of the people, who place in them entire confidence. The French as well as the Irish hold them in the same respect."

Fabre decided to enter into negotiations with the Redemptorists, officially, the Congregation of the Most Holy Redeemer, an order that had been founded in Naples in 1732 by Saint Alphonsus Maria de Liguori, a successful lawyer who gave up his practice to become a priest. And on March 19, 1884, the bishop announced his decision to redraw the geographic boundaries of St. Ann's. He removed five hundred families from the overflowing Griffintown church and assigned them to two new parishes, St. Gabriel's in Point St. Charles and St. Anthony's in St. Henry. The change, he knew, would upset Father Hogan and the close-knit congregation of good old St. Ann's, for thirty years the heart of Griffintown.[5] Irish Sulpicians had served as pastors at St. Ann's since the church first opened its doors in 1854, and the Griffintown Irish had formed strong bonds with all of the priests from their native land. Each one was a *soggarth aroon,* a devoted, beloved priest who shared their history and their politics as well as their faith, and each one was eventually forced to part reluctantly from his parishioners.

St. Ann's first pastor, Rev. Michael O'Brien, from County Tyrone,

Parishioners of St. Ann's revered their Irish-born priests,
the Rev. Michael O'Brien, the first pastor, and his successors,
Rev. Michael O'Farrell and Rev. James Hogan.

had worked so tirelessly for the poor Catholics of Griffintown that his
own health broke down. And his successor, the eloquent Rev. Michael
O'Farrell, had endeared himself to his parishioners with his gentle,
beguiling personality. But not long after the assassination of his close
friend D'Arcy McGee, the priest was recalled to St. Patrick's against
his wishes, a heartache for him and his congregation. In July 1869, he
left the Sulpician order and moved to the United States, where he
became pastor at old St. Peter's in New York City, and, in 1881, Bishop
of Trenton, New Jersey.

Then there was Rev. James Hogan. "He was no administrative genius,
perhaps not a pulpit orator," a parish history concedes, but "his genial-
ity and genuine interest in the people and their problems was recipro-
cated, on their part, by a deep affection. He became truly the guide,
philosopher and friend of his parishioners."

Christian charity, and perhaps discretion, kept Bishop Fabre from naming in his letter the Irish priests who, he believed, had not measured up. But Rev. Hogan, known to enjoy a drink or two, likely stood at the top of His Lordship's list of "unsatisfactory" administrators. Father Hogan's fighting Irish spirit had led to more than one clash with the bishop over the Irish turf of St. Ann's, just as Father O'Brien and Father O'Farrell had tangled with Fabre's predecessor, Bishop Bourget.

During his visit to Montreal in 1870, Rev. Michael Buckley had noticed an antipathy between his compatriots and French Canadians so deep that, although he had come from Ireland to raise funds for a cathedral in County Cork, he did not even try to solicit donations from French Catholics. "In many places efforts have been made by the ecclesiastical authorities to blend the two nationalities, but oil and water are not more dissociable," he observed.

In fact, friction between Irish and French Catholics had led to many notable confrontations, not just in Montreal. One famous scandal arose in 1850, in Burlington, Vermont, where the two groups shared St. Mary's Church, after the Irish refused to allow the French Canadians to build a separate church on parish property.

Even where language was not an issue, Irish Catholics across North America were demanding their own parishes and priests of their own nationality. In New York and Philadelphia, in the last half of the nineteenth century, at least half of the city's Catholics belonged to "national parishes," rather than attending the local church with a mixed congregation, although many bishops disapproved of the separate parishes, which increased the visibility of the newcomers and made them more vulnerable to discrimination. (In an effort to encourage assimilation, Bishop John Fitzpatrick of Boston actually discouraged the formation of new Catholic schools, hospitals and other institutions from 1846 to 1866.)

Irish national churches caused yet another headache for bishops. In the United States, the Germans, Poles and other ethnic groups, observing the success of the Irish, began to request parishes of their own. In a few cities, schisms occurred when emigrant groups defied the bishop and organized their own parishes and tried to appoint their own priests.

But in Montreal the need for English-speaking priests gave urgency to the Irish demands for separate churches. In the late 1850s, the Irish priests began pressing for a new church for their compatriots in the city's east end, who were then sharing a chapel in the lower level of a school in the predominantly French district known as the Quebec Suburb. (Montreal's Irish Catholics now made up a third of the population and although a heavy concentration lived in Griffintown, significant numbers had settled in neighbourhoods across the city.) Resentments, it was rumoured, had even led to fistfights between the Irish and French congregations sharing the chapel, dedicated to St. Bridget of Ireland. In January 1859, Fathers O'Brien and O'Farrell started a fundraising campaign. The priests assumed that, if they found the money, Bourget would permit them to construct a new church. By March 1867, the Irish community had raised £800. But the bishop, for reasons he would not disclose, refused to allow construction to proceed.

After waiting for nearly a decade, the Irish lost hope. On Sunday, March 10, 1867, the Irish priests issued a call from the pulpits of St. Patrick's and St. Ann's, inviting all donors to a meeting to determine what to do with the money they had contributed, which, having been invested, had grown from slightly more than $4000 to nearly $40,000. The decision: The funds would be invested in the new St. Patrick's Hall and the shares would be donated, in equal parts, to the St. Patrick's Orphan Asylum and Irish Catholic charities in St. Ann's Parish. (The shares would turn out to be a poor investment. The concert hall, a stunning example of Irish architecture, burned down and stockholders suffered a loss, receiving only fifty-five cents on a dollar.)

Bishop Bourget eventually approved the construction of St. Bridget's Church in the city's east end, six years later. Now he wanted the money. On June 29, 1873, he wrote a letter to the trustees of the St. Patrick's Orphan Asylum, telling them he thought "it would be gracious" for them to restore the funds to the church project. The trustees consulted a lawyer and informed the bishop that they lacked the legal authority to divest the funds.

Another six years passed. On June 8, 1879, Bourget's successor, Bishop Fabre, wrote to the superior of the Sulpicians, Joseph-Alexandre Baile, advising him that "the money collected more than twenty years ago by O'Brien and O'Farrell for the building of a church for the Irish in the Quebec Suburb is now in the hands of Father Dowd, director of the St. Patrick's orphanage, and Father Hogan, rector of St. Ann's." The bishop intimated that said money should be handed over at once for the church. The priests reiterated their legal position. But the matter did not end there. On January 15, 1885, the St. Patrick's orphanage board met to discuss a claim from Rev. Lonergan, the parish priest, and the *fabrique* (parish council) of St. Mary's Church, demanding the payment of the money—with interest. The dispute eventually went to an ecclesiastical court. On December 1, 1887, the orphanage won the case.

Behind the battle over money for an Irish church lay a long-standing power struggle between the Gentlemen of St. Sulpice and the bishop of Montreal. In the early days of settlement, the Sulpicians—appointed seigneurs of Montreal in 1663—owned and controlled the entire island, which they ran as a single parish from their grand church of Notre Dame. As the French population grew, the Sulpicians built new churches, but treated them as "branches" of the vast parish of Notre Dame. That historic arrangement lasted for over a century and allowed the powerful society of priests to retain both their spiritual and civil authority to perform and register births, marriages and deaths.

But the appointment of Jean-Jacques Lartigue as the first bishop of Montreal, in January 1821, threatened the Sulpicians' power. Though church law gave the bishop authority over the Sulpicians, the priests refused to cede control of their sprawling historic parish.

Lartigue's saintly, but more demanding successor, Bishop Bourget, was determined to loosen the Sulpicians' hold. In 1866, he announced his intention to divide Montreal into several parishes, each with a fixed territory. The parishes would fall under the authority of the bishop, as in every other Catholic diocese around the world.

Under the bishop's plan, St. Ann's would be designated an English-speaking Catholic parish. (In fact, the Sulpicians had once tried to offer services in both languages at St. Ann's Church, but gave up because of the ill will that led to physical confrontations between the two groups.) But St. Patrick's, spiritual centre of the Montreal Irish, would become a bilingual parish. No longer permitted to draw parishioners from across the city, the grand church on the hill would serve the three thousand Catholics—half Irish, half French—within its now limited boundaries.

Bourget's decree angered Father Patrick Dowd, proud pastor of St. Patrick's. And the displeasure of the unofficial "bishop of the Irish" was evident as he read the announcement, as required, from the pulpit on Sunday, November 25, 1866. His most famous parishioner, D'Arcy McGee, took up the cause. The next Sunday, December 2, six thousand Irish Catholics rallied on the church grounds to hear McGee speak out against the bishop's decision: "We have contended with many problems, with poverty and with prejudice. Now 30,000 strong, we stand in danger of disorganization, division and prostration. It is a question of self-preservation. The most natural administrative boundary to our parish is language," McGee argued.

The threat to St. Patrick's came while the Irish priests were pressing the bishop to create the city's third Irish church. In addition, Montreal's Irish Catholics—almost one-third of the population of the city and 90 per cent of the English-speaking Catholic population—felt slighted by the bishop, who had influenced the decision to close St. Patrick's Hospital, providing in its stead two English-speaking wards in the French-speaking Hôtel-Dieu. The archbishop of Quebec declined to rule on the sensitive case and referred the disgruntled Irish to Rome.

In March 1867, McGee travelled to the Vatican, one of a delegation to ask Pope Pius IX to save St. Patrick's Church for the Irish. He presented their case to the Pope in an audience on March 25. On the eve of Confederation, McGee argued the importance of the decision that would set a precedent "for all bilingual areas across the new nation." Six years later, Rome's judgment came down on the side of the Irish.

ON APRIL 21, 1884, FATHER HOGAN wrote a polite letter of resignation to Bishop Fabre, and rumours began to swirl through the Irish community. Father James Whittaker, the assistant at St. Ann's, confronted the bishop, who admitted that he had asked the Redemptorists to take over the parish.

On June 13, Father S.P. Lonergan wrote a letter of protest to the bishop:

> Your Excellency,
> You have called in strangers. By this action you virtually declare incapable the nine Irish priests you have in your Episcopal city. Or I might say better that you give to understand that by misconduct they are unworthy of your confidence. If they were incapable, why were they ordained? If they are culpable, why have they been allowed to exercise the ministry? For if they are capable and good priests, I cannot understand why you should prefer strangers to them.
> . . . . It is deplorable to have to talk like this to your Lordship. I shall probably cause pain, but I would consider myself guilty of cowardice, if I did not speak according to my conscience.
>
> With sentiments of the greatest respect,
I remain, your humble servant,
S.P. Lonergan, Parish Priest.

Then, on June 17, 1884, seven other Irish priests overlooked by the bishop—J.J. Salmon, pastor of St. Gabriel's; S.P. Lonergan, pastor of St.

Mary's; J.P. Kiernan; F. Fahey; J. Whittaker, acting pastor of St. Ann's; P.F. O'Donnell; and Wm. O'Meara—joined the protest and wrote a letter of complaint to the bishop in which they stated: "Your petitioners regard no charge more detrimental to their interests than the advent of the Redemptorist Fathers to St. Ann's Parish."

But the Redemptorists, skilled preachers renowned for their retreats and novenas, had made a powerful and lasting impression with their first mission in Canada, at St. Patrick's Church in Montreal, in late 1865, during the Fenian crisis. Impressed by the congregation's response to the priests' powerful sermons, three Canadian bishops had already invited English-speaking Redemptorists from the United States to direct parishes with large Irish emigrant populations—St. Patrick's in Quebec City in 1874, St. Patrick's in Toronto in 1881 and St. Peter's in Saint John.

After a brief exchange with the Redemptorists at Baltimore, however, Bishop Fabre opted to bring French-speaking Redemptorists from Belgium to St. Ann's in Griffintown. It was an odd choice, bound to alienate the Irish. Seventy years later, the bishop's decision remained a puzzle to the anonymous author of a parish history: "It may seem strange that [he] should place in charge of a purely Irish parish, most of whom were directly from Ireland or by descent, a generation removed, priests from another country, not too familiar, to say the least, with the language of their parishioners. . . . a missionary order." His Grace's private correspondence would later reveal that he "resented the idea of parish income flowing to the United States."

The foreign priests did not receive the traditional Irish greeting, *céad mile fáilte* (a hundred thousand welcomes). On Thursday, September 4, 1884, after a long transatlantic journey, Redemptorist Fathers Jean Catulle and Guillaume Godts walked down the gangplank onto the busy Montreal wharf and found their own way to the presbytery at 32 Basin Street in Griffintown. Rosaries clicking under their black cassocks, the French-speaking Belgian priests mounted the steps of the greystone building and knocked on the door of St. Ann's rectory, praying, perhaps, for a warmer reception than the one the Redemptorists had received initially at St. Patrick's in Quebec City, where suspicious parishioners refused to relinquish control of church deeds and money.

Father James Whittaker, the acting pastor, greeted the newcomers and handed over the keys and parish books to Father Catulle, the superior. French-speaking Redemptorists now had charge of good old St. Ann's, an English-speaking Irish parish. "To say the least, they were not received with band and banner," a church historian notes.

BY THE END OF SEPTEMBER, three more Redemptorist priests, Reverends Edward Strubbe, Arthur Caron and van der Capellen, as well as three lay Redemptorist brothers, had arrived. Father Catulle delivered his first sermon on Sunday, September 14, to a sullen congregation curious to hear what the priest they called the "Dutchman" had to say. The stocky, handsome pastor acknowledged his parishioners' sorrow over the loss of their Irish priests and dared to promise: "What they were by birth, we will be by heart." Led by Father Catulle, the new parish team immediately began to implement their ambitious program of spiritual and social services.

Once the official shock had passed, the Redemptorists soon found an ardent Irish congregation willing to listen to their dramatic sermons filled with stories of saintly temptations and glory and threats of purgatory and hell, and to be consoled by their almost continuous round of parish missions, retreats, novenas, pilgrimages and spiritual exercises. The priests organized several sodalities: pious lay groups, popular in Ireland, that met weekly for religious instruction and prayer.

And in the spring of 1885, the foreign priests won the hearts of the Irish when they commemorated the Famine emigrants who had died in the fever sheds in Black '47 with a solemn requiem mass and a public pilgrimage. Parishioners, including descendants of the victims, filled the church, heavily draped in mourning for the sad but consoling ceremony. The entire congregation then marched in procession to the Black Stone, an immense boulder, with a plaque honouring the six thousand buried in the mass graves. The rugged monument, sometimes called the Irish Stone, was erected in 1854, after workers accidentally unearthed bones during the construction of the Victoria Bridge. The Redemptorists' ceremony established an annual, unbroken tradition known as the "Walk to the Stone."

Early in 1885, construction began on a new three-storey red-brick monastery on Basin Street. The existing greystone pastor's residence was too small to accommodate the Redemptorists' plans for a seminary and novitiate to train priests and students. They needed a chapel, refectory and common rooms for a large community of priests.

The priests' ambitions for the community led to a flurry of expansion over the next few years. In 1887, they established a home for the aged in Goose Village and appealed to the Little Sisters of the Poor, a Belgian order dedicated to the care of the elderly, to serve the elderly Irish of St. Ann's and neighbouring parishes. In 1889, they constructed a new school, St. Alphonsus, for children living in that part of the parish across the Lachine Canal, also known as Victoriatown. The priests also added a brick extension and a third storey to St. Ann's Academy for Girls on McCord Street.

Changes to the church proved more controversial. In 1888, Father Catulle hired parishioner Patrick McDermott, an architect and contractor, to renovate and enlarge St. Ann's. The wooden galleries that ran along two walls of the church were removed to allow more light to shine into the interior, as well as to reduce the strain on the walls, the risk of fire and the temptation to little boys who threw things down on the pews below. Many parishioners bemoaned the loss of two rows of trees and lawns at the entrance, removed to make way for a thirty-two-foot extension at the front of the building. In 1890, three bells were installed on the church's new tower.

But before they built a monastery, before they repaired and built schools and before they renovated the church, the Redemptorists delivered on the promise Father Catulle made in his first sermon—to provide the young men of St. Ann's with "an organization of their own." The priest's goal was in tune with a progressive religious movement of the times: to save youths' souls and build character through organized sports and cultural activities. North America's first Young Men's Christian Association had opened in Montreal in 1851. Even the police chief saw the need for amusements for the young men of the city, calling in his 1885 report for temperance workers to provide alternatives to the numerous saloons, especially those with boxing halls and billiard tables, that led youth down "the path of crime."

On a Sunday afternoon in January 1885, several dozen youths showed up at St. Ann's Hall to listen to Father Strubbe's plans for a young men's society. The eloquent, energetic thirty-seven-year-old priest from Bruges outlined an ambitious program of sports, choirs, musical and dramatic productions, debates, lectures by prominent citizens and other cultural pursuits. The young men—many of them carters or factory workers with little schooling—would run the society themselves, with his guidance as spiritual director. That afternoon, enthusiastic members elected a slate of officers and appointed a committee to draft a constitution and bylaws.

The society set up a base in St. Ann's Hall; they installed a temporary gymnasium, erected a stage and painted several sets of scenery for dramatic performances. But it soon became evident that the 350-square-foot meeting room on the top floor of the boys' school was inadequate. The Redemptorists decided the St. Ann's Young Men's Society needed its own, brand new, building. To raise the money, the priests proposed a stock plan; in May 1885, they invited potential investors to buy fifty-dollar shares that would bear interest at the current bank rate. The entire capital would be returned to the shareholders in instalments over five years. Despite some initial hesitation, twenty supporters—including

Father Catulle, member of Parliament J.J. Curran, and R. McShane—volunteered to finance the project.

The Redemptorists hired Patrick McDermott and Son as contractors. McDermott Jr., a member of the society, kept careful watch when construction began on June 1, 1885, on Ottawa Street, on a lot adjoining the boys' school. The cost of the project ballooned from the initial estimate of $6,000 to $11,000 after the priests decided to buy an adjacent property and expand the size of the building by a third. The Redemptorists were proving to be every bit as capable as l'abbé Marois had predicted.

But the summer of 1885 brought a series of crises that would shake Griffintown, and add urgency to the priests' plans to engage the parish youth. The first incident occurred on Sunday, July 19. Constables Andrew O'Neill and John Malone had just started their shift on the Murray Street beat at six in the evening when they noticed three young men, obviously inebriated, quarrelling on the sidewalk a short distance away. O'Neill would later identify them in court as Charlie Considine and two of the Hamilton brothers. The constables reached the youths—members of St. Ann's Parish—just as another policeman, Sergeant McCambridge, on his way back to the station at the end of his shift, approached from the opposite direction.

The police told them to move on. But the youths refused and after Constable O'Neill gave William Hamilton a shove, he started to remove his coat, as if ready to fight. The sergeant ordered the constables to take him to the police station. And when Hamilton resisted O'Neill's attempts to put him in chains, Malone stepped forward to hold him. O'Neill would later testify that while he was putting the chains on Hamilton, Considine dashed into a nearby yard and reappeared with a six-foot pole and, uttering "a fearful oath," demanded that they release Hamilton. He then took a swipe at Sergeant McCambridge and fled.

By this time, some twenty or thirty people had gathered and were trying to prevent the police from taking Hamilton to the station. In the midst of the struggle, thirty-year-old Constable Malone, hit on the back of the head by a brick, slumped to the ground. Information collected from witnesses at the scene pointed to Considine as the culprit.

Constables Beattie and O'Neill found him about an hour later, half a mile away at the home of an acquaintance, Patrick Barrett, a labourer. Barrett's wife, Norah, later testified that she met Considine for the first time as he was trying to escape from her house by jumping out a window. After a struggle in an upstairs bedroom, Considine was arrested and charged with aggravated assault.

Constable Malone suffered a concussion as a result of his injury and spent the next few days in a coma, attended by doctors at his Colborne Street home. He regained consciousness a number of times on Friday and Saturday, and there were glimmers of hope he would pull through. Around four o'clock on Sunday afternoon, he opened his eyes and appeared to recognize his wife, Mary Hanlan, who was cradling their nine-month-old baby in her arms. He whispered, "Goodbye," and slipped back into a coma. He died at three the next morning, surrounded by doctors and Redemptorist fathers from St. Ann's.

After Malone died, the police charged Charlie Considine with murder. News of Malone's death sent a wave of grief and shock through Griffintown. The community was so close-knit that O'Neill, the arresting officer, was a good friend of the Considine family.

At the time of his arrest, Considine flippantly told O'Neill he had enough influence in city council to get off. But the handsome twenty-year-old, represented by J.J. Curran, the respected Irish Catholic lawyer and MP for St. Ann's, looked apprehensive when he appeared in court on September 16 for his murder trial.

The trial was interrupted in the afternoon while one of the doctors who had treated Malone was on the stand. A health worker arrived to announce that a family member of one of the jurors had been diagnosed with smallpox. The judge discharged the jury and the courtroom was fumigated.

The trial resumed the following day with a new set of jurors. The judge also closed the courtroom to spectators to help prevent the spread of smallpox, preventing Considine's supporters from attending.

On Monday, September 21, another juror took ill with "Canadian cholera." The judge discharged the second jury. The case would resume on November 9.

Montreal was by now in the middle of another major epidemic, the most serious since the cholera outbreak of 1854 that killed 1,186 residents. The first case, diagnosed by doctors at Hôtel-Dieu in February, caused no alarm. Smallpox broke out in Montreal every year. Nearly five thousand city residents, mostly children, had died of the disease between 1872 and 1881. But in April, after a sharp increase in the number of cases, the Board of Health offered free vaccinations for what appeared to be a more virulent outbreak. By May 1, more than twelve thousand had volunteered for the shots.

But smallpox continued to spread. Travellers and businessmen began to avoid the stricken city. By mid-August, the plague had taken 120 lives, forty victims were hospitalized, and an estimated four hundred cases were under treatment at home. The Board of Health decided to make vaccination compulsory. Those who refused to comply would face a fine of twenty dollars or a jail term.

Dr. James Hutchinson, public vaccinator for St. Ann's Ward, immunized more than two thousand patients at his Wellington Street office in the first two weeks after his appointment on August 24. He saw another rush for vaccinations in mid-September, after the Grey Nuns reported that they had discovered more than fifty unreported cases in the west end, several of them in Griffintown.

Smallpox killed 150 residents of St. Ann's Ward in 1885, a relatively small toll compared with the predominantly French-speaking working-class neighbourhoods of St. Mary's and St. James wards where 2,157 died. The Irish listened to the priests who told them to obey the vaccination order. But many French Canadians resisted vaccination; they also refused to bring their sick to the isolation ward. The poor, unable to pay the fine, were jailed. Health officers faced verbal abuse and violence when they tried to enforce quarantine. On September 30, when a health board worker tacked a placard on an infected house in the east end, a woman rushed out, grabbed it and tore it up. Her husband followed, loudly accusing the placarder of assaulting his wife.

A crowd gathered at the scene of the dispute, and by evening it had swollen into a menacing swarm. Around seven o'clock, the protestors set out to take revenge on the authorities. The rampage began with an attack on the east end health office, where they broke all the windows and ransacked the building. The mob proceeded to vandalize the houses of several doctors (one of them the city's medical health officer), an alderman and a drugstore; they also set several fires before descending on City Hall and smashing its windows. The crowd targeted the nearby *Herald* offices before dispersing. But the disturbance continued, and the mob reassembled to complete the destruction of the east end health office. Carting boxes of smallpox placards and sulphur disinfectant into the street, they lit a massive bonfire, then torched the building. The police managed to quell the riot by one a.m., with the help of the Victoria Rifles and other volunteer regiments.

More than three thousand Montrealers died in the epidemic that ended early in 1886. But the disease was on the wane—the number of deaths had decreased from sixty to fourteen a day—by November 8, 1885, the opening day of the St. Ann's Young Men's Society's new headquarters at 1107 Ottawa Street.

The handsome, three-storey, red-brick building topped with a mansard roof stood smack up against the parish boys' school, on a property that was roughly the size of a doubles tennis court. A gymnasium filled the entire ground floor. The second and third floors held a reading and a meeting room, a library, a spacious games and recreation room

The library and the reading room at St. Ann's Young Men's Society headquarters.

and living quarters for the janitor. The building boasted gaslights and what one newspaper called "the most improved hot water apparatus" for heating, a luxury in Griffintown.

The Young Men's Society also renovated St. Ann's Hall. They added a new sloped floor to improve the audience's view of the stage and installed a door leading from the third storey of the new building into the theatre on the top floor of the adjoining boys' school. And, with new seating, a reporter decided, "It is now one of the coziest and complete halls in the city."

There was much fanfare and ecclesiastical hoopla during the day-long celebration of the society's new building. Members attended morning mass together at St. Ann's Church at seven, then gathered at the hall for breakfast. At ten, they walked back to church in a procession led by a marching band for a high mass. The solemn blessing of the building took place at one o'clock, followed by a celebratory dinner—tickets one dollar—attended by the society's members, friends and guests, including several dignitaries.

J.J. Curran addressed the gathering. The kindly, forty-three-year-old mutton-chopped lawyer—due in court to represent young Considine the next day—delivered a witty, erudite speech tracing the "trials, tribulations and triumphs" of Ireland, before offering his congratulations on the "building of the spacious new structure where the young Irish Canadians of the district could meet for mutual improvement, for the development of their mental and muscular forces and to prepare themselves for the battle of life; to enable them to wage it honourably for

John Joseph Curran, distinguished Quebec Superior Court judge, author, Conservative member of Parliament, and Solicitor General. Born in Griffintown in 1842, he was one of eleven children of an Irish blacksmith.

the benefit of the land in which they lived and the grand old land from which their forefathers came."

The day concluded with vespers at St. Ann's Church, where Bishop Fabre sang the benediction and blessed the society's new flag. The inauguration ended the following evening, November 9, with the society's first choral concert.

That morning, when Considine's murder trial resumed, his team of lawyers, led by Curran, demanded his acquittal, arguing that it would be unlawful to subject their client to a second trial. The judge ruled against them and the trial proceeded. But numerous discrepancies arose as the witnesses repeated their testimony for a third set of jurors and faced yet another cross-examination. In summing up the case for the jury, the judge admitted he had never heard such contradictory evidence. The jury acquitted Considine of the murder of Constable Malone.

An Irish Night! At St. Ann's Hall!

Grand Irish Drama, in Five Acts,
-Entitled-

The Irish Eviction!

-or-

The Land Agent's Fate!

Vividly portraying the struggle with
Landlordism in Ireland at the present day

The posters for the St. Ann's Young Men's Society's first stage play, *The Irish Eviction!*, appeared all over Griffintown in March 1887. At 7:30, half an hour before the curtain rose, organizers had to stop selling tickets. More than one thousand people had filed through the heavy green doors of St. Ann's Hall for the society's St. Patrick's Day concert on Thursday, March 17, plunked down fifty cents—twenty-five cents for children—and tromped up the four flights of noisy metal stairs to the third-floor theatre. But the hall only seated eight hundred, so more than two hundred disappointed ticket-holders headed back into the cold, dark, snowy streets.

Act I opened with news of Parnell's arrest, the Irish Catholic hero "thrown again into one of England's prison-hells." (Parnell had, in fact, been arrested on October 14, 1881, for inciting tenants in Ireland not to pay rents.) Now a heartless land agent, Alfred Belmont, comes to evict Jerry McCarthy, a tenant on the estate of Squire Hamilton, a typical Irish landlord.

BELMONT: Oh, for the love of Heaven, delay your work for a few days, as my poor wife is dying!
McCARTHY: Dying, or not, out she must go at once.
(The Crowbar Brigade moves in to level the cottage and, when McCarthy bravely tries to protect his home, the land agent assaults him.)

"Every hit made against landlord oppression in Ireland was lustily cheered," the *Montreal Daily Star* reported the following day. "The performance was highly creditable to the society and showed that great care had been taken in working up the different characters."

From the outset, the St. Ann's Young Men's Society reflected its members' love of Ireland. The society always mounted Irish plays, often written by society members. Many of Ireland's most distinguished politicians, journalists and authors came to Griffintown at its invitation—Michael Davitt, a founder of the Land League, and William O'Brien, journalist and MP, among them.

Until the arrival of the Ancient Order of Hibernians, no other Irish organization in Montreal, and there were many, marked the anniversary of the death of the Manchester Martyrs. The staunch Irish nationalists of Griffintown maintained the innocence of the three Fenians, sentenced to hang by the British in 1867 on flimsy evidence, after a policeman was killed during a failed attempt to free two leaders of the Irish Republican Brotherhood en route to prison in Manchester, England. Every year, on November 23, the Young Men's Society presented an Irish entertainment and invited a prominent Irish Canadian to deliver a patriotic address.

The society's concerts—featuring Irish songs, dancing, comedy skits and drama (usually a tragedy and almost always set in Ireland)—drew sold-out crowds and favourable attention in the press. In December 1888, the *Gazette* theatre critic gave a high rating to *Falsely Accused, Or, Waiting for the Verdict*, about a young Irish farmer charged for the murder of a wealthy landlord, saving his highest praise for the leading man, J.J. Gethings, comparing the Griffintown resident to Wilson Barrett, a world-renowned British actor.

The society's name also appeared in the columns of the Irish-American press, notably New York's *Irish World* and the *Boston Pilot*. In March 1888, the society staged the tragedy *Robert Emmet*, about the mythic Irish hero, an idealistic young Protestant aristocrat sentenced to death by the British after leading an abortive uprising in Dublin in 1803. On March 31, the influential *Irish World* gave the production a glowing review.

The St. Ann's Young Men's Society quickly became one of the most popular and prestigious Irish organizations in the city. Members found an outlet for their talents and took pride in their achievements. In 1902, the society staged *The Abbot of Dungarvan*, a play scripted by member James Martin. (Martin wrote four plays: *The Pride of Killarney, The Rebellion of '98, Siege of Limerick* and *O'Rourke's Triumph*.) By then, the society had moved its popular theatrical productions to the Monument National, a large playhouse on St. Lawrence Boulevard, to accommodate large audiences from across the city.

The society excelled in sports, too. Most of the players from the championship Shamrock Lacrosse Club—almost all of them from St. Ann's Parish—belonged. Brennan, Taugher, Hoobin and other celebrated athletes played for society teams. The famed Harry Hyland, a Griffintowner who starred in Canada's earliest pro hockey leagues, helped win several trophies for the society.

All young men of the parish had access to the library, gym and other facilities at St. Ann's Hall, and those eighteen and over were eligible to join the society, after they underwent an initiation.

"Stand up, stop smoking, throw away your chewing gum, and no more talking. I will do all the talking from now on. This is . . . serious and I want no laughing. This is a Young Men's organization. . . . One of its important rules is discipline, that is respect of the laws and rules." So spoke the degree warden, responsible for preparing candidates for presentation to the executive. Then, according to the ritual format described in the society's annals, he put prospective members through fifteen minutes of drills, teaching them to march in the form of a cross— a Catholic symbol of spiritual salvation and the society's emblem.

The Young Men's Society banned drinking on its premises, no doubt influenced by Father Strubbe, an ardent temperance advocate. The priest frequently appeared before city commissioners to oppose liquor licences and to report any infractions of the law in Griffintown. His efforts led to several raids on saloons that served alcohol on Sundays and to shutting down grocery stores that sold liquor illegally.

The Redemptorists gave the Young Men's Society significant discretion in the management of its building. But, in a rare imposition of priestly authority, Father Schelfhaut, a new arrival from Belgium, shut the society out of the hall on February 15, 1896. "To our great astonishment we were informed by the Rev. Brother Prudent that he had received strict orders to have the doors leading to the Entertainment Hall locked and so prevent us from holding our matinee on Saturday, the 15th of February," the society's secretary wrote in March, in an impassioned eight-page letter to Father Catulle and Father Strubbe. "We were exceedingly incensed at the unwarranted and uncalled for action of the Rev. Father Schelfhaut."

The priest met with the society's executive, but declined to give a specific reason, only hinting that the organization was not Catholic enough, nor large enough. "He told our president that we should have five hundred members in our society," the secretary stated in his letter. "Now, Rev. Father we are . . . 215 in number, all of good character and we [consider] this number . . . very high [compared to] St. Anthony's Young Men's Society [with] only forty on its Roll. St. Mary's Young Men's Society has eighty. St. Patrick's, twenty." In fact, the society, conscious of its reputation, had expelled at least one hundred members they had deemed unsuitable, a move that had made them some enemies within the parish.

But the Young Men remained loyal to Father Strubbe, giving him an overwhelming vote of confidence at one heated meeting: "All of our two hundred and odd members were ready to stand up and pledge their loyalty and love to him for his untiring zeal, his self-sacrifice and his prudent care."

The popular, dynamic Father Strubbe had gained the respect and devotion of the entire parish. Known as the "great bazaar priest," he organized hugely successful annual fairs. One, in 1891, ran for ten days and attracted people from across the city. Besides the standard booths— cigar and refreshment stands, fortune tellers, fish pond, tombola, wheel of fortune—parishioners staged concerts, operettas, cantatas and torch-light parades with brass bands to bring crowds to St. Ann's Hall every night. The mayor and other local dignitaries attended many of the events, some combined with elaborate dinners featuring pâté de foie gras and other elegant fare.

And, in what might be a first for any church bazaar, the *St. Anne's Fair Journal,* a daily eight-page newsletter illustrated with engravings, was published and sold during the ten-day event. Miss Katie O'Brien edited the witty, well-written publication, inspired by Father Strubbe. The *Fair Journal* contained features and profiles of local interest, as well as Irish-themed short stories and poems written by parishioners.

The St. Anne's Fair Journal, *a newsletter that ran
Irish-themed short stories and poems written by parishioners,
was issued daily during an elaborate ten-day church bazaar in 1891.*

The benevolent Rev. Father Edward Strubbe, a zealous temperance advocate, organized the St. Ann's Young Men's Society in 1885.

In spite of initial reservations, St. Ann's, under the Redemptorists, had become a dynamic centre of Irish Catholic culture, with its own network of award-winning sports teams, choirs, and musical and dramatic productions. The humble Griffintown parish could rival the great national parishes of Boston and New York.

FATHER STRUBBE BROKE THE NEWS to the young ladies of the Sodality of the Children of Mary, gathered for a regular monthly meeting in St. Ann's Hall in the fall of 1901. The venerable priest's voice trembled as he told them that, after nearly eighteen years in the parish, the superior at the Redemptorist Mother House in Belgium had summoned him back to his native country for a new assignment. The letter ordering his sudden recall had arrived that very afternoon. He was obliged, he told the teary-eyed members of the sodality, to embark for Europe immediately.

A few days later, the St. Ann's Young Men's Society escorted Father Strubbe to a farewell reception at the parish hall, where admirers filled every seat and spilled out onto the streets. "There was not a dry eye in the place," reported parishioners who listened to the laudatory speeches recalling the priest's long service, as he watched, visibly emotional. The next day parishioners and friends lined the entire route to the harbour, seeking the beloved priest's parting blessing. Throngs filled the wharf and a number of St. Ann's Young Men sailed with him as far as Quebec.

Father Strubbe's boat, the *Numedian,* was already well on its way to Brussels when word arrived that he was to remain at St. Ann's after all. His superiors had listened to a citywide protest at his removal. But it was too late and he returned to Belgium, where he would later say that he found himself "a stranger in his own land."

In 1904, his superiors decided to send him back to Montreal. Word quietly spread through St. Ann's that Father Strubbe would soon return to the parish. For an entire week, John Kane made daily trips to Bonaventure Station. The elderly gentleman met every train, watching and waiting, hoping to catch first sight of the *soggarth aroon.* Early one morning, Rev. Father Rioux, rector of St. Ann's; Charles Strubbe, a nephew; and a few of Father Strubbe's friends from St. Ann's joined the old man on the platform. Father Strubbe had travelled from Antwerp to New York on the SS *Finland.* At 7:15 a.m., accompanied by his brother, also named Charles, a resident of Montreal, who had travelled to New York to meet his ship, the priest finally made an appearance at the railway station. Kane's face lit up when he caught sight of the priest. The old gentleman shook Father Strubbe's hand and presented him with a fine shillelagh as a welcome home gift.

PART THREE

Take Me Back to Griffintown

EIGHT

The Irish Below the Hill

And, though we've sought another shore
We're Irish yet! We're Irish yet!
—William Henry Drummond

HERBERT BROWN AMES DREW A STRAIGHT LINE across a map of Montreal, along the invisible boundary that separated the city's well-to-do from the lower classes. The high ground—the area at the top of the map, where the city's wealthy elite lived on the leafy avenues hugging the slopes of Mount Royal—he named the "City Above the Hill." The district at the bottom of the map, under the CPR train tracks, he called the "City Below the Hill." It covered roughly one square mile and encompassed parts of Point St. Charles and St. Antoine Ward, and all of Griffintown.

Ames lived above the line, in an elegant house on Bishop Street, in Montreal's exclusive Golden Square Mile, home to some of Canada's wealthiest citizens, up and away from the workers who cobbled boots and shoes in his profitable factory on the edge of Griffintown. But

An aerial view of the City Above the Hill in 1896,
looking north from Griffintown.

the tall, mild-mannered son of privilege decided to zero in on their gritty neighbourhood, where, he wrote, "the tenement house replaces the single residence and the factory with its smoking chimney is on every side." The largely Catholic inhabitants of the City Below the Hill had found an unlikely, though somewhat sanctimonious advocate in the Protestant businessman. "No one deserved to live in such squalor," wrote Ames, a practical idealist who was convinced that improving the living conditions of the poor could also add to the bottom line: "Society as a whole would be better off if its workers, made happier, were more productive."

Born in Montreal in 1863 to wealthy American parents, Ames had attended the exclusive Amherst College in Massachusetts in the 1880s, an era when social reformers had taken up the cause of the working class in industrial cities in Europe and the United States. The infamous tenements of New York, Boston, Philadelphia and other metropolises, home to hundreds of thousands of Irish emigrants, had caught the attention of so-called "muckraking" journalists. American intellectuals were grappling with the evils of the city: corrupt politicians and the squalid housing conditions of the urban poor.

Ames returned to Montreal in 1885 determined to fix the long-neglected slums in his own city. "Most of the residents of the upper city know little—and at times seem to care less—regarding their fellow-men in the city below," he wrote. "The citizens of Montreal should, for a time, cease discussing the slums of London, the beggars of Paris and the tenement house evils of New York, and to understand more perfectly the conditions present in their very midst."

In 1896, Ames, then thirty-three, decided to take a measure of the living conditions of the workers in the City Below the Hill. He would use the emerging science of statistics to unearth social problems and provoke action. In the autumn and early winter of 1896, Ames organized Canada's first house-to-house sociological survey. His team of canvassers went knocking on doors in the City Below the Hill. Their questions were numerous and detailed: What's your religion? Country of origin? Place of worship? Family size? Occupation? Income? Number of boarders? Number of rooms in the house? Bathtubs? And much more. The investigators visited factories and commercial establishments, too, and tallied up the number of workers. They counted taverns, churches and schools. They carefully recorded each response, along with their own observations.

The results first appeared in a series of ten articles in the *Montreal Star* in 1897 and, later that year, in a book called *The City Below the Hill*. The groundbreaking work painted a detailed portrait of the working class living on the west side of Montreal. Ames, a facts-and-figures man, illustrated variations within the district with charts and maps.

The survey included a rough cross-section of Montreal's three main ethnic groups, with a population that was 42 per cent French Canadian,

33 per cent Irish and 21 per cent of British origin. (The remaining 3 per cent were mostly European.) But the Irish predominated in the district of Griffintown. In its core residential area, in the vicinity of St. Ann's Church, the proportion of Irish soared to 69 per cent. And it was there, among the Irish, that he found the most dramatic results.

In 1882, George Grant's *Picturesque Canada* declared, "The Irish population of Montreal take a high stand in business, politics and society. They number in their ranks many successful merchants and large capitalists, and have leading representatives in all the learned professions."

Yet Ames's survey proved what many had long suspected: Griffintown was the poorest area in the City Below the Hill. The district did have a "well-to-do" minority—7 per cent of Griffintown families earned more than twenty dollars a week (a substantial income at the turn of the century), compared to 15 per cent of residents in the larger district. But roughly 60 per cent of Griffintown's families scraped by on just six dollars a week, while the average weekly income of families in the City Below the Hill was slightly more than ten dollars.

Ames established a poverty level—what he called "the point where comfort ends and poverty commences"—at six dollars a week, the minimum wage for an unskilled labourer. In the City Below the Hill, 10 per cent subsisted on less than five dollars a week. This "submerged tenth," Ames noted, relied on "neighbourly sympathy" to survive. In the heart of old Griffintown, the percentage of families with incomes below five dollars a week soared to 24 per cent—or one in every four.

Two months after the initial survey, Ames's canvassers returned to question roughly half of the "submerged tenth"—the poorest families in the City Below. In this second round, interviewers probed for the causes of their poverty. More than half of the poor blamed their sad circumstances on a lack of steady employment; 34 per cent were unable to find regular employment in the off-season, while another 28 per cent could find no work at all. Most were unskilled labourers who worked in construction or on the wharves during the summer and looked for odd jobs in the winter. "When spring arrives, overdue rent and debt at the corner grocery have so mortgaged the coming summer's earnings that saving becomes impossible," Ames explained. Loss of a breadwinner through old age, illness or death had pushed nearly a third of families into destitution: 9 per cent were too old to work; another 9 per cent, too ill; and the 8 per cent of families headed by a widow lacked a breadwinner.

Based on his canvassers' observations, Ames asserted, "In seven per cent of cases visited drunkenness was clearly at the bottom of the trouble." He found a "startling average" of one licensed liquor store for every 219 persons in the City Below the Hill. He checked for a link between alcohol and poverty by comparing the number of liquor stores in the poorest part of Griffintown with the number in the less poverty-stricken Point St. Charles neighbourhood. The survey found one liquor store for every 160 persons in Griffintown, compared with one in 240 in Point St. Charles, leading Ames to conclude, "Wherever poverty and irregularity are most prevalent, there the opportunities for drunkenness are most frequent." Still, he declined to point to intemperance as a cause of irregular employment and poverty. He took the stance—progressive for the times—that it might be an effect of hardship.

Griffintown, not surprisingly, was the most overcrowded district in the City Below. Density in a ten-block area next to St. Ann's Church reached 173 people per acre, almost double the rest of the City Below and more than four times that of the upper city. In a single block on Young Street, five hundred souls were dwelling in slightly more than two acres.

Still, as Ames pointed out, Griffintown was not as seriously congested as the slums of New York, Boston and other American cities. Density in New York City's poorest neighbourhoods typically exceeded three hundred persons to an acre, much higher in some of the five-storey clapboard rookeries, like the notorious "Gotham Court," also known as "Sweeney's Shambles," and the "Big Flat," a tenement on

Mott Street that sheltered more than a thousand men, women and children. Montreal's small residential buildings—typically two-storey rowhouses with one family above and a second below—were "more conducive to health and good morals," Ames concluded. But he deplored the ramshackle rear dwellings crammed into some of the yards behind the district's typical row housing: "If one desires to find where drunkenness and crime, disease and death, poverty and distress are most in evidence in western Montreal, he has only to search out the rear tenements."

Ames saved most of his outrage for "that relic of rural conditions, that unsanitary abomination, the out-of-door-pit-in-the-ground-privy." By 1896, modern plumbing graced virtually every house in the upper city. Yet, nearly fifty-eight hundred privies remained in use in the city of Montreal. In Griffintown, three-quarters of households relied on communal privies.

Montreal's notorious death rate remained high at the time of Ames's survey in 1896, exceeding those of the teeming metropolises of London, Paris and New York. But it varied widely within the city, from 22.47 per thousand in the City Below to 13 per thousand in the upper city.

Ames found to his surprise that, overall, St. Mary's and St. Jean Baptiste—two French-Canadian working-class wards on the east side of Montreal, which he did not include in his survey—fared worse than St. Antoine and St. Ann's, the two wards in his survey. And there were significant differences within the City Below. The overall mortality rate in Griffintown—at 24.62—was only slightly higher than the average for the City Below. Ames also identified four "districts of death" within the City Below—two of them in Griffintown—where the mortality rate soared to more than 30 per thousand. Not unexpectedly, the four areas also scored the highest density, overcrowding, most rear dwellings and privy pits.

The idealistic Ames believed that lives could be saved if landlords provided safe, sanitary accommodation. He was also convinced that a capitalist could help his fellow human beings—and turn a profit—by investing in decent housing for workers. In 1897, he set out to prove his theory by building Diamond Court, probably the first model housing complex in Canada, at the corner of William and Colborne streets. The location, he calculated, was "within half a mile or ten minutes walk of industrial establishments employing over 12,000 persons." He chose Griffintown for his experiment because "in this region the need at the present time is greater than in any other locality within our nether city and because if success can be here attained, it will be certain elsewhere."

Diamond Court housed thirty-nine families in four separate, solid-brick blocks, two or three storeys in height. Each building had a shared front entrance with a gaslit lobby and inside stairways leading to three-, four-, five- and six-room flats. The modestly priced rental units were equipped with a stove, a sink, a washtub and water closet, and, oddly, a central drain in the concrete kitchen floor. A small courtyard featured a garden and electric lighting, and a resident janitor maintained the premises. "A healthier community it is difficult to find," Ames bragged. He projected a 5 per cent return on his investment and hoped other investors would follow his lead and build decent housing for workers. But none took up the challenge.

In 1898, Herbert Ames entered politics. He won a seat on city council and, as an alderman for St. Antoine Ward, worked to improve the living conditions of the poor by calling for a ban on privies and rear tenements, as well as fines and even demolition of properties when landlords failed to meet health standards. He served on city council for eight years and as chairman of the Board of Health's hygiene committee from 1900 to 1904. Ames's long crusade to rid the city of outhouses earned him the nickname "Water Closet Ames." But change came slowly: a decade later, hundreds of privies still stood in the City Below. Ames, meanwhile, had moved on. In 1904, he switched to federal politics and spent the next fifteen years as a Conservative MP for St. Antoine. In 1919, he was appointed financial director of the newly formed League of Nations in Geneva.

Ames's timing had been right—or so it seemed. He and other reformers on Montreal city council had launched their ill-starred campaign to
improve conditions in the City Below the Hill during an extraordinary
economic boom that would run, with a few falters, until the Great
Crash of 1929.

MONTREAL'S SO-CALLED GOLDEN AGE began in the 1880s, with the construction of the Canadian Pacific Railway. The city became the heart
of the new transcontinental line that opened up the Canadian West.
Hundreds of thousands of immigrants poured into the country, and
through Montreal, between 1896 and 1914. Unlike in previous migra-
tions, the Irish formed only a small fraction of the unprecedented flood
that brought Ukrainians, Poles, Italians, Czechs and numerous other
nationalities to Canada. Most boarded trains for the Prairies, where
they settled on the vast, open plains.

Montreal moved well ahead of Toronto, its closest rival in the
expanding economy, to become the undisputed metropolis of Canada.
The port of Montreal thrived, becoming the second largest in North
America after New York, as trainloads of cattle and wheat arrived from
the West, for shipment around the globe. Grain elevators went up
along the Lachine Canal and local manufacturers prospered in the bustling commercial centre. Impressive office buildings and fashionable
retail stores set up shop along St. Catherine Street in Montreal's "new
downtown" anchored by Windsor Station, the imposing new terminal
built by the CPR in 1886 on the southwest corner of Dominion Square,
just a few blocks north of Griffintown.

Despite the city's growing prosperity, Montreal's fractious city council, divided along ethnic, religious and class lines, paid little attention to
the inferior housing conditions and public sanitation in working-class
neighbourhoods. Ames and other reformers made little headway in a
municipal government where graft, bribes and patronage had become

An 1880 photograph of James McShane, the controversial Griffintown businessman and politician known as "the people's Jimmy."

the norm. In 1909, a Royal Commission into the administration of the city concluded that it was "saturated with corruption."

Irish Catholics, caught between the French-speaking majority and the prevailing Anglo-Protestant business elite, often had to fight for their share of the power and the spoils. In New York and Boston, the notorious ward bosses of Tammany Hall, a long-established fraternal society, helped the Irish win elections by promoting Irish candidates and delivering Irish votes, through an informal system of favours and patronage. But even the infamous Tammany Hall might have been stymied by the complex dynamics of Montreal's demographics.

Griffintown always elected Irishmen. Typically, colourful, long-serving politicians, like James McShane, a local livestock dealer, stockbroker and a member of the Shamrock Lacrosse club. He represented St. Ann's Ward as a councillor and alderman for nearly twenty years, as a member of the Legislature between 1878 and 1892, and as a federal MP in 1896. Raucous outdoor election rallies, replete with brass bands, gave voters ample opportunity to support their candidates, perhaps none so popular as McShane, "the people's Jimmy," who had fought for the Irish Catholic day labourers "squeezed out" in the competition for city work in the winter months in the late 1880s. The folksy politician inspired fierce loyalty, and when he ran for mayor against a French-speaking incumbent in 1891, his campaign song, "When Jimmy McShane gets Mayor," suggests he also raised hopes for a share of the spoils of victory:

> *Come all ye voters from Griffintown,*
> *Point St. Charles and elsewhere,*
> *We're going to run a prominent man*
> *To represent you as mayor. . . .*

> Chorus:
> *We'll buy all the bootblacks a brownstone front,*
> *The drivers will go on a tare;*
> *We'll make all the Aldermen carry a hod,*
> *When Jimmy McShane gets mayor. . . .*

> *And when election day is won,*
> *We'll light our torches bright;*
> *There never was a sight in Griffintown,*
> *As there will be that night. . . .*

McShane won the 1891 election, and he served a second term as mayor in 1892, winning by acclamation with the support of French-speaking Conservatives. But the following year, he lost the mayoralty to a French Canadian by a mere 156, questionable, votes. The Griffintown politician refused to surrender the position, or the chain of office. It took a court order to pry the necklet away. (McShane's reluctance was perhaps understandable, given the widespread election shenanigans of

Dancers at one of St. Ann's famed annual St. Patrick's Day concerts.

the times and the city's dubious record. In 1892, Ames, head of the Volunteer Electoral League, organized a door-to-door survey of five Montreal wards and discovered that the city's voting list included the names of three hundred dead and four hundred non-residents.)

As the years passed, Irish Catholics experienced even greater difficulty hanging on to political power. For a few decades after the arrival of the Famine emigrants, English-speaking Montrealers had held a majority in the city. But in the final decades of the nineteenth century, as rural Quebecers continued their exodus to the city to work in the rapidly expanding manufacturing districts on the east side, French-speakers increasingly outnumbered anglophones. By the 1880s, they began to dominate the municipal government, while the influence of the anglophones declined, mostly at the expense of the Irish, since the English and Scots tended to hold on to their positions.[6]

Irish Catholics may have lost some political clout but they maintained a vocal and visible presence in the city, much of it centred in Griffintown. The Shamrock lacrosse and hockey clubs fielded championship teams; the St. Ann's Young Men's Society now staged their original dramatic productions uptown, in the Monument National, to accommodate their citywide audience; and Irish concerts and lectures—many in the cause of independence for Ireland—drew crowds to St. Ann's Hall.

Montreal's St. Patrick's Day parades had grown ever larger and more impressive since the first procession in 1824. As the Irish spread out across the city, new parishes and associations joined the line-up, bringing out thousands more marchers, and their attendant brass bands, willing to brave snow, sleet and frigid March winds to demonstrate their solidarity and, increasingly, their nationalist politics. Home Rule had been gaining momentum in Ireland and among Irish expatriates in North America throughout the 1890s. And in 1892, one of its staunchest supporters, the Ancient Order of Hibernians, established its first division in Montreal. Rallying to the motto of "Friendship, Unity, Charity," the AOH drew hundreds of members in Montreal, with a solid base in Griffintown. In 1899, one newspaper account paid special attention to the influential society, calling its "1500-strong" contingent, dressed uniformly in black coats and silk hats, the "most notable" in the parade, remarking that their "soldierly bearing brought frequent applause."

The AOH, rooted in medieval Ireland, had assumed the role of protector of priests by 1565, after the British began to impose the Penal Laws, legislation aimed at disenfranchising Catholics. Beleaguered Irish immigrants opened the first North American branch of the Ancient Order of Hibernians, a benevolent society open to "men of Irish birth or descent," in New York City in 1836, for mutual protection against anti-Irish Catholic bigots. The first Canadian branch opened in Toronto in 1889; within a few years, there were four branches in that city, as well as others in Quebec City and the Maritimes (although its membership dropped significantly in Toronto in the years leading up to the First World War). Run by lay Catholics, the AOH regularly attended religious services as a group, though its strong ties to the nationalist movement in Ireland often earned the disapprobation of the clergy.

In Canada, too, AOH members fought injustice against the Irish. In 1900, they joined the St. Patrick's Society and other Montreal Irish organizations in a long legal battle with the Grand Trunk after the railway moved the Black Stone, the cherished monument to the six thousand typhus victims buried in Goose Village, to make room for additional tracks near the bridge. In 1911, the railway finally agreed to return the Black Stone to a spot fifteen feet east of its original location, but the memorial site was reduced to a quarter of its original size. In 1909, fifty-two years after Black '47, the AOH, led by the Quebec chapter, erected a monument at Grosse Isle, with engravings in English, French and Irish, honouring the thousands who died on the island. Only the Irish inscription blames "foreign tyrants" and an "artificial famine" for their deaths.

Montreal's Irish community remained strong and vocal, but by the turn of the century it had spread out. In 1901, only one out of every three Irish Montrealers lived in Griffintown. Large numbers of second- and third-generation Irish had moved into white-collar clerical jobs, many in the railways. Electric streetcars had made the suburbs more accessible and many had moved to Point St. Charles, Verdun, or "over the hill" to Notre-Dame-de-Grâce and other new developments.

The so-called flight to the suburbs had eroded many Irish immigrant neighbourhoods across North America. South Boston proved an exception as chain migration from Ireland continued to boost the population of the tight Hibernian community. But in Toronto, Irish Catholics had for the most part assimilated into the English-speaking city. The upwardly mobile had moved on and the city's old Catholic emigrant neighbourhoods now had mixed populations, as more recent arrivals from Europe replaced them.

But the Irish in Montreal faced a unique situation. As the population of the city grew, becoming increasingly French-speaking, the gulf between the two linguistic groups deepened. The differences were seemingly reinforced by the tendency to live apart, French Canadians predominating on the east side of the city, English Canadians on the west. But the "two solitudes," so aptly depicted in Hugh MacLennan's 1945 novel, tell only part of the story. New ethnic neighbourhoods appeared in the early decades of the century as Europeans arrived, and struggling emigrants tended to form their own solitudes, just as the Irish had done before them. Montreal took on a more cosmopolitan flavour, with a small Chinatown around Bleury Street and Mordecai Richler's famed St. Urbain Street Jewish neighbourhood to the north. All would fade away after a generation or two, as the newcomers found their footing and a way out, mostly into the English-speaking mainstream. The population of St. Ann's Ward dropped slightly, to 21,835 in 1901, from a high of 23,003 ten years earlier, and it became more diverse, as Italians settled into Goose Village, or Victoriatown, as some called it.

Still, Griffintown endured, its Irish Catholic heritage intact. Hard times had forged deep bonds and an "us and them" mentality that many never lost, and that kept bringing them back after they had moved "over the hill." The crucible of Griffintown had produced nuns and priests, politicians and playwrights, champion lacrosse players and musicians. Yet no one expected artistic talent—or much of anything— to emerge from the City Below the Hill. Even well-meaning outsiders like Ames failed to look beyond the surface of poverty.

In the fall of 1896, when Ames's canvassers knocked at the Coonans' door at 41 Farm Street in Point St. Charles, they found a family of nearly average size and income. William Coonan, 46, and his wife, Mary Ann, had three daughters, Daisy, 15, Eva, 13, and 11-year-old Emily, and two sons, Thomas and Frank. William, born in Griffintown in 1850, worked as a machinist for the Grand Trunk Railway, a steady job that enabled him to buy a modest house near the shops. Like more than two-thirds of the residents of the City Below the Hill, the Coonans were neither well-to-do, nor part of the so-called "submerged tenth."

Ames's survey took no measure of the talents and aspirations of the residents of the City Below the Hill, nor of the lively, dynamic Irish Catholic community that revolved around St. Ann's Parish. By 1896, the nuns at St. Ann's Academy on McCord Street had noticed Emily Coonan's talent and encouraged her to sketch elaborate chalk designs on the blackboard. Barely into her teens, Emily painted a portrait of the popular Father Strubbe, as well as several icons for the church. Her brother, Thomas, a future judge, attended St. Ann's Boys' School.

Like many in the district, the Coonans made sacrifices to educate their children. William would walk several miles to the library and carry home armloads of books for his family. Thrifty Mary Ann set aside money for Eva's piano lessons and Emily's art classes. And when Emily showed promise, the family scrimped to pay the tuition at the Conseil des Arts et Manufactures, and later, in 1905, at the prestigious School of the Art Association of Montreal. Yet Stephen Leacock would write—in a vivid expression of a view widely held "above the hill"— that in "the tumbled slums of Griffintown, people wouldn't know a Corregio from a Colorado Claro [cigar]."

The community spirit had survived, but so had traces of discrimination. "There was a stigma. We were from the wrong side of the tracks," recalled Kaye Lyng, who grew up in Griffintown. Lyng remembered how, on her way home from school—she went uptown to St. Patrick's— one businessman used to throw a few pennies her way, he felt so sorry for her, probably because she and her brothers and sisters wore second-hand clothes. And there were hardships: there was no bathtub in the cramped second-storey flat on Prince Street, where her family lived, but her mother, Annie O'Donnell, would allow no complaints. If Lyng or any of her five brothers and sisters grumbled about bathing in a metal washtub in the middle of the kitchen, she would remind them how lucky they were to live in Griffintown, where they had an indoor toilet.

In Ireland, where O'Donnell grew up and her parents still lived, they didn't even have privies—they would go out in the fields. "They could grow nothing on that island," Lyng recalled.

Annie O'Donnell often told her children about her life in Ireland, her childhood home in a thatched cottage on a tiny island off the coast of Donegal. She told them how the clergy in the old country were much more strict than the priests at St. Ann's. Once, O'Donnell had confessed to a priest that she had attended a wedding in a Protestant church, and he made her walk miles and miles every day for her penance.

But Annie O'Donnell never told her children the true reason she emigrated to Canada. She took that secret, that shame, to her grave. Kaye Lyng discovered, many years later, that her mother had left Ireland in disgrace. She'd had a baby, sired by a priest who visited the island to hear the family's confessions. He raped her behind an outbuilding, while her parents, brothers and sisters waited in line to confess their sins. Her parents raised the child as their own, and she emigrated to Canada. O'Donnell landed in Griffintown in 1904 and went into service for a wealthy Westmount family. She quickly learned English after her arrival in Montreal, but she always spoke Irish in the confessional box. None of the priests at St. Ann's understood a word.

A few years later, she married Thomas Lyng, a recent emigrant from Kilkenny who worked as a day labourer for the city. O'Donnell stayed home to raise their children, taking in Irish boarders to supplement her husband's erratic income. (One of the boarders, a relative, James Lyng, later became a top official with the Montreal Catholic School Commission. A high school now bears his name.) When the Depression hit, Thomas Lyng could find no work at all, so O'Donnell would rise before dawn, trek a few miles up Beaver Hall Hill to clean offices, returning in time to get her children ready for school and make breakfast for the boarders. She kept that job until she turned seventy.

However difficult her circumstances, O'Donnell continued to send packages to her hard-pressed parents. In the summer of 1932, the Lyngs took their six children to Ireland to spend the summer with relatives. Kaye Lyng remembered staying with her grandparents and meeting the child she would eventually learn was her sibling. Years later, she recalled that the thatched cottage was charming but Spartan. "We had nothing in Griffintown but they were poorer than we were. I have happy memories of Griffintown."

"We were poor, but we didn't know we were poor," recalled Charlie Blickstead, born in Griffintown in 1906, to a German-born father and an Irish mother who passed on her brogue to her son. "We were warm, well-dressed and we always had lots of food in the house. The shelves in the cellar on Duke Street were always lined with pickles and barrels of apples and potatoes. My mother rented out two rooms on the second floor."

Blickstead's father worked as a printer. "My mother, God love her, had her hands full because in those days the father did nothing, you know. The women had to work like slaves. They did the washing by hand, they scrubbed the floors by hand. But my mother would say, 'I was never so happy as when I had one in me belly and one on me hip.' They were rugged people."

Hard work and stubborn independence saw the Blicksteads and the Lyngs and the Coonans, like most Griffintowners, through hard times. But no one would turn a needy soul away. Charlie Blickstead never forgot the day Arabian Ryan knocked on their door and asked his mother, "Mrs. Blickstead, have you got a pair of trousers for me?" She didn't have it in her heart to turn him away empty-handed. "My mother gave him my father's good trousers and he got half way down the street and he sold 'em. But the worst was my father's trousers. When he couldn't them find, and my mother said, 'Aw, God help 'im. . . .'"

Then there was Wingy Munro, with one arm and no place to stay. So Emmett's Ball Club let him sleep in their hangout on the second floor of an old warehouse. "That's Griffintown for you," said Charlie Blickstead. "No one knew him, but 'You could stay here.' So summer time comes, he's still sleeping on the bench."

Mattie Crowe lived in the cellar of McConnell's Saloon. Sometimes, Blickstead recalled, Crowe could be seen walking down the middle of the street, finely dressed in the castoffs of the proprietor's four sons, singing a little ditty like a Pied Piper with all of the children following him. "There were a lot of unfortunates in Griffintown," Blickstead said.

HERBERT AMES WASN'T THE ONLY SOCIAL REFORMER to take an interest in Griffintown. In the summer of 1908, Rev. J. Stuart Jamieson, a Presbyterian minister at the Nazareth Street Mission, decided to reach out to the local youth. But it was their disruptive behaviour, not their poverty, that caught Jamieson's attention, after a gang of boys on a corner outside the mission drowned out his sermon with their mouth organs one hot August evening.

Jamieson consulted Owen Dawson, a juvenile court worker, about his idea of starting a club for the troublesome lads. The minister may have overstated the dangers of the street corners, calling them "the one place of all where youth is contaminated," but his belief that a positive influence and a place to spend their spare time might prevent them from sliding into a life of delinquency reflected the philosophy of the times. The federal government had recently passed the Juvenile Delinquents Act, heralding a rehabilitative approach to youth crime. And Dawson and a group of influential businessmen had established Shawbridge Boys' Farm, a new reform school, northwest of Montreal. Now they would turn their attention to Griffintown.

Two nights after their first conversation, the Presbyterian minister and his friend Dawson met with fifteen boys on the corner and proposed the idea of a club. All of them showed up for the first meeting in September 1908, in a side room of the mission at the corner of Wellington and Nazareth streets. Each boy promised to return with a friend the next week. Jamieson and Dawson took up a collection and bought the boys sweaters with the club's crest. Athletics provided

*Members of the Griffintown Boys Club, then called
the Nazareth Street Club, meet at a vacant grocery shop.*

the main attraction in the early months, and club members met on
Tuesday nights and Sunday mornings to play baseball, hockey or football. Membership was limited to thirty, to allow the volunteers to get to
know the boys. "The boys at first regarded the Club as merely a conve-
nience, a place where they could get something for nothing," Jamieson,
the club's vice-president, observed in the 1910 report. "If threatened
with expulsion for bad behaviour they would quickly reply 'I don't
care.'" But, after a few months, they noted, dozens of eager youngsters
had to be turned away for lack of space.

On May 1, 1909, the club moved into an old grocery store on
Wellington Street: "A long, narrow dingy room with a shower bath in a
cupboard, a filthy yard behind, and a sick woman overhead," according
to one club report. But members spruced up the new quarters, demolished counters and shelves, and installed gym equipment and a shower

bath—"a very necessary treat for some of the lads"—and assembled a small collection of books. A benefactor donated a piano. Meetings increased to three evenings a week. Friday sessions began with a half-hour "practical talk," followed by gymnastic drills on the bars, trapeze or punching bag. Boxing quickly became the favourite pastime.

In the summer of 1909, organizers took the boys on the first of many outings to the country. "Some of the youngsters had never seen lakes and rivers," wrote Dawson in the club's first annual report, published in 1910. Mrs. J.H.R. Molson, one of several wealthy patrons, organized summer camps for the children. James Cyril "Flin" Flanagan, a Montreal dentist and one-time McGill football hero, provided free dental care. In the fall of 1909, two female volunteers rented a vacant store a few doors east of the boys' club on Wellington Street and started the Griffintown Girls Club, with about forty-five members. "Dawson had a lot of opposition as the local kids thought he was trying to make sissies out of them, so every once in a while the club would be wrecked," one report noted.

Still, Dawson found much to admire, as well as to correct, in the rough-edged Griffintown lads. "Most of the boys we are trying to help have sunk to a very low level, and it is not uncommon to find boys under fifteen habitual thieves, or others who have begun drinking and smoking at the age of eight or ten," he noted in his 1910 report. Many did not go to school and few worked.

The following year, Dawson reported: "Probably our most difficult task has been to keep the boys steadily employed; not because they are lazy or positions are scarce, but on account of the ease with which a boy can make a living dishonestly. The numerous warehouses, coal yards and freight sidings which abound in our district offer great temptations for theft. . . . In the boy's mind, the monotony and small pay of routine work is not for a moment to be compared with the more adventurous life."

Cocaine use became prevalent in Montreal in the fall of 1912, and six of the club's members took up the habit. "We soon found that half a

Lunchtime at the St. Ann's Day Nursery.

dozen of them were fast becoming addicted. . . . We were able to take prompt action, and cocaine is now practically unknown in Griffintown. We might add, too, that about a dozen of the older lads have signed the pledge." Dawson's solution was to keep the boys occupied. To join the club, members had to undergo an initiation and take a pledge that included the promise: "I will try to be steadily employed in some work."

In 1911, the boys' club moved to a spanking new $10,000 building on Shannon Street. The newly named Griffintown Boys Club—the first of Canada's boys clubs to operate out of its own building—boasted a gym with a small stage, a reading room and games (sitting) room with an open fireplace, a small library, much-used shower baths and locker rooms and a small shop. The Griffintown Girls Club rented a large room at the back of the building, with a separate entrance.

But while the club's well-to-do directors tended to patronize the working-class youth, the organizers took a soft-sell approach to religion.

"Few of the boys are members of a church. The only feasible arrangement in a movement of this kind is to try and teach the spirit of religion by indirect methods," the club's secretary, Hugh A. Peck, wrote in his 1910 report.

Still, by 1913, few of the popular club's 115 members were Catholics. Suspicious of the influence of Protestant organizers, the priests and Brothers of St. Ann's forbade the children of the parish from attending the club, steering them instead to youth activities in the parish hall.

But St. Ann's pastor, Father George Daly was worried too about the children he had seen wandering around the neighbourhood. "I found that many married women had to go to work, since through illness or desertion of the husband these mothers were obliged to support their families," he recalled much later. "During the absence of the mother, the children were playing in unsanitary backyards or in the streets of the slums."

The priest noticed a vacant lot at the corner of Eleanor and Ottawa streets, and made a deal with the owner, a member of the parish. He then lobbied the Montreal Catholic School Commission to construct a kindergarten building. Next, he had to find a religious community willing to run it. Several orders declined the task. "Is it for the poor?" Mother Mary Julian, Mother General of the Sisters of Providence, asked when Father Daly approached her about the project. When he said yes, she answered, "We will go." In July 1914, four members of the nursing order moved to Griffintown to run the new St. Ann's Kindergarten and Day Nursery.

A few days after their arrival, Fathers McGuiness and Cullinan went to bless the Sisters' convent. But the two priests hesitated to knock on the door of the little yellow cottage on Eleanor Street. This house appeared too small, too humble, even for nuns who had taken the vow of poverty. The priests stood on the sidewalk, wondering if they had the wrong address, until one of the Sisters eyed them from a window and opened the door. When they saw her black habit, one said to the other, "The nuns live here?"

The convent—the nuns called it their "beautiful mansion"—had two rooms and a little kitchen downstairs; upstairs, a dormitory, shared by the four resident nuns, and a "dear little chapel," just big enough for an altar and four prie-dieus.

St. Ann's Kindergarten and Day Nursery, one of the first in the city, opened on July 26, 1914, when the nuns began to care for the children of working mothers. Then, in September, they welcomed 166 pupils for preschool classes. The Sisters of Providence also undertook the care of the poor and the sick in Griffintown. On August 3, within days of their arrival, the nuns made their first home visits. But the needy, aware of their reputation, had already begun to knock on the convent door. One poor, ailing old woman named Margaret asked the nuns to take her in. "Since our works consist in day nursery and visiting the sick and poor, we had to send her away disappointed," the convent's annalist wrote in their journal. Around four o'clock the same day, a panicky woman ran to the sisters and pleaded for help for her dying mother. Finding her in a "sad state," two nuns "fixed her up as best they could and she fell off to sleep."

The Sisters of Providence saw it as their special mission to assist the dying and, in that role, they encountered some of Griffintown's saddest and sometimes eccentric characters. On May 9, 1915, the sisters received an urgent call to the home of a recluse who lived across the street from the convent. The sisters helped soothe the dying old woman, put her to bed and bathed her. A priest came to anoint her and she died the next morning. "The sisters did not remain, as there were many of the women around with her. It was reported she had lots of money, so that was another reason why the sisters did not remain," the annalist wrote.

Father Daly told the nuns that the old woman had willed her money to the church, and he asked the nuns to look for it. "As the house was not very orderly, this was quite a task. It was Sunday so we got a dispensation as the landlord wanted to get in. It was a kind of little store so the sisters got to work. It took them all week with windows and doors

The Sisters of Providence ran a day nursery in their convent (left) and taught classes in the adjacent St. Ann's Kindergarten school on Eleanor Street.

closed and the odor was unbearable. But they found $3,700, thrown here, there and everywhere. In boxes, bags, sewn in an old petticoat. . . . They found boxes and boxes of pennies but had to boil them in peas and soda to get them clean and afterwards soak them in coal oil and rub them separately. We had lots of fun over it but I tell you the sisters who worked there were very tired indeed. Father Daly gave $200 to Sister Superior and the coppers and silver amounted to another $100. It is not every week we make that much."

On May 20, 1915, the nuns moved their residence and the day nursery into an old house adjacent to the kindergarten, purchased by the Providence community. The next day the men came to tear down the "beautiful mansion." Fifty-one-year-old Sister Donald—born Mary O'Brien, in Manchester, New Hampshire—arrived on October 23 and took charge of the new parish clinic, with a waiting room, an examining room and a dispensary, in the kindergarten building. By the end of the year, attending physicians had seen 453 patients, and the nuns had handed out 460 prescriptions.

In 1915, the seven Sisters of Providence made 1,774 visits to the homes of the sick and 1,630 to the homes of the poor, handed out 987 meals and donated $1,866.60 in goods and money to the needy. To raise funds for their charitable works, the nuns followed the example of Mother Gamelin, the saintly Montreal widow who founded their order, and went door to door in the neighbourhood, seeking donations. In August 1915, generous Griffintown residents contributed $400—nearly $10,000 in today's currency—to the poor in their midst, a stunning feat given the record-high unemployment and inflation that were prevalent during the recession from 1913 to 1915.

As the early decades of the twentieth century unfolded, world events— the Great War, a global pandemic, and even Ireland's troubles—would demand even greater sacrifices and new tests of loyalty, not just for the Irish of Griffintown, but for those across the country.

"HOME RULE FOR IRELAND." Newspapers splashed the Irish nationalists' dream come true across their front pages in May 1914. After decades of promises and setbacks, John Redmond, president of Ireland and leader of the Irish Parliamentary Party, announced that Ireland's long-sought independence had become a reality with the passage of his Home Rule Bill, slated to become law after passing a third and final reading in the British House of Commons.

The government had given its consent, but Home Rule still faced a formidable obstacle in Northern Ireland. There, vehement loyalists, backed by the Orange Order, had been gearing up to block the movement, "using all means which may be found necessary." In 1912, after the introduction of the bill, its opponents formed a militia, the Ulster Volunteers (organized a year later into the Ulster Volunteer Force), and began to train their 100,000 members in marching drills and to import rifles from Germany. In 1913, nationalists from the south responded by creating a rival militia, the Irish Volunteers, drawing on the Gaelic

League, the Ancient Order of Hibernians, Sinn Fein and the clandestine Irish Republican Brotherhood for its soldiers. Ireland appeared to be on the brink of civil war.

Meanwhile, the outbreak of the First World War dimmed the hopes for self-government for Ireland. When Britain declared war on Germany on August 4, 1914, Redmond agreed to postpone Home Rule until the end of the conflict. He also stood in the House of Commons and pledged Ireland's support in the war effort.

The Ulster Volunteer Force soon formed its own regiment, the 36th (Ulster) Division, in the New British Army. But Redmond's call to arms for the British caused a split in the Irish Volunteers. Most of the 160,000 members, Redmond supporters, broke away and formed the National Volunteers. As many as 40,000 of these served in the British army during the war, although suspicious officials refused to let them form their own regiment like the Ulster Volunteer Force. But Irish rebels had an old adage: "England's difficulty is Ireland's opportunity." The few thousand remaining Irish Volunteers, now controlled by the radical Irish Republican Brotherhood, plotted a rising while England was preccupied by war.

The news and the rumours out of Ireland created anxiety among the nationalists of Griffintown. Irish expatriates in North America had not only watched the long battle for Home Rule, they had provided moral and financial support to the nationalist cause, channelled through the Ancient Order of Hibernians, the United Irish League and other nationalist groups. The AOH had also offered to help recruit and train men for the Irish Volunteers by forming a branch for members who aspired to "a knowledge of military discipline." One resentful Orangeman from Belfast, quoted in *The New York Times,* blamed Irish Americans for the success of the Home Rule movement, stating, "If we could get rid of Irish Americans and then could banish the priests, we'd settle the whole Home Rule question in a day."

Ireland's crisis became Canada's concern. In August 1914, after Canada followed Britain into the war, the government looked uneasily at the country's Irish Catholics, particularly in Montreal, a one-time bastion of Fenianism, where ties to Ireland had endured. Would they side with Ireland's rebels? The AOH in Canada, run independently of the U.S. organization, did not have a military division, nor did it condone the American order's extreme pro-German stance. (Much to the alarm of the authorities, AOH extremists in the United States had declared their support of Germany in the battle against Britain.) But the influential organization's strong statements in support of Home Rule and the Irish Volunteers were enough to raise doubts at a time of war.

It was a question of loyalty—Irish Catholics' loyalty to the British—that drew hundreds to a mass rally in St. Ann's Hall on September 13, 1914. And Britain received that night in Griffintown, an unprecedented promise of support. "This is a great struggle for the world's freedom. In such a fight could there be any doubt for which side the Irish heart would beat?" declared the Hon. Charles Joseph Doherty, Canada's minister of justice and MP for St. Ann's riding. He called on the audience—members of the city's United Irish League—for "absolute, unqualified and enthusiastic approval of the stand taken by John Redmond as leader of the Irish people, in the crisis that had come upon the world."

Doherty spoke on the stage at St. Ann's Hall—trod by so many fiery Irish patriots—backed by Father Daly, Dr. J.J. Guerin (a former mayor of Montreal) an Irish MPP, two Irish aldermen, and several other distinguished members of the Irish community, in a strong show of solidarity. "I am not apologizing that we take part with our former enemies, but present friends, the people of Great Britain," said Dr. Guerin. "With the Home Rule we are to get, our interests will be entirely bound up with Great Britain."

Never had such words of support for England been spoken in St. Ann's Hall, or cheered with such enthusiasm. The event, the *Gazette*

The Irish Canadian Rangers aimed to demonstrate their commitment to "Britain's War" in this First World War recruitment poster.

reported, "must have astonished the walls of St. Ann's Hall, so long devoted to Home Rule oratory." At the end of the meeting, all stood to sing the Fenian anthem, "God Save Ireland"—and "God Save the King."

Irish Canadians from every province responded to the call of duty. By 1917, nearly four thousand Canadians of Irish descent had enlisted in the Canadian Expeditionary Force, roughly 10 per cent of the total recruitment. Thousands more served in their own ethnic units. In 1915, the Toronto Irish, both Catholics and Protestants, formed the 110th Irish Regiment of Canada, taking the motto "Fior Go Bas" (Faithful Until Death). British Columbia mustered two Irish Canadian units: the Irish Fusiliers of Canada, mostly Ulstermen, and the British Columbia Regiments (Duke of Connaught's Own). The 121st (Western Irish) Battalion, a unit of the Canadian Expeditionary Force, was recruited in New Westminster, B.C.

Both the Toronto 110th Irish Regiment and the 121st (Western Irish) Battalion went overseas in 1916, where members were reassigned to other battalions and used as reinforcements, many of them in Irish units. They suffered a casualty rate of more than 60 per cent, in some of the most brutal battles of the First World War.

Montreal's Irish community also rallied to the cause. In August 1914, the Hon. Charles Doherty, the Rev. Gerald McShane, pastor of St. Patrick's Parish, and ten other Irishmen gathered in the office of lawyer H.J. Trihey to organize an Irish militia, known as the 55th Regiment, the Irish Canadian Rangers. Trihey, the thirty-six-year-old former captain of the Stanley Cup–winning Shamrocks hockey team, took command of the regiment, intended strictly for home defence. Volunteers of Irish descent, Catholic and Protestant, donned uniforms sporting a shamrock on the cap and a harp on the collar, and attended evening drills. On April 24, 1915, more than four hundred men stood ready for inspection by the governor general, HRH the Duke of Connaught, on Fletcher's Field, with a forty-piece band in attendance, as well as a drum and bugle corps and a squad of eight stretcher-bearers.

It was a strong demonstration of Irish fealty, somewhat offset by the AOH and the St. Ann's Young Men's Society's marches in honour of the anniversary of the Manchester Martyrs, an anti-British tradition that had a whiff of treason during a time of war. But as the war progressed and the need for troops in Europe increased, the Montreal Irish stepped up their efforts.

In the spring of 1915, the Irish Rangers 55th Regiment assembled "C Company," also known as the Irish Canadian Company, for the 60th Overseas Battalion of the Canadian Expeditionary Force. Nearly four hundred soldiers of "C Company," including Sergeant-Major Bryant, Quartermaster Sergeant Corbin, Sergeant George Weyman, Walter Hanley and others from Griffintown, sailed for France with the 60th on November 5, 1915, proud to hold the honour of being the first Irish Canadian unit sent to the battlefields of Europe. Hanley, a member of the St. Ann's Young Men's Society, suffered several serious wounds and spent time in a prisoner-of-war camp.

Later that year, the Irish Rangers raised their own overseas battalion, known as the 199th Irish-Canadian Rangers—later renamed the Duchess of Connaught's Own Irish Canadian Rangers—under the command of Lieutenant-Colonel H.J. Trihey. By early 1916, three dozen Irish Canadians—Catholic and Protestant—from the city's business, finance and professional elite had signed up as officers. But the Easter Rising, one of the most pivotal events in the history of modern Ireland, would throw a shadow over the general recruitment slated to begin on May 1.

On Easter Monday, April 24, 1916, militant Irish republicans staged a rebellion in Dublin. Some 1,250 Irish Volunteers and members of the Irish Citizen Army marched through the streets at midday, past puzzled Dubliners, and seized fourteen strategic buildings, bridges and other installations across the city. From a makeshift headquarters at the General Post Office, rebel leaders proclaimed the new Republic of Ireland.

Armed only with rifles, they had gambled that the British, preoccupied by the war in Europe, would pull out of Ireland. But the government called up the troops stationed in the city and sent in four army divisions to crush the uprising. The military surrounded the rebel strongholds and, armed with heavy artillery and supported by a gunboat in the River Liffey, they launched an attack. The ferocious battle lasted several days, culminating in the bombing of central Dublin on Friday, and the killing of one thousand citizens and more than five hundred soldiers. The rebels finally surrendered. Dubliners, most of whom did not support the uprising, jeered and booed as the British marched them off to prison on April 30. But public opinion shifted dramatically a few weeks later, after reports that fifteen rebel leaders had been executed by firing squads after secret military trials. The war of independence had begun.

Back in Montreal, reports of Britain's brutal and continuing suppression of the rebels, martial law and executions after the rebellion disturbed and disillusioned many of the Irish who had previously supported the war. Why fight for the liberty of a foreign nation when Ireland itself remained under British rule?

The Irish Rangers stepped up their lagging campaign. They plastered posters on streetcars, they erected military displays in Dominion Square, and they issued "I helped to serve" buttons to women who delivered a recruit. And prominent Irishmen sounded the call to arms at public meetings, several of them in Griffintown. Three members of St. Ann's Young Men's Society, George and James Kelly and Patrick Cherry, joined the Rangers in 1917 and served in France, where James Kelly earned a Military Medal for bravery. By the end of the war more than two dozen members had signed up, several of them conscripted.

In April 1917, the AOH invited Montreal's Irish organizations to a religious demonstration on the anniversary of the Easter Rising—a bold move, given the times. In a report to the St. Ann's Young Men's Society, the president, W. O'Reilley, paid tribute to "the men who were martyred in Dublin," and to the fight for Irish freedom. "I am sorry to say, gentlemen, that this cause is still left in abeyance and I must say it is [our] most sacred duty . . . to secure for [Ireland] what our forefathers have even laid down their lives for." O'Reilley declared that the parade had been a success, even though it "was not attended by the majority of our members, owing no doubt to some kind of misunderstanding that was worked up on the byways and highways of our parish." Irish nationalism had become a sensitive issue in Griffintown.

The Irish Rangers never mustered a full battalion, but outrage over Britain's brutal treatment of the rebels may not have been the only cause for the lacklustre response. Heavy recruitment by other regiments had already shrunk the pool of eligible recruits. And the Irish must have been in poor shape—many who did volunteer had to be turned away for physical reasons. On Monday, July 31, 1916, the *Gazette* reported that nearly one thousand willing volunteers had been rejected on medical grounds and the Rangers had run out of "I offered to serve" buttons.

Meanwhile, industrial wages were rising in Canada, and other regiments across the country were also having trouble attracting recruits to the low-paying military.

The Rangers also faced the hostility of French Canadians opposed to the war. In one recruitment drive, on August 24, 1916, a fight broke out after French-Canadian opponents heckled the Rangers. One Private Flannigan knocked out a policemen who tried to arrest him during the melee.

On May 18, 1917, the Hon. Charles Doherty, an honorary member of the St. Ann's Young Men's Society and a frequent visitor to Griffintown, stood in the House of Commons and introduced the Military Service Act, one of the most contentious in the history of the country. The conscription bill, which passed on July 24, split the country along linguistic and other lines, with French Canadians in Quebec firmly opposed and English Canada largely in favour. At first, French Canadians had supported the war. The Royal 22nd Regiment—a new French-speaking unit based in Montreal and popularly known as the "Van Doos"—accepted its first recruits barely a month after Canada entered the conflict. But many Quebecers lost, or never had, any enthusiasm for "England's war," while Irish Canadians were apparently divided on the issue.

Conscription became the central issue of the December 17, 1917, election. In Griffintown, it was one of the hardest fought campaigns since D'Arcy McGee's battle for the riding against Fenian forces in 1867. Doherty, the incumbent and architect of the conscription law, faced two Liberal Irish opponents in the St. Ann's riding: Daniel Gallery, a former MP and alderman, and the anti-conscription candidate, Dr. J.J. Guerin, Montreal's last Irish mayor, elected in 1910. "Doherty's an Irish traitor!" became a favourite taunt of hecklers at rowdy political meetings in St. Ann's Ward.

A brawl broke out at the back of St. Ann's Hall during Doherty's speech at a constituency meeting on November 19, 1917. Several disturbers were ejected but returned to the hall and disrupted the meeting with their hollering.

Home Rule for Ireland!

Home Rule for Griffintown!

At one point, the husky Griffintown-born alderman, Thomas O'Connell, chairman of the meeting, went down to the back of the hall, plunged into the middle of a fistfight and broke it up. Another scrap began when one man told another he was not Irish—a serious insult to a second- or third-generation Irishman in Griffintown. "I'm more Irish than any man in this hall," he retorted, before starting a fight that, according to the reporter on the scene, "overturned several rows of chairs and mixed police and opposing factions in an inextricable confusion."

One questioner wanted Doherty to explain why twenty-five thousand soldiers were being kept in Dublin instead of being sent to the front. Doherty had no answer and said he was not responsible for that.

"Well, you want us to take their place," the man shot back.

Nevertheless, Doherty won the election and the traditional Irish riding of St. Ann's became one of only three ridings in the province to vote for conscription. Although the Union government, an emergency coalition formed by Conservative Prime Minister Robert Borden in 1917, had shrewdly enhanced its chance of success by redrawing electoral boundaries across the country. St. Ann's riding was expanded to include Verdun, reducing the Irish to a minority—only eight thousand of the constituency's fifty thousand voters. But a street-by-street breakdown of the polls printed in the *Gazette* the day after the election shows that old St. Ann's—the area bounded by William and Wellington streets and from Duke to McCord—gave more votes to the anti-conscription Irish candidate, J.J. Guerin, than to Doherty.

Conscription in Canada took effect on January 1, 1918. And it was one of several crises that led organizers of Montreal's St. Patrick's Day parade to consider cancelling the annual event. The committee quarrelled bitterly over the propriety of celebrating while so many young men were fighting a war, and Ireland's civil war only added to the unseemliness. But Donald Pidgeon, historian of the United Irish Societies, says there was another reason for the cancellation of the parade—one that does not appear in official minutes—and that was the fear of conscription agents: "Many of the Irish Catholics would not fight for England and they would not attend." The issue was put to a vote and, with strong support from the AOH, the committee decided to hold the parade. But on March 6, after the death of John Redmond, leader of the Irish Parliamentary Party, the committee reconsidered its decision. An official notice subsequently appeared in the *Gazette* stating that, out of respect for Redmond, the parade had been cancelled.

But the AOH and the St. Ann's Young Men's Society decided, on the contrary, that the annual St. Patrick's Day procession should take place as "a mark of respect to the memory of John Redmond." Determined to maintain the continuity of the parade, which had been running in Montreal since 1824, they defied the committee. "The Society decided to hold a parade of their own and on Sunday evening the Society in a body marched to St. Ann's Church where a sermon was preached that was very edifying to us Catholic Irishmen," states the Young Men's Society annual report for 1918. There were no marching bands and many parishes and Irish associations did not participate, nor did they follow the usual uptown route, but on Sunday, March 17, diehard marchers from the Young Men's Society and the AOH donned their top hats and paraded through the streets of Griffintown. As for conscription agents, tradition has it they would dare not set foot in the old Irish stronghold.

SEVEN MONTHS LATER, a lone priest followed by two acolytes walked through Griffintown's deserted streets, his arms raised, holding aloft the sacred host, chanting the Latin benediction, *O Salutaris Hostia*. The faithful knelt piously in doorways along the route, many bearing black mourning crepe. The Spanish flu epidemic had spread across North America and the Montreal health department had ordered all the churches and schools in the city to close for four weeks. Now church bells tolled, as processions of priests set out across the city to bless the houses and people stricken by the disease.

The pandemic took at least 20 million lives, many more than the number lost on the battlefields of Europe, as it swept around the globe between March 1918 and June 1920, even reaching remote Pacific islands and villages on the coast of Labrador. The deadly virus began to roll across Canada in September 1918, likely carried into the country by the movement of troops in the final months of the war. The disease spread from east to west, following servicemen as they boarded trains for cities, towns and farms. By the spring of 1919, it had killed as many as fifty thousand Canadians, taking its worst toll in Quebec with nearly fourteen thousand victims.

Montreal, a major transportation hub, was the hardest hit of any Canadian city. By the end of November, more than three thousand residents had died. In mid-October, at the peak of the outbreak, between one hundred and two hundred people were dying every day. Coffins were piled in rows along the roads near cemeteries. As in many parts of the world, the epidemic led to a shortage of coffins, hearses and undertakers. City officials dealt with the backlog of dead bodies by adapting a trolley car to transport coffins to the cemetery.

Funeral homes were hiring carters to transport victims. A Griffintown carter, James Patrick Feron, opened one of the district's first funeral parlours at 111 McCord Street, after the epidemic. Jack McCurran, a young Irish emigrant, landed in Griffintown just before the outbreak. "My grandfather brought him over from Ireland. He helped out one time, burying them, and he got the flu and died. He was 28," recalled his cousin, Kitty Lynch.

Jack and Mary Taugher, owners of a cigar and candy store at the corner of McCord and Wellington, lost five of their thirteen children in the epidemic. And when the kindergarten reopened on November 12, after an eight-week absence, as many as sixty pupils failed to return. More than half of the flu's victims were healthy adults. Many children were left orphaned and unclaimed by relatives because of their exposure to the flu. The Sisters of Providence took care of several Griffintown children until places were found for them in St. Patrick's Orphan Asylum.

While the flu raged during the autumn and winter of 1918, the priests of St. Ann's answered constant calls to minister to the sick and dying. One of them, Father Francis Corrigan, died in the epidemic. The nuns had closed down the clinic at St. Ann's kindergarten following the instructions of the health authorities. The city set up emergency hospitals. But the nuns and Brothers of the parish all volunteered to care for the sick. The Sisters of Providence turned the kindergarten into a distribution centre for donations of medicine, food, bedding, clothing and money for destitute victims. The nuns, accompanied by volunteer social workers, made 1,654 home visits. They brought meals, changed bedding and washed dishes, caring for 218 sick and standing vigil at thirty-two deaths. Three of the Sisters caught the virus, but survived.

The Griffintown Club also set up a relief station during the flu epidemic. Director Ralph A. Cusack found one family in a state of near starvation after both parents contracted influenza and were unable to care for themselves or their little son. "Many families in this district who were never before in need have been forced to ask for aid. Frequently the wage-earner has been stricken, and loss of wages has resulted in financial disaster," he told the *Montreal Star* on October 30.

The club initiated a number of social services in the postwar years. Saturday morning kindergarten classes began in 1918. And in 1920, volunteers opened a cafeteria in the girls' branch to serve light lunches to the factory girls working in the district, to save them from "loitering about streets and buying inferior food at tuck shops." The club's director and volunteers also began to visit the homes of their members, to assess their family environments and to enlist parents' cooperation. They found many in difficult circumstances.

The Griffintown Club had seen a dropping off in its senior membership during the war years. Thirty-six members enlisted and several others working at munitions factories were unable to attend regularly. In the final months of the war, it closed entirely. But by 1920, the club had more than two hundred members and a long waiting list to join. And, in 1921, the director expressed satisfaction that eighty-two of the 207 who regularly attended the club were in school and the rest were working.

Father James Farrell, a Redemptorist priest who grew up in Griffintown, had gone to the club—off limits to Catholics—only once to play basketball. His father, a railway worker, died in the 1918 flu epidemic, while his mother was pregnant with their sixth child. Like many eight-, nine- and ten-year-old boys in Griffintown, he attended St. Ann's School and worked at part-time jobs. He worked at Mr. Scott's stable on Young Street, sweeping out stalls, fetching water for the horses, carting and other odd jobs.

When he was twelve, Farrell got a job on Gallery's Bakery wagon. He also worked at Pesner's, delivering groceries, sold used sacks to the ragman (for about two cents) and —an adventure for a young boy— hunted for scrap metal. "There was a big, abandoned iron foundry over on Murray Street. We scrounged through the earth there; every once in a while you would come up with a real chunk of metal. A man came by and collected this stuff, he would weigh it, and you might get 20 cents for it," he recalled.

Farrell's mother took in boarders, most of them newly arrived Irish emigrants. Farrell remembered one nervous tenant named Frank in the early 1920s—a time of turmoil in Ireland when many men wanted for murdering soldiers fled the country—who kept telling him and his brothers: "Anybody comes looking for someone with this name—you don't know him, you've never heard of him."

Unrest in Ireland after the Easter Rising in 1916 led to a flurry of emigration. A number of newcomers took up residence in Griffintown, not all of them rebels on the run. Others, like Terry Flanagan's Belfast-born father, who had become tired of political instability, headed for New York City at the end of the war. A sailor like his father before him, Flanagan found work on a Standard Oil ship. On one trip, in 1926, young Flanagan docked in Montreal. There, at a dance in the Catholic Sailors' Club in Old Montreal, often frequented by young people from nearby Griffintown, he met Margaret Corway, his future wife. Marriage had to wait—Margaret's mother had died and she had to care for her five younger siblings. Flanagan refused to return to his troubled, native Ireland.

BUT THE FIRE OF NATIONALISM continued to burn in many Montreal Irish hearts. In 1919, a number of Griffintowners travelled across the border to Ogdensburg to attend a fundraising dinner featuring Éamon de Valera—the mathematics professor turned revolutionary who had led a battalion of Irish Volunteers in the failed Easter Rising. The Sinn Fein leader, born in America to an Irish mother and a Spanish father, had escaped imprisonment in England and spent a year and a half touring the United States, raising more than £1 million for Sinn Fein and the cause of independence in Irish strongholds such as New York, Boston and Chicago. Much of the money went to the Irish Republican Army, formed in January 1919, in the wake of the failed uprising.

Republican sentiments had surged in the early 1920s, as Ireland lurched into civil war and the Black and Tans, the reviled British soldiers sent in to help the Royal Irish Constabulary quell the rebellion, targeted civilians. The St. Ann's Young Men's Society provocatively carried the Sinn Fein flag of the Irish Republic in the 1920 St. Patrick's Day parade. A steady snowfall did not deter nearly ten thousand marchers from participating in the 1921 march, "the biggest ever known in

Montreal," according to the *Star*. The procession ended with a mass at St. Ann's Church, where a special collection was taken up "for those suffering for the cause of liberty." Father Thomas Heffernan preached about "the brutal act of a tyrannical law in Ireland" and asked the overflowing congregation to join in prayer, for "it was by divine intervention the Irish question might be settled." Still, there were cracks forming in Irish unity: the *Star* also noted that de Valera supporters did not participate in the parade "because of difference of opinion over money collected in Canada for the cause."

St. Ann's Young Men never lost their love of dear old Ireland but the dream of Home Rule began to fade by the late 1920s. The civil war ended in 1923 and Ireland was partitioned; Northern Ireland remained part of the United Kingdom, while south gained self-government, as a dominion of the Crown. In 1926, de Valera grudgingly accepted the new Irish Parliament in Dublin, still loosely tied to England.

The Young Men's Society, meanwhile, began to turn its attention to the history of the Irish in Canada. In 1927, it entered a special float in the St. Patrick's Day parade, featuring a reproduction of the Irish settlement of St. Columban established in the Laurentians, north of Montreal, by Father Phelan in 1836.

As war receded, many of the Griffintown Irish started looking to the future for a more comfortable, modern life "over the hill." Montreal was spreading out, and in October 1926 the Farrells moved to Rosemount, then a new suburb north of the city, with fresh air and open spaces. Farrell's mother's health had deteriorated and her doctor blamed the fumes from the Montreal gasworks, just a block from their house on Ottawa Street. So they didn't wait until May 1, the city's traditional moving day. "We did what they call a moonlight—when you didn't bother too much about the year's lease—and just took off," Farrell recalled. "My brother and I hated Rosemont," he said. "There was nothing to do there. In Griffintown, in the big yard, right down the steps at the back of our house on Ottawa Street, you could watch blacksmiths. You could wander around and make your own fun. Griffintown had everything—trains and boats and the canal."

The wealth and ease of the "roaring twenties" skipped by the old neighbourhood, but residents caught the era's buoyant mood and thirst for change as the economy began to pick up in the 1920s. Griffintown had a head start on the illegal liquor trade that attracted flocks of American tourists to Montreal during Prohibition. Illegal stills proliferated in Griffintown during the few years (from 1914 to 1919) that Quebec banned the sale of spirits. Cliff Sowery, director of the boys' club, recalled that after the Mounties raided a large one, set up by rumrunners during the American Prohibition, they "allowed the neighbours to dismantle it and all of Griffintown was drunk for two weeks." But longtime resident Charlie Blickstead remembered one—of many—from an earlier time, built into a fence in a backyard on Ottawa Street, behind a loose board marked by an arrow.

Blickstead left Griffintown, the first time, for adventure. "I said to my friend, Ernie, 'Let's get the hell out of here,'" he recalled, explaining how, in 1923, he set out for New York City on a whim. "I have twenty cents in my pocket. We walk down Smith Street, cross the Victoria Bridge and we're on our way to New York City. In those days, there were very few cars, so we walked." When he returned a few years later, after several odd jobs, including a stint in the circus, he decided he wanted to join the fire department. "My mother got my sister to talk to the parish priest, and he spoke to Alderman O'Connell. A couple of days later, I was on the fire department."

Blickstead lived in Griffintown for a few more years until his family moved up to St. Michael's Parish. But the Blicksteads, like most who left the City Below, kept strong ties to Griffintown. Lena played the organ at St. Ann's Church for nearly forty years. And Charlie wrote long poems immortalizing the colourful neighbourhood of his youth; the gritty cobblestone streets peopled by the likes of Jimmy Rafferty, the peddler who bobbed nervously on his cart, while housewives picked through his produce, wizened and black from standing out in the winter. Hook-the-Hat, the wacky old woman who pulled hats off passersby with her walking stick. Jockey Duggan—so-called because he was tiny—who spent his days at Mooney's store with a bottle of whiskey, and Davie Finn, Pokey Leahy, "Senator" Whelan and dozens more.

> *To survive in Griff, you had to be sturdy,*
> *I remember the Gypsies, the hurdy-gurdy.*
> *And the man with the drum, the one-man band,*
> *The tin-type photographer, on Chaboillez Square,*
> *St. Ann's Young Men, and the annual Fair.*

In 1920, at the age of thirty-five, artist Emily Coonan sailed to Europe on a National Gallery of Canada travelling scholarship, the first ever awarded. (She won it in 1913, but postponed the trip because of the war.) By the 1920s, she had gained considerable acclaim for her painterly, impressionistic portraits, landscapes and interior scenes. In 1924, her *Girl in Dotted Dress* was chosen for the British Empire Exhibition. In 1925, the National Gallery in Ottawa purchased *San Frediano Gate, Florence,* one of three of her works in their collection. Coonan's paintings appeared in exhibits with the Group of Seven, and she shared a studio with the celebrated Beaver Hall Hill Group. But she never moved out of the City Below the Hill.

Yet even the Redemptorists considered abandoning Griffintown in the 1920s for a parish in the Town of Mount Royal, a new upscale suburb on the other side of the mountain. Industry and the railways were threatening to encroach on Griffintown's residential areas, but St. Ann's pastor, Rev. Arthur Coughlan, decided against a move. "Attendance at the services is quite large [over 4,000] so that it seems to me it will take many years for the parish to be practically wiped out, as some predict will happen," Coughlan wrote, in a letter quoted in *Redemption and Renewal,* Paul Laverdure's history of the Redemptorists in Canada. "The parishioners are mostly of the poorer classes. The Redemptorists should work with them, as St. Alphonsus would want."

And, as it turns out, the seminarians at the Redemptorist monastery at St. Ann's enjoyed living in Griffintown, too. As Laverdure notes, "The many outings, the poetry, the oratory, the meetings with parishioners, the escapades from the upper windows of St. Ann's, the clandestine smoking, and the punishments and expulsions of the unruly ringleaders all became part of [its] oral history. . . . Experiences [that] helped lighten the intensive spiritual training."

A Twentieth-Century Urban Village

Oh, take me back to Griffintown,
Griffintown, Griffintown.
Oh, take me back to Griffintown,
That's where I long to be
Where my friends are good to me.

SISTER DONALD WOKE TO THE SOUND of shattering glass around midnight on Saturday, June 11, 1932. The short, plump, sixty-eight-year-old nun slept in the dispensary, a little cottage in the yard behind the Sisters of Providence convent on Eleanor Street. Loud squawks followed the tinkling glass and confirmed Sister Donald's suspicions: thieves had broken into the nuns' chicken house. She rushed out into the yard to confront them. One had already fled; the other was scaling the fence, attempting to escape. But two neighbours, responding to Sister Donald's cry for help, caught him and held him until the police arrived.

It was a minor misdemeanour: two chickens killed, one wounded. And the crime occurred in the depths of the Great Depression when more than one-quarter of Canadians had lost their jobs, a dismal number that went as high as one-third in Montreal. Still, the judge showed no mercy. It was the youth's third offence, so he sentenced him to six months of hard labour. "Poor boy! Would that his severe punishment make him understand at last the dangers of the path he has taken," Sister Florine, the superior, reflected in the convent's annals.

The Sisters of Providence had done their best to feed the hungry. In 1930, the nuns living in the small Griffintown convent served 15,251 meals and distributed $355.69, in cash and goods, to the unemployed who knocked on their door. In the first six months of 1931, they handed out thirty-three thousand meals. "Every morning these poor people gather at our door to receive a lunch," Sister Florine wrote in the annals on June 29, 1931. "We prepare the packages the night before: for each, two slices of bread and jam and two others with meat or butter for Fridays. Little by little, the number of needy has risen to around 350 and we have even had to call on the aid of the police to maintain order." But by the end of June 1931, the nuns, who funded their charitable works through their small teachers' salaries and donations, had nothing left to give.

The church, not the government, had always served as the traditional safety net of the poor in Quebec. Religious orders and parish and lay organizations, such as the St. Vincent de Paul Society, had fed and clothed and housed the needy. But the Great Depression exhausted most of their resources. As the crisis persisted, the kind-hearted nuns, like many religious communities, had to turn away the ever-increasing numbers of destitute lining up at convents and presbyteries across the province, begging for a handout.

The stock market crash of 1929 had set off a spiral of misery, hurling suffering in uneven measures across the country. On the Prairies, farmers went bankrupt as the price of wheat plummeted below the cost of seed; some managed to hold on to their once fertile fields only to watch them wither in a decade-long drought. Forced off the land, thousands flocked to the cities in search of work.

Large cities suffered, as factories and businesses adjusted to the economic collapse by laying off workers and slashing wages and hours. And Montreal, the city with the country's largest workforce, suffered the worst unemployment. Tens of thousands rode the rails to the barely beating industrial heart of Canada. Armies of unemployed, many of them transients, stalked the streets looking for jobs.

Politicians faced increasing pressure to act as the crisis deepened. In June 1930, Parliament passed the Unemployment Relief Act, intended to provide wages—not welfare—to the growing army of unemployed by subsidizing public works initiated by the provinces and municipalities. In Montreal, thousands of labourers were hired to construct landmarks such as the Chalet on Mount Royal, as well as more utilitarian projects like viaducts, public baths and toilets. The latter were dubbed "Camilliennes" in honour of soft-hearted Mayor Camillien Houde, who spent $40 million on public works during the 1930s. Houde once said that he wept when he thought of the "poor labourer who has not work, shelter or food."

Griffintown got its own Camillienne—an elegant art deco–style public restroom—in Gallery Square Park, at the entrance to the new Wellington Tunnel dug under the Lachine Canal. The tunnel, another Depression-era make-work project, replaced the old Wellington Street Bridge. It created hundreds of jobs, though many of the workers came from outside the district. And the tunnel, some say, marked the beginning of the end of Griffintown, since hundreds of residents were forced out of their homes when the city expropriated several blocks of houses and a large tract of land in front of St. Ann's Church to build it. Hundreds more would be displaced in 1938 when the CNR constructed an elevated railway track through Griffintown, linking the new Central Station (completed in 1943) with the Victoria Bridge, eradicating entire streets and numerous houses and industries in its path.

But by 1932, many provinces and municipalities could no longer afford to pay their share of public works. In debt-ridden Montreal,

Houde's political opponents attacked his extravagance and he lost the mayoralty in the April 4, 1932, election. Voters also turfed two dozen "Houdite" aldermen. But Griffintown voters stood steadfastly behind Thomas O'Connell, one of the mayor's supporters and their lone voice in a city council dominated by French Canadians, and re-elected him for the thirteenth consecutive time. In fact, O'Connell—responsible for the tunnel project—was all but acclaimed at his nomination meeting a month earlier. Hundreds of supporters jammed St. Ann's Hall, singing "When Irish Eyes Are Smiling" and cheering "Erin Go Bragh!" as they presented him with a petition with three thousand signatures, encouraging him to stand for office.

The popular Conservative politician had represented the district since 1906, winning seven elections by acclamation. A member of the St. Ann's Young Men's Society and one-time field captain on the Shamrock lacrosse team, the local plumbing contractor also enjoyed the support of the clergy, who at voting time would remind parishioners that "hell was red and heaven was blue." He also counted Dr. Conroy, a Griffintown physician, among his most vocal advocates. Father Tom McEntee, O'Connell's nephew, recalled how the doctor made a house call to him during the campaign. After treating the young boy, Conroy stepped onto the balcony at the corner of Ottawa and Murray streets to harangue passersby with one of the alderman's famous slogans—warning them that if they failed to vote for O'Connell they would be eating snowballs that winter. And on the night of the election, after Dr. Conroy delivered Betty and Buster Broden's second son, they took his advice and named their baby Thomas Connell Broden.

In 1932, with most provinces and municipalities unable to afford more public works for the unemployed, the federal government reluctantly introduced a new Relief Act. The federal, provincial and municipal governments would share the cost of welfare, but the municipalities would dispense the aid. By 1933, close to 1.5 million Canadians, or roughly 15 per cent of the population, were receiving government relief.

The amount of assistance and how it was delivered varied considerably across the country, as each municipality grappled with an unprecedented rush of desperate citizens.

The Quebec government decided, at first, to distribute relief to the poor, as it had in the past, through religious and lay charitable organizations, such as the St. Vincent de Paul Society. (The new funding enabled the Sisters of Providence to resume their distribution of food to the needy. In 1932 the nuns handed out 28,315 meals to the hungry.) But the sheer numbers of unemployed in the Depression proved too much for those traditional channels. In 1933, the government decided to assist the needy directly. By February 1934, more than a quarter of a million people—28 per cent of the population of Montreal—were living on public assistance.

Unemployed workers faced an intensive investigation, including a home visit, to establish that they were indeed destitute. Assistance rarely took the form of cash. Most often, the city handed out vouchers for food and other essential items, and paid rent, gas and electricity bills directly. Relief payments invariably failed to provide a decent standard of living. In 1933, Montreal relief agents allocated $21.88 a month for food for a family of five, at a time when the Canadian Welfare Council calculated that a balanced diet would have cost $35.17. And the relief proved to be short-lived. In 1936, Quebec decided to discontinue welfare and return to a work-for-relief system after the federal government reduced its share by 25 per cent. And the deprivation increased as the economy continued its freefall.

Still, those Griffintown families fortunate enough to keep their jobs lived comfortably enough in the Depression. Deflation lowered the cost of living by as much as 25 per cent, compensating somewhat for wage cuts and reduced hours. The price of bread fell to five cents a loaf, hamburger to ten cents a pound. These prices were, however, small consolation to the large number of unemployed or to the carters, longshoremen and other low-wage and seasonal workers living in the district. In Montreal, labourers faced a discouraging 60 per cent unemployment rate during the Depression, as construction nearly came to a halt and activity at the port and on the railways declined.

Frank Higgins ran the municipal corporation's yard on Murray Street, hiring day labourers to shovel snow, sweep streets and tackle construction projects in the summer. "Big Frankie," a blustering bully of a man, took his job seriously, driving around Griffintown on Sundays to make sure the streets were clean and berating the sweeper who had missed a piece of litter.

A phone was a luxury, but Paddy Boyle's father, a city labourer, installed one to make sure he didn't miss a call from Higgins. Then he would send a note to the rest of the crew who didn't have phones. Young Paddy would be sent on the errand: "Bring this over to Mr. Cartwright. Tell him we got a hole to dig tomorrow."

Trucks had not yet replaced horses on the streets of Montreal, and right through the Depression many Irishmen sought employment as carters. "The only people who had food them days was people that owned horses," recalled Leo Leonard, owner of the Griffintown Horse Palace. "They'd get calls to go to work at 2:00 and 3:00 in the morning."

Frank Hanley kept two horses in a stable and earned his living as a carter. At the best of times, carters—and they were numerous in Griffintown—earned an adequate, if erratic, living. In the thirties, Hanley (who was the cousin of a prominent local politician of the same name) took odd jobs as he found them, with grocery stores, coal companies and other businesses that managed to stay afloat in that decade. Sears, the butcher, paid him six dollars a week to make deliveries; he also hauled wood and coal for Tougas. His son John loved to accompany his father on his rounds. One wintry day in 1934, the five-year-old hopped into the wagon and sat on top of the cargo, his father and uncle chuckling as the horses clip-clopped through Griffintown.

Some twenty minutes later, the horses slowed down. Young John looked up, shocked to see where his father had stopped. "The name on the gate said P&H Feron," he recalled. "Somebody had died on a ship and the Hanley brothers were transporting him to Patrick and Hank Feron—undertakers. I see them taking the body out. 'What was I sittin' on?' I ask. The poor man, I was sittin' on his head. I ran home and I cried for a week. I thought he was coming after me."

During the Depression, Frank Hanley found only sporadic employment. Forced onto relief, he had to feed his large family on eleven dollars a week. "Our rent was $10 a month, so you got one [dollar]," his son John recalled. "My mother would make us porridge and molasses, molasses and bread. We didn't know what steaks were. My grandmother had six or seven boarders. They paid her and she'd give us stuff to eat. In the winter, if a window got broken, it'd get patched with cardboard."

Many in Griffintown slid further down the economic ladder. Though Henry O'Toole—a ten-year-old when the stock market collapsed in 1929—did not steal the nuns' chickens, "I used to rob vegetables and coal," the Second World War veteran admitted years later. His family struggled even before the economy collapsed. O'Toole's father, a bartender, had to support seven children on eighteen dollars a month—at a time when the Canadian Welfare Council set the poverty level at $1,040 a year. "There was no relief. Bread and molasses was a good meal," he recalled. For a time, the family lived in a three-room flat on Murray Street, though they did not stay long in Griffintown, or in any one place, often moving on when rent came due. Every month was moving month for the O'Tooles.

The other Frank Hanley was twenty years old when the stock market crashed. He survived by standing in breadlines and collecting relief by working for the municipal corporation, shovelling sidewalks and other manual labour, for eight cents an hour. It was while he was working as a maintenance worker at Griffintown's Basin Street Park that he won his first battle with city hall and got a taste for politics. The city had decided to close one of the two rinks. Hanley decided to embarrass the politicians. He gathered several dozen raggedy children and invited the

Gazette to take pictures of them skating on the canal. Red-faced councillors decided to keep the rink open. Ten years later, Hanley would launch a thirty-year career as an alderman and MLA for St. Ann's Ward.

Frank Hanley was born in Griffintown on April 5, 1909, the first of Bella and John Hanley's four children. A five-foot-four-inch leprechaun of a man, with a roguish grin and a witty tongue, he cultivated the image of a stereotypical fighting, drinking, stage Irishman. "My father worked at Dow Brewery," he said in an interview, typically offering up mischievous details: "He was a checker, so he used to hand out a coupla cases extra. We stole a lot of beer from Dow Brewery, the Hanleys." His parents ran a candy store on Young Street. They also worked as caretakers at St. Ann's Kindergarten.

With characteristic hyperbole, Hanley described Griffintown as "a place that was all fun and no work. Nobody worked. Everybody played at that time—and stole." Three generations of Hanleys lived in one big house on Ottawa Street. "The coal docks were right on Ottawa Street. The man in charge would overload the truck and we used to jump on the back and throw the coal off and the women would come out with their buckets and pick the coal up and take it into the house."

Hanley claimed that the Christian Brothers "evicted" him from St. Ann's Boys' School at a very early age. "I hated school. I started a lot of trouble. Every hour in school I used to ask to go see my father at his candy store right near St. Ann's School. The Brother got fed up and said, 'Go stay with your father.'" In another telling, Hanley said that the Brothers punished him after he skipped school on St. Patrick's Day and, without asking their permission, rode his pony in the parade instead of walking with his class.

The versatile Hanley took up boxing and held the city and provincial flyweight titles from 1921 until 1924. He also played the banjo and performed a soft-shoe routine in a minstrel show at a Peel Street theatre. "Oh, I was a dancer. I had my patent leather tap shoes and my bandy legs." He earned ten cents a dance—and the nickname "Banjo."

Before he entered politics, Frank Hanley did a stint in a minstrel show at a Peel Street theatre. He earned ten cents a dance and the nickname "Banjo" for his soft-shoe routine.

He also worked for a blacksmith, returning freshly shod horses to their owners. A heap of blarney led to a five-year stint in the United States as a stable groom and eventually as a jockey on the major North American circuit. "I'm just back from Meadowlands," the fast-talking, eighty-pound Hanley told a horse-trainer he met at a Montreal race-track. "The one who gives me the best offer, I'll work for."

Hanley left for Maryland and rode in five states, and in Cuba, before returning to Montreal in 1930, when he got too heavy to work as a jockey—and because: "One day they asked me to leave. You know why? I fixed a race. Poor suckers like Mrs. Moriarty upstairs betting her money and the race was fixed. We had a lot of fun fixing races. The price was very low then. We got $2 a winner."

Nobody typified the unconventional nature of Griffintown more than Frank "Banjo" Hanley. But Griffintown residents' spirit set them apart—and not just during the Depression.

St. Ann's Church remained at the heart of the urban Irish village of Griffintown. And the priests stood at the top of the hierarchy. The Redemptorists held sway from the pulpit with their dramatic sermons. Like Ireland's *soggarth aroons,* they touched all aspects of life: counselling parishioners on matters spiritual and financial, dragging drunken husbands out of bars, and, in one rare instance, buying a bicycle for a poor boy whose father had just died.

The Redemptorists provided what assistance they could, but rumours of quiet desperation persisted. The destitute were burning their shutters and inside doors to stay warm. Children were walking miles to the market, scouring the ground for a cabbage leaf, a carrot or a potato that might have fallen from a vendor's cart. One hard-up father couldn't afford twenty-five dollars for a coffin for his three-year-old, so staff and members stayed up late and built one in the Griffintown Club woodworking shop.

Griffintown needed hope. Father Bartley, St. Ann's rector, encouraged his parishioners to turn to Our Mother of Perpetual Help. The Irish had faith in the Mother of God. They knew she had worked a miracle at St. Patrick's, a Redemptorist parish in Quebec City, many years earlier. On May 30, 1876, when a fire swept through their poor Lower Town neighbourhood, hundreds of Catholics held a picture of Our Mother of Perpetual Help up to the approaching flames. More than a thousand homes were destroyed, but those shielded by Mary remained untouched.

On Tuesday, September 29, 1931, hundreds of faithful filled St. Ann's Church for a special devotion to the Virgin, with prayers and hymns and a veneration of the sacred picture. Father Bartley held up the icon and encouraged the troubled souls of St. Ann's to entrust their sorrows to the sad-eyed Madonna. Their urgent prayers filled the church, hundreds of worried, desperate voices breathing a collective prayer to Our Mother of Perpetual Help. Then, with a call for silence, the priest allowed a few minutes for private intentions. Heads bowed, the people of St.

Ann's found expression for their despair, the hope of a miracle and, perhaps, the blessing of peace.

The faithful returned to St. Ann's Tuesday after Tuesday to pour their hearts out to Our Mother of Perpetual Help. Griffintown neighbours knelt side by side in church, seemingly lost in their own problems, but aware of the troubles of the person in the next pew: the father of seven standing hunched at the back of the church, who had lost his job; the widow seven months pregnant, left penniless when her husband suddenly died; the young mother struggling to raise her two children in a small flat down near the canal, on her meagre pay as a counter girl at the cafeteria in the Queen's Hotel. While they waited for God to work miracles, they helped each other.

Everybody scrimped. Most knew, and used, all of the well-worn tactics of the poor to survive the Dirty Thirties. Newspaper served as toilet paper. Cardboard slipped into a shoe could stop the rain from coming through a hole. Meters could be jacked to cut down the electricity bill. A bureau drawer made a fine baby's cradle. Children stood on the sawdust-strewn floors at Pesner's meat counter and, following their mother's instructions, asked the butcher for a bone "to feed the dog." Mothers sent children to ask about day-old bread at the bakery. Women took in laundry and made room for boarders. Families shared their homes, and children went to work. Children snacked on bread with mustard or ketchup.

"We were very poor, but we didn't know it because everybody else was the same," recalled Iris Howden, a child in the Depression. "We always had food on the table, a roof over our heads." Be thankful for what you have, mothers would tell their children. Many Famine survivors had told their children and grandchildren no stories of starvation, or of the horrors at Grosse Isle. Now, decades later, hunger still remained unmentionable.

But it was hard to fool the neighbours in close-knit Griffintown. On some blocks, as many as twenty flats overlooked the same backyard.

People didn't lock their doors. "People would chase us and we'd run through a house," said Tommy Fitzgerald, recalling his boyhood days. "They could be having lunch and somebody would whiz by and nobody would blink."

Families shared layers of interconnecting galleries and staircases, and the ups and downs of life. In a rare suicide attempt, Mr. M., a widower with two young daughters, climbed onto the roof of the shed in the yard behind his house on Ottawa Street. He stood on a kitchen chair and shouted out to the neighbours sitting on their galleries: "I'm going to hang myself."

"You made sure all the neighbours had something to eat," Iris Howden recalled. "My mother would make a stew that could feed an army. She'd bring supper down to the family with six kids. Somebody else would bring lunch." Her father, Arthur Howden, luckily worked right through the Depression, delivering kegs of beer for the Black Horse Brewery on a wagon hauled by one of the company's trademark stallions. But his steady wages had to feed his twelve children.

The Howden girls each had one tunic, one white blouse, and one set of underwear and brown stockings. "They were washed every night and you wore them the next day. My mother used to put newspaper on the table, for a tablecloth. We used to read it while we were eating. We didn't have blankets. My mother put overcoats on us in bed," said Iris. "But she fed a family down the road who had nothing."

Hard times, however, did not dampen a sense of occasion. One Irish housewife on Murray Street was known to buy a roll of bologna and invite the neighbours for Sunday dinner, Frank Dougherty recalled. She would make a tub of mashed potatoes and slice the bologna like a pot roast. To accommodate her children—twelve sons—she tore down an archway between two rooms and filled the long space with a row of beds, no space between them. The boys slept head to toe.

"Everybody was poor, but some were poorer than the rest," remembered Woppy Kelly. Nothing marked the difference more than clothes.

The well-to-do employed dressed fashionably; some comfortably off women owned a fur coat. White-collar workers wore respectable suits, occasionally second-hand, taken in here and there by a resourceful wife or mother. One CPR employee from Griffintown got along with one pair of shoes, one suit, a white shirt and a tie. Many people relied on the salesmen from St. Lawrence Boulevard who went door to door selling clothes and dry goods on credit. At the end of every month, the salesmen returned to collect a small payment. As Gerry Harkin, a widow's son, who grew up in Griffintown during the Depression with seven siblings, said, "They got the money when you paid them."

Redpath Sugar's large cotton sacks, emblazoned with the company slogans, were cut up and used for dish towels, pillowcases—even homemade underwear. Bleach would eventually fade the bright red lettering, although one pair of bloomers danced on a clothesline on McCord Street, the word "sweet" intact long enough to cause talk in the neighbourhood.

"First up, best dressed" was more than an old Irish saying. In large families, siblings would hide their clothes from each other. The poorest children went to school in torn clothes, or stayed home because their parents could not afford to buy them shoes or warm jackets. But even those who owned little more than the clothes on their backs struggled to keep them clean. If not, they faced merciless teasing, like the four young brothers from one hapless family on Eleanor Street, nicknamed Rinso, Oxydol, Lux and Tide.

But then, most everybody in the neighbourhood had a nickname: Tweet Brennan and Windy Reid, Bunny Kehoe, Rob-the-Plank Kelly and Ha-Ha Murphy, who punctuated every conversation with loud gales of laughter, even at funerals. Nellie Howden, the "Queen of Griffintown," a rough old woman with a heart of gold and a penchant for swearing and drinking. And Johnny Fish: "What's the weather, Johnny?" children would ask respectfully, as he strode through Griffintown in the 1940s and '50s. Johnny Fish's real name was John O'Hearn. But, spoken with a thick Irish brogue, O'Hearn sounds like "a herrin'," so naturally everyone called him Johnny Fish.

Many an argument broke out when landlords came calling. In the 1930s, the Shea family owned a block of houses on Ottawa Street. Rents were low for their gaslit flats, though they sometimes inadvertently tried to collect it twice. One Shea brother would come calling on the first of the month, collect the money, then head to a tavern. Another brother, noticing that the rent hadn't been deposited in the family's account, would knock on the door more aggressively, demanding payment.

Many landlords took pity on their poor tenants. After her husband died, Mrs. Dougherty could no longer afford the rent on her large two-storey flat on Murray Street. The owner sympathized with the young widow, mother of an eleven-year-old son and pregnant with twins, and he reduced her rent to fifteen dollars a month. But he also blocked off a doorway and installed a kitchen upstairs, creating a second flat and cutting her space in half.

Children scavenged the neighbourhood for firewood, rummaging behind factories and warehouses for discarded crates, carting home bits of wood and cardboard to grateful parents. Frank Doyle walked the railway tracks, hunting for the bits of coal that fell from fast-moving trains. Sometimes a sympathetic crewman would throw a shovelful onto the ground at the boy's feet. Frank Marino, an employee at a coal yard on Bridge Street, loaded his pockets at the end of each workday, bringing the small pile of briquettes to a needy widow with seven young children. Little Tommy Fitzgerald and his friends used to go to the same the coal yard. They took turns climbing through a hole in the fence and passing coal out to the boys on the sidewalk, who put it on their coasters. Parents relied on the pennies their children earned on paper routes, running errands and collecting bottles. Young boys and girls would line up outside Pesner's and offer to take customers' groceries home on a coaster.

Griffintown offered adventure, too, to daring lads. A dip in the Lachine Canal was a rite of passage. Most boys, and a few girls, ignored warnings from parents and police and made clandestine trips to "Griffintown Beach," where they swam in the murky, oily waterway that snaked behind the factories and warehouses. The truly daring dove off the top of Black's Bridge, a railway overpass.

Many children dropped out of school as early as grade three. Eight-, ten-, and twelve-year-olds worked full-time, six days a week, in the railways, factories and other companies as messengers, bookkeepers, or guard boys. Kitty Lynch quit school early to work on an assembly line at MacDonald's, shredding hot tobacco: "The first job was terrible. But then I got on to the cigarettes—that was all right. But you worked Saturdays—all for seven dollars a week."

But at the end of a hard week's work, the Irish would lose themselves in music. On Saturday nights, neighbours could count on a singsong at the Doyles on Ottawa Street. Kitty Lynch from across the street, or maybe Leo Durocher, would play piano, while Jimmy McArthur crooned "Pal o' Mine" and Eddie O'Brien rendered a hammed-up "Julia Donohue." Everyone joined in for "Oh, Take Me Back to Griffintown," an anonymous adaptation of a traditional song popular in Irish emigrant communities. (Old-timers in the Miramichi remember another version, "Oh, Take Me Back to Bartibogue," about an early Irish settlement in New Brunswick.) One memorable night, so many neighbours gathered for a singsong at Kitty Lynch's parents' house on Young Street that some of the men decided to lift her mother's piano out the window of the main floor flat and onto the street so everyone could join in.

On fine summer evenings, all of Griffintown spilled out onto the sidewalks. Families would gather at their front door—if they had one— to chat with neighbours and passersby. Kids squeezed three or four on the narrow stoop; kitchen chairs were pulled onto the sidewalks; grannies rocked on rockers. Now and then, an old man might take an occasional swig from a beer bottle tucked discreetly into a paper bag between his feet. The housebound hung out the windows, arms propped on cushions, craning their necks to catch the action on the street, now and then shouting remarks to a passerby below or to another head sticking out a third-storey window halfway down the block.

It was not unusual to hear a little harmonizing on the corner, maybe a mouth organ. One corner quartet called themselves the Bunkhouse Boys and took their act to nightclubs. On Dalhousie Street, bits of "Danny Boy" and Tin Pan Alley tunes would float through Mrs. Flanagan's open windows. In the distance, a shout, a police siren or the racket of railway workers shunting boxcars on the tracks down by the canal filled the air.

"You couldn't sleep because it was so hot so you'd be out till all hours sitting on the steps," recalled Betty Bryant. Harold Galley and his pals would sit on the doorstep on Ottawa Street, near Eleanor, telling stories and singing songs until one or two in the morning. Or until Mrs. Keily, who lived upstairs, opened her shutters and threw a bucket of water on them.

The Griffintown Irish always had their pride. "They wouldn't take charity," Cliff Sowery, director of the Griffintown Club, told a news reporter many years later. "I was good at collecting clothes from places like Westmount and NDG [Notre-Dame-de-Grace]. I'd have a room full of stuff and spot a man walking in the winter with no coat on or with cardboard in his shoes. I'd have to tell him, 'Look, I got to get rid of all this stuff and you'd be helping me if you would take some of it away.'"

In February 1930, the Griffintown Club opened a brand new four-storey building on Shannon Street. Sir Edward Beatty, chairman of the CPR and the club's honorary patron, officiated at its opening on Monday, February 24. The Welfare Federation funded the club and provided a free dental clinic, as well as baby and prenatal clinics, on the premises. During the Depression, volunteers cooked and served meals to 250 needy children every day.

Twenty years after its founding, St. Ann's priests, brothers and nuns—suspicious of any Protestant influence—still forbade Catholic children from attending the popular Griffintown Club. In the early 1930s, Mary O'Connell, a grade four student at St. Ann's, was sent to the parish priest for punishment after her teacher learned she had visited the "Protestant" club. Father Joseph O'Hara meted out the usual penalty: Mary was expelled from school for a few days, and she had to promise never to go back to the club. But after listening to complaints from a number of parents, Father O'Hara—an Irish-born priest, new to the parish—decided to visit the club. He then relented and told the Brothers to let the children go if they wanted to.

By 1938, membership had increased to more than sixteen hundred, many of them Catholic. At seven o'clock, when the club opened for the evening, dozens of kids would be lined up at the door, waiting to get in to play pool, ping-pong, darts or badminton. Many unemployed boys spent hours in the club's workshop, equipped with parts and tools and books, making balsa-wood model airplanes. Cliff Sowery taught them how to build crystal radios and one- and two-tube battery sets. Friday night movies in the gym cost a nickel. Some kids covered their pennies in tinfoil but no one was turned away. After the movie, the band would set up for a dance for the older crowd. Sowery played the accordion in the Griffintown Orchestra, a group that included, at different times, two saxophones, a violin, a piano and drums.

BOXING HAD ALWAYS BEEN one of the Griffintown Club's main attractions. The sport's popularity soared after six Canadian boxers came home from the 1920 Olympic Games in Antwerp, Belgium, with five medals—one gold, two silver and two bronze. The manly art had acquired an aura of glamour in the years leading up to the Depression. Jack Dempsey, heavyweight champion of the world from 1919 to 1926— and a sometime ditchdigger of Irish ancestry—had found fame and fortune in the ring. The beloved slugger inspired working-class lads across North America, perhaps none more than the boys of Griffintown.

Griffintown lads took the sport seriously, training faithfully, often running miles at a stretch. The club's ambitious young fighters won numerous city, provincial and national amateur championships in the 1920s: Stanley Knight, the smart, courageous young fighter from Griffintown, winner of the 100-pound championship of Montreal, who died of appendicitis in November 11, 1933, at the age of nineteen; Tony Mancini, the dark-haired little scrapper from Goose Village, who represented Canada in the 1932 Olympics at Los Angeles, and won the provincial welterweight championship for the second time in 1933 and the Canadian welterweight title.

Cliff Sowery had dreams of his own when he headed to the Griffintown Club in 1929 to train with the resident boxing coach, Dr. Gibson Craig, an intercollegiate welterweight champ. Like the other aspiring boxers slamming their fists into the club's punching bags, Sowery, then a twenty-three-year-old factory hand, planned to fight his way out of the working class. Born in England, he came to Canada in 1912 at the age of six, when his widowed mother gathered up her seven sons and two daughters, and emigrated from Wareham, a picturesque coastal town in Dorset, to Saint John. The family moved again, this time to Montreal, and by 1921 the Sowerys were living in a flat on Rozel Street, in Point St. Charles. A restless, rebellious youth, Sowery first ran away from home at eleven, then a dozen more times, once making his way out west, where he worked as a cowpuncher. Another time he went to sea on a merchant ship. At home, the sports-loving Sowery played lacrosse, hockey and baseball. And when he went to work as a mail boy for Belding Corticelli, a thread manufacturer, he played goalie on the company soccer team. At sixteen, the five-foot-eleven, 160-pound middleweight found his niche when he tried boxing, starting out with Jimmy Gill, a trainer on Charlevoix Street.

He later switched to the Griffintown Club to prepare for a pro bout at the Montreal Forum. But Sowery let his ambitions slide after he witnessed the drive of the local fighters. "I saw so many kids with guts and determination in the gym there, but with no polish, I started training 'em and forgot about my own career," he told veteran sportswriter Tim Burke years later. Sowery volunteered as boxing coach at the club, while working at Northern Electric. When he lost his factory job at the beginning of the Depression, the club hired him as a boxing instructor.

In 1930, Sowery signed up for a five-year stint with the U.S. Marines. He proved to be a promising amateur boxer in the service, before returning to the Griffintown Club as physical director. Later as executive director, the devoted Sowery took on many roles—father figure, counsellor, social worker. But perhaps none so brilliantly as boxing instructor, the role that would win him a place in Canada's Boxing Hall of Fame.

Joe "Kid" Coughlin, one of the toughest fighters to come out of Griffintown, made a late but stunning debut under Sowery's tutelage. He entered his first tournament in his late teens and won five straight fights in the city's novice championship—knocking out all five opponents in the 122-pound division. The rugged Irish slugger moved awkwardly in the ring. Coughlin simply tore into his opponents with an unrelenting barrage of smashing punches.

Nothing stopped the fearless boxer—dubbed "Griffintown's Fighting Fool" and "Comeback Joe" by Montreal sportswriters. More than once, Coughlin went down on a count only to pick himself up off the canvas and knock out his opponent. The hard-as-nails boxer ignored injuries. "He had a tooth knocked out. Do you know how he got it fixed?" his sister Annie Wilson recalled. "He got a piece of ivory out of the Griffintown Club piano and fixed it himself. You'd never know the difference."

Sportswriters would call it the funniest boxing match in the history of Montreal, but Griffintown's Joe Coughlin looked deadly serious as he stood in his corner, waiting for the gong. The square-jawed slugger had knocked out one local hero; now he wanted to wipe the grin off Johnny Pope's face.

Pope, Montreal's lightweight champion, nicknamed the "Clouting Clown," came out punching—and joking. The veteran boxer talked as fast as he fought and soon had the crowd rollicking with laughter. The turning point came in the fourth round. Pope put out his right hand, feigning a handshake. Coughlin fell for the trick. He reached out to his rival, who quickly delivered a left hook and a powerful smashing right to the head that sent Coughlin sprawling across the canvas. The Griffintown up-and-comer went down to a count of six. Incensed by Pope's trickery, he sprang back in the final round. But despite what one sportswriter described as "a whirlwind of fighting," Coughlin lost that match in November 1934.

Four months later, six hundred fans turned out to watch Coughlin seek revenge against Pope in a five-round rematch in St. Zotique Parish Hall. This time, Coughlin stayed alert for Johnny the Clown's tricks. An exuberant Pope took the first round with long swinging blows. The next three rounds went to Coughlin. Pope, close to defeat, rushed back in the final round with a powerful uppercut that broke three of Coughlin's lower teeth. "Joe recuperated quickly and at the end of the round was once more driving Pope back with stiff jabs," wrote a sports scribe.

Coughlin's wide, mangled grin at the end of the match showed his satisfaction at beating his rival. Blood poured out of Pope's mouth and nose but, one newspaper reported, "As is his happy way, he smiled through the gore and congratulated his rival heartily."

Coughlin won the Montreal City Amateur Championship in 1934 and 1935, and the Quebec 147-pound welterweight title in 1934 and 1935. He also earned a chance to qualify for the Olympic boxing trials and for the Empire Games in 1934.

Sowery often praised his protege's "granite jaw and raw courage" and encouraged the hard-hitting lightweight to take up professional boxing. Midway through the Depression, Coughlin opted for a steady job with the CNR as a brakeman instead. But through most of the 1930s, the handsome Irish lad's legendary courage thrilled spectators in the amateur rings of New York, Boston, Montreal and Toronto.

Boxing fans long recalled the memorable night when Coughlin met Walter Young, winner of the 1937 Boston Marathon. "The first throw in the second round was by Walter. He raced across the ring as soon as the bell sounded. Joe didn't even have time to stand erect, when Walter hit him with a beautiful right-hand haymaker. Joe fell flat on his back and to the crowd's amazement stood straight up on his head, and then fell flat on his face. Joe was out colder than a mackerel. He finished the round and in the final heat with both boys on the verge of a knock-out. Joe's fighting spirit gave him a well-earned victory and the provincial championship. It was certainly one of the best fights ever witnessed around Montreal," wrote one reporter.

In May 1936, Sowery organized the Junior Golden Gloves, Montreal's first juvenile amateur boxing championships, at the Griffintown Club. He ran the event big-league-style, like Chicago's famed Golden Gloves tournament. Fights went three rounds, each lasting a minute. The young sluggers, all under sixteen, some as young as seven, sparred with boys within five pounds of their own weight, from the skimpy 50-pound class to the hefty 108-pound division, later raised to 115 pounds.

For five nights in a row, more than five hundred spectators crammed into the Griffintown Club gym to cheer on the youngsters. The press covered the inaugural Junior Golden Gloves, with one enthusiastic reporter praising "outstanding bouts" and participants' "rare gameness and skill." Sowery's proteges claimed eight of the ten titles. The tournament became an annual event, copied and written about in Ottawa, Boston and Winnipeg, as the press took note of potential stars.

ONE BLOCK WEST OF THE GRIFFINTOWN CLUB, across the great divide of Colborne Street, the St. Ann's Young Men's Society appealed to the community's loftier ambitions. Its well-stocked library, and its flourishing literary, debating, dramatic and choral groups conferred prestige on its members. Not that the two organizations were mutually exclusive. Many Griffintown Club Members, like Joe Coughlin, belonged to both. He and hundreds of other Irish youth had covered the walls and filled the showcases of St. Ann's Hall with trophies in baseball, lacrosse, basketball, and other sports. But the Young Men's Society took greater pride in its cultural achievements. "The glorious thing . . . is that the finest things of mind and soul have kept pace with the purely physical life of the Society," R.J. Hart wrote in 1934, on the occasion of the Redemptorists' golden jubilee in the parish.

In 1935, the St. Ann's Young Men's Society—by then the oldest organization of its kind in North America—celebrated its fiftieth anniversary. And while there may have been a touch of exaggeration in the society's boast that "it has been fifty years a breeding place of genius," it could count doctors, lawyers, teachers, businessmen, priests, politicians, cabinet ministers and judges among its membership.

The anniversary year brought fresh triumphs: St. Ann's intermediate baseball team won a provincial championship. The dramatic section drew huge crowds to its annual St. Patrick's Day concert at the Monument National, featuring *Heart's Desire* by the popular American playwright Anne Nichols. Forty-five new members enrolled in the society. But at the annual meeting in April 1935, president John Cullen declared that the previous year "from a financial point of view can be termed as a failure." The society experienced lean years in the 1930s, with a falling off in attendance at its paid activities.

The Depression also saw changes in Montreal's St. Patrick's Day parade, with participating organizations eliminating floats to reduce expenses. But despite sleet or snow, and in the face of widespread economic distress, the Irish turned out in increasing numbers and enthusiasm. The Griffintown contingent numbered in the hundreds. The St. Ann's Young Men's Society, grand in dark dress coats and high hats,

St. Ann's Parish dramatic society, 1919.

with shamrocks and shillelaghs, walked in lockstep, flying silk banners and followed by their traditional Irish jaunting cart, a marching band and the students of St. Ann's Boys' School.

A lucky few managed to achieve every Griffintown lad's dream—to ride a pony in the parade. "It was quite an honour," says Harold Galley, who rode a pony on loan from the O'Donnells' cartage company in three parades; the first was in 1935, when he was eight years old. The privilege, when approved by the Brothers, also meant an escape from weeks of daily drills under the direction of the sturdy, mustachioed Major Long, adjutant in the Irish Rangers in the First World War, who trained them to walk with military precision in the parade.

IN THE 1920S AND 1930S, Father Richard Baines would stride briskly along the sidewalk, brandishing a cane, and if a girl went by wearing a short skirt, he'd give her a whack on the back of her legs and an admonishment: "Go home and put on some clothes." To children out too late, he'd say, "Get in the house, it's after nine o'clock." Another priest, who was dubbed "Father Flashlight," would shine a light on embarrassed young couples snuggling in shadowy doorways.

Every Irish mother prayed that one of her sons would enter the priesthood. And God heard their prayers. Griffintown produced dozens of priests, nuns and Brothers—and at least one bishop. On May 17, 1930, the Pope appointed Gerald Casey Murray as Bishop of Victoria. His consecration took place in his beloved St. Ann's on May 7, 1930.

The Irish revered their priests—and spoiled them. Art Broden remembered the royal treatment his uncle, Father Alf Cloran, a Redemptorist stationed at Saint John during the war years, received on his visits home to Montreal. "He'd have thick steaks, and of course, he'd throw a pound of butter in the skillet. He ate like it was going out of style." Family members would give him their ration tickets for sugar and butter.

That the priests were human amused and surprised devout Catholics. "Father Cloran had friends in high places. His big friend, Eddie Quinn [was] in charge of all the boxing and wrestling at the Montreal Forum. As kids, we went to watch the wrestling in box seats. He also had a friend, another Irishman, who ran Madison Square Gardens. He preached fire and brimstone to the rest of us, but he was living high off the hog," said Broden in an interview.

Father Francis Kearney, probably the most beloved of priests, arrived at St. Ann's in 1938, at the age of forty-six. The Westport, Ontario, native had served at Redemptorist missions and parishes in Ontario, Newfoundland, Saskatchewan and New Brunswick, before his assignment to St. Ann's. Except for a brief posting in London, Ontario, and three years as a navy chaplain, Father Kearney spent the rest of his life there.

Humble and humane, Father Kearney became even more accessible when a serious heart condition, diagnosed in 1952, limited his activities. He would spend most afternoons sitting on the stone steps of St. Ann's, chatting with neighbourhood children, waving and offering

Father Francis Kearney, one of St. Ann's most beloved priests.

a friendly "Hello, lovey," to passersby. Taxi drivers would salute him with a toot of the horn. And in a quiet moment, he would hear a parishioner's confession.

Long lineups formed outside Father Kearney's confessional, while no one stood outside the other five, where sterner priests waited for penitents. He issued the lightest of penances, rarely more than one Hail Mary. He would also tell a joke, or maybe ask if he could put your little brothers and sisters in a garbage can. Father Kearney's friendliness spooked those counting on the anonymity promised by the confessional's screen. Frank Dougherty had barely begun his confession, "Father I accuse myself of—" when Father Kearney interrupted, asking, "Is that you, Francis?"

Preparation for First Communion, First Confession and Confirmation—the sacramental triple crown—began in grade two. The Sisters of Providence created a state of high anticipation. Girls dreamt of veils and white dresses. "You wait for your First Communion, like you wait for your wedding day," recalled Iris Howden. Gerald O'Connell's landlady outfitted him for the occasion: "When I made my First Communion, they took me out and they dressed me in white—suit, shirt, even the shoes in white."

The children would walk in solemn procession down the main aisles of St. Ann's and file into pews on the left and right. Near the end of the high mass, they would proceed to the marble altar rail and stick their tongues out to receive the host. After mass, the communicants would make their rounds, and admiring neighbours and relatives would give them gifts of money.

The priests preached that missing mass on Sunday, a mortal sin, could lead to eternal damnation. But punishment came more swiftly for the pupils at St. Ann's Boys' School. If the Brothers found out they did not go to church, they would get the strap.

In the days before compulsory school attendance, the Christian Brothers did their best to educate their often reluctant students, sometimes heading out into the lanes and alleys and canal banks to track

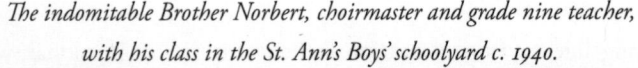

The indomitable Brother Norbert, choirmaster and grade nine teacher, with his class in the St. Ann's Boys' schoolyard c. 1940.

down truants. Tough disciplinarians, the Christian Brothers—many of Irish descent—ran St. Ann's Boys' School with an iron hand—and the strap. "Brother Henry gave everybody the strap the first day," recalled Frank Doyle. "'Everybody, line up. Bang. Bang. Now that's what you're going to get if you act up.'"

Sometimes, the students tried to intimidate the teachers. At the beginning of one school year, in the late thirties, Frank Dougherty recalled that one of his classmates, a husky lad and a boxer, strode confidently up to their lay teacher, a rookie from a wealthy suburb, and told him: "You take it easy on us, or you'll have a bad time." Dougherty and the other boys waited to see what would happen next. But Mike McNamara, a teacher from Griffintown who overheard the ruckus from an adjoining classroom, did not hesitate. He strode to the back of the class and punched the bully. "From then on that class was under control."

McDonnell's (later called the Coffee Pot), a popular corner store across the street from St. Ann's Church, filled up with churchgoers on Sundays and after Tuesday devotions. It was a long tradition. John Taugher, coach of the Shamrock lacrosse team, opened the cigar and candy store, then called Taugher's, in the 1880s. The Irish would congregate in the shop after mass, knowing that King Brady and other members of the popular lacrosse team were sure to be there, talking about their latest game.

When the after-church crowds cleared away, Griffintown's elderly Irish bachelors—and the dozens of priests who lived in the rectory and seminary on Basin Street—kept the Coffee Pot busy. If the choirmaster needed a singer or two for Benediction, she could usually find a volunteer from the crowd that hung out there: Jimmy McArthur, John Dancey, Eddie Brennan and his brother, Tweet, or Bunny Kehoe, a grinning leprechaun barely more than five feet tall, a weigh-scale man who tried to pass as a fireman in his government uniform. Kehoe, a fine amateur actor, liked to lock himself in the washroom and produce enough sound effects to replicate a brawl.

ABOVE: *Hanging around McDonnell's, a favourite neighbourhood haunt later called the Coffee Pot.*
BELOW: *Peggy McDonnell (left), co-owner of McDonnell's restaurant, with her mother, Mrs. Mary Taugher.*

Gambling was illegal, and rampant, in Montreal until late in the twentieth century. Businessmen and lawyers played barbotte (a dice game) in fancy uptown establishments and tony suburban casinos, placing hundreds of dollars for a throw of the dice on baize-covered tables. Montrealers could gamble at hundreds of small operations around the city, where they could illegally but easily bet on horses and sports, or buy Irish Sweepstakes tickets, or play roulette, blackjack, baccarat, craps and barbotte.

In Griffintown, the most popular game was craps. A favourite location was a laneway on Ottawa Street, across from St. Ann's Kindergarten, on Saturdays and Sundays after mass. Games often lasted for three or four hours. The first round might see eight-year-olds throwing the dice for a few pennies. As the pot grew bigger, older guys would join in, betting nickels and dimes, then paper money, fives, tens and twenties. They would usually pick one of the kids to be "king's man"—to hold the money.

The boys fought for the honour, and for the tips—a quarter or fifty cents, depending on the size of the pot. Don Kelly collected thirty-two dollars on his best day. But if the lookout whistled a warning that the police were coming, the king's man had to run and hide the pot. "I could go over roofs, down stairs, climb fences and never touch the ground until Wellington Street," says Kelly. "Once the cops were gone, I'd come back with the money. I wouldn't want to be the guy who said I lost it climbing the roofs." Meanwhile, the players could pick up the dice, run into the back door of a nearby flat, say "How do you do?" to its occupants and stroll out the front door when the coast was clear. The police couldn't enter a house without a warrant, so it was a foolproof way to avoid arrest.

Most of the time the gang outside Irene's, a big, musty store at the corner of Colborne and Ottawa streets, and a favourite haunt of local boxers, simply ignored the police. "The cops would come by, say, 'Hey guys—break it up.' The guys would say, 'Take a hike.' That was it—the cops took a hike," says Harold Galley.

It was harder to dismiss the priests. One afternoon, Father Edward Boyne strolled into the lane when some St. Ann's boys were playing craps. "It's none of your business," Woppy Kelly told him. The burly priest reached down, grabbed the dice, dropped them into the sewer and walked away.

A number of blind pigs operated in the district, and at least one was owned by a god-fearing man. Mike Pearson, a devout Catholic, bought the Arrawanna Tavern, a low brick building on Bridge Street, across the canal from Griffintown, in 1929. And by the 1940s, the bar—its name taken from the title of nineteenth-century American composer Theodore Morse's improbable hit song about an Irishman courting an Indian maiden—had become one of the most popular in the area. Despite the law prohibiting the sale of liquor on the Lord's Day, Sunday was one of its busiest days. Men would stop by for a drink, entering by the back door—but only if they had been to church. Pearson would ignore the law of the land, but he wouldn't allow a customer who had missed mass to buy a drink.

As late as the 1940s, wakes were still held at home, with the deceased laid out in an open coffin in the parlour. Sometimes the bodies were prepared in the home. But often Feron's, the local undertakers, would remove the corpse to their funeral parlour for embalming, then bring it home for the wake, often making a long, awkward climb up a narrow staircase to a second- or third-storey flat, or hoisting it up and through a window.

It was not uncommon for neighbours to take up a collection to pay for a burial. During the Depression, a funeral cost about twelve dollars—out of the reach of most families. Griffintowners often turned to Feron's. "When my grandfather opened the business, he never sent bills," says Bernie Reid, Feron's current manager. "People didn't have the money so my grandfather extended credit to anyone. People paid when they could."

Grieving families hung black crepe on their front door to mark a death in the family. Passersby, even children, unacquainted with the deceased, would drop in to pay their respects, rap on the door, enter and kneel at the coffin and say a prayer.

Friends and relatives kept a three-day vigil beside the body. The family would serve sandwiches, liquor and, in earlier times, set out clay pipes and tobacco. Mourners would pay their respects, then linger and share stories about the deceased. The noise level would rise as visitors filled the parlour and the kitchen and the hallway, sometimes spilling out onto the front steps and the back gallery. Laughter might soften the sadness as talk drifted to old times or the latest boxing match. Or somebody might pull out a mouth organ or play the spoons, *clickity-clack,* on his knee or arm. Charlie Blickstead's verses recall some of the good times:

> *Always six candles surrounded the coffin,*
> *At the height of the wake, you'd be dyin' from laughin'*
> *And Dan Murphy's poems would bring on a tear.*
> *While Dan Duffy'd hang from the chandelier.*

> *Mike Finnigan's wake, who thought he would die,*
> *Uncle Pat had a few, then thought he'd drop by.*
> *He's crooning a hymn, in his Irish soprano,*
> *In the darkness he kneels, to face the piano.*
> *On leaving he tells them, "I'm sending a wreath,*
> *Poor Mike's lookin' grand, such a fine set of teeth."*

In Ireland, many priests frowned on the wake as an occasion of sin. And long nights of drinking, it was often rumoured, led to shenanigans at a few Griffintown vigils. Art Broden tells another story of his uncle, Jackie Taugher, who attended a home wake with some inebriated pranksters: "The joke was, the first one of the gang to pass out—they take the stiff out of the coffin and put the guy that passed out in the coffin. Of course, the guy comes to, and there's a candle burning. . . . He loses it and they have to call an ambulance." A dozer might also wake up to find his face had been painted with black shoe polish.

As late as the 1930s, at the end of the two- or three-day wake, a huge black funeral carriage pulled by black horses wearing big black plumes would pull up at the door to transport the body to church. The dead received a solemn, dignified requiem at St. Ann's. Frank "Fingers" Feron would lead the way, as pallbearers heaved the casket into the church. The priest would meet the procession and bless the coffin. The dirges would sound from the choir loft as the coffin rolled noisily down the aisle on a creaky bier, followed by altar boys bearing candles and incense.

After the funeral mass, mourners would follow the casket on foot through the streets of Griffintown to the home of the deceased. They would stop and place flowers at the door before proceeding to the cemetery, a familiar place to the Griffintown Irish, many of whom made it a custom to visit the dead each week after Sunday mass.

Griffintown had its ghosts, too, the Headless Woman being the most famous. Mary Gallagher, many believed, continued to stalk the district, looking for her head, chopped off in a brutal murder in a William Street flat in 1879. Johnny Fenlon remembered, as a boy in the 1930s, standing with his father, Constable Bartholomew Fenlon, outside No. 7 station on Young Street when Johnson, an old hunchback—one of the few people "known" to have seen the headless woman—came to tell his father about the latest sighting. "I remember him saying to my father, 'I saw it and took to my heels.'"

"Firecracker Day" was the most popular tradition. Victoria Day, May 24, always ended in a blaze of glorious, unauthorized street fires on almost every block. Griffintowners stockpiled fuel months ahead. It was an open conspiracy. The Irish took delight in flouting the authorities. Even grannies quietly saved cardboard and wooden boxes, newspaper, scrap wood, old tires—anything flammable. The stashes ballooned after

May 1, Montreal's traditional moving day, as old chesterfields, chairs and other discards joined the pile. Norman Howden, who helped light bonfires in the middle of Murray Street near his boyhood home in the 1930s, remembered, "We had a ball. We burned everything—furniture, pianos, old cars."

Father James Farrell remembered how at age eight or nine he would act as a lookout, standing on the sidewalk at the entrance to the lane and watching for the beat cops. Meanwhile, in the backyard, behind the long block of rowhouses on Young Street, his fourteen-year-old brother, Bill, and his friends were loading an old bedstead with wood scraps, discarded furniture and all the other junk they had stashed away for Firecracker Day. As soon as young Jim gave the signal, they sprinkled it with coal oil, ran it out to the middle of the street, put a match to it—and disappeared.

Giddy neighbours from the crowded block gathered around that illicit bonfire on May 24, 1925; some threw more fuel or firecrackers into the flames. Minutes later, the No. 3 fire engine raced down the street, sirens blaring. Firemen jumped off the truck, hauled out the hose and extinguished the blaze, only to see another one flare up down the street or around the corner.

The celebrations started early. The first firecracker exploded shortly after dawn. Intermittent snaps and bangs ricocheted around the neighbourhood during the day. By early evening, the acrid smell of spent firecrackers hung over streets strewn with bits of red wrappers. Pedestrians making their way along crowded sidewalks had to jump and dance to avoid the Big Berthas and Red Rockets little boys threw at their feet. As a boy, Frank Hanley, future MLA and city councillor, liked to throw them under horses' feet. Little girls twirled sparklers, tracing smoky filaments in the dusky sky. Anticipation filled the air. Everyone was waiting for the bonfires.

After dark, all over Griffintown piles of wood and flammable junk would suddenly appear in the middle of the road. A quick-footed

Ladies of the Sodality of the Children of Mary
walk in the annual Corpus Christi procession.

lad would pour on some fuel, drop a match and fade into the crowd. Dozens witnessed the lighting of the fire, but none could, or would, identify the instigators. By the end of the Depression, the Irish were starting to lose the wild ways of their emigrant predecessors, but they still retained their impulse to tweak the authorities.

Griffintowners took perverse pride in their rowdy Firecracker Days. Most were gentle, church-going souls who simply saw no harm in the occasional shenanigan. A few weeks later, even the pranksters would turn out to pray and sing hymns in street processions to celebrate the feast of Corpus Christi—a tradition of Catholics around the world. Parishioners who lived along the route put statues and holy pictures in their windows, or set up little altars on the sidewalk. "The men in our little block always put up an altar in our laneway," Betty Bryant recalled. "Granny and my uncles and cousins were all Protestant but they loved the procession and the altar."

Shutters sported a fresh coat of green paint; windows sparkled. Some shopkeepers, and even Protestants, decorated their stores and houses with flags, flowers, draperies and streamers.

Members of No. 3 fire station on Ottawa Street built the grandest altar of all. It took them a week to hammer together the multilevel wooden platform next to the station. By the time they were finished, the altar—backed by rows of evergreens trucked in for the occasion—was resplendent in artfully draped white cloth and baskets of spring flowers.

For the feast of Corpus Christi, the priests, members of the Sodality of the Children of Mary, the St. Ann's Young Men's Society, schoolchildren, altar boys and the parish choir would assemble outside St. Ann's Church. Singing hymns and reciting litanies, the procession would make its way through streets thronged with respectful observers, as it had for much of the history of the parish. When they reached the firemen's altar, the procession would stop. The priest, holding the sacred host—encased in a golden ciborium and protected by a golden canopy held aloft by four white-gloved Knights of Columbus—mounted the steps for the Benediction. To the solemn strains of *Tantum ergo,* the celebrant would raise the host and the crowd would bow their heads in veneration. The smell of incense would waft through Griffintown: a scent that to the Irish, a people of many contradictions, was as sweet as the smell of firecrackers.

TEN

❧

Griffintown Goes to War

We're living the most exciting existence a man can live in wartime . . .
God protect you all, as well as us, till we meet again.
—Edward S. Supple, a gunner in the Royal Canadian Artillery,
British 8th Army, in a letter from the battlefields of Europe
in the autumn of 1943

Margaret Dowling waved a casual goodbye to her mother before stepping out into the early morning drizzle on Tuesday, April 25, 1944. The sixteen-year-old hopped a streetcar and headed uptown to the office where she worked as a clerk, as if this were like every other day since the beginning of the war. Margaret's mother, Delia Dowling, worked the night shift as a cleaner at Windsor Station. And that morning, as usual, the fifty-six-year-old widow had returned home in time to make breakfast for her only daughter before retiring to the room they shared in an Ottawa Street boarding house, expecting nothing more than to catch up on her sleep.

Daily life in Griffintown had changed dramatically since the outbreak of the Second World War in September 1939, when the country was still mired in the Depression and nearly 1 million Canadians, one-tenth of the population, remained unemployed. Times were hard, perhaps nowhere more so than in Griffintown, a struggling district in a near bankrupt city where numerous factories remained idle and more than one hundred thousand residents subsisted on meagre relief.

But the war had put the jobless back to work. Almost overnight, the hopeless men who had wandered from city to city in search of non-existent jobs disappeared off the streets. Thousands of unemployed men, young and old, had marched into recruiting centres and emerged with the promise of a paycheque and a uniform. Within a month, the Canadian forces grew from fewer than ten thousand to seventy thousand. "Half of Griffintown lined up before they even opened, all standing in line on St. James Street," John Hanley Jr. said in an interview. "My father went overseas right away." There are no official statistics for the number of applicants from the district, but none would dispute the strong, enthusiastic turnout from Griffintown. And many sailed to Britain with the earliest convoys of the 1st Canadian Division in December.

But they also served who stayed behind. During the course of the war, Canadian factory workers would produce a staggering $11 billion worth of military equipment—a massive arsenal of guns and ammunition, airplanes, ships and tanks and other supplies, for the Allied forces. The initiative came from Ottawa. Soon after the conflict began, British Prime Minister Neville Chamberlain asked the Canadian government to train twelve thousand pilots a year. Canadian Prime Minister William Lyon Mackenzie King agreed and also promised, under the British Commonwealth Air Training Plan, to supply thousands of fighter planes. King made the commitment, an almost overwhelming task for a nation with such a tiny air industry, because he believed it would eliminate the need for Canada to muster a large army. The cagey politician wanted, at all costs, to avoid conscription, an issue that had divided the country in the First World War and would certainly do so again.

Armed with lucrative government contracts—more than $50 million in the first four months alone—manufacturers across the country geared up their factories and scrambled to find and train the hundreds of thousands of workers needed to fill war orders. In Montreal, idle factories—including many in the Griffintown area—sprung into action and mobilized the city's industrial workforce, one of the largest in the country. And, as the armed forces drained the country's manpower, thousands of women joined the assembly lines that rolled out military planes and bombers, corvettes and minesweepers, aircraft carriers and radar equipment, tanks and shells, machine guns, artillery, uniforms and camouflage material, tent canvas, bandage cloth and sundry other essentials for Britain and the Allied forces.

An ocean separated Canada from the battlefields, but government authorities took measures to secure the coasts and strategic ports, including Halifax and Montreal, a major centre for the production of munitions. Canadians could not escape reminders that the country was at war. Official posters warned them of sabotage and spies, or urged them to buy Victory Bonds. More ominous were the periodic blackouts and air raid tests, preparation for a possible German invasion.

Signs of war seemed especially prominent in Griffintown. The army had turned a local elementary school into a military training centre. Soldiers stood guard along the Lachine Canal, in the railway yards, on nearby Victoria Bridge and at other potential targets. Terry Flanagan, born in 1935, remembers watching the long troop trains pulling out of the newly built Central Station, from his family's Dalhousie Street flat. "It was directly opposite the railway overpass, that dreadful scar that divided Griffintown in half. I could sit in my bedroom at night and look out the window and watch all the trains go by. They were on absolute level with us. During the war years, we saw all the soldiers going out." He also recalls seeing the wounded soldiers returning home at the old Bonaventure Station on nearby Chaboillez Square, on walks with his mother: "I remember going up to that old wooden building

Soldiers guard a railway bridge on the Lachine Canal in 1939. Officials increased security on the home front after the outbreak of the Second World War.

and there wouldn't be any great big brass bands playing and they'd be taking fellows off the train and carrying them out to ambulances."

Liberators, Flying Fortresses, Martin Marauders and other bombers routinely scraped the skies over Montreal. The city had become a jumping-off point for the thousands of military planes that Britain ordered from American aviation plants. The Atlantic Ferry Organization, a civilian operation, took delivery of the planes at a base near Dorval Airport and hired pilots to fly the new aircraft across the Atlantic, a risky but routine mission that was transferred to the Royal Air Force in 1943 and renamed Ferry Command. Still, the threat of an attack on Canada seemed remote, and the sight of several bombers flying over the city on the rainy morning of April 25, 1944, would not have caused any alarm.

But around 10:30, a four-engine B-24 Liberator that had taken off from Dorval a few minutes earlier on its maiden flight suddenly lost altitude as it ascended over Mount Royal. At a height of five or six hundred feet, the pilot abruptly changed course and pointed southward, in an apparent attempt to make an emergency landing in the St. Lawrence River, less than two miles away. It was a short, perilous hop that would take the crippled aircraft over the heart of the city and Griffintown.

The bomber continued to lose altitude as it rumbled over Peel Street. Pedestrians watched in alarm as the Liberator swooped within inches of the Post Office building at the corner of Peel and St. Antoine, then careened over the roof of Bonaventure Station. A moment later, the tip of the right wing hit the top of the Dow Brewery, a block away. Barely a thousand yards from the river, the bomber began to disintegrate as it flew over Griffintown. "A piece of the wing, or something, fell on each side of me," a man heading down Colborne Street later told a reporter. "I sure stepped on the gas in a hurry."

The pilot—Flight-Lieutenant Kazimierz Burzynski, a Polish Air Force hero who had logged more than a million miles—skimmed chimneys and rooftops as he fought to keep the crippled aircraft aloft for the last six hundred yards to the river. The plane zoomed low over St. Ann's Boys' School, over the heads of students lined up along the fence near Colborne Street, at the end of recess. On Murray Street, cantankerous old James Higgins sat on his gallery and waved angrily at the pilot, shouting that he was flying too low, after the plane nicked off the knobs at the top of the bay windows in his block.

St. Ann's Church had just emptied after morning devotions when the low-flying plane roared past, below the steeple. The vibrations rattled the windows of McDonnell's across the street and sent frightened customers rushing out of the restaurant. They watched in horror as the pilot, his path blocked by Black's Bridge, a bulky iron structure over the Lachine Canal, circled back over Griffintown and made another attempt to reach the river.

The disintegrating bomber fought to stay aloft. Flames shot out the side of the aircraft as the pilot lurched over houses and factories,

*Aftermath of the terrible plane crash into a block of houses
at the corner of Shannon and Ottawa streets on April 25, 1944.*

slicing off chimneys and lightning rods. Griffintown residents watched, terrified, as the sinking aircraft narrowly missed the New City Gas Company building on Ottawa Street, then struck the top of a shed in the Quebec Hydro-Electric Commission yard. The impact tore off part of a wing and sent an engine crashing onto the roof. The building caught fire and Albert Lanctot, a fifty-one-year-old electrician working in the shed, ran to the nearest exit. "The whole place was on fire before I made two steps," Lanctot told a newspaperman the next day. "I ran for my life and jumped an eight-foot fence, something I never thought I could do. Then I tore off my flaming coat."

Seconds later, at 10:33, the bomber crashed into six houses across the street, one of them the flat where Lanctot lived as a boarder. The plane slammed into the Shannon Street block with such terrific force that it pushed right through the building and stripped off the back wall of a row of houses facing onto Ottawa Street. The plane burst into flames and exploded, flinging chunks of flaming wreckage in all directions. Fuelled by more than two thousand gallons of gasoline in the aircraft's tanks, the fire quickly spread to nearby houses. Within minutes, flames engulfed the entire block and thick clouds of smoke billowed over Griffintown.

The five-man crew—three of them Polish Air Force officers on loan to the Royal Air Force—died in the crash, one of the worst air disasters in the history of Montreal. Only two people emerged alive from the smoking rubble of the Shannon Street building. A soldier pulled Mrs. T. Hébert to safety through a window. Lucien Tison jumped from a second-storey window, clad only in his underwear. The thirty-eight-year-old night-duty war worker, who was badly burned, was asleep when the plane ripped into his house.

Several residents managed to escape from the damaged houses on Ottawa Street. After the back wall of her home collapsed, Mrs. Leo Paul Pigeon escaped from the third floor, down the front stairs of the burning building. "I was lying in bed reading when the back wall came crashing down inches from me," Pigeon told a reporter. "The whole building shook." Half of the house had gone and the back stairs had disappeared. A passerby, seventeen-year-old James Carroll, ignored the smoke and flames and rushed into the neighbouring flat to look for survivors. He found the elderly Mrs. Mary Anne Parker on the second floor and carried her to safety. He risked his life a second time to save old Mrs. Mary Stevenson, on the third floor. Delia Dowling, asleep after her night shift, died in the burning house.

A whim had prompted Happy Furlong, a sixty-five-year-old calèche driver who boarded in the same rooming house as the Dowlings, to go out and buy a quart of beer shortly before 10:30. By the time Furlong returned, his shattered boarding house was in flames.

Broken electrical wires hung loose. Telephone lines in the vicinity of the crash went dead. "The lights went out," recalled Frank Doyle, then an 11-year-old student at St. Ann's Boys' School. "We heard this big noise, boom, right over the school, it shook the place. Brother Edward, our teacher, said, 'Stay here and pray.' We could see the black smoke."

Brother Edward Hogan went down to see what happened. He had rung the bell at the end of recess and sent the students back to class, two-by-two. The last of the boys had just entered the building when the plane crashed a block away. "Part of the tail was leaning on the outside of the fence where I had lined up the boys. That's how close it was," Brother Hogan recalled. "The airplane people told us it was miraculous. The plane cleared the school by 30 feet."

By noon, firemen had managed to contain the flames. And the search began for the bodies of the missing, believed to be in the flattened buildings. Frantic residents rushed home to make sure their families and friends were safe. Throughout the day, thousands of churchgoers walked past the crash site on their way to the Tuesday devotions at St. Ann's. By evening, thousands of people filled the streets surrounding the tragic scene.

One of the first bodies retrieved from the steaming wreckage was that of thirty-eight-year-old Constable Philippe Lemieux, a familiar face in the district. The married father of three was last seen dashing into a burning house. Margaret Dowling had rushed home from work as soon as she heard news of the crash. She stood, teary-eyed, on the sidewalk across the street, as firemen searched the ruins of her home. Eventually they came down the stairs carrying her mother's shrouded remains on a stretcher.

The Wells brothers, Walter and James, had also hurried home after the crash, only to find their Shannon Street boarding house crushed to the ground and engulfed in flames. The grief-stricken James Wells waited for three hours in the pouring rain, shocked and dazed, as the firemen searched for his missing wife and three-year-old son; Walter's wife, Betty, also died in the crash. They were among the ten civilians, including four women and two children, who perished in the disaster.[7]

*A Griffintown family throws a party for soldiers who helped
with rescue efforts after the April 25, 1944, plane crash.*

Across the street from the crash site, the Griffintown Club opened
its doors to survivors, policemen and firemen, reporters and photogra-
phers, and a steady stream of fathers, mothers and children inquiring
about family members. Neighbourhood women opened their homes
to the injured and their rescuers, and served them coffee, tea and sandwiches. They also brought heaping plates of sandwiches to the club and
donated their ration tickets for coffee, cream and sugar to the survivors
and their families, as well as to volunteers.

A few weeks later, on May 13, the Toronto *Globe and Mail* published
a tribute to their generosity: "We do not know what racial strain now
predominates in Griffintown. It used to be Irish, and the backbone of
many a famous Shamrock lacrosse team," J.V. McAree wrote. "Whatever it is now, its women are the sort of which other Canadians can be
proud." The crash of the bomber in the "densely crowded" Griffintown,

he pointed out, had much the same effect, though on a completely different scale, as bombs in European cities.

"Many a Griffintown housewife cleared her shelves of rationed goods," he noted. "Four hundred of Griffintown's sons are overseas, and their mothers thought nothing of giving their last bite and supp, as it might be, to other war sufferers. So, when speaking of Quebec, please remember that Griffintown is in Quebec, and that the women of Griffintown take no back seat to any other group of patriotic mothers in Canada."

Early on the afternoon of the crash, the Royal Air Force Transport Command issued a statement from Dorval headquarters: "There were no passengers or mail, but the aircraft carried approximately six hundred pounds of freight. The cause of the accident is not at present known, but a board of inquiry has been convened." On April 28, a coroner's inquest declared the deaths accidental. The RAFTC undertook an official inquiry.

Rumours circulated that the bomber had been sabotaged and that one of the crew had bailed out of the plane and gone missing. The mystery deepened after it appeared that the downed Liberator had been transporting a huge cache of gold coins. That story began about three weeks after the crash, when a fire warden found a ten-dollar gold coin while he was cleaning up the site. The news spread and several dozen men, women and children converged there over the next few days. Some brought lanterns and stayed after dark. Gerald Harkin estimated at the time that about 180 pieces of gold were found. He reported in the *Griff News* that a six-year-old found one and sold it for a quarter.

Officials never confirmed or denied the reports, although the British Treasury did ship gold and securities to Canada for safekeeping during the war. Some observers concluded that the coins must have been hidden in one of the houses. But others scoffed at the idea that a resident of Griffintown would, or could, hoard a fortune in gold. Some skeptics denied that any gold coins at all had been found at the site. "There were gold coins and gold bullion, marked Germany and Switzerland, all over the ground. I saw them, I was there," Rita Earle insists. Earle, twelve years old at the time of the crash, said that military police kicked her off the site, although one of her friends, she said, managed to put a coin in his shoe before he ran off.

A few weeks later, another disaster threatened Griffintown. On Friday, May 5, a spectacular fire broke out at a Canada Steamship Lines warehouse on the canal bank, near Ottawa Street, shortly after three p.m. The blaze, sparked by a welder's torch, ripped through the single-storey freight shed in a minute, trapping a dozen longshoremen between the fire and the Lachine Canal. Masses of black smoke darkened the sky as the contents of the 2,400-foot-long steel structure fuelled the inferno. Repeated explosions rocked the neighbourhood for several minutes as huge steel drums of alcohol and oil blew up, and were hurled hundreds of feet into the air.

Several employees escaped the flames by diving into the canal and swimming to the next dock. A freighter crew rescued a number of others, then quickly cast off and moored a safe distance away. There were no deaths or injuries in the three-alarm fire, but damages exceeded half a million dollars. Most of the goods destroyed in the fire—shell casings, wire, rope, mechanical equipment, airplane parts, canned and dehydrated food—were destined for military use overseas. Large quantities of sugar, tea and other rationed commodities were also lost.

Intense heat and smoke kept spectators at a distance, but thousands lined the wharves from across the canal to watch the fire. The sound of exploding liquor bottles continued for hours after the flames were put under control.

Griffintowners suffered a third shock on Tuesday, September 5, 1944, when an earthquake hit the Montreal area. The eruption, at 12:39 a.m., shook houses, rattled dishes and cracked ceilings. Terrified residents ran crying and screaming into the streets in their nightwear. In wartime, when government posters illustrated with rats warned citizens to "Keep Your Trap Shut" and "Starve Him with Silence—War Secrets," paranoia was understandable. One fellow was convinced the French Resistance had caused the quake, Pin Provost wrote in a Griffintown Club newsletter. He also told of one little girl crying, "Mom, the Germans are here. I knew they were coming. I knew it."

The fire and the earthquake added to the pervasive sense of doom that darkened the war years. In Griffintown, as in many communities across the nation, gloomy newspaper headlines and official casualty lists dampened spirits. By the time the plane slammed into the ill-fated block at Shannon and Ottawa streets, nearly two dozen young men from the club alone had died in the service of their country. The victims of the bomber crash—indirect casualties of the war—added ten more names to Griffintown's growing tally.

Initially, many joined the military for the money. Paddy Doyle's half-monthly pay stub for June 30, 1942, shows that the army private had earned $16.67 that week, plus a $6.75 bonus: significantly more than the five dollars or so he would have earned at home as a labourer for the city. And more than the paltry two or three dollars in relief the government allotted to unemployed single men during the Depression.

But money alone could not account for the district's high participation. Patriotism and adventure also drew many recruits. Nearly five hundred young men from the Griffintown Club alone, more than a third of its membership, joined the armed forces.[8] As the war continued, many more young men enlisted as they came of age, following fathers, uncles and older brothers into the army, navy and air force. Many families saw two or three sons go overseas. Nine sons enlisted from one family on Ottawa Street.

Some, like Danny Doyle, lied about his age to get into the navy when he was seventeen; he couldn't wait to join his brother, "Chubby," his Uncle Paddy and his buddies overseas. Adventure, a sense of duty and patriotism too, drew many Griffintown recruits. Many had Irish names—Brennan and Connolly, Stacey and Sullivan. And although they took pride in their Irish heritage, this was Canada's war and they

ABOVE: *James "Chubby" Doyle, Paddy Doyle and Danny Doyle enjoy
a chance meeting at a British military base during the Second World War.*
BELOW: *Paddy Doyle's army pay stub.
His income more than doubled after he enlisted.*

PERIOD ENDING	5709
JUN 30 1942	
WAGES	16.67
COMMISSIONS Bonus	6.75
TOTAL	23.42
DEDUCTIONS:	
ADVANCES	
NAT. DEF. TAX	
UNEMPLOY. INS.	90
WAR SAVINGS	
GROUP INS.	
H. & A. INS.	
UNIFORM	
LOCAL FEES	
SECURITY DEP.	
MISCELLANEOUS	
NET TOTAL	22.52

were fighting for their country. Griffintown servicemen fought on all fronts: in Britain, Europe, the Mediterranean, North Africa and the Far East. They served on naval ships in the Battle of the Atlantic, piloted bombers over enemy territory and filled Canadian ranks in every major battle: in the Battle of Hong Kong on December 8, 1941, hours after the attack on Pearl Harbor, where they were hopelessly outnumbered against the Japanese; at the disastrous raid on Dieppe in 1942; at the fierce Battle of Ortona in Italy's "Bloody December" of 1943; in the D-Day landings on the beaches of Normandy in 1944; and in the gruelling Battle of the Scheldt in Belgium and the Netherlands. Some, like Lieutenant-Commander Charles Blickstead, assumed senior roles. A director of the Montreal Fire Department, he joined the Royal Canadian Navy in 1944 and was assigned to the post of chief fire commissioner.

MINDFUL OF QUEBEC'S LONGSTANDING OPPOSITION to compulsory military service, Prime Minister Mackenzie King had declared in 1939 that there would be no conscription. At first, when eager recruits, including a significant number of French Canadians from Montreal, were rushing to join the army, navy and air force, it looked like an easy promise to keep. But, by the spring of 1940, the Allied forces appeared to be losing the war. Hitler's troops had advanced against Denmark, Norway, Belgium and the Netherlands. By mid-June, the Germans occupied France, and Italy had joined forces with Hitler. The need for reinforcements took on new urgency, and English Canadians were clamouring for a stronger military force to protect a vulnerable Britain.

At the same time, enlistment fever had cooled. Army pay had begun to pale in comparison with the remunerative jobs in Canada's booming munitions industry. In June 1940, Parliament passed the National Resources Mobilization Act—a sweeping piece of legislation that allowed the government to appropriate the property and services of its citizens for the needs of war. Ottawa then ordered all Canadians aged sixteen and over to register for possible national service. The government simply wanted an inventory of the country's manpower—or so the federal politicians said.

Quebec nationalists suspected that King had taken the first step toward overseas conscription. On August 2, 1940, Montreal Mayor Camillien Houde refused to comply and openly encouraged his fellow Quebecers to ignore the National Registration Act. Three days later, the RCMP arrested the popular politician as he was leaving city hall. He would spend the next four years as a prisoner in internment camps. (Clement Toner, the Irish carter who hauled Houde's baggage from Fredericton to the camp at Ripples, New Brunswick, 20 miles east of the town, counted 27 pieces of luggage: small comforts for behind the barbed wire.) Houde easily won back the mayoralty in an election held shortly after his release in August 1944.

Meanwhile, King cautiously eased Canadians down the slippery slope toward conscription. The first home-defence conscripts, thirty thousand men aged twenty-one to twenty-four, were called up in October 1940 for one month of compulsory military training at hastily constructed army camps across the country. In March 1941, the instruction period was extended to four months, and draftees were trained alongside volunteer recruits. A short time later, "trainees" were forced to remain in the army indefinitely and were posted in home-defence units. The army now had two classes of soldiers: "A," or "Active," soldiers willing to take on overseas duty and "R," or "Reserve," men, reluctant conscripts for home service, called Zombies by their sneering colleagues.

But the need for reinforcements became critical after the Japanese attack on Pearl Harbor in December 1941. And in April 1942, Griffin-towners, along with other Canadians, had an opportunity to state how far they were willing to go for their country when King, still wary of breaking his promise, decided to hold a referendum on conscription. Not that he would implement it, even if he had a mandate, stated the

GRIFF
NEWS

Published Monthly by GRIFFINTOWN CLUB for its men in the armed forces.

Masthead of the Griff News, *a monthly newsletter written by members of the Griffintown Club for their men overseas during the Second World War.*

prime minister in the one of the most ambiguous quotes in Canadian history: "Not necessarily conscription but conscription if necessary."

Canadians gave King permission to break his promise: 65 per cent voted for conscription. But the referendum revealed a deep split in the country: 73 per cent of Quebecers voted against conscription, while, in the rest of Canada, 80 per cent endorsed mandatory military service. In Montreal, the vote split along linguistic lines, with English-speaking districts strongly in favour and French against.

In St. Ann's Ward, the results were close, with 53 per cent voting yes. But a closer look at the polls shows a split within the riding. Residents of old Griffintown supported conscription by a resounding 75 per cent. The difference suggests a growing separation from the French-Canadian majority. Nevertheless, while Quebec nationalists staged protests and went on a rampage in Montreal, breaking windows in recruitment offices, many French Canadians from Griffintown enlisted. At least two of them, Lieutenant-Corporal Art Renaud of the Royal 22nd and Private Maurice Demers of the Royal Canadian Army Service Corps, lost their lives.

Despite his new mandate, King did not order any conscripts to go overseas until 1944, after the Canadian infantry suffered severe casualties on D-Day and in the invasion of Normandy. Pressured by military leaders who threatened to resign if the government did not provide reinforcements, he finally agreed to the draft of sixteen thousand home-defence soldiers. Some thirteen thousand reluctant conscripts were shipped to Europe, but only 2,463 faced action on the front.

From the first days of the war, Griffintown supported its boys overseas. Every month, members of the Griffintown Club shipped packages of cigarettes to more than four hundred servicemen overseas. A mothers' group organized rummage sales and raised money to send Christmas parcels.

As the war dragged on, the club decided to reach out to its military men with a newsletter. The first issue of the *Griff News* appeared in April 1943. Every month until the end of the war, the staff and members of the club sent the eight-page *Griff News* to the boys in the trenches, airfields and naval stations.

"Service Mail"—excerpts of letters from the front—became one of the most popular features in the *Griff News*. "We snatch the chance to write when we can," W.H. Parsons wrote from the Mediterranean. "I am writing this from a foxhole. There's one thing about these foxholes: the sergeant major has a job to find you if there is a dirty job around."

George Grimshaw, a member of the Royal Rifles of Canada, spent four years as a prisoner of war in Japan, one of 1,975 Canadians who were captured on Christmas Day, 1941, after the Battle of Hong Kong, and were forced to perform slave labour in POW camps, mines and shipyards. One of only 1,418 of the 1,975 Canadians to survive the ordeal, Grimshaw sent a letter to the Griffintown Club that played down the extreme hardship. In the letter, received on September 11, 1943, but postmarked June 11, 1942, he wrote that he was "in good health and passed the time by playing softball and volleyball."

In a letter that appeared in July 1944, Frank Burton said he'd received the *Griff News* just after he boarded a ship for the D-Day invasion on June 6. "It sure was welcome. It took my mind off a lot of things that I think all the boys were thinking about. I think I was the first one to bring the *Griff News* to France. It came through a lot with me and it is

Brothers George (left) and James Grimshaw, raised in Griffintown, both joined the Royal Rifles of Canada. George spent four years in a Japanese prisoner-of-war camp.

a little worn now from the salt water we waded through to get ashore [at Normandy] and a little ruffled from being in my pocket. The first week was sure hell, and I was in some tight spots, but I came out so far with only with a few scratches from barbed wire. I think we have Jerry running in his own direction."

The writers—staff and volunteers—did not avoid bad news. "Liberator Falls in Griffintown Killing Fifteen" read one headline in the May 1944 edition. The newsletter also included a brief report on the Canada Steamship Lines fire, "one of the biggest in Griffintown"; and, a few months later, an item about the earthquake, lightened with an anecdote: "An old drunk who was passing by bumping into every pole he came to for support asked what all the racket was about. Told it was an earthquake. He said, 'Go on, you're crazy. It was me. They just threw me out of the St. James Hotel.'"

Most issues contained a mix of local happenings and sports, information about club activities, births, deaths and marriages, plenty of humour, nostalgia and warm, morale-boosting letters of pride and appreciation, all doled out with the slap-happy style of the guys on the corner.

The *Griff News* also offered a glimpse into life on the home front. With Griffintown's top boxers—Joe Coughlin, Charlie Cunningham and other champions—off fighting the war, the *News* revisited the club's past glories in the ring, and predicted future stars, with young Gus Mell getting most attention: "Gus Mell should bring Griff's name where it used to be in the boxing game. . . . Mell is a member of Air Cadets 49th Squadron and the Griffintown Boxing Club. Press men who have seen this boy in action [predict] a good future in the ring. He has TNT in his hands."

The war boom had brought a measure of prosperity to Griffintown. Jobs were plentiful and Canadian factory workers' incomes rose steadily from $975 a year in 1939 to $1,500 in 1946. At the same time, strict price controls, monitored by the federal Wartime Prices and Trade Board, kept inflation in check. Still, as Theresa Mott explained in the *Griff News* in April 1944, because of rationing, the standard of living had not improved much since the Depression:

> You will all remember the days when you or someone belonging to you had to go every week to a dingy little office and give your life's history to some fellow . . . and then if you were lucky you got a small pittance which was not enough to keep half the people it was supposed to alive. . . . Today there is plenty of money. . . . Most everyone is making a half decent pay. But the funny thing is that we have no more than we had in the Depression. You can't buy butter today: not because you haven't got the money, but because you have no ration coupons. Sugar, tea, preserves, yes, and even liquor is rationed. If some of you boys were home and wanted to get a bottle of beer you would really know what rationing meant.

The boys overseas learned about Griffintown's aspiring Royal Canadian Air Force pilots. The club's popular Air Cadets, G Squadron No. 49, had more than one hundred members. Another eighty boys under age twelve belonged to the junior cadets. An old Spitfire fighter plane, donated to the club at the beginning of the war and stored in an empty lot behind the building, allowed the cadets to simulate flight and examine an airplane engine. In their neat blue uniforms, they always drew a crowd as they practised marching drills behind their brass band.

"We girls want a chance," Dorothy Stacey wrote in a *Griff News* editorial, demanding a female air cadet squad. "We don't want to fight particularly, but we do want to do our part. Why not give us a chance to show what we can contribute to Canada's war effort?" A girls' corps, she argued, could provide basic training in drill and physical culture, as well as first aid, home nursing, office work (stenography and filing), driving and anti-aircraft detection—war duties that were already being performed by women in the British Isles. By January 1944, fifty girls had formed a cadet corps—the Canadian Auxiliary Service Corps had introduced cadets for girls in 1943—and met for drills every Tuesday night.

The war offered women everywhere new roles and a taste of independence. By 1945, more than fifty thousand women had enlisted, though were most assigned to cooking and clerical jobs, only gradually being given more traditional male tasks as drivers and signal workers. Despite the Griffintown girls' eagerness to contribute to the war effort, any glimmerings of feminism were lost amid the yearning for the men overseas. So many eligible young men had enlisted that the club cancelled its regular Friday night dances. The Fairyland Theatre on Notre Dame Street helped fill the void with *Mrs. Miniver* and other romantic war-themed movies. The radio's anxiety-making news reports and sentimental songs like Vera Lynn's "We'll Meet Again" kept feelings high.

The number of marriages in Canada soared in the war years, and many Griffintown couples joined the march to the altar. Some brides followed their new husbands. But more often the war parted the newly-weds, and teary farewells became a familiar scene in train stations across the country. Many wives and mothers fell to weeping again when a government telegram delivered tragic news.

Slightly more than 1 million Canadians fought in the Second World War, and forty-two thousand lost their lives. Griffintown suffered a proportionately high toll, with twenty-eight casualties from the club alone. Many of them very young: Corporal James Michael Vincent Dilio enlisted in the Victoria Rifles on the day war was declared. Transferred to the Tank Corps, he died in action on August 5, 1943, at the age of twenty-one. Michael Gerald Edmund Donoghue, a twenty-one-year-old pilot officer, died on January 21, 1944. A letter from Jim Connolly appeared in the *Griff News* after the death of his brother, Leo, a sergeant in the RCAF, on February 25, 1944: "We had a nice funeral. Only two of the crew survived the crash. The pilot could have bailed out but got back into his seat and did his best to set the aircraft down easy. Leo was unconscious when they got him out and he died the following afternoon."

STILL, MONTREAL HAD A FRIVOLOUS SIDE, even during the war. In a celebrated October 15, 1944, *Maclean's* article, sportswriter Jim Coleman called it the "Paris of North America," claiming that "demon rum may be rationed in other sections of the country but there is enough medicinal spirits in Montreal to float the entire Atlantic fleet up St. Catherine Street. . . . Tired businessman, expatriates who have fled briefly from the more arid sections of the country, money-heavy war workers and young men and women of the armed services keep the merry wheels spinning. . . . It is more than probable that it is enough to make the boys in France and Italy gag slightly—but this is part of the 'Home Front' in September 1944."

But there was another group that servicemen resented even more—

zoot-suiters, the dandies who called them "suckers" for going to war. When the *Griff News* reported that Pete Levery, a sometime Griffintown boxer, was a zoot-suiter, it brought "howls of protest." The long-haired young Montrealers who adopted the zoot-suit fad were largely, but not all, French-Canadian war resisters. Their gaudy attire, inspired by jazz musicians, flouted the laws of good taste as well as government regulations. During the war, restrictions were placed on pant cuffs, patch pockets, and even women's skirt lengths, in order to save scarce fabric, thread and buttons for military use.

Hanging from exaggerated, wide padded shoulders, the long, loose jacket of a zoot suit reached almost to the knees. It was worn over voluminous, extra-high-waisted trousers that narrowed at the ankles. A wide-collared shirt, flashy oversized tie and a wide-brimmed hat completed the colourful outfit. A long watch or key chain, strung from the belt, was an optional accessory. In the lingo of "hep cats"—1940s swing enthusiasts—it was "the drape shape with the reet pleat and the stuff cuff." Sailors saw the zoot-suiters as cowardly and unpatriotic.

In the spring and summer of 1944, soldiers and zooters frequently fought on the streets in downtown Montreal, as well as in St. Lambert, on the south shore, and in LaFontaine Park, in the east end of Montreal. The violence escalated in late May, with a series of incidents culminating in a riot in Verdun on June 3, after the navy set out looking for zooters.

Some four hundred sailors, at least a few Griffintowners among them, searched St. Catherine Street bars and pulled their extravagantly dressed enemies out of their favourite haunts to beat them up. As the evening wound down, more than a hundred sailors headed west, to the Verdun Pavilion, a dance hall and a known zooter hangout. The patrons barricaded the doors and cowered inside, but the sailors battered down the doors and instigated a brawl that lasted for more than an hour, causing numerous minor injuries (not to mention the indignities to several zooters who had their fancy clothes torn off their backs). The police arrested four civilians; the navy's shore patrol detained several sailors.

Griffintown's tough reputation followed the boys overseas. In April 1945, J.H. McCarthy, a dispatch rider in Europe, complained that he had to convince servicemen from other parts of Montreal that the district had changed: "They have the idea that all we do is stand around corners waiting for some unfortunate fellow to pass so we can beat him up, but I am gradually teaching them they are all wrong."

A strong affection for the old neighbourhood emerged in many servicemen's letters. At Roger Harkins's request, in April 1944, the *Griff News* printed a few verses of the sentimental singsong favourite, "Oh, Take Me Back to Griffintown":

> *Griffintown, Griffintown.*
> *That's where I long to be*
> *Where my friends are good to me*
> *Hogan's Bath on Wellington Street*
> *Where the Point bums wash their feet*
> *Haymarket Square, I don't care anywhere*
> *For it's Griffintown for me.*

And in November 1943, navy man Chubby Doyle, unhappy about a mess hall assignment, sent in lyrics for a song he wrote about Griffintown, to be sung to the tune of "Dear Old Pal of Mine":

> *Oh, how we miss you, good old Griffintown,*
> *And think of you most, when's the light's turned down*
> *All the fun that's in you, and our loved ones with you,*
> *You know we're with you*
> *For there's just one Griff.*

But Griffintown was changing dramatically during the war years. Early in 1944, Cliff Sowery warned of an unsettling transformation: "I wonder how many of you will want to settle down in Griff after travelling around the world. The powers that be have given us a beautiful new railway station [Central Station] but the approaches to it have wiped out a big stretch of Griffintown. This district in the heart of Montreal seems destined to become an industrial centre, and we hope that plans for its people are as carefully made as are plans for cities which have the most advanced town planning."

"Our Griffintown has been torn to pieces in the last ten to fifteen years," Tom Murphy warned in the May 1944 issue. Murphy estimated that between demolitions and expropriations, half of the houses in Griffintown were now torn down. Murphy lamented the loss of the Haymarket. "Today the CN trains pass over the spot where all the good ballplayers in Griffintown played at one time or another. . . . A little farther down the street they cross over our old softball field at the corner of Ottawa and Nazareth streets."

"You can tear down the buildings and the houses in any district, but you cannot tear down the spirit of the people who inhabit that district," he wrote optimistically. "The days of Griffintown slipping backwards instead of advancing can be stopped if each and every one of us united our efforts after the war to make our Griffintown the place which we would all love to see it again. The center of political power, sports, and above all, happy home life, that it has been in the past and will be again in the near future, we hope."

But the war years—and the plane crash and Canada Steamship Lines fire and the earthquake—had made Griffintown, and Griffintowners, more vulnerable. In 1944, the Redemptorists tried to boost the community's spirits by installing a bowling alley in St. Ann's Hall. Hockey star Gordie Howe, MP Tom Healy and city councillor Frank Hanley attended the opening night in October. Bowling alleys enjoyed a heyday across North America in the postwar years, and Griffintowners filled the lanes every night of the week. But it would take more than a popular pastime to revive Montreal's urban Irish village after the Second World War. Although affection for the old neighbourhood remained intact, war had changed the soldiers arriving at Bonaventure Station in 1945. Once they stepped off the trains from Halifax and passed the welcoming bands, they found themselves in a different Griffintown and a changing city.

ELEVEN

Leaving Griff

So loath we part from all we love
From all the links that bind us . . .
—Thomas Moore

THE ODDS WERE AGAINST THE KID from Griffintown. Gus Mell, a nineteen-year-old rookie with barely a year in the pro rings, appeared to be no match for Sal Bartolo, the National Boxing Association's world featherweight champion. Sure, the gutsy Mell had won ten consecutive fights after winning the Canadian featherweight crown in June 1944. And, yes, he had evened the score with a technical knockout in a rematch after Jerry Zullo knocked him flat in ninety seconds in a fight at Boston Garden on March 12, 1945. But the twenty-eight-year-old Bartolo, a veteran slugger, had fended off all pretenders to his crown for more than a year. On Friday, April 13, 1945, nearly nine thousand boxing fans filled Boston Garden, ready to root for Bartolo, the hometown favourite.

Once the fight started, the crowd went wild with cheers, but not for the "Pride of East Boston." Mell's whirlwind style, his unrelenting storm of left hooks punctuated with jolting rights to body and jaw, undermined the 128-pound champ and awed the fans. The non-title fight lasted the full ten rounds and, in the end, Mell, a 132-pound underdog, took the decision.

The upset victory rushed Mell to third spot in the world featherweight rankings—and into the limelight. Back in Montreal, the hometown press heaped praise on the city's new boxing hero: "Bartolo relied mainly on his vast boxing skill and two-handed barrages near the end of each round but he couldn't keep Mell out. The kid out-boxed him and, at times, outslugged him," the *Montreal Standard* reported. "Mell boxed beautifully and punched hard with both hands to win one of the greatest ovations ever heard in the history of Boston Gardens."

The good-looking Irish lad had proved himself a contender. A shot at the crown, fortune and fame seemed almost inevitable, the *Standard* predicted in a laudatory article the day after the fight: "It has long been apparent around Montreal that Gus Mell had class. The kid from Griffintown, who only a few months ago, was helping support his fatherless home through meagre pickings from $25 preliminaries, has hit the jackpot. A title bout with Bartolo is now inevitable and the $7000 he garnered as his share of last night's $22,000 gate will be chicken feed beside what's to come. The kid is already on fistian's glory road—and only 19."

Pictures of Mell went up all around the club. A few days after his victory over Bartolo, the club's directors rewarded their promising young protege with a signet ring and a rare lifetime membership.

Mell spent most of the summer training for his next big fights. On weekends, he went for rides in country in the brand-new car he bought with his winnings. Gus "Pell" Mell, the "Pride of Griffintown," stood at the top of Canadian boxing rankings. It was just a matter of time, his neighbours and friends believed, until he took the world title—and showed the world what the Griffintown Irish could do.

Disappointingly, Mell would lose his much-anticipated rematch

*Griffintown boxer Gus "Pell" Mell, a contender for the
world featherweight title, trains for a big fight in November 1945.*

with Bartolo—a title fight on May 4, 1945, in Boston. "Bartolo defeats
Mell" shouted the banner headline in the next day's *New York Times*.
Mell had missed his first chance at a world title by a whisker. Never
mind. The quiet-mannered boy from Colborne Street had made the
big league. He was fighting the best in his weight class. Admitting
Bartolo was his stiffest competition, he told reporters he wanted a rubber match. "I can take him all right. I know most of his tricks now."

Mell still had high hopes. By the end of September he had defeated three name fighters—and beaten Bartolo a second time. Sportswriters started to compare him to the likes of Joe Louis, Sugar Ray Robinson and Johnny Greco. Dave Egan wrote in the *Boston Daily Record*, on September 24, 1945: "Mell has many of the attributes of the star of the future. He reeks color, he is a deadly puncher."

THE SWEET SCENT OF OPTIMISM blew through Griffintown's careworn streets in the spring of 1945. Gus Mell had just come back from Boston flush with the promise of future glory, a contender, if not yet a world champion. Then, just a few days later, on May 8, came the euphoria of VE Day, the declaration of victory in Europe. In fact, the news of Germany's surrender broke on Monday, May 7, and overjoyed Canadians didn't wait for the official ceremony planned for the next day. In downtown Montreal, offices emptied as tens of thousands poured into the streets for a spontaneous celebration, with an explosion of ticker tape and confetti, cheering and flag waving, singing and dancing, to the tune of church bells, sirens and honking car horns. Fighting would continue in the Pacific through the summer, but at least in Europe the war was over. Griffintown's sailors, soldiers and flyboys would soon return from overseas. It would be like the good old days. And, for a time, it was. But the end of the Second World War marked the beginning of the end of Griffintown.

Homecoming was bittersweet. Old gangs started reappearing on the corners, nostalgic for the dozens of pals who would never come home. Some veterans bore serious war wounds. In July, the *Griff News* reported that Leo Durocher was back sitting in the bleachers at the Basin Street park, watching baseball, but he faced a series of operations to remove shrapnel from his lungs. Archie Pearson laughed off the injury that forced him to use a cane and wear slippers, blaming the army for marching him all over the country.

Many who had left as boys had grown up at war. A large number of Griffintown veterans had enlisted to escape the Depression and none wanted to fall into poverty again. "Tell the boys to keep their guns, to insure that we don't go back to the pre-war standard of living," Jim Connolly wrote in a darkly humorous letter from Europe in April 1945. Many returned to jobs in the railways and local factories. Some took advantage of veterans' programs to continue their education. But others had dropped out of school as early as grade three to help support their families during the Depression, and with little education they had trouble finding a decent, steady job.

"Oh, Take Me Back to Griffintown" may have been one of the most popular songs for homesick boys at war, but many returning veterans did not linger long in the old neighbourhood. The postwar passion for progress and the shiny-new made the district's rundown housing, with its antiquated plumbing, seem an embarrassment, hopelessly behind the times.

The last of the privies had disappeared by the 1930s. Bylaws had forced landlords to install indoor toilets, which they did, sometimes awkwardly. But few landlords updated their properties and many houses still did not have bathtubs or hot running water. Mothers continued to plop children into metal washtubs in the middle of the kitchen. Adults sought out the public showers in St. Ann's bowling alley, the Griffintown Club, O'Connell's Bath on Duke Street or Central Station.

Many of the houses were hard to heat. "My father used to get up and keep the fire going all night," says Iris Howden. "The belly of that old woodstove was red!" The Galleys had three stoves in their ten-room house on Eleanor Street—one at the front entrance, another in the kitchen and a third at the top of the stairs, near the bedrooms. The family had to leave the water running so the pipes wouldn't freeze. In the morning, they took the block of ice out of the sink and put it in the icebox.

Like many of his buddies, Gerald O'Connell, an ex-navy man, married and moved to a new bungalow in Pointe Claire, one of several rapidly expanding suburbs west of the city. Some convinced their parents to follow them, and the Irish began to trickle out of Griffintown, typically heading west to Point St. Charles, Verdun and Notre-Dame-de-Grâce, or NDG, as Montrealers called it, though they returned in large numbers every week to attend St. Ann's Church, to participate in the St. Ann's Young Men's Society, the sodality and other parish activities, and to visit family and friends who stayed behind.

The ties that kept the Irish in Griffintown were beginning to unravel. Thousands stayed, some too poor to move, but many were too attached to the familiar old neighbourhood and their beloved St. Ann's Church to think of leaving. Others simply preferred the district's convenient location, near the centre of the city. In 1946, Betty Bryant, then a twenty-three-year-old secretary, and her sister, Irene, convinced their mother to move out of their tiny flat on William Street into a much larger, newer house in Verdun. Six months later, the family returned to Griffintown, to a house on McCord. "She couldn't stand it, so we had to move her back," said Bryant. Young people, too, refused to join the flight to the suburbs. They swept and scrubbed bumpy oilcloth floors, they applied a fresh coat of colour to walls thick with a century's worth of paint and wallpaper, and they settled in to raise another generation.

While one of Canada's oldest Irish settlements defied the forces of time, Montreal indulged in a postwar love affair with modernity. By the time Expo 67 opened its doors to the world for Canada's centennial, the city had become a bustling metropolis with a cosmopolitan European flair. The Lachine Canal, the ancient handiwork of Irish labourers, once the key to the city's prosperity, had slipped into irrelevancy in 1959, with the opening of the St. Lawrence Seaway. Montreal's impressive new port, one of the largest in the world, expanded and renovated to handle year-round shipping, could now accommodate the supersized commercial vessels that travelled the 2,355-mile waterway. In

1960, the opening of a new terminal at Dorval International Airport, the busiest in the country, clinched its role as the gateway to Canada. And the industrial districts along the canal began to decline as traffic shifted to the impressive Port of Montreal.

The city's skyline rose to the occasion with the completion of Place Ville Marie in 1962, at the time the largest, most innovative office complex in the world. Designed by renowned modernist architect I. M. Pei, the office tower's cruciform shape echoed the cross on Mount Royal. It soared forty-two storeys up from a vast public plaza above an innovative subterranean shopping mall with an underground link to Central Station. A huge rotating light at the top of Place Ville Marie waved long arms of light over the mountain, the city and, through the spaces between the thickening forest of skyscrapers, into Griffintown.

Happily ignored by urban planners and developers, Griffintown had become an anachronism, and in the 1950s the lively, close-knit, largely English-speaking enclave, barely a mile from the glitter of Peel and St. Catherine streets, enjoyed a last hurrah.

Shiny, long-finned Chevys wheeled the '50s into Griffintown and parked the future on its narrow streets, in front of century-old lace-curtained doorways or in backyard sheds and stables. Old-timers embraced the new, but held on to the past. When Bunny Kehoe, who never learned to drive, won a fancy new car in a raffle, he put his prize up on blocks in a garage on Young Street. Ninety-year-old Sarah Higgins, daughter of Famine emigrants, sat in her rocker, snuff box in one hand, rosary beads in another, watching boxing on one of the first television sets on her block.

Griffintown housewives watched *Leave It to Beaver*'s June Cleaver cook dinner on a modern electric range, then retreated to their own nineteenth-century kitchens with iceboxes and woodstoves and wringer washers. A few holdouts clamped a wringer to a washtub balanced on two kitchen chairs and did their laundry by hand on a scrubbing board. In the winter, towels and longjohns were hung to dry on a line strung

NHL Detroit Red Wings attend a rosary service broadcast from
Our Mother of Perpetual Help Shrine at St. Ann's Church, c. 1954–1955

across the kitchen, or draped over the backs of chairs, the oven door or the stovepipes.

A few rear dwellings, decried by Herbert B. Ames more than half a century earlier as "abominations," remained standing. One Ottawa Street resident kept a rooster and chickens in a communal backyard, chopping off their heads with an axe on a block of wood near the sheds. Leo "Clawhammer" Leonard kept horses in his Griffintown Horse Palace, a stable built in 1834, one of the last in the city.

Father McElligott, the parish priest, had reason to worry about the future of St. Ann's Church. He knew that dozens of once-flourishing emigrant Irish parishes in New York, Boston, Philadelphia, Baltimore and other American cities, as well as in Halifax, Quebec, Kingston and

Toronto, were rapidly diminishing, as the second and third generations assimilated and drifted away from the urban core to large, mixed parishes in the suburbs. Even the churches of South Boston faced challenges as new populations moved into the famously Irish enclave.

Closer to home, the bells of St. Edward's Anglican Church had already stopped ringing over Haymarket Square. The small congregation, only five hundred parishioners, half of them living outside the neighbourhood, could not afford repairs to the stately structure at the corner of Inspector and St. Paul. They put the building up for sale after a final Sunday service on October 1, 1950. It sold in November 1952.

But the Redemptorists, encouraged by high attendance, ignored the threat to the parish and proceeded with extensive renovations in preparation for a celebration of St. Ann's centenary in 1954. Father James Farrell, born across the street from the church, preached the keynote sermon at a special mass during the week-long festivities, which included plays, concerts and banquets attended by several thousand former residents, and numerous celebrities.

St. Ann's, a rare survivor, continued to thrive. Many parishioners who had moved out of Griffintown frequently returned on Sundays and Tuesdays and participated in parish organizations, as if they had never left.

> *Mary help us, help, we pray;*
> *Mary help us, help, we pray;*
> *Help us in all care and sorrow,*
> *Mary help us, help, we pray.*

Thousands of voices, young and old, strong and quavering, joined in the surging strains of *Mother Dearest, Mother Fairest*, competing with St. Ann's organist, Lena Blickstead, pulling out all the stops on the powerful Casavant organ. At 5:15 on Tuesday evenings in the 1950s and '60s, St. Ann's Church was jammed. The weekly devotion to Our Mother of

Perpetual Help, introduced by the Redemptorists in the bleak days of the Depression, had become a tradition that attracted Catholics and Protestants from across the city.

By 1951, more than 5 million people had attended what came to be known as "the Tuesdays" and placed more than 20 million petitions at the shrine to Our Mother of Perpetual Help. To accommodate the growing crowds over the years, the Redemptorists added extra services. By the 1950s, there were six—the first at 9:30 a.m., the last at 9 p.m. The city ran special buses for the thousands of Montrealers—many of them non-Catholics—who made the regular weekly pilgrimages to St. Ann's, where they placed their petitions on the altar and lined up to light a float in front of the miraculous icon of Our Mother of Perpetual Help, after the service.

The brogue that once dominated the district had softened to a gentle lilt (some now called it a Griffintown accent). And a postwar influx of Italian and other European immigrants helped French Canadians out-number the Irish in old Griffintown. But the neighbourhood never lost its Irish character. Never was this more obvious than in the weeks leading up to March 17, the feast of Ireland's patron saint. St. Ann's Hall reverberated with the *clickety-clackety-stomp* of the tap dancers rehearsing for the annual Irish concert, with Italians and Ukrainians competing for a place in the lineup of Irish colleens and gossoons.

Griffintown's streets hummed on St. Patrick's Day morning. The St. Ann's contingent would assemble outside the hall on Ottawa Street before heading uptown to take their place in the parade. Marshalls organized the merry confusion as top-hatted marchers and bands and ponies and the jaunting cart hurried to find their place in the lineup. Young boys outfitted in green satin scurried around on ponies and horses decorated with softball-sized kelly-green rosettes, trying to control them amid the noise of the band tuning up for the "Wearing of the Green" and "Come Back to Erin."

By the 1950s, many members of the Young Men's Society lived in other parishes, but they always returned to St. Ann's for the parade. Don Pidgeon, the United Irish Societies' historian, grew up in Griffintown and remembers the warmth of the reunions. St. Ann's Young Men, in dark overcoats, white silk scarves and top hats bedecked with shamrocks, walked in lockstep down the painted green line on St. Catherine Street, behind silk banners, brass bands and the jaunting cart. Priests and dignitaries waved from shiny black Cadillacs. The traditional shenanigans would resume at the Queen's Hotel after the parade.

Firecracker Day hijinks continued to light up the street every May 24 through the 1950s and beyond. Griffintown's everyday street life lost none of its verve, with the gangs on the corner seeming to take their cue from the plucky comic characters in the *Dead End Kids,* the *East Side Kids* and the *Bowery Boys,* three popular movie series in the 1940s and '50s. Hollywood had transformed the historic Bowery Boys—the notoriously vicious New York City gangs that had terrorized Irish Catholics a century earlier—into a group of good-natured young ruffians from New York's gritty tenements, not unlike those of Griffintown. Actor Leo Gorcey, star of more than sixty of the movies, played the leader of the gang, an aspiring fighter variously named Muggs Maloney or Slip Mahoney—a ready hero for scrappy Griffintown boys with Irish names and Golden Gloves ambitions.

Registrations for the club's Junior Golden Gloves hit a record high in 1948. Gus "Pell" Mell had, by then, won the hearts of Boston fight fans. His name—eventually added in April 1975 to the New England Boxing Hall of Fame—was always a box-office draw in the city where he had a fan club, and needed the protection of a police escort on his way in and out of the ring, to keep from getting mobbed by exuberant admirers. Expectations of Mell's imminent riches inspired poor boys' dreams of punching their way to fame and fortune. And many young sluggers continued to make their way to the Griffintown Club from across the city and beyond, to train and fight in the renowned annual tournament in the postwar years.

ABOVE: *Donny Marry, Leo Mason, Jackie Kelly, Herbie Mines and (front) Jimmy Kelly walk under the banner of the St. Ann's Young Men's Society in the 1955 St. Patrick's Day parade.*
BELOW: *Kindergarten children in the "Hop, One, Two, Three," the traditional opening number of the St. Patrick's Day concert, in 1949.*

Gus Mell shared the limelight with several other local boxers who rose to prominence in the ring. Armand Savoie, a fireman's son, grew up at the corner of Ottawa and Colborne streets, only a brick's throw from the Griffintown Club. In 1948, he won both the provincial and Canadian featherweight titles and, later that year, represented Canada at the Olympic Games at Wembley Stadium in London, England. Savoie turned pro in 1950 and went on to fight 103 matches in Canada, the United States, England and Ireland. He won the Canadian light-weight title on September 24, 1951. On July 7, 1952, he picked up the Canadian welterweight title in a bout with Johnny Greco, only to lose it in a rematch on August 26. His impressive career record—57 wins (KOs 30), 40 losses and 6 draws—eventually earned him a place in the Canadian Boxing Hall of Fame.

Griffintown's Marcel "Rocky" Brisebois appeared in Canada's first televised boxing match on February 8, 1954. Oddsmakers favoured Brisebois—the national welterweight champion from 1952 to 1954—in the title fight against Claude Fortin. And the Griffintown boxer, said to make a novena at St. Ann's Church before most of his fights, hand-ily dominated his opponent. But two judges called it a tie and the third gave it to Brisebois. Officials declared the fight a draw, despite an official rule that the majority should rule. Brisebois' manager loudly objected, chanting "We wuz robbed" in nine dialects in the space of a minute, and saying: "Two judges give the fight even and one scores it for Brisebois. Need I say more?" The *Herald's* headline read "Fuzzy draw decision puzzles boxing fans."

Two weeks later, Brisebois went into the ring for the last time for a scheduled match against Reggie Chartrand. Only twenty-four, Brisebois had racked up a spectacular record in his 114 pro bouts—96 wins, 14 losses and 4 draws. Then he hung up his gloves in frustration and walked away from the sport forever.

In the early 1950s, Frankie Fitzgerald, another young Griffintown boxing champion, decided to enter the pro ring after competing in the

Empire Games in Vancouver. But he found his career blocked before it even started. Despite a certificate of health from a medical doctor, the Quebec Boxing Federation declined to qualify him for the ring, citing his faint heart murmur. "Cliff Sowery was getting too powerful," Fitzgerald said. Griffintown boxers could no longer count on fighting their way out and up. The rules had become arbitrary—both in the ring and out. And Griffintowners lost, even when they had won.

The district had already suffered a major blow. On October 27, 1953, just months before Brisebois appeared in the controversial televised fight, the venerable boys' club shut its doors forever. Never mind that the noise and chatter of the more than four hundred children and teens filled its gym, workshops and activity rooms six nights a week. After reaching a peak of nearly two thousand in 1946, membership had declined to about eight hundred in 1953; now mostly Catholics, many French-speaking. The club's directors wanted to redirect its funds to a location with a large English-speaking Protestant population, to focus on "non-sectarian" work. (Dow Brewery bought the property and, three years later, demolished the club and turned it into a parking lot.)

TIMES MAY HAVE BEEN CHANGING, but Frank "Banjo" Hanley, popular city councillor and MLA for St. Ann's Ward, still fought for his constituents with all the chutzpah of a Tammany Hall ward boss. "Go see Hanley" was a byword for residents of Griffintown and Point St. Charles. Like an old-time ward-heeler, he would fix parking tickets. "Oh yeah. I'd just call this fellow on Senneville St. and say, 'No parking tickets on him, he's a good guy,'" he said in an interview. He also helped hard-up constituents in need of a job or a handout. "I probably gave out one hundred dollars a week to these people."

Griffintowners had always counted on their local politicians to cut through Montreal's partisan politics and find jobs for Irish Catholics with the police, fire and other city departments. And many, like Buster

"Republic of Hanley" election campaign poster.

Broden, owed their careers to Hanley. He got Broden—a dead ringer for Art Carney, the comic character who played sewer worker Ed Norton on the 1950s *Jackie Gleason Show*—a job in the sewers. Broden shared the comedian's deadpan humour, but, with Banjo Hanley's support, he advanced much further than Norton. Broden eventually became a master electrician by enrolling in a correspondence trade school, and he earned several promotions in Montreal's water department, eventually assuming responsibility for the sewers in the whole west end, a position that came with a station wagon and a chauffeur.

In return, Banjo expected Broden to hire unemployed Irishmen. From time to time, he would call and say, "I'm going to send someone over. I want you to give him a job," Broden's son Connie recalled. But not all of them made ideal employees and Buster had to cover for a number of Hanley's proteges, many of whom liked to drink on the job. Broden's sewer crew had to watch water levels in a dozen or so sewage basins in their area. The men would drop a pail of water into the sewer as a gauge. "And in the bucket were quarts of beer. It kept the beer cold," said Connie, a retired brewery executive and former Montreal Canadiens player and NHL scout.

Buster would go down into the sewer stations to check on the guys. "And the guy would be asleep or drunk. Somebody would get disciplined, and, of course, the mother of the person who was disciplined would phone Banjo, and then Banjo would phone my father."

But the men proved loyal to Buster. "On one occasion, they brought him home to my mother, and announced that poor Buster got gassed in one of the manholes in Verdun—turned out he got gassed in the tavern," said Art Broden, Buster's older son. "If my mother would have ever found out, she would have killed him and the poor guys that brought him home."

The boys were loyal to Hanley, too, often helping him win elections. The showboating Irishman knew how to woo voters. "I kissed more babies and attended more wakes, Irish wakes, French-Canadian and even Protestant wakes, than all of my opponents put together," Hanley boasted to a reporter after he retired. Although one relative remembers a snub: "When my Johnny died, he sent somebody else, a French fellow, to write in the book. He got everything wrong." Still, few could argue the politician's claim: "The people loved me." And, just to be sure, during summer campaigns, Hanley's team would organize street dances on Young Street and show movies on large screens in Gallery Square. His outrageous shenanigans—he managed to dupe Jimmy Durante, Pierre Trudeau and other celebrities into campaigning for him—infuriated the authorities and won the devotion of his constituents in the riding he called the "Republic of Hanley."

Hanley entered municipal politics in 1940, winning his first election by acclamation. Shortly after taking office, he impressed Mayor Camillien Houde—also famed for outrageous behaviour—by settling a potential garbage strike. His solution: half the workers would perform the additional end-of-day tasks demanded by the city and return the horses to their stables, while the other half stayed behind and drank beer. The two groups would take turns. So began the brilliant career of a populist Irish politician.

He went on to win more than a dozen consecutive elections, often in a landslide, and represented St. Ann's Ward on Montreal city council from 1940 to 1970 and in the Quebec legislature from 1948 to 1970. Asked the secret of his success at the polls, Hanley stated: "You don't take chances. You bring more ballots to the box than you have on the list. You go up to Côte-des-Neiges [cemetery] and take down names of people. Of course, other people did it for me." Montreal had a long history of wild elections. Few passed without reports of goons, telegraphing—padding voting lists with names taken from headstones—and other tactics. And Hanley's supporters were no more adept at stealing and stuffing ballot boxes than their rivals.

In one 1940s election, Hanley's boys kidnapped a candidate planning to run against him. The would-be opponent was walking along Notre Dame Street, heading to City Hall to register the day before nominations closed, when a car pulled up alongside and two goons grabbed him and pushed him into the trunk. They held him prisoner in a poolroom for twenty-four hours, until the deadline passed. "I don't know who kidnapped my opponent," Hanley told a reporter many years later. "But it sure made my campaign much easier. Less bother."

Hanley remained an independent during his three decades in politics: "I guess that is the Irish in me," he explained. The ultimate pragmatist, Hanley supported whichever party happened to be in power, aiming to garner as much of the patronage spoils as he could for his constituents. It was a strategy that led him to embrace Maurice Duplessis, the controversial Union Nationale leader and premier of Quebec who swept into power on August 17, 1936, ending the Liberals' thirty-nine-year reign in the province. Duplessis led a crusade against communism with his infamous 1937 Padlock Law, which gave the government power to lock up the premises of anyone suspected of promoting the movement. That law, as well as Duplessis' strong Quebec nationalism, raised the ire of many anglophones. But the Church and Irish Catholics, including his cabinet minister, T.J. Coonan, MLA for the Montreal riding of

St. Laurent (and brother of artist Emily Coonan, both raised in St. Ann's Ward) supported the premier. Hanley saw Duplessis as an ally: "I was very friendly with Duplessis and we got along very well," he stated in a 1985 interview for the *Canadian Parliamentary Review.* "He was the best Prime Minister I have ever known. He was very charitable and very good to the minorities but he just was not liked by the English."

Hanley was also a strong supporter of Camillien Houde, the self-styled "Cyrano de Montréal." The popular mayor presided over Montreal during the freewheeling '40s and '50s, when many police and politicians turned a blind eye to the city's booming gambling dens and bawdy houses, provided that they shared in the profits.

In 1948, Montreal lawyer Pacifique Plante, better known as Pax Plante, tried to shut down the party with an investigation into the city's police force and municipal politicians. He published his findings in a series of sixty-two articles that ran in *Le Devoir* over a three-month period, beginning on November 28, 1949. The exposé, written with the help of journalist Gérard Filion, revealed details of underworld activities protected by police. The scandalous revelations led to a public inquiry. In September 1950, Justice François Caron began the hearings in a probe that would take four years. Meanwhile, Plante, for a time head of the morality squad, and Jean Drapeau, another earnest young lawyer, continued the crusade to close down Montreal's myriad blind pigs, bookies, gambling dens and prostitution rings.

On October 28, 1954—three weeks after Caron published his damning report on the Montreal administration—Drapeau won the mayoralty in a landslide victory. But the reformist mayor lost the next election, in 1957. Drapeau's clean-up campaign, including a restriction on the hours of liquor establishments, met fierce resistance from senior police and city officials. And Hanley, who often served as acting mayor, provided some of the strongest opposition. Indeed, the Irish politician had made a plea to legalize gambling in his maiden speech in the provincial legislature in 1948. But the former jockey's persistent defence of gambling as a harmless activity outraged Drapeau—and led to a long-lasting political feud.

In 1956, Drapeau tried to sway Catholic voters in St. Ann's riding against Hanley by sending them a letter quoting Pope Pius XII's encyclical on politicians, in an attempt to show that Hanley was unfit for public office. And the diminutive councillor was twice dragged out of city hall, kicking and shouting, by police on the orders of Mayor Drapeau. In 1960, the blarney-mouthed Irishman attempted to filibuster a budget amendment that would have hurt his constituents by cutting municipal jobs and recreation facilities. The ex-jockey was ejected a second time in 1969, when he got carried away in his fight against a bylaw permitting the sale of horsemeat.

But Quebec's Quiet Revolution would eventually silence the "Voice of the Irish." Hanley lost an important ally with the death of Premier Maurice Duplessis in 1959. (The premier had bankrolled Hanley's 1956 election campaign, to counter Drapeau's strong opposition to the outspoken Irishman.) By the end of the 1960s, Hanley, the Irish and indeed the province's entire anglophone minority would lose considerable influence under Duplessis' successor, Jean Lesage. Power would shift emphatically to the francophone majority as the province sought greater autonomy, loosened its ties to the Church and focused on preserving French language and culture. In Montreal, heated language debates preoccupied the dwindling English-speaking population, only a third of whom, in 1961, were bilingual. (In 1961, French Canadians made up 64 per cent of Montreal's population of 1.7 million.)

Drapeau returned to the mayor's office in 1960 with an imaginative vision for the city. He launched a breathtaking series of public works: the Place des Arts, the Montreal Symphony Orchestra's magnificent new home, completed in 1964; the swish new subway system, opened in 1966; and several other public works that would transform the city in preparation for Expo 67. But Drapeau, bent on creating a sophisticated, modern metropolis, willingly sacrificed historic buildings to widen streets and make room for dozens of high-rise offices and apartments, as well as his architectural wonders. Alarmed at the loss of the city's heritage, activists organized to protect Old Montreal. By then, Drapeau had turned his attention to Griffintown.

Mayor Drapeau delivered the first in a series of lethal blows to the neighbourhood in 1963, when the City of Montreal rezoned almost all of Griffintown for industrial use. The change prevented owners of existing residential properties from rebuilding if a house burned down or was demolished. It also removed any incentive to maintain them. Gentrification—the salvation of working-class districts across North America—became illegal in Griffintown. The Drapeau administration never explained the reason for the change but its implication was clear: the city wanted to depopulate the district.

Rumours spread that Drapeau was trying to eliminate his long-time foe, Frank Hanley. "Drapeau pulled all the houses down, so Frank wouldn't have any more voters," says a cousin, John Hanley Jr. If so, the tactic worked. One after another, blocks of houses fell victim to the wrecking ball; some were paved for parking lots, others left vacant. The City of Montreal, notorious for ignoring bylaw violations in Griffintown, began to condemn unfit dwellings while ignoring fire-prone junkyards and other hazardous industries in the area.

In 1964, St. Ann's lost fifteen hundred parishioners when the city bulldozed Victoriatown, a working-class enclave on the other side of the canal, at the entrance to the Victoria Bridge. The small outpost of six residential streets known as Goose Village had risen on the site of the old fever sheds. City planners preparing for Expo 67 erected the Autostade football stadium on part of the land. It was torn down in 1970, and Goose Village became a sea of asphalt, with a new street grid and new French street names.

Once again, the city attempted to relocate the Black Stone that marks the mass grave of the Irish Famine emigrants. The enormous boulder, on Bridge Street in Goose Village, presented an obstacle to the city's plans to widen and straighten the approach to the Victoria Bridge in preparation for Expo 67. Montreal's Irish societies fought the move and, in June 1966, both parties agreed on a compromise. The historic monument would remain in place, on a small traffic island stranded in the middle of the busy four-lane road.

The attack on Griffintown continued. In 1965, the city planners decided to route a new elevated highway through the middle of the neighbourhood. In May, the City of Montreal expropriated several blocks of houses and businesses, almost a third of the district. It ordered fifty families out of their homes and tore down the O'Connell Bath to make room for the Bonaventure Autoroute, linking the city centre to the Expo site.

In January 1967, one Griffintown landowner made a belated attempt at gentrification and renovated a rundown block of century-old row-houses on Mountain Street, across from St. Ann's Church. Frank Hanley praised the project for bringing back "some of the happiness of the old community," and, with characteristic overstatement, called it "a little bit of Westmount in Griffintown." But so many dwellings had been flattened by then that the once bustling district had taken on the forlorn air of a bombed city. One sad consolation: the rubble-strewn vacant lots opened up vistas of Mount Royal.

Next came the assault on the schools. The Montreal Catholic School Commission closed St. Ann's Boys' School and the kindergarten in 1965, and moved all the children—boys and girls—into St. Ann's Girls' Academy on McCord Street. Three years later, the commission closed that school too, despite protests from the pastor and parents. Neighbourhood children were bused to schools in another district a few miles away.

By 1970, Griffintown's population had fallen to fifteen hundred souls. Like many longtime residents, Nellie and Arthur Howden ignored, as long as they could, the notice to leave their flat on Murray Street. "My mother was the last one out. They were tearing houses down around her," says her daughter, Iris Howden. The Howdens found a flat on a nearby street, but they were soon forced out of that one too.

"They wouldn't tear down the church, would they?" parishioners asked each other as they stood on the steps of St. Ann's each Sunday. The church continued to draw large crowds for its Tuesday devotions, as well as on Sundays. But in 1969, the bishop asked the Redemptorists to close their mission in St. Ann's Parish. The priests held the last of their famous Tuesday devotions to Our Mother of Perpetual Help on August 19. On Sunday, February 1, 1970, at the end of the final mass, the last teary-eyed parishioners walked out of their beloved church and the doors of St. Ann's shut forever.

Under the terms of their 1884 contract, the Redemptorists relinquished the church, house and garden—built on Sulpician land—to the bishop. The chancery office immediately called for demolition tenders. In early June, a salvage company crew began to dismantle the interior of the church and rectory. Within two weeks, the church was an empty shell.

Bulldozers and excavators rumbled into Griffintown on Monday, June 15, 1970. Like a convoy of army tanks, they wheeled into place around St. Ann's Church, rattling windows, squealing and shaking the ground. Amelia Murphy stood in the small crowd on the corner across the street, watching, angry and disbelieving, as the demolition crew prepared to tear down her beloved church.

Diocesan authorities claimed that costly repairs, a dwindling congregation and the city's lack of interest in preserving the historic structure made it impossible to maintain the 116-year-old church. Mourning parishioners questioned the ecclesiastics' decision. No one could deny that St. Ann's congregation had shrunk, but many former parishioners returned to their old neighbourhood for mass on Sundays, boosting regular attendance. "And look at the Tuesdays," they said. The novena— which once attracted five thousand people every week—continued to draw a crowd.

Anger and a sense of betrayal led to talk of a conspiracy: "St. Ann's would still be standing if it were a French church," parishioners, past and present, grumbled among themselves. "They could have maintained it as a shrine." Instead, the popular Tuesday devotions—and Lena Blickstead, St. Ann's venerable organist—were transferred to St. Patrick's Church. In the early '60s, Vatican II had begun to discard Catholic traditions beloved by the devout Irish. Now they would lose their church. And, some, even their bearings: in a city with a legacy of religious intolerance, in a district where Catholics had been forbidden to attend a boys' club founded by a Presbyterian, Catholics and Protestants were now encouraged to pray for Christian unity.

Mrs. Murphy sat by the window of her house, built in 1854, the same year as St. Ann's, and watched, heartbroken, as the church came apart, brick by brick. The heart of Griffintown, where the hard-luck Irish had sought solace and miracles, was soon reduced to rubble. But not without resistance: the demolition crew broke three cables as they swung their wrecking balls at the stubborn steeple.

A last-ditch effort to preserve St. Ann's rectory failed. The archbishop's office temporarily halted the demolition, but gave a citizens' group less than a week to raise the funds needed to convert the thirty-two-room, three-storey brick building into a community centre or low-rent apartments for the elderly. McGill architecture professor Joseph Baker argued that the loss of the historic building would be a tragedy. In a June 10 telephone interview, Canon Jules Delorme, an assistant to the archbishop, had told a local newspaper reporter that "personally, I wouldn't want it even if someone gave it to me for nothing." The abandoned building burned down in November 1970.

An appeal to save the St. Ann's Kindergarten building also proved futile. The Montreal Catholic School Commission turned down a request to save the sound fifty-year-old building for use as a community centre. Officials tore down the sturdy structure and left the site empty. But the Griffintown People's Association (GPA), after much

*St. Ann's Church is
demolished in 1970.*

lobbying, eventually won permission to convert the "Camillienne," the Depression-era comfort station at the entrance to the Wellington Tunnel, into a youth centre.

By the fall of 1970, Griffintown's population, reduced to about a thousand, had been stripped of its schools, churches and recreation centres. English Catholics were forced to crowd into a makeshift chapel in a former classroom in St. Ann's Academy for Sunday mass. The Congrégation de Notre-Dame nuns, strict taskmasters in their time, were sentimental enough to play their recording of the bells of St. Ann's from loudspeakers on special occasions.

Perhaps the descendants of fiery Irishmen prone to rioting had become "too Canadian" in their attempts to save their historic neighbourhood. They took a reasoned approach in their campaign to save existing buildings and construct new housing on vacant land. They enlisted experts:

Joseph Baker, as well as other professional architects and CMHC specialists. They submitted detailed architect-designed blueprints for new low-cost housing. (The city had built subsidized housing in other fading neighbourhoods.) They suggested zoning changes that would encourage the rehabilitation of old housing. They lobbied government officials at every level, municipal, provincial and federal, and presented a workable plan for reviving their beleaguered neighbourhood. The response: three small federal grants; the first, to operate a day camp for Griffintown children; the second, to pay local youth to paint and do small home-repair jobs; the third, to support their ongoing "political dealings" with the City of Montreal.

Irish tempers did flare on at least one occasion. On March 24, 1972, a dozen people—politicians, municipal officials and members of the GPA—gathered around a conference table in a former classroom in the historic St. Ann's Academy. A faint scent of chalk dust and beeswax, and a heady sense of anticipation, filled the air as Griffintown waited to hear the city's response to their proposals. Nothing, as it turned out. City officials responded by presenting a statistical survey revealing that only 387 families, or about eleven hundred people, still lived in Griffintown. And only three of the 365 remaining homes met municipal standards.

Pressed by the residents, the bureaucrats conceded that the city could force landlords to meet municipal standards through city bylaws. But the city had no plans to do so. One municipal politician dismissed the Griffintown group's demands as "unrealistic." The federal representative regretted that the issue was beyond his jurisdiction. The meeting exploded when politicians and officials told residents to look for low-income housing in other parts of the city.

"The 'English from the other side of the canal,' as the residents of Griffintown have long been called, quarrelled last night with three municipal councillors and one federal MP, about the future of their disadvantaged neighborhood," *La Presse* reported the next day, with a certain condescension. The French newspaper also quoted Danny Doyle, president of the Griffintown People's Association: "The citizens of Griffintown want one thing: 'To live with dignity, honour and pride.' We don't want to move. We are attached to our neighbourhood and count on living here."

In the end, no government stepped in to save Griffintown. The historic Irish neighbourhood had few claims in a city and province hinting at separation from Canada. In the early 1970s, anglophones were fleeing Quebec, following their employers, corporations large and small, to Toronto and other Canadian cities, to escape the province's increasing hostility toward the English minority. Hanley lost his seat in the provincial legislature to Liberal George Springate in 1970. Looking back on his loss, the first in his long career, the venerable politician admitted that his opponent had paid more attention to the issue of separatism than he did: "The people were scared."

Few of North America's old Irish settlements outlasted spirited Griffintown. In the last half of the twentieth century, most historic Irish neighbourhoods in the United States had gradually given way to the flight to the suburbs, urban renewal and gentrification. Boston's Southie, one of the most well-known working-class Irish Catholic neighbourhoods in the United States, persisted, but it lost much of its traditional character as numerous housing projects and gentrification brought in a more diverse population.

Yet none faced such swift, deliberate annihilation as Griffintown. By 1974, most of the district's housing had been destroyed. (Only 212 flats remained. Diamond Court, built by Herbert Ames in 1897 as a model of decent housing for workers, was also torn down.) The population had dropped to 546 people. In March 1974, the Sulpicians put St. Ann's Academy up for sale. The historic school, the last of the parish buildings, meticulously maintained by the Congrégation de Notre-Dame nuns, was knocked down in 1980. St. Ann's Parish was quietly dissolved in 1982.

Photographer David Marvin documented the destruction of Griffintown in his journals and poignant photos, finding a parallel to his personal decline into depression and deafness. (Marvin committed suicide in 1975.) By the mid-1970s, Griffintown had become a wasteland. Only a few rows of houses still stood here and there, on Mountain, Ottawa, Murray and Barré streets, in a desolate sea of vacant lots and low-slung industrial buildings.

Like the ghost villages of Ireland deserted during the Famine, Griffintown's lifeless streets and sidewalks, and the corners where tough Irish lads once stood, had an eerie, empty echo. Carters' horses clip-clopping over cobblestones, the solemn strains of the choir slipping out of St. Ann's wooden doors, the pulsating rhythms of tap dancers heel-stamping the stage of St. Ann's Hall, the *whip-bang* of firecrackers, police whistles and mouth organs, shouts and laughter and slamming shutters—the sounds of the once teeming neighbourhood had faded into memory. The Irish had come and gone. Griffintown died and Montreal lost its Irish heart.

Hundreds of thousands of Irish emigrants had passed through the neighbourhood since the early nineteenth century. Tens of thousands in the Famine years arrived stripped of everything but their spirit and humanity. Only a fraction settled in Griffintown with the canallers and their descendents, and other, later, arrivals. Among the poorest and hardiest of Erin's exiles, they endured floods, fires and plagues, and earned an honest living through grinding labour.

D'Arcy McGee and Charles Parnell and other great figures of history had walked through its streets. But Griffintown raised up few heroes of its own, finding instead a collective power by banding together in strikes and protests to fight for their rights, influencing the future of their new country, yet earning barely a mention in the history books.

In 1990, city officials renamed a section of Griffintown "Faubourg des Recollets," further obscuring the presence of the Irish. A few years later, Montreal's Irish community successfully fought a proposal to rename the neighbourhood's streets. And in 2000, the Irish won one more concession: Griffintown-St. Ann's Park, a grassy triangle outlined by the stone foundations of the old church, its park benches arranged in rows, as if facing the old marble altar.

From the beginning, Griffintown was like an island, ringed by the river, the canal, and railway tracks, hemmed in by factories. It was a way station for the neediest of emigrants. A few had sorrows so deep that their troubles filtered down and resurfaced in the poverty and social ills of their descendants. The dream of the New World eluded others, though they found comfort in the close-knit community.

Gus "Pell" Mell never won a world title. His boxing career started to careen out of control when Johnny Williams knocked him out in the second round of a fight at Boston Garden on April 24, 1953. A weakness for alcohol slowly undermined his powerful fists. Sheer talent and dedication kept the gifted boxer in the pro ring for fourteen years and more than seventy-five fights. "That left hook kept me in business when I didn't have anything else," he explained to veteran sportswriter Tim Burke.

Mell attempted a comeback as a middleweight in 1957, finally retiring from the ring a short time later. Widely acknowledged as one of Canada's greatest boxers, Mell spent the rest of his life working on the Montreal docks as a longshoreman and checker, and later as a cooper, repairing broken boxes and bags. He died on November 12, 1975, at the age of forty-nine, after a lengthy illness.

Yet most of the Irish and their descendents survived—and thrived—against all the odds. They worked their way up and out of Griffintown to prosperity and even prominence. But success often came with a sense of loss. Griffintown was an enigma: a slum to outsiders, and a haven for those who lived there; a district with a reputation for fighting and for selfless generosity; a place of hardship and laughter, where distrust of authority went hand in hand with deep religious faith.

To visit Griffintown today is to find a handful of rundown brick buildings, etched and weary with time and soot, to sense within the old walls the thousands of brave and hopeful emigrants running from poverty and persecution. Listen to the trains rattling over the tracks and imagine the foghorns of the ships that once slid through the canal dug with Irish sweat. Sorrow and hardship and suffering were all around and yet, in the midst of it all, grew kinship, caring and belonging. In Griffintown, people were all they needed to be, both Irish and Canadian.

CLOCKWISE FROM TOP LEFT: *Ellen Ahern Maher with her daughters, baby Margie and Patricia, c. 1930. Maher with Jim Broden on Young Street, c. 1925. Danny Doyle (on tricycle) with Patsy and Ruth Sheridan (rear) and Patricia and Margie Maher.*

TOP: *St. Ann's Boys Choir, c. 1945.*
BOTTOM: *The author (top row, second from right)*
with playmates in a back yard on Ottawa Street.

ACKNOWLEDGEMENTS

Let this be my tribute to the people of Griffintown, to the generations of Irish emigrants and their descendants who inspired me, as a child, to write this book, and to the scores of former residents who helped me keep their spirit alive by sharing their stories, photographs and mementos. Special thanks to Terry Batten, Paddy Boyle, Iris (Howden) Boyle, Arthur Broden, Connie Broden, Ken Broden, Betty (Bryant) Tanney, the late Frank Doyle, Terry Doyle, Frank Dougherty, Rita Earle, Father James Farrell, the late John Fenlon, Mike Fenlon, Frank Fitzgerald, Tommy Fitzgerald, Terry Flanagan, Harold Galley, Madeleine (Harkin) Galley, the late Catherine Gleason, the late Frank Hanley, John Hanley, Gerald Harkin, Margaret Harris, the late Dolly Higgins, Lily Higgins, Brother Edward Hogan, Brother Vincent (Nicholas) Hogan, Norman Howden, Sonny Howden, Rose Johnson, Anthony (Woppy) Kelly, Don Kelly, Kathleen (Harkin) Kelly, the late Peggy Kelly, Agnes Lamothe (Sister Agnes Marie), Kitty Lynch, Kaye Lyng, the late Margie Maher, Patricia Maher, the late Father Thomas McEntee, the late Amelia Murphy, Thelma (Pidgeon) Normandeau, Gerald O'Connell, Bill O'Donnell, the late Henry O'Toole, Lucy O'Toole, Tommy Patwell, Bernie Reid, Sister Patricia Ryan, Tom and Peggy Sclater, Louise (Guile) Scott, Mike Scott, Mary (O'Connell) Timmins, Jimmy Twerdin, Bill Wilkins, the late Annie Wilson, and many others. I am especially grateful to Charles Blickstead for his poems, songs and entertaining jaunts through the old neighbourhood;

to Gordon McCambridge and Don Pidgeon, the United Irish Societies' historian, for their generous assistance and encouragement; and to Leo Leonard, a font of local lore and owner of the legendary Griffintown Horse Palace, for his help and hospitality.

Dozens of historians, archivists, librarians and researchers kindly helped me assemble material on the history of the Irish in Montreal and in Canada, the essential backdrop for the story of Griffintown. Many thanks to Marie-Claude Béland at the Providence Archives in Montreal; Denise Caron, planning adviser with the City of Montreal's Bureau du patrimoine; Louis-Maris Côté at the Christian Brothers' Archives in Laval; Brother Walter Farrell at the Christian Brothers' Archives in Toronto; Sylvie Grondin at the Montreal Municipal Archives; Sophie Lemercier at the Anglican Diocese of Montreal; Mother Raymonde Sylvain at the Archives of the Congrégation de Notre-Dame in Montreal; Mary Kilfoil McDevitt of the Catholic Diocese of Saint John, NB; and François Nadeau at the Archives of the Soeurs Grises in Montreal. A few deserve special mention: Father James Mason, director of the Archives of the Edmonton-Toronto Redemptorists, and archivist M.C. Havey gave me liberal access to the records of St. Ann's Parish, and a warm welcome. Father Jacques Monet, an eminent author and historian, and director of the Canadian Institute of Jesuit Studies, broadened my perspective on the political role of the Irish in Montreal by steering me to some key research papers. Marianna O'Gallagher, a distinguished author and historian of the Irish in Quebec, always open to my queries, helped me track down an elusive photo. Farrell McCarthy, editor of the *Shamrock Leaf,* a publication of the Irish Canadian Cultural Association of New Brunswick, acted as an unofficial consultant, always ready to suggest leads and sources of information. Nora Hague, Senior Cataloguer at the McCord Museum, offered valuable advice in the selection of photos and illustrations.

I am especially indebted to Peter Toner, professor emeritus at the University of New Brunswick at Saint John and a foremost authority on the Irish in Canada, for reading the manuscript. His erudition and wit helped me escape a number of errors, as well as maintain my delight in the subject.

Researcher George Serhijczuk has won my heartfelt appreciation for his diligent efforts that helped me cover more ground, more quickly. I also relied on Ottawa researcher Beryl Corber for her speed and enthusiasm in retrieving obscure details from Library and Archives Canada.

I want to acknowledge the support of my former editors and colleagues at *Maclean's,* especially Tony Wilson-Smith, then editor-in-chief, for placing my first story about Griffintown on the cover of a national magazine, and to Peter Kopvillem for his encouragement and deft editing.

The talented and professional team at HarperCollins has gained my respect and admiration for turning my manuscript into a carefully edited, handsome volume. Many thanks to production editor Allegra Robinson for overseeing the process.

To my editor, Phyllis Bruce, I will remain forever grateful for inviting me to write a book about the Irish and for guiding its development.

Nor could this book have been completed without the support and encouragement of my late father, Danny Doyle; my mother, Muriel Doyle; my children, Alana and Paul; and my husband, Tom, who helped in so many ways, most of all by standing by me during my long immersion in Griffintown.

NOTES

1 [page 2]: Statistics for the Famine emigration are rife with disparities and contradictions. According to the reports of Alexander C. Buchanan, Chief Emigration Agent at Quebec City, one of the most authoritative sources, 98,649 emigrants set sail for Quebec in 1847. (Another 16,000 embarked for Saint John, New Brunswick, British North America's second largest port. And roughly 142,000 Irish set out for the United States.)

Buchanan estimated that six out of seven of the emigrants entering Quebec that year originated in Ireland. (The remainder came from England, Scotland and Germany.) More than 50,000 of the Irish had sailed directly out of Ireland, from eighteen different ports. But at least 20,000 had travelled first to England and boarded transatlantic vessels at Liverpool, a major port.

According to Buchanan, 16,825, or roughly 17 per cent of the 98,649 emigrants who embarked for Quebec in 1847, failed to reach their destination. The agent reported that 5,282 died on board ship, either during the crossing or in quarantine, and another 11,543 died in hospital after landing. He counted 3,452 deaths at Grosse Isle, 3,350 in the fever sheds of Montreal and 8,732 in hospitals at other Canadian centres.

Sévigny and Charbonneau note that official statistics reported by the Executive Council are slightly higher than those in Buchanan's report. The Executive Council figures indicate that as many as 17,477 of the 98,649 emigrants who embarked for Quebec perished, 5,293 of them on the voyage. These too may be conservative numbers. In "The Irish Emigration of 1847 and Its Canadian Consequences," Rev. John A. Gallagher states, "Semi-official estimates based on the computation of those who tended the fever patients, especially at Grosse Isle and Montreal, would place the mortality between 20,000 and 22,000." Nor do these estimates include the roughly 2,000 deaths among the 16,000 Irish who sailed to New Brunswick.

2 [page 52]: There are also discrepancies in the number of victims reported at Grosse Isle. At the end of the calamity, Dr. Douglas reported 4,294 burials on the island—3,452 people who had died on the island itself, and another 842 who had died on the ships waiting in quarantine. But the inscription on a monument at the island cemetary places the number of deaths at 5,424, one of the highest estimates.

3 [page 65]: In 1767, McCord and a few other merchants organized a petition for a general assembly, an idea that irritated the Governor, Sir Guy Carleton, who believed that representative government was "impossible...in the American forests." In a letter to Lord Shelburne, British Secretary of State, on January 20, 1768, the Irish-born Carleton singled out "one John McCord who wants neither sense nor honesty" and crowed that "his lucrative trade has lately been checked, by enclosing the barracks to prevent the soldiers getting drunk at all hours of the day and night."

4 [page 175]: Britain, concerned about its holdings in North America after the Rebellions of 1837 and 1838, had forced the shotgun wedding of Upper and Lower Canada. But French Canadians bitterly resented the fact that, although Upper Canada had only 450,000 inhabitants compared to Lower Canada's 650,000, the two provinces had an equal number of seats. And all sides remained suspicious about the balance of power between the elected Assembly and the members of the Legislative Council, appointed by the Governor General.

5 [page 212]: In the traditional hierarchical structure of the Catholic Church, the Pope delegates authority over specific geographic areas, or dioceses, to his bishops. Bishops are responsible for hiring (and firing) pastors and priests in parishes within their boundaries. Many of the priests working in Catholic parishes are so-called "secular" priests, that is, ordained men who practise their ministry in a diocese under a bishop. But sometimes, a bishop will invite priests from a religious order to run a parish. Religious orders—and there are hundreds of them within the Catholic Church—are made up of groups of men or women who take vows and live a communal, spiritual life as priests or brothers or nuns, usually devoted to a specialized task, such as missionary work, caring for the sick or the aged, or teaching. Religious orders generally fall under the authority of the Pope.

6 [page 249]: According to a study by Paul-André Linteau, the Irish in 1881 held eight of the city's 28 positions; 10 of the 37 seats in 1888, and only two of 33 in 1912. Meanwhile, the French representation increased from 12 seats in 1881 to 21 in 1888 and 22 of 33 in 1912.

7 [page 323]: The victims included Mrs. Delia Dowling; Mrs. Walter Wells, 26; Mrs. Victor Geoffrion, 59; Mrs. James Wells, 20; three-year-old James Wells, Jr.; Mr. T. Hébert and his 18-month-old daughter; Edgar Forget; Aurore Larochelle, 53; and Victorien Marchand, 34. (The last three were war workers from Farnham, Quebec, who were living in local boarding houses.)

8 [page 327]: Of the club's 1,295 members (children and youth), 478 enlisted and 28 died in the war.

A NOTE ON SOURCES

Chapter One

For background on the exodus of the Irish to British North America, I turned to Cecil Woodham-Smith's *The Great Hunger,* one of the most detailed and compassionate accounts of Ireland during the Great Famine. I also drew on C. O'Grada's *The Great Irish Famine,* P. Gray's *The Irish Famine,* C. Kinealy's *The Great Irish Famine: Impact, Ideology and Rebellion,* D. Hollett's *Passage to the New World: Packet Ships and Irish Famine Emigrants, 1845–1851,* E. Laxton's *The Famine Ships: The Irish Exodus to America, 1846–51* and T. Coleman's *Passage to America.* Marianna O'Gallagher's *Grosse Ile: Gateway to Canada, 1832–1937* and *Eyewitness: Grosse Isle 1847* (with Rose Dompierre), both indispensible references, helped me lay the groundwork for the sections on the arrival of the Irish in Quebec.

Details of the *Avon* and other Famine ships' port of origin, length of passage, date of arrival, number of passengers, deaths at sea and in quarantine are listed in a report dated March 31, 1848, by the chief Emigrant Agent, A.C. Buchanan, published in the *British Parliamentary Papers* and reproduced in O'Gallagher's *Eyewitness: Grosse Isle 1847*; and other sources.

The Elgin-Grey Papers 1846–1852, edited by Sir Arthur Doughty, offered insight into the government's perspective through the correspondence, reports and other documents of the officials grappling with the crisis. *1847: Grosse Isle, A Record of Daily Events,* by A. Sévigny and A. Charbonneau, helped steer me through the sea of conflicting dates, facts and figures, inevitable during such a tumultuous year.

For the arrival of the Irish in the centuries before the Famine, I turned to W. Spray's "Reception of the Irish in New Brunswick" and other essays in *Talamh An Eisc,* edited by C. J. Byrne and M. Harry; *New Ireland Remembered: Historical Essays on the Irish in New Brunswick,* edited by P. M. Toner; and T. M. Punch's *Irish Halifax: The Immigrant Generation, 1815–1859.* Robert J. Grace's comprehensive *The Irish in Quebec: An Introduction to the Historiography* helped round out the story of the early arrivals. Names and numbers of the first Hibernians appear in John O'Farrell's "Irish Families in Ancient Quebec Records," a speech to the St. Patrick's Society of Montreal in 1872, in the Concordia University Archives.

Biographical information on John McCord is gleaned from P. Miller et al.'s, *The McCord Family*; the *Dictionary of Canadian Biography Online*; and Leon Trépanier's "La Famille McCord" in *Vox Populaire.* A copy of the letter from Sir Guy Carleton that comments on McCord is in the McCord Family Papers at the McCord Museum.

Chapter Two

The title of this chapter is taken from the inscription on a Celtic cross commemorating Irish Famine victims at Middle Island in Miramichi, NB. The words are a translation of "Bron, Bron, Mo Bron," an Irish line in "The Bird of Christ," a poem published in 1896 under the pseudonym Fiona Macleod. The introductory quote is taken from "The Irish Emigration of 1847," a lecture given by Father Bernard O'Reilly in New York in 1852, reprinted in J. A. Jordan's "The Grosse-Isle Tragedy and the Monument to the Irish Fever Victims, 1847."

The scenes on Grosse Isle are reconstructed from information in numerous sources. The most relevant include M. O'Gallagher and R. M. Dompierre's *Eyewitness: Grosse Isle 1847*, a comprehensive collection of official reports, documents and letters from the clergy, staff and officials at the quarantine station; J.A. Jordan's "The Grosse-Isle Tragedy and the Monument to the Irish Fever Victims, 1847" and A. Sévigny and A. Charbonneau's *1847: Grosse Isle*. The testimony of Father Bernard O'Reilly, Father William Moylan, Dr. George Douglas and other witnesses is taken from the Special Inquiry into the Management of the Quarantine Station at Grosse Isle, published in the *Journals of the House of the Legislative Assembly of the Province of Canada*, Appendix (R.R.R.), 1847.

Letters from Father B. McGauran and Father E-A Taschereau are from the Archives of the Diocese of Sainte-Anne-de-la Pocatière and were translated and reproduced in O'Gallagher and Dompierre's *Eyewitness: Grosse Isle 1847*.

The Brien and Reilley children appear on a list from the Catholic orphanage of Quebec in the archives of the Grey Nuns, Les Soeurs de la Charité de Quebec, reproduced in O'Gallagher's *Grosse Ile: Gateway to Canada*. The records include the names of the children's parents and their place of origin, as well as the names and locations of their adoptive families.

In 1832, three American doctors—Samuel Jackson, Charles D. Meigs and Richard Harlan—travelled to Canada to investigate the cholera epidemic and published their findings in the *Report of the Commission Appointed by the Sanitary Board of the City Councils to Visit Canada for the Investigation of the Epidemic Cholera, Prevailing in Montreal and Quebec*. This report supplied details on the outbreak and spread of the disease, the condition of the hospitals, and other pertinent information. Historical background and statistics are drawn from several sources, including G. Bilson's *A Darkened House: Cholera in Nineteenth Century Canada* and M. O'Gallagher's *Grosse Ile: Gateway to Canada, 1832–1937*. Numerous anecdotes originated in the pages of the Montreal *Gazette*, *Canadian Courant* and other newspapers.

The account of the typhus epidemic in Montreal in the summer of 1847 is based on reports in the city's newspapers, including the *Gazette*, *La Minerve*, *Les Mélanges Religieux*, the *Pilot*, *Montreal Witness* and *Transcript*, as well as materials from the Montreal Municipal Archives, including minutes of Montreal city council meetings, reports from the Board of Health, the Chief of Police and the *Report to the Citizens of Montreal of the Committee appointed at the Public Meeting of the 13th Instant, under the Resolutions then adopted, calling for the Establishment of an Immigrant Station Below the City of Montreal*.

Depictions of scenes in the fever sheds draw on firsthand accounts of volunteers who tended the Irish, most notably from *l'Ancien Journal*, vol. 2, 1847, the Grey Nuns' historic record of their daily lives and work, as well as other letters and documents in their Montreal archives. Soeur E. Mitchell's *Mère Jane Slocombe* and Father E. Lecompte's *Les Jésuites du Canada au XIXe siècle* and *Lettres des nouvelles missions du Canada, 1843–1852*, edited by L. Cadieux, helped complete the picture. (Excerpts from *l'Ancien Journal* and other French texts are the author's translations.) John J. Kenny, the United Irish Societies' historian, quoted Mother McMullen's appeal to the nuns in his "Address given at the Ship Fever Monument, Bridge Street, Montreal, May 25, 1975;" he also related John Loye's story about the emigrant girl who wandered away from the sheds.

For additional background, I turned to T.P. Slattery's *Loyola and Montreal;* George Rex Crowley Keep's *The Irish Migration to Montreal: 1847–186;* and Rev. John A. Gallagher's "The Irish Emigration of 1847 and its Canadian Consequences," in the *Canadian Historical Association Report*, vol. 3, 1935–36, among other sources. The excerpt from Bourget's pastoral letter of March 1848 is the author's translation.

Rev. Ellegood's reflections are taken from his undated article "Sixty Years of Progress in Montreal," found in Library and Archive Canada's Edgar Andrew Collard Fonds. The story of John Easton Mills' wife's premonition of his death is told in a Collard column titled "Montreal's Martyr Mayor" in the *Gazette* on November 15, 1947, and in Woodham-Smith's *The Great Hunger*.

The letters from John Mullowney, James Dougherty and Bryan Clancy, emigrants from Sir Robert Gore Booth's estate, were included, along with several others, in the Third Report of the Select Committee on Colonization from Ireland. The Clancy letter also appeared in Gray's *The Irish Famine*.

Chapter Three

The Dictionary of Canadian Biography Online provided essential biographical information on the major figures of the early years, notably Marie-Claire Daveluy's article "Jeanne Mance," Jules Bazin's "Pierre Le Ber," and Elinor Kyte Senior's "Thomas McCord." E.-Z. Massicotte's "La première chapelle de Sainte-Anne à Montréal" in the *Bulletin des recherches historiques*, February, 1942, helped round out the portrait of Le Ber.

For the story of the evolution of the Nazareth Fief into the Irish district of Griffintown, I drew on *L'Hôtel-Dieu: Premier hôpital de Montreal*, an official history of the Sisters of the Hôtel Dieu; Robert Lahaise's *L'Hôtel-Dieu du Vieux Montréal*, and P. Miller et al.'s *The McCord Family: A Passionate Vision*, an essential reference and the source of details on the McCords' incomes, debts and expenditures. Several other works helped complete the picture, including Gilles Lauzon's "Du Faubourg Sainte-Anne au Quartier des Écluses: Faits saillants concernant l'évolution du secteur" (a historical paper prepared for the Societé de developpement de Montreal in 1996); Leon Trépanier's 1953 series, "The Nazareth Fief," "Griffintown" and "La Famille McCord," in *Vox Populaire*, and Claude Perrault's *Montréal en 1781* and *Montréal en 1825*. I also drew on notary documents from the Archives National de Quebec à Montreal. The Thomas McCord letter excerpted here is in the McCord Family Papers at the McCord Museum in Montreal.

The section on the Lachine Canal is based on information from a number of sources, notably Gerald Tulchinsky's *The Construction of the First Lachine Canal, 1815–1826*, Normand Lafrenière's *Canal Building on the St. Lawrence River: Two Centuries of Work, 1779–1959*, and N. Bosworth's *Hochelaga Depicta*. Details of the Lachine Canal opening ceremony are taken from accounts in the *Canadian Courant* and the *Montreal Herald*, both on July 21, 1821.

Of the numerous treatments of navvy culture, the following stand out: Ruth Bleasdale's "Class Conflict on the Canals of Upper Canada in the 1840s," (*Labour/Le Travailleur*, Spring 1981); Kenneth Duncan's "Irish Famine Immigration and the Social Structure of Canada West" (*Canadian Review of Sociology and Anthropology*, vol. 2, 1965); and Peter Way's "Evil Humors and Ardent Spirits: The Rough Culture of Canal Construction Laborers" (*Journal of American History*, March 1993). I consulted Stanley Bagg's account books at the McCord Museum for information about the canallers' alcohol purchases.

The narrative of the canallers' strike is based on the *Report of the Commissioners Appointed to Inquire into the Disturbances Upon the Line of the Beauharnois Canal, during the summer of 1843*, as well as press reports in the Montreal *Gazette*, *La Minerve*, *Les Mélanges Religieux*, *Montreal Transcript* and *L'Aurore des Canadas*. I also consulted R. Boily's *Les Irlandais et le Canal de Lachine: La Grève de 1843*, H.C. Pentland's "The Lachine Strike of 1843" (*Canadian Historical Review*, no. 3, 1948), and William N.T. Wylie's "Poverty, Distress, and Disease: Labor and the Construction of the Rideau Canal, 1826–32." Details of the violent election in the spring of 1832 are taken from a special inquiry appended to the *Journals of the House of Assembly of the Province of Lower-Canada*, 1834.

The story of Montreal's first Irish Catholic congregation and its priests draws on O. Maurault's *Marges d'histoire* and numerous other sources, including: *The Story of Seventy-Five Years: St. Patrick's Church, Montreal, 1847–1922*; *The Story of One Hundred Years: St. Patrick's Church, Montreal , 1847–1947*; J. J. Curran's *Golden Jubilee of the Reverend Fathers Dowd and Toupin with Historical Sketch of the Irish Community of Montreal*); and "The English-Speaking Catholic People of Montreal," in *L'Eglise de Montreal, 1836–1986: apercus d'hier et d'aujourd'hui*. Rev. James Danaher's "The Reverend Richard Jackson, Missionary to the Sulpitians" (*Canadian Catholic Historical Association* Report, 1943–44) provided background for the sketch of Father Jackson.

The section on the Irish of St. Columban and their priests is based on information in C. Bourguignon's *Saint-Colomban* and the Rev. L. P. Whelan's "The Parish of St. Columban" (*Canadian Catholic Historical Association* Report, 1837–38).

Chapter Four

The account of the calamitous fire in Griffintown on June 15, 1850, is largely based on reports in the *Gazette*, the *Pilot*, *Montreal Transcript* and *L'Avenir*. Bishop Bourget's pastoral letter is in the Archives of the Catholic Diocese of Montreal; the excerpt that appears here is the author's translation from the French. Broomfield's visit to Canada is described in *First in the Field*, an official history of the Phoenix Assurance Co. His letters, in the firm's archives, are reproduced in D. M. Baird's *The Story of Firefighting in Canada*.

The experiences of workers John O'Rourke, Charles Weir, Richard Powers and Patrick J. Dalton, as well as the comments of John James McGill and journalist Arthur Short, are drawn from the Royal Commission on the Relations of Capital and Labour in Canada, vol. 5, which contains the evidence of hundreds of witnesses who testified on working and living conditions in Quebec. The section on the building of the Victoria Bridge is based on information in chief engineer James Hodges' *The Construction of the Great Victoria Bridge*, and in *Victoria Bridge*, by S. Triggs et al.

The story of St. Ann's is based on parish histories and other documents from the Archives of the Edmonton-Toronto Redemptorists, the Christian Brothers Archives in Toronto and Montreal, and the Archives of the Congrégation de Notre Dame in Montreal. I especially relied on *Centenary: The Story of One Hundred Years: St. Ann's Church, Montreal*, John Loye's "The History of Griffintown and St. Ann's Parish" in *Golden Jubilee Humber: Redemptorist Fathers at St. Ann's*, 1934, and Brother Mactilius's "St. Ann's, Montreal" in *A Short History of Schools of the Christian Brothers in Montreal, Quebec and the Maritimes*.

Information on Griffintown's Protestant churches and the movement of their populations was gleaned from a number of sources, most notably Rosalyn Trigger's "Protestant Restructuring in the Canadian City: Church and Mission in the Industrial Working-Class District of Griffintown, Montreal" in *Urban History Review*, Fall 2002.

The sales contract for the Sulpicians' Mountain Domain is reproduced in Brian Young's *In Its Corporate Capacity: The Seminary as a Business Institution*, an account of the priests' worldly activities. Crime statistics are drawn from annual police reports in the Montreal Municipal Archives. Extensive coverage in the *Montreal Star* provided the material for the description of the infamous murder of Mary Gallagher, whose ghost lived on as Griffintown's Headless Woman.

The replay of the July 13, 1870, Shamrocks Lacrosse Club game is drawn from an account by Rev. Buckley in his *Diary of a Tour in America*, as well as reports in the *Gazette* and the *Evening Star*. For background on the team, I turned to D. Morrow's *A Concise History of Sport in Canada* and B. Pinto's *Ain't Misbehavin': The Montreal Shamrock Lacrosse Club Fans, 1868 to 1884*.

Chapter Five

The accounts of the floods are based largely on news reports from the Montreal *Gazette*, the *Evening Star*, the *Montreal Daily Star*, the *Montreal Daily Post*, *True Witness*, the *Catholic Chronicle* and the *Globe*. The story of Rev. Ellegood's stranded flock appears in a history of St. Stephen's in the Anglican Archives, as well as in the *Daily Witness*, May 28, 1898. Rev.

Ellegood wrote his own account of the harrowing incident in "Sixty Years of Progress in Montreal," an undated article about his lengthy ministry found in Library and Archives Canada. Collard also related the incident in a *Gazette* column. The report of the 1841 Royal Commission investigating the floods at Montreal is in Library and Archives Canada.

This chapter also benefits from the technical information and political implications illuminated in Christopher G. Boone's "Language Politics and Flood Control in Nineteenth Century Montreal," in *Environmental History*, July 1996.

Chapter Six

The extensive coverage in the Montreal *Gazette*, as well as in the *True Witness* and *La Minerve*, provides the basis for the narrative of Gavazzi's infamous visit to Montreal. Robert Sylvain's "Le 9 juin 1853 à Montréal: Encore l'affaire Gavazzi," in *Revue d'histoire de l'Amérique française*, no. 2, 1960; and T. P. Slattery's account in *Loyola and Montreal* are the most comprehensive of the many historical references consulted. Quotes from Gavazzi's speech and the passage from Henri Émile Chevalier's novel *Les Derniers Iroquois*, which appear in Sylvain in French, are the author's translations.

The discrimination against Irish Catholics in eighteenth-century Newfoundland is explored in Murray Nicolson's "Catholics in Newfoundland," in *Catholic Insight* January/February 1996, also the source of the Michael Keating anecdote. Terrence M. Punch's "Larry Doyle and Nova Scotia," a chapter in *Talamh An Eisc*, deals with anti-Catholicism in that province. Several Montreal histories note the sharing of a church by Catholics and Protestants in the late eighteenth century. Frank Dawson Adams gives the most detailed account in his *History of Christ Church Cathedral*.

The description of the 1844 election relies on press coverage, especially the Montreal *Gazette* and the *Transcript*. Jacques Monet, S.J., provided context on the politics and strategies of the controversial by-election in his extensive writings on the subject, including "La Crise Metcalfe and the Montreal Election, 1843–1844," in the *Canadian Historical Review*, March, 1963, and *The Last Cannon Shot*. The letters from Delisle to Daly and from Lord Metcalfe to Lord Stanley are in Library and Archives Canada.

The *Globe*, the Montreal *Gazette*, the *St. John Morning News* and other newspapers offered up details of violent incidents involving Irish Catholics and Orangemen. The description of the notorious 1849 riot in Saint John is based on a number of accounts, notably Scott W. See's "The Orange Order and Social Violence in Mid-Nineteenth Century Saint John," in *New Ireland Remembered*. My primary source for background on the Orange Order was C. J. Houston and W. J. Smyth's *The Sash Canada Wore*. The Hackett incident is based largely on news reports in the Montreal *Gazette* and the *Evening Post*, as well as accounts in *The Dominion Annual register and review for the 12th–20th year of the Canadian Union* and in J. C. Fleming's *Orangeism and the 12th of July Riots in Montreal*.

The description of the burning of the Parliament Building is drawn from numerous historical works and newspaper accounts. Alfred Perry's memoir appeared first in the *Montreal Daily Star*, Carnival Number, January–February 1887. Information about the role of the fireman and fire companies in the nineteenth century came from several sources, including D. M. Baird's *The Story of Firefighting in Canada;* Bruce D. Redfern's *The Montreal Fire Department in the Nineteenth Century;* and John C. Weaver and Peter De Lottinville's "The Conflagration and the City: Disaster and Progress in British North America during the Nineteenth Century," in *Histoire Sociale/Social History,* November 1980.

The biographical information on D'Arcy McGee is gleaned from numerous sources, the most important being T. P. Slattery's *The Assassination of D'Arcy McGee.* Many details on the elections and other events in McGee's political career are drawn from newspapers, including: the *True Witness and Catholic Chronicle,* the Montreal *Gazette,* the *Montreal Herald,* the *Evening Star, Montreal Daily Witness, Canadian Illustrated News, Toronto (Mackenzie's) Weekly Message* and *New Era.* McGee's comment on the "miserable town tenantry" of the New York Irish is quoted from his essay *The Irish Position in British and Republican North America.*

The section on the Fenians draws on Peter Toner's groundbreaking *The Rise of Irish Nationalism in Canada,* Hereward Senior's *The Fenians and Canada* and David A. Wilson's "The Fenians in Montreal, 1862–68: Invasion, Intrigue and Assassination," published in *Eire-Ireland: Journal of Irish Studies,* Fall-Winter, 2003.

Chapter Seven

Bishop Fabre's correspondence and Father Hogan's resignation letter are from the Archives of the Edmonton-Toronto Redemptorists. Biographical information on the Irish Sulpicians is drawn from parish annals and histories. The role of the Redemptorists at St. Ann's is covered in Laverdure, *Redemption and Renewal.*

J. J. Curran's two books—*The St. Patrick's Orphans Asylum* and *Golden Jubilee of the Reverend Fathers Dowd and Toupin with Historical Sketch of the Irish Community of Montreal*— deal with the controversies at St. Bridget and St. Patrick's parishes. The chapter also draws on the Rev. Gerald Berry's "A Critical Period in St. Patrick's Parish, Montreal, 1866–74," in the *Canadian Catholic Historical Association Report,* 1943–44, and Rosalyn Trigger's "The Geopolitics of the Irish-Catholic Parish in Nineteenth-Century Montreal," in the *Journal of Historical Geography,* no. 4, 2001.

Sources for the conflicts in Irish American parishes include *The American Catholic Parish: A History from 1850 to the Present,* edited by J.P. Doan, and T.H. O'Connor's *Boston Catholics: A History of the Church and Its People.*

The account of the Considine murder trial is based on newspaper reports and a court transcript. Sources for the smallpox epidemic of 1885 include the report of the Montreal Board of Health and newspaper reports.

Information about the activities of the St. Ann's Young Men's Society was drawn from their annual reports and minutes, as well as from the *St. Ann's Young Men's Society: Golden Anniversary Presentation.*

Chapter Eight

Herbert Brown Ames's statistics and analysis of Griffintown's standard of living are taken from his 1896 sociological survey, *The City Below the Hill*. Numerous sources, most notably Melanie Methot's "Herbert Brown Ames: Political Reformer and Enforcer," in *Urban History Review*, Spring 2003, provided background on the man and his times. To round out the picture of Montreal politics at the turn of the century, I turned to, among others articles, Alan Gordon's "Ward Heelers and Honest Men: Urban Quebecois political culture and the Montreal Reform of 1909," in *Urban History Review*, March 1995, and Paul-Andre Linteau's "Le Personnel politique de Montreal, 1880–1914: evolution d'une elite municipale," in *La Revue d'histoire de l'Amérique française*, Autumn 1998. The Mayor Jimmy McShane anecdotes and campaign song were found in the Montreal Municipal Archives.

Descriptions of life in Griffintown in this chapter are based on my interviews with former residents Kaye Lyng, Charles Blickstead, Father James Farrell, Terry Flanagan and Gordon McCambridge. Biographical information on artist Emily Coonan and her family comes from several sources, most notably Karen Antaki's Concordia University exhibition catalogue *Emily Coonan (1885–1971)*. The story of the origin and early years of the Griffintown Club is drawn from its annual reports in the Rare Book Collection of the McClennan Library at McGill University. The annals of the Sisters of Providence, held in their archives in Montreal, contain the details of the founding of St. Ann's Kindergarten and the nuns' charitable works.

The Irish Uprising, 1916–1922 proved to be one of the most useful references on Home Rule and Ireland during the First World War. The section on the position of the Irish in Canada draws on Robin B. Burns's "Who Shall Separate Us? The Montreal Irish and the Great War" in *The Untold Story: The Irish in Canada*. However, I arrived at a different conclusion from Burns in the interpretation of the 1917 election for St. Ann's Ward.

Also helpful were Brian P. Clarke's *Piety and Nationalism: Lay Voluntary Associations and the Creation of an Irish-Catholic Community in Toronto, 1850–1895* and Bruce S. Elliott's "Irish Catholics" in the *Encyclopedia of Canada's Peoples*.

For an account of the formation of the Montreal Irish militia, I relied on *The Irish-Canadian Rangers*. Descriptions of the meetings in St. Ann's Hall, the Private Flannigan incident and the election results are based on reports in the *Gazette*.

I consulted Mike Cronin and Daryl Adair's *The Wearing of the Green: A History of St. Patrick's Day* and M. E. Regan's "Montreal's St. Patrick's Day Parade as a Political Statement: the rise of the Ancient Order of Hibernians, 1900–1929" on the politics of the parades and the role of the AOH. Credit for the story of how Griffintown saved the continuity of the Montreal parade goes to Donald Pidgeon, the United Irish Societies historian. The St. Ann's Young Men's Society 1918 annual report confirms his account.

For background on the Spanish flu in Canada, I consulted, among other articles, Mark Osborne Humphries' "The Horror at Home: The Canadian Military and the 'Great' Influenza Pandemic of 1918," in the *Journal of the Canadian Historical Association*, no. 1, 2005. Details of the flu's impact on Montreal and Griffintown are gleaned from a number of sources, including the St. Ann's Parish Annals in the Archives of the Edmonton-Toronto Redemptorists, annual reports of the Griffintown Club, the Montreal *Star* and interviews with former residents.

Chapter Nine

The story of Sister Donald's encounter with the chicken thief appears in the *Annals of Providence,* also the source of the nuns' charitable works during the Depression. For background on the role of government and relief measures during the 1930s, I referred to a number of sources. The most pertinent include Hertel La Roque's *Camillien Houde: Le p'ti gars de Ste-Marie,* Louis-Martin Tard's *Camillien Houde: Le Cyrano de Montreal,* Terry Copp's "The Montreal Working Class in Prosperity and Depression," in *Canadian Issues,* Spring 1995, and the *Official City Relief Book* in the Montreal Municipal Archives.

My depiction of life in Griffintown is based on interviews with dozens of former residents of the district, including Paddy Boyle, Iris (Howden) Boyle, Arthur Broden, Connie Broden, Betty (Bryant) Tanney, the late Danny Doyle, the late Frank Doyle, Frank Dougherty, Father James Farrell, the late John Fenlon, Frank Fitzgerald, Tommy Fitzgerald, Terry Flanagan, Harold Galley, Madeleine (Harkin) Galley, the late Frank Hanley, John Hanley Jr., Gerald Harkin, Norman Howden, Sonny Howden, Anthony (Woppy) Kelly, Don Kelly, Kathleen (Harkin) Kelly, the late Peggy Kelly, Leo Leonard, Kitty Lynch, the late Margie Maher, Patricia Maher, Gordon McCambridge, the late Father Thomas McEntee, Mary O'Connell, Gerald O'Connell, the late Henry O'Toole, Bernie Reid, the late Annie Wilson, and many others.

The portrait of Frank Hanley is based on two personal interviews. I also reviewed the City of Montreal's three-volume clipping file covering Hanley's thirty years in politics, Kenneth Johnstone's feature "Nights and Days of a Ward Boss," in *Maclean's,* June 2, 1962, and Lynda Steele's "Frank Hanley: Independent," in the *Canadian Parliamentary Review,* Spring 1986.

Chapter Ten

The account of the April 25, 1944, plane crash in Griffintown is based on newspaper reports from the *Gazette,* the *Montreal Daily Star,* the *Montreal Daily Herald, La Presse,* and *The Globe and Mail* as well as interviews with Brother Edward Hogan, the late Frank Doyle, Billy Higgins, Harold Galley, Rita Earle and others living in Griffintown at the time.

For statistics and information about the military and federal programs during the Second World War, I consulted C. P. Stacey's *Arms, Men and Governments: The War Policies of Canada 1939–1945;* J. L. Granatstein's "Arming the Nation: Canada's Industrial War Effort 1939–1945;" Daniel Byers' "Mobilising Canada: The National Resources Mobilization Act, the Department of National Defence, and Compulsory Military Service in Canada, 1940–1945," in the *Journal of the Canadian Historical Association,* vol. 7, no. 1, 1996; and R. MacGregor Dawson's *The Conscription Crisis of 1944.* I turned to news reports from the *Gazette,* Serge Marc Durflinger's *Fighting From Home: The Second World War in Verdun, Quebec* and W. Weintraub's *City Unique: Montreal Days and Nights in the 1940s and '50s* for the clashes between the navy and the zoot suiters.

The *Griff News,* written by residents of the district for those who went overseas, provided a rich source of information about life at home as well as in the trenches and battlefields.

Interviews with John Hanley Jr., Terry Flanagan, Kitty Lynch, Leo Leonard and others helped round out the picture of wartime in Griffintown.

Chapter Eleven

The story of Gus Mell's boxing career is based on extensive news clippings from the *Gazette,* the *Montreal Star,* the *Montreal Standard* and *The New York Times;* also the source of information about fighters Armand Savoie and Marcel "Rocky" Brisebois."

For background on the Montreal municipal politics that ultimately led to the demise of Griffintown, I consulted Brian McKenna and Susan Purcell's biography *Drapeau;* Pax Plante's *Montréal sous le régne de la pègre*; R. Jones's *Duplessis and the Union Nationale Administration*; R. Rumilly's *Maurice Duplessis et son temps;* H. Kaplan's *Reform, Planning, and City Politics: Montreal, Winnipeg, Toronto* and Garth Stevenson's *Community Besieged: The Anglophone Minority and the Politics of Quebec.*

I tracked the fight to save the district in the records of the Griffintown People's Association—minutes, reports and correspondence with federal, provincial and municipal officials; the *Report of the Community Design Workshop of the McGill School of Architecture,* prepared under the direction of Professor Joseph Baker, the Annals of St. Ann's Church in the Archives of the Edmonton-Toronto Redemptorists, the Annals of St. Ann's Convent from the Archives of the Congrégation de Notre Dame, and photographer David Marvin's "Griffintown: A Brief Chronicle," in *Habitat,* vol. 18, no. 1, 1975. Marvin's own story and his personal connection to Griffintown is told in the NFB film *Albedo.*

A SELECT BİBLİOGRAPHY

Ames, Herbert Brown. *The City Below the Hill.* University of Toronto Press, 1972.

Atherton, William Henry. *Montreal 1535–1914.* Montreal: S. J. Clarke, 1914.

Baird, Donal M. *The Story of Firefighting in Canada.* Erin, ON: Boston Mills Press, 1986.

Bilson, Geoffrey. *A Darkened House: Cholera in Nineteenth-Century Canada.* Toronto: University of Toronto Press, 1980.

Boily, Raymond. *Les Irlandais et le Canal de Lachine: La Grève de 1843.* Ottawa: Leméac, 1980.

Bosworth, Newton, ed. *Hochelaga Depicta: The Early History and Present State of the City and Island of Montreal.* Montreal: W. Grieg, 1839.

Bourguignon, Claude. *Saint-Colomban: Une épopée irlandaise au piedmont des Laurentides.* Sainte-Sophie, QC Éditions d'ici là, 2006.

Bradbury, Bettina. *Working Families: Age, Gender, and Daily Survival in Industrializing Montreal.* Toronto: University of Toronto Press, 2007.

Burton, Anthony. *The Canal Builders.* London: Methuen, 1972.

Byrne, Cyril J., and Margaret Harry, eds. *Talamh An Eisc: Canadian and Irish Essays.* Halifax: Nimbus, 1986.

Cadieux, Lorenzo, ed. *Lettres des nouvelles missions du Canada, 1843-1852.* Montreal: Editions Bellarmin, 1973.

Clarke, Brian P. *Piety and Nationalism: Lay Voluntary Associations and the Creation of an Irish-Catholic Community in Toronto, 1850–1895.* Montreal and Kingston: McGill-Queen's University Press, 1993.

Coleman, Terry. *Passage to America.* Middlesex, UK: Penguin, 1974.

Collard, Edgar Andrew. *Montreal: The Days That Are No More.* Toronto: Doubleday, 1976.

Cronin, Mike and Daryl Adair. *The Wearing of the Green: A History of St. Patrick's Day.* New York: Routledge, 2002.

Daley, Caroline, and Anna Springer. *Middle Island: Before and After the Tragedy.* Miramichi, NB: Coast to Coast Publications, 2002.

Dolan, Jay P., editor. *The American Catholic Parish: A History from 1850 to the Present.* NewYork: Paulist Press, c.1987.

Dorwin, Jedediah Hubbell. "Montreal in 1816: Reminiscences of Mr. J. H. Dorwin." *Montreal Daily Star,* February 1881.

Durflinger, Serge Marc. *Fighting from Home: The Second World War in Verdun, Quebec.* Vancouver and Toronto: UBC Press, 2006.

Elliott, Bruce S. "Irish Catholics," in *Encyclopedia of Canada's Peoples,* edited by Paul Robert Magocsi. Toronto: University of Toronto Press for the Multicultural History Society of Ontario, 1999.

Gallagher, Thomas. *Paddy's Lament: Ireland 1846–1847, Prelude to Hatred.* New York: Harcourt Brace, 1982.

Gibbon, John Murray. *Our Old Montreal.* Toronto: McClelland and Stewart, 1847.

Giffard, Ann. *Towards Quebec: Two Mid-19th Century Emigrants' Journals.* London: Her Majesty's Stationery Office, 1981.

Gournay, Isabelle, and France Vanlaethem. *Montreal Metropolis 1880–1930.* Toronto: Stoddart and Canadian Centre for Architecture, 1998.

Grace, Robert J. *The Irish in Quebec: An Introduction to the Historiography.* Quebec: Institut Québécois de recherche sur la culture, 1993.

Gray, Clayton. *The Montreal Story.* Montreal: Whitcombe & Gilmour, 1949.

Gray, Peter. *The Irish Famine.* New York: Harry N. Abrams, 1995.

Guillet, Edwin C. *The Great Migration: The Atlantic Crossing by Sailing-Ship since 1770.* Toronto: T. Nelson and Sons, 1937.

Hodges, James. *The Construction of the Great Victoria Bridge.* London: J. Weale, 1860.

Hollett, David. *Passage to the New World: Packet Ships and Irish Famine Emigrants, 1845–1851.* Abergavenny, U.K.: P. M. Heaton Publishing, 1995.

Houston, Cecil J., and William J. Smyth. *Irish Emigration and Canadian Settlement: Patterns, Links, and Letters.* Toronto: University of Toronto Press, 1990.

———. *The Sash Canada Wore: A Historical Geography of the Orange Order in Canada.* Milton, ON: Global Heritage Press, 1999.

Jenkins, Kathleen. *Montreal: Island City of the St. Lawrence.* New York: Doubleday, 1966.

Jordan, J. A. "The Grosse-Isle Tragedy and the Monument to the Irish Fever Victims, 1847." *Quebec Daily Telegraph,* August 15, 1909.

Keep, George Rex Crowley. *The Irish Migration to Montreal: 1847–1867.* McGill University, MA Thesis, 1948.

Kinealy, Christine. *The Great Irish Famine: Impact, Ideology and Rebellion.* New York: Palgrave, 2002.

Lafrenière, Normand. *Canal Building on the St. Lawrence River: Two Centuries of Work, 1779–1959.* Ottawa: Supply and Services, c1983.

Lahaise, Robert. *L'Hôtel-Dieu du Vieux-Montréal.* Montreal: Editions Hurtubise, 1973.

Lapointe-Roy, Huguette. *Charité bien ordonnée: Le Premier réseau de lutte contre la pauvreté à Montréal au 19e siècle.* Montreal: Boréal, 1987.

La Roque, Hertel. *Camillien Houde: Le p'tit gars de Ste-Marie.* Montreal: Les Éditions de l'Homme, 1961.

Laverdure, Paul. *Redemption and Renewal: The Redemptorists of English Canada, 1834–1994.* Toronto: Dundurn Press, 1996.

Laxton, Edward. *The Famine Ships: The Irish Exodus to America, 1846–51.* New York: Henry Holt and Company, 1997.

Leblond de Brumath, Adrien. *Histoire populaire de Montréal depuis son origine jusqu'à nos jours.* Montreal: Granger Frères, 1890.

Lecompte, Édouard. *Les Jésuites du Canada au XIXe siècle.* Montreal: Messager, 1920.

Lieberson, Goddard; with a foreward by Eamon de Valera. *The Irish Uprising, 1916-1922.* New York: Macmillan, 1967.

Mackay, W. Donald. *Flight from Famine: The Coming of the Irish to Canada.* Toronto: McClelland and Stewart, 1990.

MacManus, Seumas. *The Story of the Irish Race.* New York: The Devin-Adair Company, 1955.

Marsan, Jean-Claude. *Montreal in Evolution: Historical Analysis of the Development of Montreal's Architecture and Urban Environment.* Montreal and Kingston: McGill-Queen's University Press, 1981.

Maurault, Olivier. *Marges d'histoire.* Montreal: Librairie d'Action canadienne-française, 1929.

McGowan, Mark G. *Waning of the Green: Catholics, the Irish, and Identity in Toronto, 1887–1922.* Montreal and Kingston: McGill-Queen's University Press, 1999.

McKenna, Brian, and Susan Purcell. *Drapeau.* Toronto: Clarke, Irwin, 1980.

Miller, Kerby A. *Emigrants and Exiles: Ireland and the Irish Exodus to North America.* Oxford: Oxford University Press, 1985.

Miller, Pamela, Brian Young, Donald Fyson, Donald Wright, and Moira T. McCaffrey. *The McCord Family: A Passionate Vision.* Montreal: McCord Museum of Canadian History, 1992.

Mitchell, Soeur Estelle. *Mère Jane Slocombe, neuvième superieure génerale des Soeurs Grises de Montréal, 1819–1872.* Montreal: Fides, 1964.

Mondoux, Soeur Maria. *L'Hôtel-Dieu: Premier hôpital de Montreal.* Montreal: 1942.

Monet, Jacques. *The Last Cannon Shot: A Study of French-Canadian Nationalism 1837–1850.* Toronto: University of Toronto Press, 1969.

Morrow, Don. *A Concise History of Sport in Canada.* Toronto: Oxford University Press, 1989.

Mountain, Armine W. *A Memoir of George Jehosophat Mountain, D.D., D.C.L.: Late Bishop of Quebec.* Montreal: John Lovell, 1866.

O'Connor, Thomas H. *Boston Catholics: A History of the Church and Its People.*

O'Driscoll, Robert, and Lorna Reynolds. *The Untold Story: The Irish in Canada.* Toronto: Celtic Arts of Canada, 1988.

O'Gallagher, Marianna. *Grosse Ile: Gateway to Canada, 1832–1937.* Ste-Foy, QC: Livres Carraig Books, 1984.

O'Gallagher, Marianna, and Rose Masson Dompierre. *Eyewitness: Grosse Isle 1847.* Ste-Foy, QC: Livres Carraig Books, 1995.

O'Grada, Cormac. *The Great Irish Famine.* Cambridge: Cambridge University Press, 1989.

Perrault, Claude. *Montréal en 1825*. Montreal: Payette Radio, 1969.

———. *Montréal en 1781* (Montreal: Groupe d'Études Gen-Histo, 1969)

Pinto, B. *Ain't Misbehavin': The Montreal Shamrock Lacrosse Club Fans, 1868 to 1884*. University of Western Ontario, MA Thesis, 1990.

Prévost, Robert. *Montreal: A History*. Translated by Elizabeth Mueller and Robert Chodos. Toronto: McClelland and Stewart, 1993.

Punch, Terrence M. *Irish Halifax: The Immigrant Generation, 1815–1859*. Halifax: St. Mary's University International Education Centre, 1981.

Renaud, Charles. *L'Imprévisible Monsieur Houde*. Montreal: Les Éditions de l'Homme, 1964.

Roberts, Leslie. *Montreal: From Mission Colony to World City*. Toronto: Macmillan of Canada, 1969.

Rumilly, Robert. *Maurice Duplessis et son temps*. Montreal: Fides, c1973.

Senior, Hereward. *The Fenians and Canada*. Toronto: Macmillan, 1978.

Sévigny, André, and André Charbonneau. *1847: Grosse Ile, A Record of Daily Events*. Ottawa: Parks Canada, 1997.

Slattery, T. P. *The Assassination of D'Arcy McGee*. Toronto: Doubleday, 1968.

———. *Loyola and Montreal: A History*. Montreal: Palm Publishers, c. 1962.

Tard, Louis-Martin. *Camillien Houde: Le Cyrano de Montréal*. Montreal: XYZ Éditeur, 1999.

Toner, Peter Michael. *The Rise of Irish Nationalism in Canada 1858–1884*. Galway: National University of Ireland, PhD thesis, 1974.

———. *New Ireland Remembered: Historical Essays on the Irish in New Brunswick*. New Ireland Press, 1988.

Triggs, Stanley, Brian Young, Conrad Graham, and Gilles Lauzon. *Victoria Bridge: The Vital Link*. Montreal: McCord Museum of Canadian History, 1992.

Tulchinsky, Gerald. *The Construction of the First Lachine Canal, 1815–1826*. McGill University, MA Thesis, 1965.

Vie de Mère Gamelin: Fondatrice et première supérieure des Soeurs de la Charité de la Providence. Montreal: Eusébe Sénécal & Cie., 1900.

Wilson, David A. *The Irish in Canada*. Ottawa: Canadian Historical Association, 1989.

———. *Thomas D'Arcy McGee: Volume I: Passion, Reason, and Politics, 1825–1857*.

Woodham-Smith, Cecil. *The Great Hunger: Ireland 1845–1849*. New York: Harper & Row, 1962.

Young, Brian. *In Its Corporate Capacity: The Seminary of Montreal as a Business Institution 1816–1876*. Montreal and Kingston: McGill-Queen's University Press, 1986.

ILLUSTRATION CREDITS

146 Photograph by George Charles Arless, 1887 (MP-0000.236.8), courtesy of the McCord Museum

151 Photograph by William Notman, c.1880 (view 1146), courtesy of the McCord Museum

156 *Canadian Illustrated News,* September 5, 1874, courtesy of the TPL (TRL)

163 Photograph, courtesy of Library and Archives Canada

168 *Illustrated London News,* July 9, 1853, courtesy of the TPL (TRL)

182 *Canadian Illustrated News,* August 1, 1874, courtesy of the TPL (TRL)

185 *Illustrated London News,* May 19, 1849, courtesy of the TPL (TRL)

189 Photograph by Ellisson & Co., 1862, courtesy of Library and Archives Canada

203 *Canadian Illustrated News,* July 21, 1877, courtesy of the TPL (TRL)

205 *Canadian Illustrated News,* July 27, 1878, courtesy of the TPL (TRL)

213 Photograph from *Centenary Story of One Hundred Years,* courtesy of the Archives of Edmonton-Toronto Redemptorists

227 Drawing from the *Montreal Daily Star,* January 19, 1895, courtesy of the Archives of Edmonton-Toronto Redemptorists

228 Drawing, courtesy of the Archives of Edmonton-Toronto Redemptorists

234 Drawing from *Saint Anne's Fair Journal,* courtesy of the Archives of Edmonton-Toronto Redemptorists

235 Photograph, courtesy of the Archives of Edmonton-Toronto Redemptorists

240 Photograph by William Notman & Son, 1896 (View-2938), courtesy of the McCord Museum, Montreal

247 Photograph by Notman and Sandham, 1880 (II-54846.1), courtesy of the McCord Museum

249 Photograph, courtesy of the Archives of Edmonton-Toronto Redemptorists

257 Photograph from the *Nazareth Street Club Annual Report, 1911,* courtesy of McGill University Library

259 Photograph [M129.38(10)-AG-Ka4.2], courtesy of Providence Archives, Montreal

262 Photograph [M129.38(02)-AG-Ka4.2] courtesy of Providence Archives, Montreal

266 Photograph, courtesy of Library and Archives Canada

289 Photograph, courtesy of the Hanley family

303 Photograph, courtesy of the Archives of Edmonton-Toronto Redemptorists

305 Photograph, courtesy of the Archives of Edmonton-Toronto Redemptorists

306 Photograph, courtesy of Frank Dougherty

308 Photographs courtesy of Ken Broden

314 Photograph, courtesy of Betty (Bryant) Tanney

319 Photograph (MP-0000.72.1), courtesy of the McCord Museum, Montreal

321 Photograph, courtesy of the Bibliothèque et Archives nationales du Québec

324 Photograph, courtesy of Glenna Morrison

333 Photograph, courtesy of Melissa Grimshaw

343 Photograph by Ronny Jaques, 1945, courtesy of Library and Archives Canada

348 Photograph, courtesy of the Archives of Edmonton-Toronto Redemptorists

352 Photograph (top), courtesy of Don and Kathleen Kelly

352 Photograph (bottom), courtesy of William Wilson

355 Photograph, courtesy of the Hanley family

364 Photograph by David Wallace Marvin, 1970 (MP-1978.186.248), courtesy of the McCord Museum, Montreal

370 Photographs, courtesy of Patricia Maher and the late Margie Maher

371 Photograph (top), courtesy of Don and Kathleen Kelly

INDEX